Teaching with a Multicultural Perspective

Teaching with a Multicultural Perspective

A Practical Guide

THIRD EDITION

LEONARD DAVIDMAN
PATRICIA T. DAVIDMAN
California Polytechnic State University, San Luis Obispo

Longman

New York San Francisco Boston
London Toronto Sydney Tokyo Singapore Madrid
Mexico City Munich Paris Cape Town Hong Kong Montreal

Publisher: Priscilla McGeehon
Production Manager: Ellen MacElree
Project Coordination, Text Design, and Electronic Page Makeup: Electronic Publishing
Services Inc., NYC
Cover Designer/Manager: Nancy Danahy
Cover Photo: Copyright ©Tony Stone Images
Manufacturing Buyer: Roy Pickering
Printer and Binder: The Maple-Vail Book Manufacturing Group
Cover Printer: Phoenix Color Corp.

Library of Congress Cataloging-in-Publication Data
Davidman, Leonard.
    Teaching with a multicultural perspective : a practical guide / Leonard Davidman and
    Patricia T. Davidman.— 3rd ed.
        p. cm.
    Includes bibliographical references and index.
    IBSN 0-321-07883-7
    1. Multicultural education—United States. 2. Multicultural education—United
    States—Curricula—Case Studies. I. Davidman, Patricia T. II. Title.
LC1099.3 .D39 2001
370.117'0973—dc21   00-037079

Copyright © 2001 by Addison-Wesley Educational Publishers Inc.

Please visit our website at http://www.awl.com

ISBN 0-321-07883-7

1 2 3 4 5 6 7 8 9 10   MA   03 02 01 00

Contents

Preface

We began writing the first edition of this text in the late 1980s and were deeply influenced by the spirit of educational reform that characterized that decade. Report after report showed clearly that teacher education programs would have to improve their preparation of prospective and veteran teachers for the various types of diversity that were fast becoming a pervasive part of America's classrooms. Today, as we begin the twenty-first century, classroom teachers routinely face increased diversity in students' ethnicity, linguistic and cultural backgrounds, family structures, socioeconomic status, learning styles, and degree of learning handicap. And more diversity, rather than less, appears to be predictable as increased numbers of immigrants from around the world join the American drama and teachers work with families suffering the consequences of new levels of economic deprivation. In addition, in 1995 as we considered possible changes for the second edition, it appeared to us that the polarization between socioeconomic status (SES), racial, ethnic, and selected cultural groups was increasing, thus reinforcing the need for teacher education programs that more powerfully and consistently prepared teachers for the polarization, segregation, inequality, and diversity that remained as persistent elements in many American schools and communities. In 1999, as we wrote the third edition, the polarization had not abated, and, indeed, had become a significant factor in national and local elections, as well as in the justice and health care systems. As we considered new content for the third edition, this polarization, as well as other threats to progressive capitalistic democracy, led us to choose content which emphasizes the historical and contemporary relationship between multicultural education and the ongoing development of our democratic society. This, in turn, led to the inclusion of material related to the development of democratic capacity in our nation's schools and youth. Thus, in chapter 1 we profile the democratic and equity-oriented work of John Goodlad, and discuss James Banks's latest definition of multicultural education. And in chapter 2 we have expanded our discussion of educational equity, added new material on gender equity, and reinforced the connection between multicultural education and democratic practice within the classroom, school, and community.

In our complex democratic society, filled as it is with new social and technological opportunities and dilemmas, the challenge to teacher educators and advocates of multicultural education is at least sixfold, and this text contains materials to help meet these challenges. What are these challenges? First, in a manner that encourages open-minded inquiry, we must stimulate in teachers a more positive attitude toward diversity. Second, we must motivate teachers to review their beliefs about multiculturalism in general and their own ethnocultural identity in particular. Third, we must help teachers identify information and tools they can use to transform the complex elements of diversity into an illuminating classroom and community database. Fourth, we must ignite in our teachers a desire to study their students in the students' full cultural context, to see them clearly as individuals whose school behavior is influenced in different ways by the family, community, and ethnocultural groups of which they are part. Our teachers will need to understand that to treat their students respectfully as individuals, they must learn about the relevant social groups in their students' lives, in both the community and the classroom. This more sophisticated perspective on individuality is an integral part of the multicultural education we espouse and a key element in the implementation process we call "teaching with a multicultural perspective." Fifth, we must help our students, future and veteran teachers, perceive the clear connections among societal democracy, democratic practices in public schools, and the reform movement/social justice dimension of multicultural education. Multicultural education, as a reform movement concerned with increasing democratic practice in a wide range of societal institutions, has had an enduring interest in the democratization of educational institutions. Finally, as more teacher educators become familiar with the idea that multicultural education, in addition to being an idea, a change process, and a national (and quasi-international) reform movement, is also a field of inquiry which is establishing itself as an interdisciplinary, university-based, academic discipline, they will need to design courses which allow for an open-minded critical appraisal of all concepts, strategies, and curricula associated with various conceptions of multicultural education. And, they will do this at the same time that they encourage their students to study what is good, right, and sensible in multicultural education. In short, the conversation about multicultural education needs to be democratic, one part inspirational, one part analytical, and persistently disciplined in its subjectivity.

To help address these challenges, the text provides a number of resources. These include a practical model for multicultural education, a set of key multicultural planning questions, profiles of eight educators whose work provides rich examples of multicultural thinking and practice, a set of curriculum case

studies that illustrate how the planning questions contribute to the multiculturalization of lesson plans and units, and a briefly annotated list of recommended
multicultural education-related websites. In addition, the text provides instruments and observation guides to help put multicultural teacher education into
practice. Included here are the Classroom Demographic Profile, the Typology
of Multicultural Teaching, the Specially Designed Academic Instruction in English Observation Form, the Ethnic and Cultural Self-disclosure Inventory, and a
set of definitions to facilitate the self-disclosure process. Relatedly, information
about a model of education developed by John Goodlad, Roger Soder, Ken Sirotnick, and other colleagues at the Center for Educational Renewal (at the University of Washington) will also be presented. This model, which provides a clear
mission for public school teachers and administrators as well as teacher educators, overlaps with and complements multicultural education, at the same time
that it brings some new ideas to the table. Finally, to help prospective and veteran teachers shape their own perspective on multicultural education, readers
will find an introduction to various conceptions of multicultural education, several sets of field-tested discussion questions and experiential activities, and an
annotated bibliography of equity-oriented teaching resources.

Extending the invitation to prospective and veteran teachers to shape their
own perspective on multicultural education is a key element in this text. With
this in mind, the *social construction of knowledge* is presented right at the
beginning of the text as a critical concept in relation to the goal of empowerment, and multicultural education itself is presented as a concept that has been
and is being socially constructed. We want to remind readers early on that all
advocates, opponents, and theorists of multicultural education develop a vision
of multicultural education that is shaped by their political values. While this
text is mainly a vehicle for learning how to think, plan, and teach with a multicultural perspective, it is also an invitation to begin or continue a journey
into the field and literature of multicultural education, and an opportunity to
develop a point of view and plan of action regarding multicultural education.
Ideally, the text and the course it is a part of will leave readers more inclined
to establish connections with multicultural education by, for example, joining
an organization, subscribing to one or more multicultural-related listservs or
journals, and/or developing a plan to multiculturalize one or more areas of
their curriculum.

To facilitate the formation of these connections, in the third edition we
have added new information regarding listservs, periodicals, and organizations
that are supportive of the basic goals of multicultural education. In addition,
we will support these connections by communicating with readers via E-mail.
To the extent possible, we will respond to E-mail questions in a timely way,
and will also place selected questions and answers on our World Wide Web
(WWW) homepage. The homepage will allow us, first, to provide new material that supplements and clarifies material in this edition, and, second, to keep
the text to a size commensurate with its purpose.

The text has been designed for flexible use in courses in which professors
are integrating multicultural education and analysis into traditional content

areas such as language arts, social studies, bilingual education, and models of instruction. It will also be useful in courses in which the instructor is emphasizing both the understanding and practice of multicultural education, and particularly the ability to design and implement units that incorporate a multicultural perspective.

In different ways all five chapters contribute to this understanding and practice. For example, chapter 1 provides the conceptual underpinning for the text by clarifying the definition and model of multicultural education espoused by the authors, and the postscript provides a brief review and extension of the ideas introduced in chapter 1. In addition, although all chapters contain traditional textlike conceptual material, chapters 2 and 5 offer experiential field-based activities and the opportunity to reflect on these excursions in the form of a journal entry. Chapter 2 also provides a deeper exploration of educational equity and empowerment, and strategies teachers can employ to promote empowerment, equity, and democratic practice in their classrooms. In chapters 3 and 4 we use multicultural planning questions and curriculum case studies to engage readers in a reality-based dialogue about the creation of multicultural education across the K–12 curriculum. Finally, in chapter 5 we take the reader one step further as we show how multicultural education can be productively linked to other important curriculum emphases, such as citizenship education, global education, and environmental education.

Except for chapter 1, the chapters in this text are organized for individual and nonsequential use. The best use of this text and its individual chapters will be determined by professors as they create their own multiculturally informed courses. We look forward to hearing from those who adopt this text and would appreciate their completing and returning to us the evaluation form in appendix 10 after using the book in their classes. In addition, we ask that readers be tolerant of three stylistic conventions that are employed at different points in this text. First, in discussing teachers in general, we alternate our use of *he* or *she* because we find that using *he/she* is awkward. Second, when referring to certain ethnocultural groups, we sometimes vary the label. For example, although we most often use the label *African American*, we sometimes use *Black American* out of respect for the diversity of opinion that still prevails in the African-American community over the most appropriate group label. With another group label we employ, *Native American*, we sometimes use *American Indian* for similar reasons. Third, in the text we alternate our use of *teachers* and *educators*. We occasionally insert *educators* to remind the reader that while teachers are the primary audience for this text, it is also written with the perspectives of administrators, counselors, and other educational specialists in mind. We hope that you will respond positively to our attempt to maintain a flexible, open-minded approach to group labels. Also, for those wishing to communicate with us via the Internet, our addresses are: <pdavidma\@calpoly.edu> and <ldavidma\@calpoly.edu>. Our homepage on the World Wide Web slice of the Internet can be accessed via http://www.calpoly.edu/~ldavidma>. For each of these three addresses, you do not type in the < and > marks. Finally, to facilitate follow-up inquiries on the World Wide Web at various places in the text we have inserted pertinent website addresses, and as with our own addresses.

ACKNOWLEDGMENTS

Although the content of this text is ultimately the responsibility of the authors, many persons have contributed in various ways to its successful production. To the many preservice candidates and classroom teachers whose questions and ideas gave us deeper insight into this project, we are deeply indebted. To the reviewers whose critiques and thoughtful suggestions made the text more readable and practical, we are especially grateful; these reviewers include:

Ceola Ross Baber, University of North Carolina at Greensboro

David Berman, University of Pittsburgh

Jesus Cortez, University of California, Chico

M. Eugene Gilliom, Ohio State University

Phyllis Goldblatt, Northeastern Illinois University

Cynthia Hammond, California State University, Dominguez Hills

Colleen Kamin, Roosevelt University

Anthony A. Koyzis, University of Wisconsin—Oshkosh

Ellen Kronowitz, California State University, San Bernardino

Natalie Kuhlman, San Diego State University

Dolinda Lybrand, Hardin State University

Jane Nicholls, Ball State University

Mustafa Ozcan, Clarke College

Valerie Ooka Pang, San Diego State University

Nawang Phuntsog, California State University

Timothy Reagan, University of Connecticut

Thomassine Sellers, San Francisco State University

Ramon Serrano, St. Cloud State University

James Uphoff, Wright State University

Rodolfo Vilaro, Northeastern Illinois University

Ray Wong, Weber State University

In addition, we wish to thank our exemplary teachers for their inspirational teaching.

We also express our gratitude to colleagues at California Polytechnic State University, San Luis Obispo, for their interest, advice, and support. Richard Warren, former department head, nurtured the project from its very beginnings, and Cindy Decker, Anita Smith, Veda Marie Flores, Ilene Rockman, David Sanchez, Mary Lou Brady, Jay Waddell, Wayne Montgomery, Patrick Sullivan,

Janice Stone, Patricia Mulligan, Bernie Troy, Donald Cheek, Mary Lud Baldwin, Howard Drucker, Susan McBride, and Robert Levison all helped in various ways.

In addition to those who inspired or enhanced the content of the text, we wish to thank those who contributed to the production of the documents that ultimately became the first, second, and third editions of *Teaching with a Multicultural Perspective: A Practical Guide*, namely Connie Rogalla, Kelly Zimmerman, and Nancy Vilkitis.

Finally, we thank our children, Rachel and Josef, for the support and encouragement they provided as we, on too many occasions, disappeared into our respective offices to work on this project.

Leonard Davidman
Patricia T. Davidman

Teaching with a Multicultural Perspective

CHAPTER **1**

The Idea of Multicultural Education: Past, Present, and Future Possibilities

CHAPTER OVERVIEW

This chapter has five major objectives. First, it will provide veteran and prospective teachers with a practical, goals-oriented model of multicultural education. Second, it will demonstrate the model's value and flexibility by highlighting the work of educators whose teaching and educational leadership fits within the model's parameters. Third, it will discuss concepts such as democracy, culture, cultural group, ethnicity, ethnic group, and multiculturalism, concepts that inform and are a part of the debate about multicultural education. Fourth, it will provide a historical perspective on the conceptions of multicultural education that are currently shaping the field. This should help educators develop a deeper understanding of the evolution that has taken place within multicultural education over the past three decades. We hope this insight will encourage educators to view multicultural education as an evolving body of knowledge, a discipline and movement to which they can contribute, and an approach to curriculum development and instruction that can and should inform their work. Finally, we hope that the information in this chapter will help readers develop a clearer sense of what they believe to be true about multicultural education, and the place of multicultural education in their overall philosophy of education.

   With these objectives in mind, we begin with introductory remarks regarding the significance of multicultural education, and then move to a discussion of selected pivotal concepts. Following this we introduce a synthesis conception of multicultural education, a conception that we developed with K–12 educators, students, and parents in mind. An introduction to the work of eight exemplary equity-oriented educators comes next and leads into a review of the definitions of multicultural education that have emerged in the United States over the past three decades. These definitions reveal the diversity and complexity that surround the term *multicultural education.* Following the definitions is a section that reviews specific factors that make multicultural education an intriguing and controversial topic, and this is followed by a set of examples which make clear that despite the complexity and controversy, it is quite possible to think, plan, teach, and administer with an informed multicultural perspective. The chapter closes with questions designed to encourage critical, creative, and positive thinking about the potential of multicultural education to make a significant difference in the in-school and out-of-school lives of students, teachers, parents, and various other community members.

INTRODUCTION

This chapter embodies a major premise of the book—namely, that teachers in the United States, and other nations on our ever-shrinking planet, will have to be insightful practitioners of multicultural education if they are to meet the multiple challenges that confront citizens in the fast-paced, fluid, highly **unequal** societies of the information era, an era characterized by what may be called advanced global capitalism. To become such practitioners, educators will need to understand various meanings of multicultural education and related terms such as *democracy, culture, cultural group,* and *ethnic group.* They will also need to realize that there are no precise, *right* definitions for these terms. What we have here, as in all the social sciences, is a set of socially constructed terms with various valuable meanings, some of which are more suitable than others for specific school settings and learning experiences. Of equal importance is the awareness that classroom teachers who consciously try to create a multicultural curriculum typically work with an emergent and eclectic conception of multicultural education, one that is colored by their own values and educational experiences. In this chapter, to help establish knowledge of these multiple meanings and possibilities, we will:

1. discuss ethnic and cultural self-disclosure in relation to a set of pivotal multicultural concepts;
2. introduce a model of multicultural education that we have constructed specifically for K–12 educators;
3. describe the work of eight exemplary educators;
4. present a set of overlapping and competing definitions of multicultural education;
5. discuss factors that help to explain why an approach to teaching as logical as multicultural education remains controversial and challenging; and
6. close with a set of intriguing discussion questions.

We hope that this chapter's information, and particularly our synthesis conception of multicultural education, will provide readers with a useful map of multicultural education. The map should help you select and formulate the goals, strategies, and definitions that will constitute your personal conception of multicultural education—the one that will guide you as you begin what we hope will be a lifelong journey into the experience, literature, media, and practice of multicultural education.

ETHNIC AND CULTURAL SELF-DISCLOSURE

We believe that educators in preliminary teacher education and graduate education programs should have the opportunity to study, discuss, and become reflective about themselves as individuals with a dynamic, unfolding, *cultural* identity, an identity that is shaped, in part, by the groups they identify with, either strongly or weakly. We believe, further, that this self-exploration and discussion should occur at the beginning of a program, within small, culturally diverse discussion groups, and should be part of the ongoing inquiry into multicultural education. This self-exploration activity, which we call ethnic and cultural self-disclosure, requires at least five ingredients, most of which have been included in appendixes 2 (p.310) and 7 (p.332).

First, in the context of a course or workshop on or related to multicultural education, educators should receive a clear rationale for this self-disclosure activity. Second, educators should have the opportunity to read and discuss various meanings of terms such as *culture, cultural group, ethnic group, race, racial group, minority group, visible ethnic minority group,* definitions that will help them as they describe themselves in terms of these socially constructed, evolving concepts. The third ingredient is a set of questions to guide the self-disclosure process, and the fourth is an open-minded, supportive environment, one in which the instructor makes clear her or his eagerness to discover how, at that point in time, the educators in the class perceive and define themselves. This activity needs a patient instructor, one who is genuinely interested in engaging students in the process of self-exploration, self-discovery, and self-disclosure, rather than one who is primarily interested in getting students to realize that they are, for example, white, lower-middle-class women who appear to have little insight into the advantage of their whiteness, or the significance of their socioeconomic status and gender. The self-disclosure process might wind up with the instructor politely questioning the self-definitions of educators who have difficulty seeing the importance of color, race, gender, and socioeconomic status (SES) in society, but this will come after rapport has been achieved. Furthermore, any probing regarding one's cultural and/or ethnic identity should build avenues to understanding rather than walls of separation and misunderstanding. Educators may experience discomfort during some of the small- and large-group dialogue, but no individuals or groups should feel that they are under direct attack, either as individuals or as groups, and this is particularly true for individuals who are deeply opposed to multicultural education, or students who have strong reservations. The fifth and critical ingredient is modeling. The instructor can set the stage for detailed, candid, probing self-disclosures by sharing his or her own self-disclosure during the introduction to the activity, and/or by reviewing what might be called the rules of polite discourse during ethnic and cultural self-disclosures.

The ethnic and cultural self-disclosure process shaped by these five ingredients should increase awareness of the influential relationship between *some* individuals and their ethnic or cultural group. The experience should leave educators more inclined to perceive students as individuals who are more or less influenced by the social groups in their classroom and society. In short, the multicultural and democracy-oriented teacher becomes a student of social groups as well as an observer of individual students, because she realizes that both are important phenomena.

KEY MULTICULTURAL CONCEPTS

Because we have included a list of key *multicultural education* concepts in Appendix 7, and will present various meanings of multicultural education later in this chapter, we discuss only a few key concepts below. We begin by examining the *social construction of knowledge*, and then draw on Brian Bullivant's views on multiculturalism and multicultural education to set the stage for a discussion on *culture, cultural group,* and *ethnic group* and a deeper exploration of ethnic and cultural self-disclosure.

The Social Construction of Knowledge

The idea that knowledge is a social construction, and more specifically that social and bureaucratic concepts and categories like race, ethnicity, illegitimacy, exceptionality, socioeconomic status, gender, and religion are based on subjective criteria invented by human beings, is critically important for teachers and their students to comprehend as they develop their moral vision and voice. As the discussion below will reveal, such knowledge and vision are strongly linked to three major goals of multicultural education: the **empowerment** of teachers, students, and parents; **cultural pluralism** (increased tolerance, understanding, and perhaps respect for individuals who manifest different views and lifestyles); and **educational equity.**

The root idea here, as expressed by Mary Kay Thompson Tetreault, is that "all works in literature, science, and history, for example, have an author—male or female, white or ethnic or racial minority, elite or middle-class or occasionally poor—with motivations and beliefs,"[1] and further that these motivations and beliefs, and the works they lead to, are influenced, slightly or strongly, by the sociocultural identity of the authors as well as by the era, nation, and language in which they work.

This awareness, particularly when reinforced by examples of the historical background and the sometimes dubious, subjective, political nature of selected concepts, should leave teachers and students more inclined to question the concepts, assumptions, and knowledge claims of various authority figures or other sources of authority. The authority figures include teachers, media pundits, political and religious leaders, scientists, authors, and other experts. Authoritative sources include dictionaries, encyclopedias, textbooks, newspapers, political and religious documents, and various electronic databases.

The analysis of concepts such as *gifted and talented learners, mentally retarded*, the *discovery of the New World, balance of trade, authentic assessment, high school dropout, sexual harassment*, the *invasion* (of Europe) by the Mongol *hordes*, and the *winning* of the *West* should make it abundantly clear that criteria and labels employed by educators, judges, social scientists, and bureaucrats to classify individuals into "objectively defined" groups are not universal or timeless. Indeed, the situation is quite the opposite: concepts and criteria vary across decades, ethnic and racial groups, national and state borders, and the rate at which conceptual categories are generated or revised appears to be quickening as use of the electronic highway increases. Thus, for example, teachers and students could learn that a child who has been determined to be *gifted and talented* in Minnesota might be considered average in Japan, where the school classification *gifted and talented* does not exist.[2] Relatedly, economist Peter Drucker's comments on the balance of trade should remind students and teachers that antiquated concepts can still play a key but misleading role in defining the conventional wisdom. In 1994, discussing the so-called American trade deficit, Drucker states that

> most people believe this country has a balance-of-trade deficit....The early–18th-century balance-of-trade concept was developed when a bright cookie had an idea. But this brilliant idea was limited to merchandise trade, and that is the only figure reported. Although this country today has a merchandise trade deficit, it also happens to have an enormous service trade surplus. The official amount is two-thirds of the merchandise trade deficit. The actual figure is probably much bigger, because the real service trade figures are simply not there.[3]

Another recent example of the social construction of knowledge, or the political use of labels to influence public opinion, occurred in 1994 when Madeleine Albright, the U.S. ambassador to the United Nations during William Clinton's first administration, tried to explain to Sam Donaldson and George Will, on ABC's *This Week with David Brinkley*, why President Clinton could order an invasion of Haiti to restore President Aristede to power without asking for the approval of Congress. Albright explained that the invasion was a "police action" and not an "act of war." The term *police action* was first used by the U.S. government to describe its military involvement in the Korean War; in that police action, over 50,000 U.S. soldiers died.

A discussion of examples such as these should increase our inclination to question, doubt, and probe. And this propensity, in different ways and for different reasons, will contribute to empowerment, educational equity, democratic education, and a greater tolerance for considering the ideas of others. The readiness to seriously and selectively question the claims of authority figures and of authoritative sources is an act of liberation. It places learners of all ages on the road to greater intellectual responsibility, autonomy, and self-teaching. It also places them knee-deep in the freedom-seeking stream in the Western political tradition, in which men and women, individually and collectively, violently and peacefully, claimed for themselves the right to exercise intellectual, political, economic, and religious freedom from various self-appointed sources of authority and oppression. The latter included royalty, various social and religious hierarchies, dictators of the right and left, and democratic institutions organized along racist, sexist, and classist lines.

This self-teaching, when it occurs, may contribute to greater educational equity—that is, greater fairness in the distribution of educational resources and possibly outcomes. In realizing their own potential for self-teaching, individuals help to create the most important educational outcome of all and experience the type of self-directed education that future economic and political leaders receive in the best schools in the United States and elsewhere. Too often, however, this critical, leadership-oriented education is only partially realized in low SES schools, when it is manifest at all.

There is, finally, another *potential* positive result that stems from a greater awareness of the social construction of knowledge. When individuals appreciate that the way *they* perceive and utilize concepts to describe reality is partially influenced by their gender, racial and religious identity, SES, nationality, or political orientation, they may be more inclined to analyze ideas, such as feminist pedagogy, evolution, or the race-conscious shaping of voting districts, that heretofore they would have likely ignored. In other words, a greater awareness of the subjective nature of their own perceptions might encourage learners to listen harder to individuals who espouse ideas that challenge their worldview, that seem odd, and that make them uncomfortable.

Now, with the expectation that the social construction of knowledge will be better understood, we can more perceptively consider the meanings of *multicultural education, multiculturalism,* and related terms. The readers' heightened awareness of the role they themselves can play in the knowledge construction process should contribute to a well-rounded, open-minded consideration of these socially constructed meanings.

The Meanings of Multicultural Education

As one begins a journey into the field of multicultural education, a logical point of departure is with the meanings of the term itself. A cursory review of the multicultural education literature shows that we are not alone in starting off with definitions. Most writers begin their discussion of multicultural education by coming to grips with one or more meanings of the term. A case in point is the work of Brian M. Bullivant.[4] We will draw on his work as we indicate why a broad and pluralistic conception of culture and cultural group will help teachers in general and advocates of multicultural education in particular.

In attempting to clarify the meaning of *multiculturalism* and *multicultural education,* Bullivant broke the word *multicultural* down into its constituent parts: *multi-* and *cultural.* Because the meaning of *multi-,* or *many,* is obvious, his main analytical work was to determine, in the context of multicultural education, the best meaning for the term *culture.* After examining several alternative meanings, Bullivant defined culture "as a social group's design for survival in and adaptation to its environment." With this definition in mind, he added that one aim of multicultural education would be "*to teach about the many social groups and their different designs for living in a pluralist society."*[5]

We are concerned about the boundaries of Bullivant's definition and his approach to establishing the meanings and aims of multicultural education, particularly as the term and reform movement have evolved in the United States. Although the analysis of the term *multicultural,* or more specifically *culture,* to shed light on the meaning of *multicultural education* appears logical, the approach is ahistorical and somewhat presumptuous in suggesting that there is only one interpretation of multicultural education out there. This approach would have had a stronger rationale if the early American creators of the multicultural education movement had gone directly from a definition of *culture* to their conceptions and operationalizations of multicultural education.

But this is not what happened, at least not within the U.S. historical context. As James A. Banks[6] and others have pointed out, the educational movement now called multicultural education was initially a set of individual and group responses to economic inequality, racism, and sexism in American culture. These responses were primarily, but not exclusively, located in the twentieth-century African-American community. However, in retrospect, it can be seen that all the individuals and groups struggling for greater equality and opportunity for members of politically disenfranchised and economically exploited groups, in the twentieth century and before, were laying the groundwork for the educational reform movement that in the United States would later be called *multicultural education.*

Because the historical roots of multicultural education preceded early definitions of *multicultural education,* and were grounded in the socioeconomic and political conditions of the day, it seems appropriate to reverse Bullivant's procedure in ways that focus more attention on these historical roots and what they imply about the meaning of *cultural.* To illustrate, we will discuss an early, influential definition of *multicultural education:* "Multicultural education [is] an educational reform movement that is concerned with increasing educational equity for a range of cultural and ethnic groups."[7] From this definition we draw three points. First, equity has been a pivotal concern for advocates of multicultural education. Second, a central proposition has been the idea that *all* students, regardless of gender, social class, degree of learning handicap, linguistic background, or ethnic, cultural, or religious identity, should have an equal or equivalent, or at least a genuine, opportunity to learn in school and, by extension, society. Finally, while the long-term goal is the equivalence of opportunity, the short-term goal focuses on developing strategies that *increase* equity and opportunities for selected groups that have been underserved. Put another way, students should not be penalized because of the various labels and social groups that together shape their social identity.

With these points in mind, we conclude that the term *multicultural* in *multicultural education* refers to various social, cultural, and ethnic **groups** that exist within the macroculture (total culture) of the United States, and a major concern for advocates of multicultural education is equity (and excellence) for all members of these groups. To the extent that studying these different groups and their *"designs for living"* or "design for survival" can provide ideas for maximizing the educational opportunities of members of these cultural groups, Bullivant's description of aims for multicultural education reinforces the equity dimension of multicultural education. However, many groups of concern to multicultural education practitioners do not have a "design for survival" that is widely shared by group members. Thus, in Bullivant's definition and use of the term *culture*, those groups without a survival program are cultureless, and yet in the eyes of many multicultural practitioners these cultureless groups are important cultural groups. Furthermore, these groups—the poor, the homeless, learners who are "at risk," the "English language learner," "women," "gay and lesbian high school students," and the "learning disabled" or "gifted" learners—do have a culture, or more precisely are part of a macroculture, the total culture of a nation.

Our Definition of Cultural Group

At this point, it should prove helpful to discuss our understanding of the term *cultural group*. As we use them, the terms *social group* and *cultural group* are synonymous; if a specific social group has an identity or label that is recognized or created in a macroculture (from within or outside the social group—autonymously or exonymously), like "Gay Americans" or "developmentally delayed/mentally retarded," "recovering alcoholics," "White Supremacists," or "African American," then that social group can be accurately described as a cultural group, and a cultural group could be an ethnic or racial group as well. This is true because any group that has a publicly recognized identity (label) becomes a cultural group within the **macroculture.** And this is true because its identity and label are facts that are negotiated or given meaning within that specific macroculture. In other words, any group that fits, or fits itself into, the macroculture's definition of group becomes, automatically, a cultural group in that macroculture. Furthermore, cultural groups that exist in one macroculture—for instance, the "gifted" or "at-risk learners" or the "criminally insane" or "Mexican Americans" or "victims of hate crimes" or the "homeless"—may not exist in some other macroculture. Or if a group such as "developmentally disabled learners" exists as a category in one macroculture, the members of this group may, by bureaucratic definition, have different characteristics from developmentally disabled learners in a second macroculture. The social construction process in two nations may lead to the same label, but embed different meanings in the label.

Implications for the Multicultural Education Conversation

As indicated earlier, this discussion about the meaning of *culture, cultural group,* and *multicultural education* has implications for the way we can invite future teachers, parents, students, and laypeople into the multicultural education conversation. To begin with, it reminds us that multicultural education is about *cultural groups* of all kinds, and particularly cultural groups that have been, or are, underserved or miseducated in one way or another, as well as *culture.* Second, the key cultural groups of concern in one macroculture (nation) or state may differ from those in another. Third, within multicultural education courses there is, because of the historical association of multicultural education and oppressed groups, a natural tendency for teachers to think about their profession in terms of the groups they will serve, and the groups that are important in their own lives. This analysis is instructive because it reveals that, right from the outset, there is a tension in the conversation between advocates of multicultural education and some of their often captive audience—namely, those future and in-service teachers who are accustomed to thinking of themselves, and their students, as citizens whose individuality counts for much more than the groups of which they are a part. Finally, we realize from this analysis that in a given society the focus of multicultural education may broaden from one decade to the next as new groups enter a society (the Hmong from Laos and Vietnam) or are invented by legislative or bureaucratic definition (the "at-risk learner" or the "English language learner," formerly called the "limited proficient English student") or are officially recognized as a group that is disadvantaged by power relationships within a society (women) and therefore in need of legislative protection pertaining to occupational opportunities, sexual harassment, child custody payments, and so on.

Our expansive meaning of *cultural group,* if accepted, may also have positive implications for teacher educators who are trying to help prospective and veteran teachers see that:

1. as individuals with a cultural identity, they are a part of a multicultural United States and therefore the multicultural equation;

2. multicultural education, broadly construed, is about democracy, equity, empowerment, intergroup harmony, and cultural pluralism for teachers as well as students; and

3. multicultural education is also a field of inquiry, one in which teachers, scholars, and advocates for multicultural education can specialize.

In short, multicultural education is for and by teachers, as well as students, parents, and other stakeholders; it encompasses and has positive implications for all individuals and groups in the United States and other nations that have their own multicultural education movements.

Developing a Positive Attitude toward Multicultural Education

In many cases when American teacher educators responsible for conveying the meanings of and rationales for multicultural education face their university audience, mainly prospective and in-service teachers, the majority of the group, often up to 70 or 90 percent, are White Americans or Americans of European descent (depending on your label preference), and the majority of this group are women, particularly in elementary education classes. In addition, the "students of color" in the class, Americans of African, Asian, American Indian, Hispanic, and Pacific Island descent, often have some values and social characteristics that overlap those of the White Americans. Thus the students of color and their White colleagues have commonalties and points of divergence, just like most of the classes they will work with in K–12 settings.

One of the commonalities pertains to their preliminary understanding or misunderstanding about multicultural education. Like many others, these students sometimes confuse multicultural education with ethnic studies, and, for many, both of these topics appear to be exclusively or largely concerned with the social and academic problems of "people of color." While somewhat understandable, given the origins of multicultural education and the recent contentious public and university debate about multiculturalism, ethnic studies, and multicultural education, this perception is both erroneous and counterproductive in terms of getting a group of largely White teacher candidates and their colleagues of color to develop a positive connection with multicultural education. And, we mean here multicultural education construed as a change-oriented model of curriculum and instruction, a model that addresses the aspirations and learning needs of *all* students, as well as parents and teachers.

We believe that a major objective of a course or sequence of courses on multicultural education should be to develop in teachers a positive personal connection with the content and goals of multicultural education. For this to occur, the course(s) will need certain characteristics. To begin with, the course content should be historically accurate, and reveal that multicultural education is for and about the teachers and their individual and group needs as well as groups they are not a part of. In addition, the course(s) should provide a forum in which teachers can safely explore and publicly speculate about their tentative cultural, ethnic, and racial group connections, their idiosyncratic individual identities, and their initial and emergent thoughts (positive and negative) about multicultural education. It would be helpful, also, if the instructor made clear, first, that the attempt to comprehend multicultural education in all its facets is a lifelong journey, and, second, that at the beginning of such a journey, many students will discover that there is a lot they don't know about African-American history, Mexican-American history, inequality in American life, and so on, and much to learn. But that is the point of the journey and the course(s); it is the attitude toward the lifelong journey that is critical and practical, rather than the unrealistic hope that teacher candidates can master a substantial part of the increasing multicultural body of knowledge prior to student teaching, or that they or veteran teachers will have developed a set of *correct* beliefs and attitudes by the end of a ten- or sixteen-week course.

Ethnic and Cultural Self-disclosure Revisited

In the context of such a course, the opportunity to explore, describe, and share one's cultural, ethnic, and racial connections can have a positive, enduring effect. As they make a sustained effort to cover some part of the traditional curriculum, K–12 and university instructors and students sometimes overlook the rich diversity—religious, gender, ethnic, racial, SES, age, lifestyle, work and life experience, language, and experience with handicapping conditions—that exists in almost any classroom. But a positive experience with cultural and ethnic self-exploration and disclosure can make a strong impression on prospective and in-service teachers. When teachers, working in small, diversely structured, cooperative discussion groups (five to six students to a group), see that their efforts to study and communicate with fellow teachers are enhanced because of the prior knowledge gained from their colleagues' self-disclosures, they will more likely create opportunities for their own students to discover each other as sources of cultural information and insight.

Part of the value of self-disclosure derives from the realization that the cultural information shared in small groups sets the stage for a deeper type of trust and rapport-building in a classroom community. It is noteworthy that this trust and rapport are linked to the broad conception of *cultural group* discussed earlier. We want our university students to see that their values and self-perceptions lead them to culturally connect with selected groups, and we want them to know we are interested in all their cultural connections, just as we want them to be interested in their student-clients' full cultural biographies.

Thus, in our courses the term *cultural group* is taken to mean any collection of people in the macroculture who share a public identity and sense of commonality. This sense of commonality is not the same as a sense of unity, or the strong sense of affinity that is felt by members of some ethnic, racial, and cultural groups. The sense of commonality merely suggests that members of the group understand that they have something in common with all members of that group and that the group has a public identity or label that can be shared. A vegetarian, for example, may share some norms and behavior patterns with all other vegetarians and may read articles and books about vegetarians but may not, at a given point in time, know other vegetarians in her community or be interested in spending time with other vegetarians. And the fact that the vegetarian's spouse and children do not choose to share vegetarianism is inconvenient but not critical.

Of course, it is likely that there are vegetarians who take their lifestyle and group more seriously; such individuals may be vegetarians on an individual as well as a group level. They may pay dues to a vegetarian organization, write articles about vegetarianism, and attend local and state meetings of vegetarians. Still, these organization-oriented vegetarians may be more connected to a healthy lifestyle and social movement than to other vegetarians as a "people." And, if they should desire, it would be fairly easy to stop being vegetarians. And vegetarians have not suffered *group* oppression because of their belief system, physical characteristics, language background, or place of origin. In this sense, vegetarians are far from being an *ethnic group,* a cultural group with a sense of peoplehood, shared history, common ancestry, and a common set of political and economic interests. Nevertheless, this vegetarian cultural connection should be treated seriously and respectfully; in no way should it be dismissed as a "mere" lifestyle identity. We know that being a vegetarian, or a legal alien, or an AIDS activist, or a conservationist, or a divorced working parent, or a pacifist, or a recovering alcoholic, or a rural agricultural-oriented American can be a critical part of a student's cultural identity for the short or long term. More important, this identity can become the lens through which a candidate better perceives the similarities and differences between himself and others who present different types of cultural, ethnic, and racial identities;

furthermore, in an accepting classroom environment, the identities students start with (the groups they identify with) may serve as catalysts for deeper insights into their full cultural biographies.

A key point to remember is that when we ask educators to engage in cultural and ethnic self-exploration and disclosure, we want them to report on *all* the cultural groups they see themselves as part of, and not just the important ones that are traditionally and still a major concern of multicultural education, because of the underserved, oppressed, or exploited status of such groups. This strategy is consistent with the idea of starting your teaching where your students are, and not where you'd have them be. Furthermore, because we encourage students to define themselves and then proceed to value those initial self-perceptions, it is also consistent with cultural pluralism, a major goal of multicultural education. Finally, this approach to ethnic and cultural self-disclosure builds positive relationships between advocates (and models) of multicultural education and our next generation of helping professionals. Although we have not studied this claim in a systematic way, our qualitative impression is that these positive human relationships help to produce professionals who have a more open-minded and positive attitude toward the content and goals of multicultural education. If such attitudes are part of what we are after in our introductory and advanced multicultural education courses, then the self-disclosure strategy discussed previously is worthy of more discussion, adaptation, and research. To promote such discussion, in Appendix 2 we list the set of questions that students respond to in the latest version of our ethnic and cultural self-disclosure form. Parenthetically, in our university classes we use the self-disclosure data in a variety of ways. For example, at the beginning of the course we use the data to form heterogeneous discussion groups. The self-disclosure reports, made in the small groups, also help each student see the rich diversity that exists in a class that on the surface may look fairly homogeneous. In addition, analysis of this class database places instructors in a better position to develop rapport with students, and to demonstrate how cultural group knowledge can be used for this and other instructional purposes.

MULTICULTURAL EDUCATION: A SYNTHESIS CONCEPTION

Perceiving the diversity that exists in classroom settings, and the significance of culture in shaping some students' learning preferences and patterns, will make some teachers more curious about multicultural education. But diversity can cut two ways; it can also frustrate, frighten, or overwhelm. The same will be true when we explore various conceptions of multicultural education later in this chapter. To diminish the potential that a variety of conceptions have to confuse the reader, we will first present a goal-oriented synthesis conception of multicultural education. Our synthesis conception is intended to serve as a conceptual map, a practical guide that teachers, administrators, and other professionals can use as they begin or continue their journey into the field of multicultural education. This map includes most of the goals that multicultural education theorists have advocated, and we think it adds up to a challenging but realizable agenda for K–12 school-based and university-based practitioners.

The conception of multicultural education that we recommend for your initial consideration is defined by seven major goals, and integrates elements from several other thoughtful conceptions, most notably those articulated by James Banks, Carl Grant, Christine Sleeter, Carlos Cortes, Sonia Nieto, H. Prentice Baptiste, Jr., and Mira Baptiste. Because of these multiple sources, we call it a synthesis conception. Although you will see in the latter part of this chapter that several theoreticians have sought to strengthen multicultural education by integrating it with other curriculum areas or concepts such as multiethnic education, global education, social reconstructionism, critical pedagogy, or Africentric education, we take a different tack. We employ a simpler goal-oriented conception, one that has served as a useful framework for K–12 and university-based educators seeking to understand and implement multicultural education in their classrooms and communities.

MULTICULTURAL EDUCATION DEFINED

We define *multicultural education* as a multifaceted, organizational, change-oriented strategy that is aimed at seven interrelated but distinct goals. These goals are (1) educational equity; (2) empowerment of students, parents, and teachers; (3) the development of a society that values cultural pluralism; (4) intercultural/interethnic/intergroup understanding and harmony in the classroom, school, and community; (5) maintenance and expansion of freedom and democracy in a just pluralistic society; (6) an expanded knowledge of multicultural education, as well as various cultural and ethnic groups; and (7) the development of students, parents, and practitioners (teachers, nurses, journalists, counselors, principals, custodians, documentary producers, bus drivers, curriculum coordinators, etc.) whose thoughts and actions are guided by an informed and inquisitive multicultural perspective (see Figure 1.1 for a visual summary).

These goals can be achieved by practitioners as well as volunteers working in public and private schools, television, the armed forces, museums, newspapers, religious organizations, movies, hospitals, private corporations, and so on. The educational process and product created by these cooperating and competing organizations is what Carlos E. Cortés calls the societal curriculum.[8] While all practitioners who work in these institutions are important, teachers and other professionals in K–12 public and private schools are the primary concern in this text. But as we focus on this population and the K–12 school-based curricula they create, we will not forget the voice of Cortés, who reminds us that "in particular, multicultural education scholars and practitioners have tended to ignore—or avoid addressing—the pedagogical implications of that powerful public multicultural educator, the mass media."[9] Thus, as we identify approaches that K–12 practitioners can employ to reduce alienation and level a heavily tilted playing field, we include strategies that make

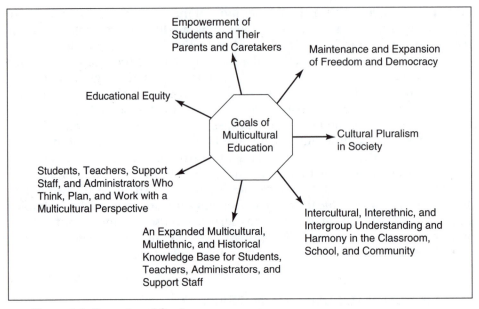

Figure 1.1 Examples of Goals

positive use of media resources as well as several that are intended to countervail such negative elements in the media as racism, sexism, and other debilitating forces in American culture.

At the classroom and school level of operation, the goals of multicultural education can be achieved by a wide range of teaching strategies, some of which are included in Figure 1.2. A more detailed list of strategies is provided in Appendix 1 (p.300), "The Typology of Multicultural Teaching." This tool was created, first, to familiarize teachers with the large number of strategies that promote multicultural education and, second, to help educators perceive that many teachers already engage in some form of multicultural education, although they may label it otherwise.

Although the typology will provide you with a set of teaching strategies that can promote multicultural education, we will also need to explore the meaning of *educational equity, cultural pluralism, empowerment, intergroup/intragroup harmony, education for freedom and democracy, multicultural/multiethnic knowledge,* and the idea of teaching (or counseling, or administering, etc.) with a multicultural perspective, to help you better understand the goals in our conception.

Educational Equity

We begin with *educational equity* because for us it lies at the heart of the modern multicultural education movement in the United States (1960s–1990s). Conceptually, it is among the most complex of the goals to explain and achieve, and for that reason it, along with democratic practice and empowerment, will

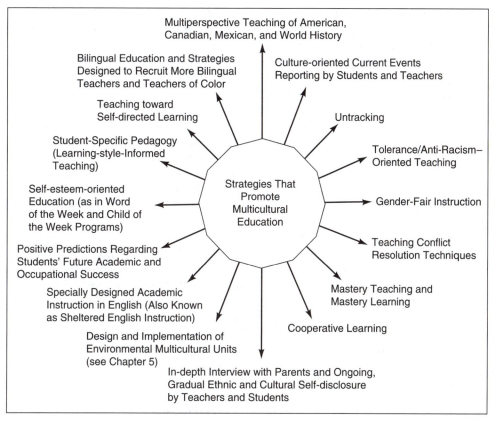

Figure 1.2 Examples of Strategies

receive a more elaborate treatment in Chapter 2. Why has educational equity been both difficult to achieve and preeminent among multicultural education goals? To begin with, in the United States we are not dealing with one centralized school system; students are educated in approximately 15,500 quasi-independent school districts. Secondly, for long periods of time, in some cases centuries, specific cultural, ethnic, and racial groups (African-American, Mexican-Americans, and women, for example) have been underserved and undermined within the overall public and private educational system. Finally, educational equity will remain a major concern and conundrum in the coming decades because of the widespread success and influence of democratic capitalism in the United States and elsewhere. While educational equity (and equality) in the United States is widely praised as an educational goal (equality of opportunity in particular), we believe that in our capitalistic democracy it is really inequality that is more deeply entrenched and valued, and if not valued at least accepted as a tolerable and inevitable result. And we have in mind here inequality of wealth, political influence, medical care, physical security (gated communities), educational opportunity, and overall quality of life. Furthermore, the longer that capitalism has been the prevailing economic system in a nation, and the longer specific families and cultural groups have had to establish their unequal wealth, the more difficult it is for contemporary school systems to create authentic equality of educational opportunity, or even rough equivalency of educational resources. Perhaps educational equity and the related concepts of equality of educational opportunity and equality under the law are best perceived as ideas which help our democratic capitalistic system maintain its equilibrium, and simultaneously allow its citizens to maintain their belief in progress, inequality, and the essential goodness of the nation. Furthermore, multicultural education, a reform movement which places educational equity and social justice at the center of its agenda, may be exactly what a system grounded in inequality needs. Namely, a movement which helps to create policies, structures, and organizations which have the potential to strengthen the 'equality of opportunity' and 'equal education under the law' dimensions of the American creed and culture.

While we will have more to say about creating equitable (fair and just) conditions in school settings in Chapter 2, it will help if we begin to clarify the meanings of educational equity here. As we do so, we should be aware that with educational equity, as with so many of the terms associated with multicultural education, we will encounter competing definitions, definitions which are, understandably, influenced by the writer's overall political orientation and specific sense of what constitutes social justice. For example, Ronald Edmond's (1979) definition of equity accepts inequality in the overall allocation of goods and services at the same time that it makes clear that a "good" society cannot ignore its poorest citizens. Edmonds wrote:

> By equity I mean a simple sense of fairness in the distribution of the primary goods and services that characterize our social order. Some of us, rightly, have more goods and services than others, and my sense of equity is not disturbed by that fact. Others of us have almost no goods and access to only the most wretched services, and that deeply offends my simple sense of fairness and violates the standards of equity by which I judge our social order. I measure our progress as a social order by our willingness to advance the equity interests of the least among us.[10]

More recently, Rebecca Powell pointed out the difference between equality of educational opportunity and educational equity, and the value of a transformational conception of equity. She wrote:

> I would suggest that learning environments that are grounded in equity are much more transformative than most of our recent reform efforts, which tend to promote *equality* but not necessarily *equity*. It is important to point out that these two terms are not synonymous; equality connotes sameness or uniformity, whereas equity implies justice. For example, providing the same level of funding to both poor and rich school districts may be "equal" but not necessarily equitable, as students in poorer school districts generally require a substantially higher level of financial support.[11]

In a similar vein, Beth Swadener, when explaining why equity, equal opportunity, and *fairness* are not synonymous, wrote that "equal opportunity is the first step towards educational equity," and "In contemporary usage....it is important to distinguish equity from fairness because members of the dominant culture have at times co-opted the term fairness in deceptive ways that are actually inequitable. For example, some argue that affirmative action and equal opportunity policies are unfair and that reverse discrimination is possible."[12] Swadener concludes her essay this way:

> Thus, the pursuit of equity in education is a dynamic process that recognizes contextual realities (e.g., institutionalized racism and sexism) and barriers to the achievement of a truly just distribution of power and opportunity, and works constantly to name, address, and dismantle systems of oppression which keep inequality in place.[13]

While accepting the value of Powell's and Swadener's definitions which emphasize the dynamic, anti-inequality, transformational potential of educational equity, we provide a more conservative interpretation of educational equity. To help illuminate this interpretation, we define *educational equity* in terms of three types of observable conditions: physical and financial conditions, the opportunity to learn, and educational outcomes for both individuals and groups. For example, when teachers and administrators try to create educational equity in a classroom, school, or school district, they will strive to make *roughly equivalent* (exact or approximate numerical equality is a social and bureaucratic impossibility) the physical school conditions under which children learn; the quality and experience of teachers and administrators, the amount of funds spent per child at each school (but some overburdened schools with higher proportions of low-SES students and "learning disabled" students should receive more rather than equal amounts per child); the opportunity for various types of learners to learn; and the educational achievement of various groups of learners within the class, school, and school district (e.g., boys and girls, Hispanics, Blacks, Whites, and Asian Americans; monolingual and bilingual learners; the economically poor and those who are more fortunate).

It is logical and important for teachers, administrators, and parents to strive to balance (make fair) or roughly equalize the allocation of resources to all classrooms and schools within a district. However, a group of teachers, administrators, and parents may be doing a superb job of creating equity conditions within the school district, while conditions of extreme inequity exist between their school district and other districts in the state or nation. This type of inequity most often results when individual school districts in a state receive a large percentage of their funds from local real estate taxes. (More on this in Chapter 2.) For the present, suffice it to say that when most teachers contemplate equity, they think about this basic ethical question: In my classroom have I created a *fair* learning environment for the (typically) wide range of learners in my charge? In contrast, when administrators contemplate equity, in addition to internal school district equity conditions, they, with the support of teachers, should be asking: Is the allocation of resources to individual school districts (and students) in my state fair, and, if not, what can I and my colleagues and professional organizations do about it?

When teachers and administrators analyze the distribution of resources, they should consider the distribution of human resources—that is, teachers and instructional aides, and the training they have received in multicultural education. This equity-related analysis is linked to the goal of cultural pluralism: when one tries to establish whether or not a group of students has had equivalent opportunity to learn, the attitudes that teachers and aides manifest toward their diverse students is a pertinent issue. And the challenging diversity we have in mind includes students who are poor, culturally and/or ethnically and/or racially different from the teacher(s), second-language learners, migrant learners, members of new types of nontraditional families, members of families where the parents are not legal residents of the United States, physically challenged or learning disabled, homeless, intellectually gifted, immigrants or refugees, heterosexual or gay, and so on. This is not a simple type of diversity; this is a stunning diversity, and we can analyze teachers' attitudes toward, and support of, students with these various characteristics, from the perspective of educational equity or a second defining goal of multicultural education—namely, cultural pluralism.

Cultural Pluralism

In a discussion of cultural pluralism as a goal of multicultural education, David Washburn's analysis of multicultural education is helpful.[14] Washburn reminds us that Milton M. Gordon identified *cultural pluralism* as one of three concepts that have helped social scientists distinguish among three different types of assimilation, the other two being *anglo-conformity* and *the melting pot.* Gordon, in his influential work *Assimilation in American Life,* wrote:

> In preliminary fashion, we may say that the "anglo-conformity" theory demanded the complete renunciation of the immigrant's ancestral culture in favor of the behavior and values of the Anglo-Saxon core group; the "melting pot" idea envisaged a biological merger of the Anglo-Saxon peoples with other immigrant groups and a blending of their respective cultures into a new indigenous American type; and "cultural pluralism" postulated the preservation of the communal life and significant portions of the culture of the latter immigrant groups within the context or American citizenship and political and economic integration to American society....Cultural pluralism....is a relative newcomer on the American scene, being predominantly a development of the experiences and reflections of the twentieth century.[15]

Cultural pluralists, then, in contrast to Anglo-conformists and advocates of the melting pot, promoted a system in which individuals could become American while they held on to aspects of their former, often European, cultural identity; in essence they desired a nation where one could participate in two cultural worlds without penalty. And this desire sometimes included efforts to protect a religious cultural identity. For example, in Oregon in 1922, in the struggle to maintain their right to form and conduct private religious schools, as well as just private schools, members of several organizations (the Catholic

Civil Rights Association, the Evangelical Lutheran Synod, Seventh Day Adventists, the Presbyterian Church, and others) unsuccessfully opposed a referendum requiring all children between the ages of 8 and 16 to attend public school. However, this "Americanization" initiative, which was supported by the Scottish Rite Masons and the Ku Klux Klan, was declared unconstitutional by the U.S. Supreme Court in 1925 in *Pierce* v. *Society of Sisters.*[16]

Significantly, the meaning of cultural pluralism has grown. Currently, when advocates of multicultural education promote cultural pluralism, they no longer think exclusively of immigrants in the process of becoming American. They think of indigenous conquered Americans whose ancestors have lived on this continent for tens of thousands of years, as well as the descendants of indentured, enslaved, and free Africans. In addition, they think of Americans who seek their full economic and political rights while maintaining a lifestyle that clashes with another, more powerful, American lifestyle/value orientation (i.e., Gay and Lesbian Americans); and they think of Americans who live within a linguistic and cultural world strongly influenced by physical characteristics, which are only dimly understood by their fellow citizens (i.e., the Deaf). Under the same pluralist umbrella we think also of Americans who are forging a new and broader cultural position and identity in the American arena (i.e., Women). In short, the groups affected by the goal of cultural pluralism in the late twentieth and early twenty-first century are far broader than the original set of European immigrant groups Horace Kallen had in mind in 1915 when he articulated the concept of cultural pluralism.[17]

Cultural Pluralism in Contemporary America

It is instructive to realize that the umbrella for today's cultural pluralism covers more diversity than the umbrella that was originally conceived. This perception helps to explain some current opposition to multicultural education. At the same time, it illuminates what is distinctive and noble about multicultural education, and education in the United States, as we enter a new millennium. One is hard put to find another nation so concerned with the civil liberties and educational rights of so broad a range of citizens.

Societies differ in the degree to which they celebrate, support, and/or tolerate diversity within their midst. Furthermore, their general orientation toward diversity influences the conditions that are placed upon newcomers/immigrants within these societies, and the way citizenship education occurs in the state-supported (public) schools in these nations. Thus, for example, we would expect schools in Saudi Arabia, Cuba, Japan, France, Northern Ireland, Nigeria, Yugoslavia, and the United States to provide different lessons pertaining to diversity in religion, political expression, bilingualism, lifestyles, and ethnic and cultural backgrounds. In other words, good citizenship as a concept and value is constructed, or infused, with different meanings in different societies.

More to the point, in contemporary American society and schools, partly resulting from the work of multicultural education advocates, good citizenship is often linked to positive attitudes about, and behaviors toward, cultural diversity. So, with cultural pluralism (and diversity) in mind, classroom teachers strive to develop in their students respect, appreciation, and/or tolerance for individuals and groups that are culturally, linguistically, and/or physically different from themselves. In this way, across 12 grades and in many different types of classes, teams of educators make a critical contribution to a society that must, of necessity, learn to value and support its considerable diversity while it simultaneously builds the critical sense of unity and cohesion that all nations, and particularly those with significant diversity, require.

It is noteworthy that, for decades, some educators have created respect, appreciation, and tolerance among *culturally different* learners by helping them discover what they have in common as they participate in developing a supportive classroom community. Worthy of note also is the fact that when teachers develop in their students a positive attitude toward tolerance and acceptance of diversity, there will usually be more intergroup harmony in their classrooms. This, in turn, will promote educational equity, primarily because of the increased ease in establishing effective cooperative learning groups. Activities that promote cultural pluralism contribute to the maintenance of a democratic society and create an environment supportive of empowerment.

Empowerment

When we specify empowerment as a goal, we have in mind a process of curriculum development and instruction that enables students, parents, and teachers (and other practitioners) to have more influence and actual power over the educational, political, economic, and social events in their own lives. For this to occur, K–12 educators, working together, must design and implement a curriculum that explicitly aims at empowerment. Such a curriculum will resemble in some respects traditional K–12 citizenship curricula, but in many schools an empowerment curriculum will, of necessity, extend far beyond the traditional citizenship curriculum. One notable area of difference pertains to the explicit study of empowerment, change, and change-agentry; a curriculum of empowerment for our new millennium will provide *all* students with experiences, attitudes, and skills that better enable them to cope with, and serve as catalysts for, change and/or preservation in their own lives and communities. In creating such a curriculum, teachers across the K–12 continuum will provide various inputs to create an overall *empowering* environment. For example, because some, or perhaps many, of their students will have little contact with empowered/empowering individuals, teachers who attempt to create empowering conditions will provide their students with:

1. *knowledge* so they can better understand the political, economic, and power relationships in the political worlds they inhabit (the local, regional, state, national, and transnational world of politics);

2. *confidence* to believe that students such as themselves can be catalysts for change or preservation in their own life and the lives of others;

3. *numerous opportunities* to become active, self-directed learners who grow accustomed to making decisions that shape the content and process of their own education;

4. *numerous opportunities* to study successful change agents and social activists so as to be better prepared to create a just society;

5. *communication skills* of all kinds, particularly those that relate to new technologies such as video and computer conferencing, E-mail, videotape production; website construction and web searches;

6. week-by-week *modeling* to provide concrete evidence of how a proactive, confident, empowered/empowering individual conducts her or his affairs in the workplace and community;

7. *validation*—that is, acceptance of and support for the cultural identities and languages they bring to class and choose to maintain. In other words, we can empower students simply by accepting that two cultures and two languages can be better than one, particularly for students who are expected to create, or choose to create, a biethnic identity (Japanese American, Jewish American, African American, Nigerian American, Italian American). We are also concerned here with students whose cultural (lifestyle) identities need support (the Gay or Deaf student or the Christian, Sikh, or Muslim student), but there are cultural identities and lifestyles that teachers cannot support and indeed will have difficulty tolerating (the White or Black supremacist or Neo-Nazi cultural group, or drug-supporting lifestyle, or antilearning/know-nothing lifestyle); and

8. *programs* that provide meaningful ways to involve parents and caretakers in an overall empowering curriculum.

Empowerment and Advocacy

There is one more critical role that teachers can play in an empowering curriculum. Because of the way political, economic, and K–12 school systems are structured in our capitalistic constitutional democracy, in the United States, we will have, into the near future at least, rich and poor schools, public and private schools, and many highly segregated schools. To a greater or lesser extent, depending on their special circumstances, students in all these schools will need teachers who are willing to be advocates for young people. Various groups in our democratic society, indeed many groups, have advocates and political action groups looking out for their special interests. And there are groups like the Children's Defense Fund (founded by Marian Wright Edelman) that focus on the needs of young people. However, the needs of pre-K and K–12 students in our society are great, and our assessment is that classroom teachers are uniquely positioned to become strong advocates for the students at their school site and *beyond*.

The content in the aforementioned educational equity section suggests issues within the school and school district which provide grist for a teacher's advocacy mill. But, how and when could educators become advocates *beyond* the school site? While there is no simple way to answer this question, we think it is helpful for educators to first recognize that educational equity does not end at the classroom or school door, and second that the economic and political policies and conditions within a community, state, and nation greatly influence the degree of equity within a school. Recall that when Ron Edmonds discussed equity he spoke of "a simple sense of fairness in the distribution of primary goods and services that characterize our social order." So, for example, if the community surrounding a school lacked a public library, or adequate health care facilities and services, or an after-school recreational program, it would be highly appropriate for some educators to work with local citizens and officials to improve the level and quality of services within the community. Although new teachers will have their hands full simply taking care of school-related tasks, it is ultimately in everyone's best interest to remember that equality of educational opportunity is a function of school as well as community resources; in short a fair school requires a fair society, a just school a just society. And empowerment-oriented educators will need to support their students in the school and community arena.

Finally, when we discuss empowerment as a goal of multicultural education, we refer primarily to the empowerment of students, but have in mind also the empowerment of parents, teachers, and other school-based practitioners, and would like to explain why. We have included parents as part of the triangle of empowerment because research has shown that when parents are involved in their children's education, student learning proceeds more smoothly.[18] Also, logic and experience suggest that students will develop a stronger belief in their ability to shape their world when they see their parents, and other community representatives, playing an influential role in school site governance councils, school district committees and boards, and similar bodies. Thus, as noted previously, teachers and administrators should find ways to increase the level of meaningful parent participation in the operation of schools. This is even more true in communities that have been historically disempowered because of racism and/or impoverished economic conditions. An effective model for developing such participation is briefly discussed later in this chapter when we review the work of James P. Comer, and we will extend this discussion in Chapter 2 when we identify strategies for involving culturally and linguistically diverse parents, and extend this chapter's discussion of empowerment.

Although other writers have emphasized the importance of teacher empowerment for the overall improvement of schools,[19] we include teachers in the triangle of empowerment because it is hard to imagine passive, unempowered teachers creating empowerment conditions for their students. Thus, when we plan for multicultural staff development, opportunities to engage in policy making and research that extends beyond teachers' own classes are pertinent. For example, finding ways to meaningfully involve teacher and parent representatives in the selection of school and district level administrators would be a step forward for multicultural education. This more inclusive process could lead to the selection of educational leaders more in touch with community and teacher aspirations. Furthermore, parents and teachers involved in such decisions should be more knowledgeable and credible when they set out to create empowering conditions for their children and students.

As you may have already begun to discern, other multicultural education goals can also play an important role in the empowerment process. For example, although the promotion of intergroup/intragroup harmony and the development and transmission of knowledge about multicultural education and various ethnic and cultural groups are quite significant by themselves, each goal can contribute to the empowerment of students.

Intergroup/Intragroup Harmony

To create intergroup/intragroup harmony in their classrooms, teachers provide knowledge, skill training, and a classroom environment that leaves individual students better prepared to live and work with members of their own social group as well as members of different cultural and ethnic groups. Because of the increasing tide of cultural and ethnic conflict in the United States and around the world, more teachers are aware that their students would benefit from a curriculum that places greater emphasis on developing positive intergroup and intragroup relationships in the context of democratic classrooms.

Parenthetically, when we speak of cultural and ethnic groups, we have in mind general cultural groups like men and women, heterosexuals and homosexuals, and immigrants and nonimmigrants, as well as umbrella groups that are more commonly associated with ethnicity, such as African Americans, European Americans, Asian Americans, Hispanic Americans, and American Indians; also included are the specific ethnic and cultural groups that are a part of these larger groups, such as West Indians (Jamaicans, Barbajans, Haitians, etc.), Mexican Americans, Cuban Americans, Korean Americans, Japanese Americans, Jewish Americans, Italian Americans, Navajo Americans, and hybrid cultural groups (ethnocultural groups), like Mormon Americans, who have taken on some ethnic characteristics.

As race- and sex-based crimes continue to increase, [20] it is timely indeed for 5–12th grade teachers and university-based teacher educators to create curriculum experiences designed to promote intergroup tolerance and harmony, and these experiences should also educate future and veteran teachers and students in grades 5 through 12 about the incidence and pervasiveness of hate crimes in the United States. For example, while the well-publicized murders in 1998 of two gay men (Matthew Shephard in Wyoming and Jack Gaithers in Alabama); the dragging death of James Byrd Jr. (African American) in Texas, and the shooting spree of white supremacist Benjamin Smith in 1999 became "national" news which served to underscore the tragic repercussions of hate, prejudice, discrimination, and racism in our society, we believe that many teachers and their fellow Americans are unaware of the weekly and total amount of criminal hate crime incidents carried out in the United States in recent years. Because such knowledge might contribute to a greater emphasis on intergroup harmony in the "official" school curriculum, we believe that teachers should be made more aware of hate crime statistics. For this purpose, the FBI's *Hate Crime Statistics Reports,* which presents data representing a bit more than 80 percent of the total U.S. population, are an excellent tool www.fbi.gov/publish/hatecrime.htm. For example, from this resource readers will learn that in both 1996 and 1997:

   a. there were over 8,000 bias-motivated criminal incidents reported to law enforcement agencies;

   b. approximately 60 percent of hate-motivated criminal incidents stemmed from racial bias and approximately 16 percent stemmed from religious bias;

   c. the total number of hate-crime incidents against Black Americans was about eight times larger than the statistic for Hispanic Americans despite the fact that the total population for these groups was roughly similar;

   d. the bulk of religious-based hate crime incidents was against Jews (78 percent); in comparison anti-Islamic incidents were 2 percent of the total; and

   e. California accounted for nearly 25 percent of the total number of hate crimes.

   Please note that in Appendix 8 (p. to come) the reader will find a more detailed analysis of the 1996 and 1997 FBI *Hate Crime Statistics Reports,* along with a set of sample invitations to inquiry.

   These types of inquiries, as well as other lessons aimed at promoting greater intergroup understanding and harmony, will help students realize that serious real-world manifestations of prejudice are a daily affair in the United States (e.g., on the average there are approximately 27 "reported" hate crimes per day), and may stimulate interest in the study of contemporary civil rights legislation. They may also contribute to empowerment because they increase the range of individuals a student can work with to achieve selected goals. At the same time, they also develop skills and attitudes that will help students survive in communities where drug-influenced crime and violence are daily disrupters of the social order. Knowledge of self and the cultural, ethnic, and racial group(s) that contribute to self-identity is a vital ingredient in the development of the positive survival attitudes alluded to above, and the multicultural/multiethnic/historical knowledge we discuss next.

Multicultural/Multiethnic/Historical Knowledge

Each year students are in school their knowledge and understanding of American and world history should increase, along with their knowledge and understanding of their own ethnocultural roots, and their appreciation of other cultural and ethnic groups. If *all* American students are taught an insightful, accurate, multiperspective American history, a history that makes clear that individuals from a wide range of cultural, ethnic, and racial groups have made significant and wide-ranging contributions to the multifaceted American macroculture, we will have accomplished a great deal. For, as James Banks has recently noted, "The most important rationale for multicultural education is to teach students an accurate view of the United States and the world," and this is a view that is "needed by all our students."[21]

   The combination of accurate historical knowledge and a deeper grasp of one's own ethnocultural roots should have a positive influence on children's sense of self-worth and their belief that they and their friends have a chance for a successful future. It may also play a role in reducing prejudice. Indeed, research has demonstrated that significant prejudice reduction can result from simple storytelling lessons in which students learn of the accomplishments of various American ethnic heroes such as Rosa Parks, Vilma Martinez, Ida B. Wells, Charles Hamilton Houston, Hubert Humphrey, César Chávez, Henry Cisneros, Malcolm X, Betty Friedan, Jonas Salk, and many others. Ultimately, the development of an increasingly sophisticated multicultural/multiethnic/historical and multicultural education knowledge base lays the groundwork for the empowerment process, the development of cultural pluralism and intergroup harmony, and the ability to achieve the multicultural goal pertaining to freedom and democracy.

Maintaining Freedom and Democracy

The connection between multicultural education and the goal of maintaining freedom and democracy has been articulated by James Banks, among others. Although the goals of empowerment and multicultural/multiethnic/historical knowledge development address similar issues, defining multicultural education in terms of maintaining freedom and democracy is an important contribution because it places multicultural education within the Western tradition. As Walter C. Parker noted, "Multicultural education itself is a product of the West. It grew out of a struggle guided by Western ideals for human dignity, equality, and freedom."[22] In the 1990s, as various critics erroneously equated multicultural education with their own, sometimes misguided, conception of multiculturalism and proceeded to describe multicultural education as an attack on Western values and ultimately divisive, illuminating the European and American roots of the multicultural education movement was a timely project.

At this point, it is timely as well to clarify the linkage between multicultural education, as a national reform movement, and another national movement which is concerned with strengthening democratic and equity-oriented practices in public schools. The organization we have in mind is the National Network for Educational Renewal (NNER) which, in its agenda for change, strongly emphasizes the "enculturation of youth into a political and social democracy" and "equitable access to knowledge for all students." We will have more to say about the NNER and its Agenda for Education in a Democracy when we profile John Goodlad in this chapter, and then again in Chapter 2 where we enumerate and discuss specific ways to strengthen and expand democratic practices in our schools and society.

While in the clarifying mode, we will make clear that while multicultural education and multiculturalism are conceptually linked, they are not exactly the same thing. Multiculturalism, for example, has been a condition and characteristic of American society from its colonial and precolonial roots. There have always been many cultural groups (multiculturalism) functioning, at some level, within the growing borders of the United States. But extreme inequality of influence, power, and opportunity has also been a pervasive characteristic of American society—this group couldn't vote, this group couldn't own land, this group could be owned, this group couldn't legally immigrate, and so on. Out of this tragic and defining crucible came the antecedents of the twentieth-century multicultural education movement, and the movement itself. Along with the movement came efforts to name it, explain it, and attack it. Thus we have multicultural education, multiethnic education, education that is multicultural and social reconstructionist, and multiculturalism, all of which have common elements such as a concern with equity, but different emphases as well.

And in contemporary society and popular literature, we often see the terms *multiculturalism* and *multicultural education* treated synonymously. While there is obvious overlap, we make the following distinction. Multicultural education as a reform movement and a change process is more focused on specific goals that relate to K–12 schools and sometimes universities. *Multiculturalism,* on the other hand, when it is used in reference to school issues, almost always pertains to intellectual conflict in the universities; it is multiculturalism versus the established canon—multiculturalists versus defenders of the status quo. Related to this usage, Michael Olneck has written that "multiculturalism remains a focal point of conflict over Euro-American dominance and continues to offer possibilities for reordering political relationships, for redefining legitimate curricular content, and for transforming established symbol systems."[23]

Multiculturalism also seems to refer to an unfolding process that, in a somewhat ambiguous manner, pertains to all the institutions in society and the entire macroculture itself. Referring to this ambiguity, Olneck noted that "the term *multiculturalism* holds multiple and often contradictory meanings. I use it as an umbrella term to refer to the wide range of curricular, pedagogical, and organizational policies and practices responsive to racial and ethnic diversity in American society and schools."[24] John Higham, a historian of American ethnicity, went a step further in explaining the confusion surrounding the term *multiculturalism* when he pointedly observed that in the 1980s and 1990s, multiculturalism had "become a policy issue in America's colleges, universities, and secondary schools without yet proposing a vision of the kind of society it wants." He extended his criticism by adding: "In view of the indistinctness of multicultural goals, it is hardly surprising that no independent assessment of what it is accomplishing has yet appeared."[25]

These quotes make clear that multiculturalism is a broader concept than multicultural education. Because of this, and because we know that there is already sufficient complexity surrounding the term *multicultural education,* we will treat the two concepts as related but distinct. Thus an advocate of multiculturalism in society and/or the universities may not be an advocate of a particular form of multicultural education, and a critic of multiculturalism may not be saying anything illuminating about multicultural education and may be unaware of the distinction between the two concepts.[26]

Let us now delve more deeply into what James Banks and we mean when we say that multicultural education is education for freedom and democracy. There is, to begin with, the contribution that multicultural education can make to the continuation and expansion of a democratic society. Regarding this goal Banks pointed out that multicultural education is education for freedom because it should help students "to develop the knowledge, attitudes, and skills to participate in a free and democratic society" and "to participate in social and civic action to make the nation more democratic and free."[27] Beyond this political contribution to a democratic society lies another, more personal, dimension of freedom. Illuminating this dimension, Banks has stated, first, that multicultural education "promotes the freedom, ability, and skills to cross ethnic and cultural boundaries to participate in other cultures and groups," and second, that "It's terribly important for kids to be able to participate effectively within their own ethnic and cultural communities, to value those communities, but also to realize the limitation of those communities."[28]

This is a difficult balance to achieve. And it is clear here that the type of cultural freedom Banks espouses, and we support, is partly what makes multicultural education so difficult for some parents and teachers to embrace. But the critical point to appreciate is that multicultural educators seek to develop ethnic and cultural pride as well as cultural flexibility and maturity. As Banks said, "we empower the Hispanic student to have the freedom to participate in African-American culture, and the Jewish student to participate in African-American culture and vice-versa. Multicultural education should enable kids to reach beyond their own cultural boundaries."[29]

With this cultural pride and flexibility in mind, we, as the parents of multiethnic children, think it would be healthy for teachers to keep two things in mind. First, when some students—for instance, Hispanic and Jewish—learn about and participate in African-American and other cultures, they may be examining their own ethnic roots. In short, in many classes teachers will be educating children whose cultural and genetic heritage is a blend of more than one tradition and gene pool.

Second, it is salient to remember that when American teachers develop in their students the knowledge, attitudes, and skills to participate in a pluralistic democratic society, and the awareness that ethnic and cultural communities place limits on their members, they—the teachers—will be fostering the students' willingness, ability, and desire to take part in and identify with the larger American society. Their students will be American, not blindly chauvinistic Americans, but Americans nonetheless. Hopefully, these students will be civic-minded, responsible, and capable of joining the main or the sidestream, and some may perceive the limitations of being "only" American in a rapidly shrinking world. Thus, in the area of identity formation, most multicultural educators support the freedom to embrace multiple identities in a fluid way. Multicultural education is about the freedom to be Muslim and American, African and American, Italian and American, or simply mainstream American, and when you push this envelope to its farthest reaches, it may also be about the freedom to embrace dual national citizenship.

The awareness of these potential multiple identities relates to the cultural and ethnic self-disclosure discussed earlier in the chapter. Unless K–6 and some secondary teachers find explicit and subtle ways to talk about ethnic and cultural preferences with parents and students, they will likely overlook many vital teaching and relationship-building opportunities.

The reader should also keep in mind that while writers such as James Banks, Carl Grant, and Sonia Nieto see the connection between multicultural education and the freedom to participate in social action to make the United

States a more democratic and free nation, other writers, from the left and right, view multicultural education and its advocates with suspicion. For example, Beverly M. Gordon wonders whether terms such as "*inclusion, multiculturalism,* and *pluralism* are used and defended in the United States because such language can assist the dominant power in maintaining its structures."[30] Gordon believes that terms such as *critical, emancipatory,* or *liberatory* pedagogy may be better descriptive terms "because they not only expand narrow frames of reference, but also make it possible for us to move our thinking from a pejorative frame to one of self-reflection, critique, and social action."[31]

One can see from these opposing viewpoints that the step from understanding the goals of multicultural education to creating a personal approach to teaching with a multicultural perspective will be challenging. For this reason, in the next three sections we will put some flesh on this approach to teaching. We will discuss what it means to teach with a multicultural perspective and to create a multicultural setting. Finally, we will describe the work of a group of educators whose research, teaching, and program creation has been informed by a multicultural perspective.

Teaching with a Multicultural Perspective

The goal of becoming a teacher who thinks, plans, and teaches with a multicultural perspective is similar to the goal of cultural pluralism in that it is strongly influenced by beliefs and attitudes an individual holds, but it is also a much broader, more inclusive goal. We can gain greater insight into the goal by addressing a basic question: What is a multicultural perspective?

A multicultural perspective is a process of thinking, a state of mind, a way of seeing and learning that is shaped by beliefs about cultural relationships and cultural competency in American history and contemporary society, or Nigerian, British, or Swedish history, depending on the nation the educator or helping professional is working in. This belief system helps teachers understand that:

1. culture, ethnicity, race, gender, religion, socioeconomic status, and exceptionality are, in complex ways, potentially powerful variables in the communication and learning process of individuals and groups;

2. to fully empower students, teachers must help them understand that the construction of knowledge is a social and evolutionary process which has been distorted and negatively influenced by systems of advantage such as racism and sexism;

3. becoming more culturally competent—that is, more successful in communicating with and helping humans who are guided by different cultural rules and norms—is a process, not an event;

4. useful ideas about teaching and living can result form cross-cultural studies and experiences. This includes studying the cultural systems and educational organizations of nations such as New Zealand, Nigeria, Mexico, Japan, Germany, and Israel, as well as the various microcultures that make up the total culture in one's nation, the macroculture. Among the former we include the cultural models of various ethnic immigrant and nonimmigrant groups in a given society;[32] and

5. the academic orientation and achievement of some of their students may be positively or negatively influenced by the "cultural model" which shapes a student's perception about his or her chances for success in a nation's economic, political, and educational opportunity structure. Although John Ogbu perceives a cultural model as a set of beliefs which shapes a *cultural group's* understanding about how its society and societal institutions function, and the group's potential for success within the society's opportunity structure, we believe that it is sensible to believe that a family or individual can also have a cultural model, and that members of a given family may work and live, side-by-side, with different cultural models—different beliefs about their individual potential for success (and their group's potential for success) in the U.S. opportunity structure.[33]

Working and growing with this belief system, educators will selectively utilize data related to culture, gender, ethnicity, and so on, as they strive to maximize the learning experience of each individual student and group in their classrooms. In addition, a multicultural perspective will lead curriculum developers and teachers to select content that shows students that the art, music, language(s), history, ethics, science, mathematics, and politics of American culture have been decisively influenced by a wide range of individuals, cultures, and ethnic groups. Beyond helping teachers focus on the major goals of multicultural education, a multicultural perspective will encourage them to examine new challenges and curriculum ideas from a much broader point of view. For example, at a workshop in which a principal was introducing a new assertive approach for helping parents meet their school-defined societal responsibilities vis-à-vis homework, reading aloud to children, and monitoring TV watching, a multicultural perspective would prompt teachers to question whether assertiveness—across the board—was a culturally logical strategy, given the range of parents they were communicating with in their local community. An assertive approach to enlist the active involvement of newly arrived, tradition-oriented Vietnamese-American parents, whose native culture does not support the idea of volunteering in community agencies or of closely collaborating with teachers in the education of their children, might stem from an ethnocentric (we-know-best) rather than a multicultural perspective.[34] Ethnocentrism can also spring from liberal impulses. For example, maintenance programs that support students' and parents' desires to remain or become bilingual can devolve from a desirable alternative for a wide range of language learners into a form of cultural insensitivity if the maintenance form of bilingual education is imposed on parents and students who, for a variety of reasons, want to focus their language learning energy on English, some new computer language, or both.

Educators should also realize that their point of view regarding multicultural education will influence major dimensions of their teaching. The teacher who works with a multicultural perspective will want to be culturally sensitive to students and their families and, therefore, will become adept at collecting, interpreting, and making instructional management decisions based on sociocultural data. This educator will also know the meaning of cultural continuity between home and school and will attempt, tactfully, to minimize or maximize this continuity, depending on the circumstances. In addition, this educator will know how to teach an accurate "pluralist" American history rather than an ethnocentric, myopic, monoculturalist history. A negative example here may be illuminating. In 1987, during a week devoted to highlighting women's contributions to American society, Mrs. White (a pseudonym), a fourth-grade teacher in our community, asked her students to conduct independent research on famous American women. She gave the students a list to help them get started. All the eighteenth-, nineteenth-, and twentieth-century women on this list were White, and the list included such notables as Ma Barker, a criminal of dubious fame. This teacher probably did not realize that her list was biased. Fortunately, using the resources now available from the National Women's History Project (NWHP) teachers can more easily provide multicultural, multiethnic lists (see Appendix 6 for more specific information regarding the NWHP). In a similar but more far-reaching example of exclusion, the editorial board of *Great Books of the Western World,* a 37,000-page, 60-volume compilation of classic texts, selected the work of 130 authors, including William Faulkner and Ernest Hemingway. Not one African-American author was included, even though the works of Ralph Ellison, Toni Morrison, James Baldwin, and W.E.B. DuBois, to name a few, are to many authorities clearly on par with those of Faulkner and Hemingway as intellectual contributions to the Western world.[35]

Creating a Multicultural Setting

Of all the new things teachers will see with a multicultural perspective, the five most important are the following: (1) the schools and society they teach in are often characterized by inequality of resource allocation and educational opportunity, (2) effective teaching is *directly* linked to multicultural education, (3) every classroom and school has the potential to be a multicultural setting, (4) all students need, and benefit from, a multicultural curriculum—multicultural education is for everyone, and (5) a classroom becomes a *multicultural setting* when the students in that room experience a multicultural curriculum. In our eyes, the *multiculturalness* of a setting is not determined by the type of students in the class; it is created by the perspective and knowledge base the teacher works with. Mrs. White's class was filled mainly with White-American children, but the students could have been mostly Black and Hispanic Americans, or the class could have been in a Catholic girls' school where all the students were Asian Americans. Whatever the color, religion, ethnicity, or gender of her students, Mrs. White was delivering a biased, monocultural unit on famous American women, and in so doing was creating a monocultural curriculum *and* setting up in her classroom a curriculum that could easily have the effect of perpetuating racism.

This point is worthy of elaboration because it is counterintuitive to many educators' notion of what the term *multicultural setting* should mean. It is understandable for educators to distinguish between a classroom that is one-fifth Hispanic American, one-fifth African American, one-fifth Asian American, one-fifth White American, and one-fifth multiethnic American, and a classroom that is, let us say, 100 percent White American or 100 percent African American, by considering the former to be multicultural and the latter monocultural. However, we prefer to describe the former as multiethnic and the latter as possibly but not necessarily monoethnic. We wish to emphasize that the average public school classroom is inevitably multicultural in terms of the groups and cultures that are found in any public school classroom. The girls and the boys have their separate "cultures"; then there are the children of various socioeconomic groups, religions, and family types, and quite likely a number of ethnic, biethnic, and/or mainstreamed students who bring their own cultural baggage to the classroom. Then there is the teacher, who, quite possibly, is a representative of the "professional education" culture. Because public school settings are inevitably multicultural in terms of the individuals and groups that interact in the classroom, the most significant multicultural question to ask is whether the students are receiving a multicultural curriculum. If they are not, then the setting is not multicultural in the critical educational sense of the term. In short, every classroom in the United States will be more or less multicultural in terms of ethnic and cultural groups (demography), but not all of these classrooms will provide a multicultural setting. The latter depends on the type of *curriculum* the teacher is implementing, and, as we have indicated, the multicultural nature and quality of the curriculum will be a function of the cultural knowledge, beliefs, and values of curriculum coordinators, principals, and, most decisively, classroom teachers.

We have talked about these values and beliefs and given some examples of what a teacher who works with a multicultural perspective will see and do; we hope we have stirred some thoughts and questions in your mind. It is time now to sharpen and extend your understanding of what it means to think, plan, and teach with a multicultural perspective by providing examples of educators who have taught and/or created programs and organizations which were influenced by their own idiosyncratic multicultural perspective.

EXAMPLES OF EQUITY AND DEMOCRACY-ORIENTED PROGRAM DEVELOPMENT

The eight educators we have selected—Phillip Uri Treisman, James P. Comer, Bruce C. Davis, Jaime Escalante, Susan K. Sherwood, Mary Catherine Swanson, Charles Vidal, and John I. Goodlad—allow us to illustrate what can be accomplished when imaginative and energetic educators accept the challenge of working creatively with a multicultural and/or democratic perspective in their program, school, or classroom. Although Treisman, Comer, Davis, Swanson, Vidal, and Goodlad each worked as a school site or program leader as they carried out their program, the lessons and inspiration provided by their work, and the work of classroom teachers Escalante and Sherwood, can easily be translated into individual classroom practice. In addition, the update on Vidal's work reveals the vulnerability of equity and democracy-oriented programs in the current complicated era of state-mandated standards and high-stakes testing.

Phillip Uri Treisman: Mathematics Educator

Our first example, Phillip Uri Treisman, a professor at the University of Texas, Austin, and formerly a mathematics educator at the University of California at Berkeley (UCB), dramatically improved the academic achievement of an assortment of individual students after analyzing the mathematics difference in achievement of two ethnic groups in the United States.

In 1975, while Treisman was working with teaching assistants at UCB, he learned that 60 percent of the African-American students at the university were failing freshman calculus, while the failure rate for Chinese students was only 12 percent. His search for the explanation of this huge difference led to a doctoral inquiry in which he employed a wide range of methods. When traditional survey and hypothesis-directed research did not yield clues, Treisman arranged to observe and videotape 20 Black students and 20 Chinese students in their dorms and other settings as they worked on their mathematical assignments.

After 18 months of observation and interviewing, he discovered that the key to the differential pattern of success was the way students interacted with each other at the university. The vast majority of Black-American students (18 out of 20) never studied with other students and attributed their success in getting into UCB to knowing how to separate studying from socializing. Treisman's description of the support-oriented pattern of study adopted by many Chinese students (13 out of 20) suggested that the isolated and individualistic pattern of study adopted by the Black-American students made it difficult for them to discover what was going on in the course and at the university.

From the "cultural" facts uncovered in his dissertation inquiry, Treisman, from 1978 to 1989, developed and refined a workshop strategy that allows students to study mathematics under the guidance of a skilled teacher within a community of peers. In an interview,[36] Treisman noted that the failure rate of Black students in calculus had dropped from 60 percent to 4 percent, and that for the last 10 years the minority students in the workshop program have done much better than other students. It is noteworthy that the UCB workshop program served students of all ethnicities, and succeeded in helping all students, most notably Latino and African Americans, who had had the highest rates of failure. Treisman noted in a 1992 speech:

> Black and Latino participants, typically more than half of all such students enrolled in Calculus, substantially outperformed not only their minority peers, but their White and Asian classmates as well. Black students with Math SAT scores in the low–600s were performing comparably to White and Asian students whose Math SATs were in the mid–700s. Many of the students from these early workshops have gone on to become physicians, scientists, and engineers.[37]

By 1995, approximately 150 colleges and universities had experimented with Treisman's workshop strategy in courses such as physics, chemistry, engineering, and mathematics.

If Treisman had perceived his calculus students only as individual Americans and not as members of ethnic groups (Chinese Americans and Black Americans) and had examined the failure and success of individual students only, he probably would never have developed the educational equity workshop strategy that has proven so successful. Treisman had to see color and ethnicity and then discover the effects of ethnic culture on study habits before he could pilot and evaluate an equity-oriented strategy. He did more than just compare the success and failure rates of one group of students against another. By not accepting the status quo, by not accepting and rationalizing the tremendous failure rate of the Black-American students as somehow linked to their lack of preparation, weaker motivation, or intellectual capacity, Treisman, unknowingly and in an embryonic manner, was beginning to work with a multicultural perspective. When he began his doctoral inquiry, Treisman was, in his own way, saying "no" to dramatically unequal outcomes, at least at the level manifest in the UCB calculus program. And then, when his doctoral inquiry did not yield useful answers to his research problem, Treisman continued to work with a multicultural perspective, using participant observation to learn whether culturally influenced norms and patterns of behavior were somehow linked to the differential patterns of achievement in the calculus classes. Finally, he developed a teaching strategy that has dramatically improved the success rate of Black-American and Latino-American students and produced positive results for other targeted ethnic groups.

Treisman's work at the University of Texas, Austin, and at UCB in the 1990s, which follows through on his earlier research, is also worthy of mention. After developing a strategy that dramatically increased the success rate of visible ethnic minority students in undergraduate-level calculus and related courses, Treisman and colleagues like Rose Asera attempted to develop a strategy that would reduce the underrepresentation of African, Latino, and Native Americans in graduate programs in the mathematical sciences. The strategy they developed is called the Summer Mathematics Institute for Minority Undergraduates (SMI), and in the summers since 1989, "this six-week residential research Summer Mathematics Institute has served approximately 30 minority undergraduate men and women who have completed with distinction two or more years of collegiate mathematics."[38] The undergraduates come from colleges and universities across the United States, and evaluation data reveal that the SMI is valuable for candidates in a number of ways. For example, despite their success with undergraduate mathematics, as a group they knew little about the content and stages of graduate education, sources of financial support for graduate study, and the fact "that minority students like themselves, with both strong academic records and faculty recommendations, would be offered support in the form of fellowships, research assistantships, or teaching assistantships."[39]

Like his earlier work at UCB, the scholarship of Asera and Treisman reveals that the process of helping "underrepresented" talent rise up to succeed in undergraduate and graduate work requires an integrated structure that includes group work, curriculum revision, counseling and guidance, the open-minded and wise recognition of color, gender, and culture, and ongoing evaluation.

To sum up, Uri Treisman was working with a multicultural perspective (educational equity) when he attacked the problem of unequal success, and he was using a multicultural perspective (knowledge of the family and cultural background of his students) when he developed a solution. In addition, by developing a pool of talented, underrepresented graduate mathematicians, he has helped to add diversity to the next generation of mathematics professors (educational equity). At no point did he directly teach about the significant cultural or ethnic characteristics of a specific group. This was not necessary. Teachers do not have to aim simultaneously at all seven goals of multicultural education to teach with a multicultural perspective, but during the year they should aim for as many as are possible.

James P. Comer: Child Psychiatrist and School Reform Leader

With our next example we examine another success story involving predominantly Black-American students and, in this instance, a creative Black-American educator as well. It is noteworthy that as this story emerged over several decades, the organizational strategy that was discovered in two predominantly African-American schools in one city had been used by hundreds of individual schools and nearly one hundred school districts to restructure their overall curriculum and school organization. When contacted in May 1995, Comer staff members reported that the Comer model, officially known as the School Development Program (SDP), was an influential force in over 600 schools in 73 school districts in 21 states. When contacted in May 1999, staff members reported that the SDP had changed its focus. Rather than focusing on change in individual schools in various school districts, the SDP now focuses on district wide reform, and in 1998–1999 the SDP had contractual arrangements with 28 school districts in 16 states. The SDP staff was directly involved with 321 schools but hundreds more from prior years continued to use the Comer model to direct their reform efforts. In addition, it is worth noting that students of various ethnicities are currently being educated in Comer Process schools. Indeed, in cities like Topeka, Kansas, and Sarasota, Florida, there are Comer Process schools in which the majority of students are White.

But this was not the case in 1968, when the story began at Katherine Brennan and Martin Luther King Jr. Elementary Schools, two predominantly (99 percent) African-American schools in New Haven, Connecticut. In 1968 these two schools were ranked near the bottom of New Haven's 33 elementary schools in achievement and attendance, and teachers were leaving the school at the rate of 25 percent a year. The parents were described as "dejected, distrustful, angry, and alienated."[40] At this point a professor of child psychiatry with the right instincts, assumptions, methodology, personal history, and historical perspective entered these two schools and became the hero of a drama that is still unfolding as more and more schools across the nation adopt the Comer Process. The protagonist in this story is Dr. James P. Comer, professor of child psychiatry at Yale University and director of the Yale University School Development Program, a component of the Yale Child Study Center. Within the space of seven years—by 1975—Comer and his Yale colleagues—and the schools' parents, administrators, teachers, and mental health specialists—had developed a plan that essentially turned these two schools around. As evidence, Comer has written: "By 1975 the program was clearly having an effect. Behavioral problems had declined, relations between parents and staff had improved and the intelligence of the children had become manifest." He adds that by 1979, the students who had once ranked lowest in achievement among the 33 elementary schools in the city had caught up to their grade level by the fourth grade, and that by 1984, "pupils in the fourth grade in the two schools ranked third and fourth highest on the Iowa Test of Basic Skills."[41]

For our purposes, three elements in this story are crucial: first, two critical realizations that lie at the core of the Comer plan; second, several of the key components in the Comer plan; and, finally, the manner in which a multicultural perspective was brought to bear in Comer's problem analysis and solution.

Comer and his colleagues realized that the essence of the problem at the Brennan and King schools was not the low achievement, low morale, and low attendance; it was the schools' failure to pay attention to the psychological development of their students and the lack of positive relationships between the schools and the schools' parents. These perceptions, along with other insights, led to the development of a carefully structured governance and management team that included all major stakeholders at each school site. The team consisted of the principal, teacher representatives, parent representatives, and a member of the school's mental health unit, and it operated with some very interesting guidelines. Team members would recognize the authority of the principal, but the principal would not push through decisions without weighing the concerns of team members, and, remarkably, decisions made by this governance team would be by consensus rather than vote. Because of the consensus strategy, most of the decisions made by the governance team resulted in ownership and buy-in by team members rather than a win or loss by one stakeholder or another. At these schools the principals shared real power with teachers, mental health professionals, and, most significantly—in these disenfranchised, alienated, economically distressed communities, in which 70 percent of the families received Aid to Families with Dependent Children—with parents.

The creation of a school governance team and a mental health team, and a comprehensive school plan based on input from all adult stakeholders, are major elements in Comer's approach to developing a productive school culture. But in what ways did a multicultural perspective contribute to Comer's analysis and solution? Let us begin with what might not be so obvious. Comer saw ethnicity (African Americans) and poverty, and recognized a distinct and unique ethnic and cultural group (African Americans) whose children were failing as students in large numbers in American schools. Comer did not choose to study several of these children or several families, a decision that would have been intellectually and ethically defensible. Instead, he and his team immersed themselves, over 12 years, in the day-to-day life of an entire school. Comer's team studied the interactions between the school and the African-American students and families who lived in a poor community—in Comer's words, "out of the mainstream." Comer's solutions, if they were achieved, would apply to poor African Americans as a group, as well as to other ethnic groups in the United States with overlapping characteristics.

Beyond selecting low-socioeconomic-status African-American families and their low-achieving schools as the focus for long-term study, Comer, like many social scientists and educators, brought a specific belief system or mind-set to this inquiry. His own life as a Black American and his academic preparation had produced a belief system that said, in effect, that culture, race, SES, ethnicity, and self-esteem could all be powerful variables in the learning process of individuals and groups. It was this set of beliefs, functioning as a multicultural perspective, that led Comer to see the problems at the King and Brennan schools as cultural in nature. In Comer's own words, "our analyses of interactions among parents, staff, and students revealed a basic problem underlying the schools' dismal academic and disciplinary record: the sociocultural misalignment between home and school."[42]

In anthropological terms, Comer and his colleagues discovered that there was discontinuity between the culture of the home and the culture of the school; this discontinuity created conflict between the schools and the families in the community; and, further, the children, parents, teachers, and administrators were all victims of this heretofore invisible clash of cultures. It was Comer's ability to see the *cultural* nature of the problem that allowed him to design a powerful, schoolwide approach to psychological, social, and academic development, an approach that attended to differences between the home and school culture as well as any problems that might arise because of the ethnic or racial differences between teachers and students.

Quintessentially, Comer's approach draws heavily on child development, relationship, and organizational change theory to create a child-centered, risk-free, trust-filled school culture that empowers students, parents, teachers, and administrators, among other stakeholders. The compelling logic of creating such environments, and the positive results accruing in schools that adopted the Comer Process brought foundation funding—15 million, for example, from the Rockefeller Foundation—to help disseminate information about the School Development Program as well as a $3.4 million, five-year, grant (1998) from the U.S. Department of Education for similar purposes.

The School Development Program, which has its roots in the work Comer carried out in 1968 in New Haven, is now the catalyst for a national movement aimed at developing a systemic approach to creating and maintaining Comer Process schools. To support this objective, a set of 15 videotapes has been developed, a School Development Program newsletter is published several times a year, conferences are sponsored, National Leadership Academies are held throughout the year, and information is also transmitted via the Internet.[43]

Bruce C. Davis: Elementary School Principal

Our third example centers on the work of Bruce C. Davis, the former principal of Emerson Elementary School in Rosemead, California. Over a nine-year period at Emerson, Davis helped to create a unique parent-involvement program. Because our conception of multicultural education has as a major objective the establishment of a strong, empowering, culturally informed relationship between the home and school, almost any parent-involvement program that is implemented in a culturally sensitive manner will provide an example of an educator working with a multicultural perspective. Davis's efforts are worthy of recognition because of the special demographic characteristics of his school and the unique aspects of his personal effort to create a dynamic parent-participation program at Emerson.[44]

In 1989–1990, Emerson Elementary had 650 students; 44 percent of these students were English learners (learning English as a second language) and 38 percent of the school's families were on welfare. In addition, the school's families spoke 19 different languages or dialects, creating an atypical and challenging circumstance for a principal interested in parent involvement. Languages used for oral and written communication included Cambodian, French, Tagalog, Thai, Burmese, German, Italian, Zapotec (Native Mexicans from Mexico), Spanish, Vietnamese, Cantonese, Mandarin, Chiu Chao, Fukinese (a Chinese dialect), and English. Since 1980, Davis and his staff have met their multilingual challenge in a number of ways. One of these is the Emerson School parent-participation program, which includes the following:

1. Each week one student from each class receives a blue ribbon for being the "student of the week," and one student receives a red ribbon for being "super-reader of the week"; these ribbons (1,470 per year), which are donated by the Parent-Teacher Association, are presented to the students every Friday during morning assembly.

2. Each teacher completes two "reason slips" per week, listing the reasons the selected students received their ribbons. Later, the principal and two home/school coordinators call the parents of each selected child; referring to the reason slips, the callers tell the parents why their child was awarded the ribbon and emphasize how proud the teacher and school are of their child.

3. School meetings that involve parents are conducted in six languages, and letters are sent home in four languages.

4. The school constantly sends home thank-you notes and letters of praise to both parents and students.

5. The school learns about parents' special skills and encourages the parents to use them at the school.

Because of these and other program elements, Emerson Elementary School has received a California Distinguished School Award, and in 1995 Davis received the American Hero in Education Award from the Reader's Digest Foundation. Once again, in a complex setting, we see a school staff joining together to involve parents in the school program. These examples from Connecticut and California should convince you that parents will support the school program when educators find creative, meaningful, and culturally informed ways to involve them.

Jaime Escalante: High School Calculus Teacher

Our fourth example reviews the strategies and accomplishments of Jaime Escalante, the remarkable and highly acclaimed mathematics educator whose work was vividly portrayed in the film *Stand and Deliver*. Our focus is on

Escalante's efforts specifically, even though we are aware that Garfield High School's successful advanced placement program in mathematics and other content areas was the creation of a team of dedicated educators, most notably Benjamin Jimenez, who worked with Escalante in mathematics. When Escalante began teaching in Los Angeles's Garfield High School in 1974, the school was predominantly Latino American (95 percent); approximately 75 percent of the student body was eligible for free or reduced-cost lunches if they chose to apply. By U.S. standards, Garfield High School served a low-SES community in 1974, and the same held true in 1987. However, one important statistic did change in the 13-year period between 1974 and 1987: the number of Garfield students who were taking and passing the advanced placement calculus exam.

It took Escalante, a Bolivian immigrant, a few years just to discover what the advanced placement examinations were all about, but when he understood the nature and rationale for the exam, he realized that the advanced placement (AP) exam in calculus could become a powerful motivational force for the entire mathematics program at Garfield. In 1977, the idea of linking the AP calculus test with Latino-American students from a low-SES high school that had almost lost its accreditation in 1975 was a bold thought, but bold is an understatement when discussing the drive, imagination, and single-mindedness of Jaime Escalante. In 1978, four out of seven of his students passed the exam. This number grew each year until, in 1987, 129 of the students taught by Escalante and Jimenez took the exam and 89 passed (66 percent). In 1987 there was no comparable high school in the United States that performed nearly as well, and Garfield students scored much better than students at most middle- and upper-class high schools in the United States. What led to this tremendous change at Garfield, and how does it relate to teaching with a multicultural perspective?

The story of Escalante's success with students taking advanced mathematics at Garfield (algebra, trigonometry, analytic geometry, and calculus) has been spelled out in detail by Jay Matthews in his book *Escalante, the Best Teacher in America*.[45] Much of what we relate here is based on an article coauthored by Jaime Escalante[46] and our interpretation of material in the Matthews book. In terms of our model of multicultural education, the goals Escalante addressed were educational equity and the creation of collaborative, empowering relationships among parents, teachers, and students.

From the very beginning, Escalante "wanted to prove that Mexican-American children with fathers who were fourth-grade dropouts could match the best seniors at Beverly Hills High School."[47] This is what equity meant to Escalante. His was not an expansive view that consciously included Blacks, Asians, and other minorities, but it encompassed the Latino cultures Escalante could identify with, and the largely Mexican-American student population at Garfield. For Escalante, equity meant that relatively poor Latino-American students would perform as well as, or better than, the children of wealthy White Americans in what he considered the most difficult of all high school subjects. In a sense, calculus became a metaphor for success, a vehicle for showing Latino-American students at Garfield, and every school, what they could accomplish if they worked hard and believed in themselves and in Escalante. Of course, Escalante worked just as hard with the Asian-American, Black-American, and White-American students who enrolled in his classes, largely as a result of Garfield's special magnet program related to computers.

Escalante also sought to establish a special collaborative relationship with and between his students. He cared about the students he worked with and gave of himself in a manner that few would or could emulate. The amount of time he invested in this program shows his dedication. Escalante and his close collaborator Jimenez were available to answer student questions before school, at lunchtime, and after school—often until 5:00 P.M. For many students and teachers, the day ended between 2:00 P.M. and 3:00 P.M. Escalante was also not shy about contacting parents, enlisting their support, and sometimes challenging them. At the beginning of the year he would call the parents of all his Algebra II students, introduce himself, and exchange pleasantries. The parents of his calculus students (starting in 1981) received another message in the form of a contract, which he asked—and expected—all students and parents to sign. With their signatures, both parents and students agreed that the student would return to Escalante's room at 2:00 P.M. for more lectures and exercises, which often lasted until 5:00 P.M. For these hours, Escalante received no extra pay. In Japan such after-school education to prepare for special exams takes place in private schools and is called *juku*. The educators who provide it are paid well. At Garfield, Escalante and Jimenez, and others who strongly identified with their students' academic success, received a different type of reward, although they would surely have been delighted to accept extra remuneration if it had been available.

Escalante and Jimenez would sometimes speak with parents about matters that related to cultural conflict and cultural pluralism. An example that involved one of Jimenez's students is particularly revealing. The student was having difficulty keeping up with trigonometry homework because she had to work as a cashier three nights a week at her parents' restaurant, which was a one-and-a-half hour bus ride from her home. When she had stopped handing in homework, Jimenez decided to visit the girl's parents, accompanied by his more experienced colleague and department head, Escalante. After Escalante explained to the parents that their daughter was bright enough to be an engineer or physicist or teacher, the father informed them that they had "the wrong picture. Women are just here to get married and have kids and that's all. She has to work."[48] Escalante informed her father that *he* had the wrong picture, that he could not force his child to work, and that Escalante might have to call the authorities. The bluff led to a compromise. The student would work two nights a week, and her parents would buy her a desk to help her do her homework. The student later passed the advanced placement calculus test and went to Princeton before returning to California State University, Los Angeles, to pursue an engineering degree. In this instance Jimenez and Escalante took a couple of extra hours to speak with a traditional Latino male about the new Latino-American culture they wanted his daughter to be a part of, a culture in which both men and women could aspire to be professionals.

In the course of his Garfield career, which ended in 1991 when he joined the faculty of Hiram Johnson High School in Sacramento, California, Jaime Escalante confronted and challenged administrators, teachers, counselors, and students. But with his students, in particular, he did so in a manner that endeared him to them. For his students he played many roles and used many tactics, but the persona that comes through most strongly in Matthews's book is Escalante as the inspirational and demanding coach of the calculus team. For him the AP exam each spring was the Olympics. He would get his team ready, and his students would behave like teammates; the fast would help the slower, and all would move forward together. His classes would have a pep rally at the beginning and receive occasional pep talks during the period as needed. At the beginning of the year he told them: "You want to make your parents proud. You want to make your school proud. Think how good it will feel to go to college and know that you did the Calculus A.P."[49] His calculus team had special jackets, a special sweatshirt, and a special affinity for hard work and winning. Like many successful athletic coaches, Escalante intuitively understood the power of a winning team and a winning tradition, together with the utility of a mystique and reputation for the coach.

In addition, like many successful teachers, Escalante spends a good deal of time organizing his classes in advance so that maximum amounts of time can be spent on creatively responding to each new group of students, and seeking out new resources (grant, texts, videos, etc.) for his students. As an example, he organizes all his quizzes *before* the school year begins.[50] Also, while he is quite strict about hard work in general and homework specifically, his high expectations are delivered in a teaching environment in which abundant humor and caring—he calls it unconditional love—are manifest.[51] Beyond his unconditional love and concern for their nutrition and general health, Escalante understands that many students, and particularly those who study in low-SES high schools, will need to be persuaded that there is a real-world payoff for the extraordinary requirements that are a part of his program. To accomplish this, he takes his students out to real-world settings to see engineers and scientists making use of calculus-related knowledge, and he brings back his former students to tell of their successes in the world of work *and* how much money they are making.

After reading Jay Matthews's book and/or Escalante's article, some observers may say that Escalante has gone too far in his exclusive focus on mathematics, while others may wonder what is multicultural about his teaching. Suffice it to say here that the synthesis approach Escalante crafted (see Figure 1.3) was (1) equity-oriented and empowering and (2) a direct and logical response to the socioeconomic, cultural, and political realities he encountered. When a teacher walks into a low-income, bicultural/multiethnic, gang-influenced environment, an environment with a very small university-oriented population, extraordinary measures are needed. In our opinion, by responding wisely to these cultural variables, Escalante in an inspiring way taught with a multicultural perspective. From another perspective, utilizing John Ogbu's terminology, Escalante offered his students the opportunity to work with a new cultural model, a new belief in what they could accomplish in the U.S. opportunity structure if they worked very hard for academic success.

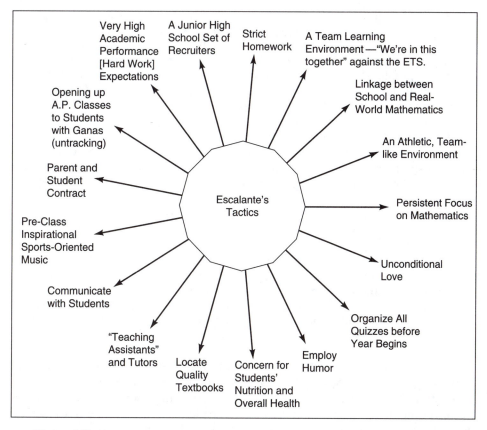

Figure 1.3

Susan K. Sherwood: Primary Grade Teacher

With our fifth example we travel to Hansen Elementary School in Cedar Falls, Iowa, to describe the work of veteran first-grade teacher Susan K. Sherwood. Hansen Elementary, located in what is commonly perceived as America's heartland, has the student population most Americans would stereotypically expect. In 1988, with about 480 students, Hansen Elementary had fewer than five African-American students, a few Asian, American-Indian, and Hispanic students, and a large (95 percent-plus) population of White-American students of varying socioeconomic status and religious backgrounds. However, along with the abundance of White students, there was a great deal of diversity for teachers to manage, and Sherwood's first-grade classroom was no exception. In her eighteenth year of teaching first grade at Hansen Elementary, this is the way Sherwood described the diversity in her classroom in an article entitled "Portrait of an Integration: A Child with Severe Multiple Disabilities Integrated into a Regular First Grade Classroom."[52]

As a teacher of young children, my perspective on this integration process was different. Every class has a wide range of abilities and problems. This particular group of twenty-one students was no different. The intelligence range as measured by the Cognitive Abilities Test was 137–168. Shane was reading at the eighth grade level; Tom was diagnosed as learning disabled; Jane was medically diagnosed as hyperactive; Micah was adept at mathematics problem solving; Erica was a six year old in puberty; Jennifer, Ryan, and Samantha were at-risk because of their home environments and past experiences. (All the students' names are pseudonyms.)

Sherwood, like many contemporary K–12 educators, accepted the responsibility of creating a caring, supportive environment for the wide range of learners she described. These students, like the others in her class, needed a special kind of environment, and, at this point in her career, Sherwood was very well prepared in terms of philosophy and skills to create such a climate. In discussing the needs of this group of first graders, she wrote:

> *All* needed to belong to our classroom community and to accept their own strengths and limitations before they could freely accept others. To develop confidence, instill love of learning, and enhance self-concept, the teacher builds on each child's uniqueness—creating a motivating and challenging environment where all children are free to work cooperatively, learn from mistakes, take risks and rejoice in accomplishments. Such a classroom community is a support system for each of its members.[53]

Clearly, this is an educator who is attending to the equity, self-esteem, and intergroup harmony needs of her students, and in so doing is creating a strong foundation for a wide-ranging multicultural curriculum. With her commitment to, and competence in, meeting the diverse academic and social needs of her students, Susan Sherwood provides a fine example of teaching with a multicultural perspective. But she is more than a fine example, and it was her willingness to work with Ann, her twenty-first student—on a full-time basis—that transformed this teacher into an inspiring model for future and current educators.

At 6 years of age, Ann was a child with severe multiple disabilities. She had suffered birth trauma, was head injured, had moderate to severe mental disabilities, had no right-field vision, and possessed a small amount of left-peripheral and central vision. She had hemiplegia to the right side of her body but was ambulatory and was verbal. She was a child who, in the past and in many schools in the present, would have spent all or a good portion of her day in a "special day class" taught by a "special" educator, a teacher who had received special training to work with severely disabled (or challenged) learners like Ann.

Jeni Moravec, the special educator at Hansen Elementary, felt that for Ann the "least restrictive environment" stipulated by federal law might be a full-time integration placement in Susan Sherwood's first-grade classroom, and she asked Sherwood to accept such a placement. Although she had no formal preparation in special education, Sherwood's belief in free public education for all students and her understanding of Public Law 94-142 (the Education for All Handicapped Children Act of 1975) suggested to her that if her classroom might be the one most likely to allow for maximum social and academic growth for Ann, then she ought to agree to the request and do her best to make her classroom the least restrictive environment. After reaching this decision, she soon discovered, to her surprise, that she was something of a pioneer in Iowa, at least in 1988. Although PL 94–142 had mandated full implementation of its provisions by 1980, Sherwood soon learned that in 1988 she was one of the few public school educators in Iowa working with a severely challenged student on a full-day basis in a regular education classroom. Several years later, Ann, the student Sherwood worked with, had completed her third year in a regular education environment, and in 1990 all the severely challenged students at Hansen Elementary were learning in regular education classrooms.

Creating Equity for Ann.   Several factors combined to make Susan Sherwood's classroom work for Ann and the other children in her class. First, on most days Jeni Moravec, the special educator, spent at least one hour in Sherwood's class working with Ann as well as other students, and simultaneously provided Sherwood with the technical and emotional support she needed, particularly at the beginning of the year. A second factor stemmed from Susan Sherwood's realization that she needed to create a team of adults to make this type of integration work. Her classroom team consisted of herself, the special educator, a parent volunteer, and a graduate student from a nearby university. In addition, the building principal and two professors served as resource people for the team, and the members of this team had to function in a special way, as she explains:

> Before working in my classroom, each [team member] had to agree to assume the role as a "facilitator of learning." Their primary purpose may have been to facilitate integration; however, any child in need was to be supported when the adult was not directly involved with Ann. In this way, children did not perceive Ann as having a special helper. Additionally because the support person was not always immediately available for anticipating and intervening prior to the natural flow of actions and consequences, Ann had to develop independence and responsibility. At times it was difficult to step back and allow Ann the opportunity to fail. Like other students she needed the freedom to fail in order to learn through trial and error.[54]

It is noteworthy that the nonhandicapped students in the class were also a significant part of the classroom team. The students served as role models for appropriate behavior, and several served in more direct facilitative roles, sometimes gathering materials for Ann and at other times firmly encouraging her to complete the task.

A third critical factor, from our perspective, pertains to class size. The school district in this instance created an environment in which educators could take action regarding equity because they were working in a classroom with the appropriate number of students. The debate about the "educational significance" of class size goes on and on, but not in our minds. Given the diversity in Sherwood's first-grade classroom, 21 students is quite ample; 30 or more students, in our opinion, would make failure for such efforts almost inevitable.

While other factors could be mentioned, the most critical one was Susan Sherwood and her belief system. She did not have to accept Ann and could easily have worked out a compromise with the special educator—"I'll take Ann in the morning, and you keep her the rest of the day." Indeed, a half-day assignment by itself would have been quite challenging. But it would not have been the test Moravec wanted, nor the chance Sherwood wanted Ann to have. Sherwood was willing to risk failure, to go beyond past practice, to accept change and continue learning. Although much of her success could be attributed to employing the correct set of strategies (the team of adults, cooperative learning, full as well as parallel participation in classroom activities), it was her belief in Ann's right to have a full-time opportunity to live and learn in a regular classroom that set the stage for success with integration and prepared the way for what will likely be Ann's later successes in living a fruitful life in an integrated world filled with people of varying strengths and disabilities. Because of their experiences with Ann, and Sherwood's modeling, all of the 21 learners in Ann's first-grade classroom will be better prepared to live with her in this integrated world, a world in which the academic, employment, and general citizenship rights of disabled citizens are increasingly well protected.[55]

Although Susan Sherwood was a modern-day pioneer in Iowa in 1988, she was also part of a slow national movement toward greater classroom integration of students with severe disabilities. In 1987 the Severely Handicapped Branch of the federal Office of Special Education funded five states (California, Colorado, Kentucky, Virginia, and Illinois) to undertake "systems changes projects," and since then has approved 11 other states. In these 16 projects the main goal has been to increase significantly the number of students with severe disabilities who were being educated in integrated learning environments— the so-called regular classroom environment.[56]

In July 1995, as we gathered material for the second edition of this text, we called both Susan Sherwood and Jeni Moravec and learned the following. Ann attended Hansen Elementary for all the elementary grades, and for the most part in each of these grades was educated in regular "integrated" classrooms. Over the course of her elementary years, she grew increasingly confident and independent. As Jeni Moravec said in a recent conversation, "When she started out she was afraid of everything. She was a small terrified dependent child. Now she is poised, self-confident, and a leader in her current classroom."

But Ann was challenged when she attempted to attend the local "regular" junior high school with her Hansen classmates. With her family's support, she tried to attend but encountered teachers and administrators who believed that she belonged in a separate special school for the severely handicapped. Ann was given a brief trial at the "regular" junior high school but received little support from the faculty. For example, one teacher remarked that Ann "couldn't even take herself to the bathroom." But Ann could; however, in a hostile environment Ann's fragile confidence withered, and she began to believe that the teachers at the junior high were right. Now, as a learner in a special segregated classroom staffed by supportive personnel, Ann has regained her confidence and she can take herself to the bathroom—as she always could. She is also a positive role model for her classmates who are not yet quite as independent and confident as she. The confidence-building years at Hansen Elementary were years well spent, and Ann's efforts to integrate her local junior high may yet open doors for physically challenged students who may follow her example. Indeed, in a July 1999 conversation, Jeni Moravec indicated that this is exactly what happened. Students from Ann's school district whose handicaps were more severe than Ann's wound up in the public junior high school mainstream. Sadly, Ann, who in 1998–1999 was in the tenth grade, has remained in the separate special school for the severely handicapped. It is conceivable that the exclusion Ann experienced for her local junior high school may result in a post–high school life that is totally removed from mainstream experiences. Ann may forever be in the sidestream, the world of residential and group homes that often involves moving away from friends and family. As educators we sometimes forget that the decisions we make with a one-year horizon have lifelong repercussions, and may diminish or destroy the very confidence that special learners and their parents need to imagine themselves as capable of entering the mainstream. Finally, it is noteworthy that Ann's Hansen Elementary classmates protested her segregated placement, wrote letters to various decision makers, and attempted to meet with the superintendent of schools. They, apparently, had learned something from their years with Ann, something that the junior high school teachers and administrators had missed, or simply did not want to learn.

Mary Catherine Swanson: Creator of AVID (Advancement via Individual Determination)

For our sixth example of thinking, planning, and creating with a multicultural perspective, we will trace the development of a project that resulted from a desegregation order in San Diego, California. In 1980, when the San Diego Unified School District was ordered to desegregate its schools, Mary Catherine Swanson was in her fourteenth year of teaching at Clairemont High School and was the chair of the English Department. Up until 1980, Clairemont High School had provided "traditional enriched curriculum to a homogeneous middle-class student population, 80 percent of whom enrolled in college." Fortunately for the rest of us, in 1980 a dramatic change occurred at Clairemont High School. A new high school drew away the most affluent students at Clairemont at the same time that 500 Latino and African-American students were bused to Clairemont for the first time. These students had "no experience with pre-college preparatory courses."[57]

In response to the new situation, Swanson developed the AVID program. Her goal was "to make underrepresented students eligible for advancement to four year colleges."[58] To accomplish this, she selected 30 ethnically and culturally diverse students who were in the non–college track to constitute the first AVID cohort; the grade point averages in this first cohort ranged from 1.5 to 2.5. Four years later, all 30 students graduated from high school with a cumulative grade point average of 3.2, and all 30 went to college—28 to a four-year college and two to a community college. Furthermore, the cohort of 30 received $50,000 in grant and loan funds, and at the end of their freshman year, the AVID students attending San Diego State University and the University of California at San Diego had a cumulative GPA of 2.46.[59]

By 1986 it was clear that the AVID project at Clairemont High School was a huge success. As a result, Swanson accepted a full-time position at the San Diego County Office of Education, where her main responsibility was to help other high schools create their own AVID programs. Once again Swanson's efforts were extraordinarily successful. By November 1996, 465 high schools in approximately 128 school districts in California had adopted AVID, and 100 high schools outside California had AVID programs. In addition, 49 Department of Defense high schools had AVID programs. And the success has continued into the 1999–2000 school year when the AVID center staff, now operating as an independent nonprofit organization, expects to be working with 900 schools in approximately 15 states and 13 foreign nations. It is noteworthy that approximately half of these sites will be middle schools, and that each of these 900 sites will have agreed to implement their AVID program in line with a set of *AVID Program Implementation Essentials* (more about these on the following page); while AVID was initially and exclusively a high school program it is now a sixth through twelfth grade program with 60 percent of its new growth in middle schools. In recognition of her important work, Mary Catherine Swanson, along with James P. Comer, was a recipient in 1991 of the prestigious Charles A. Dana Award for pioneering achievements in health or education; along with the honor each recipient receives $50,000. More specifically, Swanson received this award for developing a teacher-led program that had given thousands of students the skills, support, and guidance they needed to fulfill their potential to pursue a college education. What are the key components of the AVID program? In 1999 the key components are almost identical to the strategies Swanson employed with her first AVID cohort, but some new significant elements have been added.

To begin with, as it is currently implemented, each AVID program has a program coordinator who is assisted in her or his efforts by a school site AVID team consisting, typically, of AVID-trained teachers, counselors, and one or more administrators.

Selecting an appropriate set of AVID students is an important first task for the program coordinator. Currently all, or the vast majority of, candidates will be high–potential underachieving students, and many of these students will be members of groups who are underrepresented in higher education. In addition, the AVID students usually come from a low-SES family, with little or no experience in higher education, and have demonstrated academic potential in writing and mathematics at the middle school/junior high school level. Although the selection process may vary from one AVID program to another, at Arroyo Grande High School in California, each eighth-grade student screened into AVID must sign a contract before being admitted to the ninth-grade cohort, and the parent(s), coordinator, and counselor will also sign the contract.

While the contract and the program coordinator and school site team are obviously important components, the AVID high school program revolves around three critical strategies. First and foremost is the AVID elective period. For four years, every day of each semester, the AVID cohort will meet during the same period to collaboratively and noncompetitively engage in small-group study of content covered in their college-prep set of courses, and offer each other support and motivation to keep on striving. Second, the AVID students "learn the writing process through prewriting, drafting, and editing formal papers,"[60] and also learn how to simultaneously record notes *and* questions as they process information delivered in lectures, films, discussions, and so on. These notes and questions become the basis of inquiry-oriented tutorial sessions during the AVID elective period; where possible, college students of color who serve as role models will lead, or participate in, these study sessions. With the initial cohort the new note-taking skills had some unanticipated effects. As Swanson notes:

> The faculty and other students in honors classes were initially skeptical. But because AVID students were such active note-takers, teachers began to view them as being serious about learning. Honors students began to accept AVID students as fellow learners and to ask about their note-taking techniques.[61]

The third critical strategy in the AVID program is known as the "AVID methodologies." Some of the teachers at participating high schools receive staff development training that shows them how to make greater use of inquiry, writing, and cooperative learning in their specific courses, and, where possible, the AVID students attempt to study with these instructors. To help ensure that these critical strategies and other key elements are in place, starting in 1996–1997 AVID staff began to train regional and district directors to certify that AVID sites were incorporating all of the AVID Program Implementation Essentials. Some of the essentials are:

1. AVID student selection must focus on students in the middle who have not previously succeeded in a college preparatory curricular path;
2. The school must be committed to full implementation of the AVID program, with the AVID elective provided as an integral part of the school day;
3. AVID students must be involved in a rigorous course of study that will enable them to meet requirements for university enrollment;
4. Methodologies used in AVID—writing, including a strong relevant curriculum, inquiry, and collaboration—must provide the basis for instruction in the AVID classroom;
5. A sufficient number of tutors must be available in the AVID class to facilitate access to rigorous curriculum, and the tutors must be trained to implement the methodologies used in AVID. The tutors should be college or university students; and
6. AVID program implementation and student progress must be monitored through the AVID Data System, and results must be analyzed to ensure success.

The complete and most current set of AVID Program Implementation Essentials, as well as other valuable information, can be accessed via the AVID homepage www.avidcenter.org or phone (619-682-5050).

Some other facts about AVID are noteworthy. To begin with over 90 percent of the students involved in AVID (over 15,000 students) have gone on to college. Second, in 1992 the program received an A+ award from the federal

Department of Education for helping to achieve the aims of the *Goals 2000* initiative. Third, Hugh Mehan has described AVID as a successful untracking intervention because the program places low- and high-achieving students in the same rigorous academic program.[62] Fourth, the AVID program, under the leadership of Mary Catherine Swanson is dynamic. It is creating new programs and strategies to help AVID schools help their high potential underachieving students. It has built, for example, an increasingly sophisticated Internet presence, carries out an ambitious program of research pertaining to AVID schools and students, and shares their results, as well as AVID-related studies conducted by other researchers, via their website and their newsletter *ACCESS*. For example, in the Winter/Spring 1998–1999 issue of *ACCESS* results from AVID's 1997–1998 survey of 580 AVID sites were shared.[63] By Spring 1998, 521 sites representing 29,799 students in 11 states and 13 foreign countries had returned their AVID survey—a 90 percent response rate which included 293 high schools, 223 middle schools, and five schools of different configuration. Among other things, from this data set AVID learned that:

1. nearly 85 percent of the 1996 graduates from AVID sites in California, Kentucky, Virginia, and the Department of Defense Dependents schools completed the requirements for four-year colleges and universities;

2. nearly 92 percent of AVID high school students were taking courses which placed them on track for acceptance into a four-year college;

3. of the 1,752 1996–1997 graduates reported on in this data set 63.4 percent had received acceptance to four-year colleges, with another 30 percent expected to attend two-year community colleges;

4. 48 percent of AVID students in middle schools which offered algebra, pre-algebra, or another college-preparatory mathematics course took such courses; and

5. 35 percent of AVID students in middle schools that offered honors courses took at least one such course.

These percentages support Gene Maeroff's observation that AVID "creates a subculture in which academic achievement is an acceptable goal."[64]

Finally, although it is not well documented, there is AVID's contribution to cross-racial and cross-ethnic interaction, and possibly harmony, in 900 schools. Although AVID's primary goal is not to create an integrated setting, students of color and their White colleagues in AVID high schools are learning to work and study together in their honors classes, and in the AVID cohorts African Americans, Latino Americans, Pacific Islanders, and others are working in cooperative learning teams in an intense, family-like atmosphere. As a program that was created in response to a desegregation order, such cross-cultural interaction must be truly satisfying to Swanson, as well as to the 900 site coordinators of AVID, who are creating a new type of equity-oriented, high-energy, high-commitment role for high school and middle school teachers across the nation.

Charles Vidal: Middle-School Principal

For our seventh example, we travel to Modesto, an agricultural town in California's central valley, to study the evolution and special characteristics of Hanshaw Middle School. Hanshaw was completed in 1991 but began to evolve in 1987 when Modesto School District voters passed a $72 million school bond. At the time the bond was passed, Charles Vidal was coordinating the Modesto Schools program which aimed at reconnecting high school dropouts with the public school system. Once tapped to be the leader of the future Hanshaw Middle School, Vidal set out to uncover new ideas for a school that would be built in one of the poorest areas of Modesto. This predominantly Hispanic neighborhood had a very high incidence of unemployment (25 percent), a high percentage of seasonal employment in agriculture, a very high teenage pregnancy rate, and a high percentage of homes in which a language other than English was spoken (about 65 percent). In addition, there were 29 police-identified gangs operating within the school's proposed boundaries. Vidal understood that within such a neighborhood his entire faculty would have to compete with these gangs for the loyalty and lives of his future students.

To gain knowledge for this complex task, Vidal studied the educational literature, visited middle schools that served similar populations, and attended various educational conferences. When these strategies did not pay off, he decided to follow the advice of Tom Peters, author of *In Search of Excellence,* who advised entrepreneurs to get close to their customers. Following this advice, Vidal visited over 500 South Modesto families to find out what kind of school these families thought their community needed. While carrying out these visits, Vidal saw "families with three and four generations living under one roof all working closely together to help the family survive." Vidal reported that these visits helped him discover key elements for the educational model and philosophy that would shape the curriculum and delivery system at Hanshaw during its first four years of existence (1991–1995).[65]

Gradually Vidal began to understand that the school he would help design would have to break with the past and the idea of business as usual. Early on, he developed the belief that for Hanshaw to meet the needs of South Modesto, it would have to create an environment and culture in which a whole set of new relationships could be nurtured and developed. He had in mind relationships between students and students, students and teachers, students and society, teachers and community, teacher and principal, school and community and health agencies, and K–12 schools and institutions of higher education (junior colleges and four-year colleges).

Nothing brought this home to him more clearly than his visits, in the late 1980s, to the other junior high schools in his school district, the schools to which the South Modesto kids were being bused prior to the completion of Hanshaw. He saw kids sitting in rows where they were encouraged to compete rather than collaborate and spent a lot of time listening to instructors— up to eight different lecturers a day—speaking from lecterns. This was completely antagonistic to the collaborative home cultures many Hanshaw students were reared in, as well as the learning needs of English learners; it also clashed with Vidal's beliefs about the type of teaching that he called brain compatible or brain friendly.

So what kind of school was created at Hanshaw? How would it break with the past, as well as the realities of other Modesto City Schools of that time? To begin with, there was a change in nomenclature and behavior. While other Modesto schools have teachers and students, Hanshaw has *community leaders* and *citizens.* The message was clear to Vidal and his staff. To be successful in their community, Vidal and his staff of 39 could not simply build a vibrant, supportive community at Hanshaw; they and their school needed to work with other government agencies and private and public organizations to redefine the surrounding community in which those 29 gangs were operating. They understood that their task was not to build a glorious kingdom on top of a mountain, located on an island that was sinking. And the student citizens would play a key role in this redefinition. Yes, many may come from poor families with little advanced education, but all would constantly be reminded that they were citizens of Hanshaw, Modesto, and the United States, and as citizens they had rights, responsibilities, and numerous opportunities. These included the right to learn, the responsibility to help others learn, and the opportunity to seriously think about going to college—at a school that would do everything it could to support them if they chose to make college their goal.

The structure at Hanshaw during the 1991–1995 period promoted these rights and responsibilities, and to some extent the 1999–2000 curriculum still does. But incremental changes began in 1996, and significant structural changes were implemented in 1999–2000 in response to new state testing requirements. For example, from 1991–1999 each of Hanshaw's students was part of a 120-student family which interacted with a team of six teachers, and teachers attempted to develop and deliver an *interdisciplinary* curriculum that would be relevant for the students and their community. In this curriculum the learning would be experiential, collaborative, and project centered, and lecturing and the use of textbooks was deemphasized.

In 1999–2000 the family structure, team teaching, and emphasis on interdisciplinary learning was replaced with a more traditional seven-period school day where textbooks were once again a key part of the curriculum and teaching by credentialed subject matter specialists in separate content-focused courses was emphasized. While the family structure and team teaching were part of a statewide emphasis to help elementary school students successfully transition into the middle school, in 1999 Wendall Chun, Modesto Schools Associate Superintendent, told us that this design never produced satisfactory test scores at Hanshaw. Thus, with an eye to the future, namely the year 2004–2005, when the seventh graders entering Hanshaw in 1999–2000 will have to pass a statewide exam in order to graduate high school, the school district decided a major change was necessary.

Other elements from the original design were also replaced or modified. For example, to promote career exploration the Hanshaw faculty made use of an exploratory wheel which incorporated a set of electives for each student. The wheel exposed all students to eight explorations in areas such as computers, chorus, robotics, arts and crafts, and hydroponics.[66] In 1999–2000 the electives were no longer a requirement for all students, and some students, such as those scoring in the bottom quartile in reading, had to take two periods of reading each day, leaving little room for any type of elective. In addition, to help promote a college-going orientation, and to help Hanshaw serve as a replacement for gang affiliation, each of Hanshaw's 120-student families was affiliated with a specific California State University (CSU) campus, and on at least two occasions each Hanshaw family visited *their* campus and heard inspirational speeches. These visits allowed students "to close their eyes and see themselves there."[67] Vidal wanted the students to realize that "college is something that is as much for them as anyone else."[68] The current principal, Ed Miller, who was a part of Vidal's early–1990s leadership team, also wants to promote aspirations for college. However, in 1999–2000 efforts to promote a college-going orientation were more global in nature and did not involve affiliation with, or visits to, CSU campuses.

Also, in the 1990s, as a part of its success orientation, the Hanshaw faculty paid close attention to the psychological needs of Hanshaw students. There was a constant stream of positive reinforcement within each class, and the entire school. As English teacher Cheryl Green-Jenkins noted, my "English students pledge to do their best, stay in school, graduate, and go to college."[69] And science teacher Craig Johnson added, the "constant boosterism—the pencils, the bus talks, the *be your personal best* slogan—might seem sappy at a more affluent school but not Hanshaw.[70] In a similar vein, social studies teacher Robert Rosenthal said, "whether or not they're performing what we want, we let them know they are worthwhile people . . . that's what self-esteem is really about at this site.:[71] In 1999–2000, according to Principal Miller, the concern with student self-esteem and life skills was still a significant part of the Hanshaw curriculum.[72] But, it seems clear to us that in 1999–2000 the Hanshaw students, and students throughout California, were getting a slightly different message, something like "Yes you are a worthwhile person but in the eyes of the state your worth is linked to a critical set of exams and no one of us can ignore this reality."

Given the changes that have occurred at Hanshaw Middle School, it is fair to speculate about this question: To what extent is teaching and administering with a multicultural perspective a part of the current Hanshaw school culture? Let us begin by noting that the original design and culture clearly resulted from a vision that was influenced by a multicultural perspective. For example, information about the local culture and other community realities led to specific elements in the curriculum design, and there was a strong emphasis on attitudinally empowering students. And teachers, who were viewed as community developers, team teachers, and creators of the curriculum, were also empowered. But, is this true about today's Hanshaw culture? In fairness, we must say that it is too early to definitively say anything about the new Hanshaw curriculum and its relationship to multicultural education. But it is clear that teachers and administrators at Hanshaw, and throughout the State of California, in 1999–2000 are more reactive than proactive, and more vulnerable than empowered. Furthermore, as the state introduces its regime of standards and high-stakes testing, along with class-size reduction in grades K–3, and the voters make bilingual education more difficult to implement, more and more it appears that school cultures are defined by outside forces. And, finally, while the regime of testing may positively contribute to increased student achievement and equity if supported by adequate staff development, tests that are truly valid, and more resources for teachers and students, the top-down process has taken away something vital from local school districts, administrators, teachers, and communities. But, the curriculum influence which has been lost can be partially regained, and the educator we turn to next has started a national organization which may be a part of the solution.

John I. Goodlad: Curriculum Leader and Organizational Innovator

For our eighth example, we turn to the work of John I. Goodlad, an educator whose varied projects have been informed by a consistent concern with equity and democracy. Across a distinguished and distinctive career which began in the late 1930s in a one-room schoolhouse outside of Vancouver, Canada, and continues at the University of Washington in Seattle, Washington, in 1999–2000, John Goodlad has held many interesting positions and been an influential voice in several educational arenas.[73] With regard to positions, in addition to being a classroom teacher, Goodlad has been a professor, an educational administrator, an active researcher (principal investigator of the *Study of Educational Change and School Improvement*, *A Study of Schooling*, and the *Study of the Education of Educators),* a well-published and influential author and coauthor (e.g., *The Nongraded Elementary School*, *A Place Called School*, *Teachers for our Nation's Schools*, *The Moral Dimensions of Teaching*, and *Educational Renewal,* among many other publications), and a change agent and creator of educational networks (e.g., the League of Cooperating Schools while at UCLA, and the National Network for Educational Renewal while at the University of Washington).[74]

With regard to influence, as Ken Sirotnick has suggested, Goodlad's scholarly, research, and change-oriented agenda has been exceptionally broad, including topics such as the form and function of schooling; the dynamics of school improvement and educational change; "the preparation of educators and the form and function of university/college units responsible for this activity; and the moral commitments to equity and excellence in education as foundational building blocks for a healthy democratic society."[75] All of these topics and research interests converge in Goodlad's latest (1985 to present) and largest change-oriented project, the National Network for Educational Renewal (NNER) and its Agenda for Education in a Democracy. This project, whose core endeavor and guiding themes overlap significantly with the goals of multicultural education, conveys important ideas for current and future educators. Below, we provide an overview of the NNER by addressing the following questions:

1. What is the NNER, how has it evolved, and what are its broad goals?

2. What is the core endeavor of the NNER, and why was this endeavor selected?

3. What are the major guiding themes of the NNER, and how do these themes relate to the broad goals of multicultural education?

4. What value does the NNER agenda hold for current and future educators?

The Four Questions. With regard to Question One, in 1999–2000 the NNER was a loosely knit national (USA) network of individual partner schools (over 400), school districts (over 100), and 34 colleges and universities in 14 states. These entities collaborated in 16 different geographical settings to help achieve the major goals and central mission of the NNER, the latter revolving around the concept of simultaneous renewal. The network, which was established in 1986 by John Goodlad and his colleagues (Ken Sirotnick, Roger Soder, and Gary Fenstermacher among others), has been supported and shaped by the Center for Educational Renewal (hereafter the Center), located within the School of Education at the University of Washington, and the Seattle-based Institute for Educational Inquiry (hereafter the Institute), an independent non-profit organization led by John Goodlad. Between 1986 and 1998 the renewal agenda defined within each of the sixteen settings was strongly influenced by policies emanating from the Center and the Institute. However, starting in 1998, with the encouragement of the Center, the NNER began the process of becoming a more autonomous organization. In 1998–1999 an NNER governing council was created with each setting having one representative, and the council has drawn up an application process which will allow for the gradual growth of the NNER.

The 16 settings currently in the NNER include the Brigham Young University—Public School Partnership, the California Central Coast Network for Educational Renewal, the Colorado Partnership for Educational Renewal, the Connecticut School-University Partnership, the Hawaii School-University Partnership, the Metropolitan St. Louis Consortium for Educational Renewal, Miami University (of Ohio), the Nebraska Network for Educational Renewal, the New Jersey Network for Educational Renewal (centered at Montclair State University), the South Carolina Network for Educational Renewal, the Southern Maine Partnership, Texas A&M University, University of Texas at El Paso, University of Washington, Wright State University (of Ohio), and the Wyoming School-University Partnership.[76] It is noteworthy that these 16 settings come from all regions within the United States, vary significantly in size and scope, and encompass a wide range of colleges and universities. The NNER colleges and universities include small private colleges, state-supported universities, large private colleges with strong religious orientations, and colleges/universities which are predominantly Anglo, Hispanic, and African American. This diversity is by design. From its inception the NNER, in part, was conceived as a large piece of action research, and one of the goals of the Center was to see how the NNER agenda and strategy would play out in a wide range of institutions. The limited size (N=16 settings) of the NNER during the 1986–1998 period was strongly influenced by this research agenda; the Center staff selected the number of settings it thought it could adequately support and study with its limited human and financial resources.

Given its geographical diversity, it's clear that the NNER, in addition to being part of a large action research project, was also designed to be a special type of national educational movement. This is supported by Gary Fenstermacher who states that the central purpose of this movement, and the work of John Goodlad, is to "strengthen the voice of democracy in the on-going discussion about the purpose and future of public education in the USA," and "restore the links between education and democracy."[77] Relatedly, Fenstermacher says that "The Agenda for Education in a Democracy aims at renewing our common and collective commitment to public education in the United States," and that in this renewal process schools, and therefore educators, "carry an enormous responsibility for fostering democratic character," character which "is vital to democratic governance."[78]

These goals illuminate the NNER core endeavor (simultaneous renewal) and will help us understand why it was selected above others (Question Two). The core endeavor of the NNER has two aspects. First and foremost, it is to promote *simultaneous renewal* within the set of collaborating partner schools, partner school districts, institutions of higher education (IHEs), and any other agencies which are involved. Simultaneous renewal connotes collaboration and improvement, among other things, and this means that all of these constituencies will help each other get better at carrying out selected tasks such as the design and implementation of K–16 service learning projects, the enhancement of K–12 students' academic aspirations and achievement, and the improvement of teacher, counselor, and administrator preparation programs. The second part of the endeavor is to decisively influence the direction of the simultaneous renewal agenda by linking it to a set of major themes and critical conditions. These guiding themes provide public schools and collaborating colleges and universities (IHEs) with ideas and values which contribute to a philosophy of education which is more coherent, compelling, and unifying. The philosophy provides a strong rationale for public schools in a democracy, and democracy within public schools.

Goodlad and his colleagues developed this two-part core endeavor as a response to research which began in 1976. Their program of research, which is reported on in *A Place Called School* (1984),[79] *Teachers for Our Nation's Schools* (1990),[80] and *Educational Renewal: Better Teachers, Better Schools* (1994),[81] revealed that:

    a. in the 1970s and much of the 1980s most K–12 schools and IHEs were carrying out independent, as opposed to collaborative, *joint* programs of improvement;

    b. creative, mutually advantageous, philosophically focused partnerships between K and 12 and IHE institutions were few and far between; and

    c. in the 1980s many K–12 program leaders and IHE program leaders lacked a clear philosophy and mission, and more specifically they lacked a mission and philosophy which linked their program content to the broader purpose of maintaining and improving democratic values and institutions within our society.

In short, the two-part core endeavor stemmed from the recognition that K–12/IHE collaboration and democratic focus were missing, and that such omissions placed public education and democracy at risk. Goodlad also recognized that to attract educators to this endeavor another set of compelling ideas on themes would be necessary. These ideas, which have been called the NNER guiding principles, cornerstone themes, and the four-part mission of the Agenda for Education in a Democracy by various authors, and their relation to multicultural education will be discussed below (Question Three).

Although the four guiding themes have sometimes been expressed and interpreted in slightly different ways, no one who is seriously committed to the NNER Agenda ignores these themes. As expressed by Fenstermacher, the four guiding themes are:

1. to facilitate the critical enculturation of the young into a social and political democracy;
2. to provide to all children and youths disciplined encounters with all the subject matters of the human conversation;
3. to engage in pedagogical practices that forge a caring and effective connection between teacher and students; and
4. to exercise responsible stewardship of our schools.[82]

While the language employed in these four guiding themes is fairly clear, some additional words of explanation may prove helpful, and beyond these words we refer readers to Gary Fenstermacher's illuminating chapter entitled "Agenda for Education in a Democracy" in *Leadership for Educational Renewal: Developing a Cadre of Leaders,*[83] as well as other chapters in that text which address each of the guiding themes.

To begin with, it is important to realize that the 'critical enculturation' theme implies much more than what is traditionally implied by instruction in civics and citizenship education. The complexity and special significance of this theme is emphasized in the NNER literature, and by NNER theorists such as Fenstermacher who wrote: "Democracy is not a natural state of the human species. It requires intentional, discerning effort to achieve and then maintain," and that for our democracy to function and flourish it "requires persons of a particular character, as well as particular skills and understandings."[84] After listing some traits associated with democratic character—tolerance, fairness, caring, openness, critical judgment, and a due regard for evidence—Fenstermacher makes this important observation: "Readying the young for democratic participation entails offering lessons in the formation of character essential to the maintenance and the advancement of democratic life. Hence the task of readying the young for democratic life is the business of all educators."[85]

With the "disciplined encounters" theme it is important to realize that this is the part of NNER Agenda which addresses equity. Indeed, other NNER theorists express this theme as 'providing equitable access to knowledge.' Reinforcing this, Fenstermacher says that this theme "calls on educators to attend to the disciplines in ways that offer all willing learners fair and equal access to the accumulated knowledge and wisdom of humankind," and further that this theme obligates schools to "provide the young with authentic opportunities to break away from the stereotyping and stratifying influences of class, race, gender, and other similar chance aspects of birth or environment."[86]

With the "pedagogical practices" theme the big idea is that educators, in order to be successful with themes one, two, and three, will need to perceive and interact with their students both as learners and fellow human beings. In many of our bureaucratic settings this is a challenging task. But, if educators want their students to care about the quality of our society's schools, neighborhoods, political structures, and human family, they will have to demonstrate consistent care and concern for the human beings they are trying to teach. In short, this theme challenges all teachers to develop teaching practices that will help to make their students hopeful, caring, and self-confident, as well as smart and intellectually curious.

Regarding the stewardship theme, it is noteworthy that stewardship is one of the concepts which makes the NNER Agenda unique among American reform movements, past and present. While many teacher education programs and contemporary reform movements focus teachers' attention on the domain in which they do their traditional and important work—the classroom—the stewardship theme encourages teachers to be concerned with the health and vitality of their whole organization, and to do something for that overall health and vitality. As Peter Block observes "Stewardship is . . . the willingness to be accountable for the well-being of the larger organization by operating in service, rather than in control, of those around us."[87] And Wilma Smith adds to our understanding by noting that "Stewards actively direct affairs to safeguard and improve something precious, and in the process, they earn a sense of fulfillment and distinction."[88] What remains to be said is that in the NNER literature it is the public schools, more than private-sector schools, which are considered to be precious. The explicit assumption is that as we protect and renew our public schools and the concept of public education, we renew and protect a major source of strength for our democracy.

To complete our response to Question Three, we turn now to the relationship between the goals of multicultural education and the NNER guiding themes, and then discuss the value which the NNER Agenda holds for current and future educators (Question Four). A quick review of our seven-goal model of multicultural education reveals substantial overlap between these goals and the NNER themes. For example, it is clear that both multicultural education and the NNER as national educational movements are concerned with the expansion of educational equity and democratic practices in school and society. In addition, the goals of empowerment, intergroup harmony, and educational equity are facilitated by the nurturant pedagogy and stewardship themes. Finally, in terms of suggesting new ideas for a personal philosophy of education, it appears to us that the NNER Agenda nicely complements the seven-goal model of multicultural education. In fact, the NNER Agenda makes multicultural education in some American regions more feasible because of the ongoing collaboration between various IHEs and school districts.

All of this points to the value which knowledge of the NNER bestows upon current and future educators. It provides them with another model and educational network they can draw on as they articulate and operationalize their own conception of multicultural education. And the NNER model, as made clear previously, adds some new ideas which educators can fold into their conception of multicultural education, ideas pertaining to stewardship, simultaneous renewal, the salience of public education in our democracy, and the idea that teaching is quintessentially and unavoidably a moral endeavor (more on this later).

These eight educators—Phillip Uri Treisman, James P. Comer, Bruce C. Davis, Jaime Escalante, Susan K. Sherwood, Mary Catherine Swanson, Charles Vidal, and John I. Goodlad—with their special projects and successes, remind us that educators can pursue selected goals within our model with different strategies. Our model of multicultural education has seven goals, and each can be pursued in a variety of ways. Furthermore, although the goals in our conception will likely remain the same, the methods to achieve them will change as the educational context changes and the teacher's multicultural perspective matures and evolves. Some of this evolution in perspective will likely arise from exposure to other conceptions of multicultural education, and with this in mind, we next review the definitions that have shaped the dialogue in the field of multicultural education since the 1960s.

MULTICULTURAL EDUCATION: AN EVOLVING CONCEPT

There are at least two ways to categorize definitions of multicultural education, and both shed light on the ongoing interpretation and evolution of this pivotal concept. In the first approach, we could examine definitions that appeared in various decades, especially the 1970s, 1980s, and 1990s. A cursory analysis of this categorization suggests that (1) definitions offered in the 1990s are more complex and include variables mentioned in the definitions from the 1970s and 1980s and (2) the definitions in the 1990s attempt to incorporate new concepts such as *critical pedagogy* and *social justice;* the latter appears to be an expansion of *education equity,* a key concept in earlier definitions. In addition, one new important definition incorporates the idea that multicultural education is a field of inquiry, a new emergent academic discipline. This definition and another that includes critical pedagogy and social justice as core elements are discussed next as we elaborate on the second approach.

The second approach to categorizing multicultural education definitions, the one we shall employ, focuses on the dominant characteristic or characteristics in the definitions. Following this scheme, we shall place definitions within five broad, overlapping categories. In the first category, *cultural pluralism* is the key characteristic, and *educational equity* is the key concept in the second category. The third category contains definitions that stress the reduction of *racism, sexism,* and other *-isms,* while the fourth focuses on definitions in which *freedom* is the core idea. Finally, in the fifth category we present definitions that link multicultural education to other philosophical movements or approaches to education; these include social reconstruction-ism, multiethnic education, critical pedagogy, and Africentric education. We will examine cultural-pluralism definitions first.

Definitions Involving Cultural Pluralism

In 1977 several examples of cultural-pluralism definitions were disseminated in *Multicultural Education: Commitments, Issues, and Applications,* a document edited by Carl Grant and published by the influential Association for Supervision and Curriculum Development (ASCD).[89] The following are located in the "definition" section of this document:

1. In educational terms, the recognition of cultural pluralism has been labeled "multicultural education."
2. Multicultural education, as interpreted by ASCD, is a humanistic concept based on the strength of diversity, human rights, social justice, and alternative life choices for all people.

Elaborating on these statements, the ASCD authors wrote that

the essential goals of multicultural education embrace: (a) recognizing and prizing diversity; (b) developing greater understanding of other cultural patterns; (c) respecting individuals of all cultures; and (d) developing positive and productive interaction among people and among experiences of diverse cultural groups.

Another definition that focused on cultural pluralism appeared in the work of Mira L. Baptiste and H. Prentice Baptiste, Jr.[90] The Baptistes, whose definition was part of a competency-based approach to multicultural teacher education, wrote: "Conceptually, multicultural education is that which recognizes and respects the cultural pluralistic nature of our society in the United States." While these pluralism-oriented definitions were being articulated in the late 1970s, another view that emphasized equity was being formulated, and examples of this type follow.

Definitions Involving Equity

The following are illustrative of the equity-oriented definitions. The first comes from James Banks, the second from Donna M. Gollnick and Phillip C. Chinn, and the third and fourth from James Banks and Cherry McGee Banks.

Multicultural education [is] an educational reform movement that is concerned with increasing educational equity for a range of cultural and ethnic groups.[91]

Multicultural education is the educational strategy in which the student's cultural background is viewed as positive and essential in developing classroom instruction and a desirable school environment. It is designed to support and extend the concepts of culture, cultural pluralism, and equity into the formal school setting.[92]

Gollnick and Chinn's definition embraces cultural pluralism as well as equity; both theirs and Banks's, like the Baptistes', suggest that for multicultural education to become a reality, the school environment must reflect a commitment to multicultural education. In this vein, in 1989 Banks described multicultural education as an institutional change process that requires changes in the total environment.[93] In addition, in 1995 in the introduction to the *Handbook of Research on Multicultural Education,* Banks and Banks perceptively modified the first definition above when they wrote:

> Multicultural education is a field of study and an emerging discipline whose major aim is to create equal educational opportunities for students from diverse racial, ethnic, social-class, and cultural groups.[94]

Later, in the same introduction, after commenting on the productive interaction between multicultural education and other interdisciplinary fields and academic disciplines, James and Cherry Banks elaborated on the above definition.

> Consequently, we may define multicultural education as a field of study designed to increase educational equity for all students that incorporates, for this purpose, content, concepts, principles, theories, and paradigms from history, the social and behavioral sciences, and particularly from ethnic studies and women studies.[95]

These definitions are significant because for the first time multicultural education is introduced as an entity which is more than a concept, process, and reform movement. And, the chapters in the *Handbook of Research on Teaching* as well as G. Pritchy Smith's *Common Sense about Uncommon Knowledge:The Knowledge Bases for Diversity*[96] present the variety of topics and knowledge which support the idea that multicultural education is a fledgling academic discipline, worthy of its place within academia. On a practical level, this means that candidates who receive some exposure to multicultural education as part of a credential or M.A. program can now earn an advanced degree (M.A., M.Ed., Ed.D., or Ph.D.) in a program where multicultural education is the major focus. For example, in 1997, Mark Drozowski, in his *Insider's Guide to Graduate Programs in Education,* listed 35 college and universities whose catalogue indicated that they offered an M.A. or Ph.D. in multicultural education.[97] Among those listed were the Universities of Washington, Massachusetts, New Mexico, Wisconsin (Madison and Milwaukee), and Harvard, UCLA, Ohio State, and George Mason University. In August 1999 we conducted an informal survey of these and other campuses. The results indicated that these campuses, and likely others, do indeed offer candidates the opportunity to earn an advanced degree where multicultural education or multicultural studies is the major component of a program of studies in broader curriculum areas such as Curriculum and Instruction; Urban Studies; Language, Literacy, and Culture; Educational Policy and Leadership; and Counseling and Psychology. For example, at the University of Washington candidates can earn an M.Ed. in Curriculum and Instruction with a multicultural education study option. In this program, in addition to other requirements, candidates will complete 9 credits in Foundations of Education-related courses, 15 credits of ethnic diversity-related subject matter outside the College of Education, and 15 credits in multicultural education courses offered by Curriculum and Instruction faculty. Within the latter group, two courses, *Multiethnic Curriculum and Instruction* and *Education Minority Youth* are required. Program materials disseminated by the University of Washington College of Education describe this option as one that is "designed to prepare teachers and other professionals to assume leadership roles in school districts, colleges, universities and other institutions that have projects, courses and programs related to multicultural education, race relations, and to improving the academic achievement of students of color." In a similar vein, but different structure, students at the University of Massachusetts can earn an M.Ed. in the Bilingual/English as a Second Language/Multicultural Education (BEM) Program. In this program, which prepares candidates for leadership roles in second language education and multicultural education, candidates can select a specialization in bilingual education, multicultural education, English as a second language, or English as a foreign language. In addition, in a highly individualized program of study, candidates at the University of Massachusetts can earn a doctorate (Ed.D.) in Language, Literacy, and Culture. Analysis of materials disseminated by this program suggests that it can be accurately described as a doctoral program in multicultural education which revolves around the concepts of language, literacy, and culture. The program materials, for example, state that the goal of the Language, Literacy, and Culture doctoral program "is to construct a diverse and collaborative community of scholars who are interested in exploring new ways of understanding language, literacy, and culture in the interest of developing more effective and equitable practices," and that the program makes use of "perspectives from fields such as anthropology, sociology, and critical studies . . . in order to reconceptualize language, literacy, and cultural practices as social and political action." Because of this emphasis we perceive the Language, Literacy, and Culture program as one that is strongly connected to educational equity and the maintenance and expansion of democracy, two pivotal goals in our conception of multicultural education. In addition, other programs with similar themes and structures at the University of Wisconsin, Madison, the University of Wisconsin, Milwaukee, Ohio State University, and UCLA indicate, first, that the study of multicultural education in advanced degree programs is not an isolated phenomenon, and second that it is accurate to describe multicultural education as a fledgling academic discipline and an interdisciplinary field of study which is establishing organizational roots in various universities in the United States.

On a more speculative level, we think it fair to observe that some interesting complexity has been added to courses in multicultural education now that it is perceived to be both a reform movement and a fledgling academic discipline. For example, the nature and direction of inquiry in multicultural education courses and programs may change as instructors and students try to help the field mature as an academic discipline. One would expect that critical and more elaborate inquiries into a wider range of multicultural issues and concepts might occur, including inquiries which examined the field and discipline of multicultural education itself. It would be interesting, for example, to find out what doctoral programs which allow for multicultural education specializations have in common and how they differ, and what type of inquiries are being conducted by doctoral candidates in these programs. How many, for instance, pertain to educational equity? And, how prominent is the study of racism and sexism in the course work of advanced degree programs in multicultural education?

With these questions in mind, it is noteworthy that despite the breadth and complexity in the aforementioned definitions, and the formulations which follow from there,[98] some advocates of multicultural education might consider them incomplete because they do not explicitly mention racism. Examples of definitions which do mention racism follow.

Definitions Involving Racism

The first two definitions in this section emerged from the work of educators brought together to carve out guiding definitions for influential organizations; the final definition appeared in a survey disseminated by Eugene Kim of California State University, Sacramento. The first one is extrapolated from Standard 2.1 of the guidelines employed by the National Council for the Accreditation of Teacher Education (NCATE) in 1979–1986; the second is from *Excellence in Professional Education,* a document created and disseminated by the Office of the Chancellor of the California State University system in 1983.

> Multicultural education is preparation for the social, political, and economical realities that individuals experience in culturally diverse and complex human encounters. . . .Multicultural education could include but not be limited to experiences which: 1) Promote analytical and evaluative abilities to confront issues such as participatory democracy, racism and sexism, and the parity of power; 2) Develop skills for values clarification including the study of the manifest and latent transmission of values; 3) examine the dynamics of diverse cultures and the implications for developing teaching strategies; 4) Examine linguistic variations and diverse learning styles as a basis for the development of appropriate teaching strategies.[99]
>
> Multicultural education is viewed as a methodology to encounter racism and prejudice based on ethnic identification and to promote positive attitudes about human diversity.[100]

Finally, Kim, in a 1987 survey pertaining to multicultural education, offered this definition:

> Multicultural education is a deliberate educational attempt to help students understand facts, generalizations, attitudes, and behaviors derived from their own ethnic roots (origins) as well as others. In this educational process students will unlearn racism (ethnocentrism) and recognize the interdependent fabric of our human society, giving due acknowledgment for contributions made by various ethnic groups throughout the world.[101]

Although these definitions clearly address racism and integrate this focus with cultural pluralism, it is noteworthy that, within this set, the concepts of equity and freedom are not mentioned at all, and each of the definitions stops short of actively preparing students to restructure society significantly. To find this more radical conception, we need to examine the definitions that link multicultural education to freedom, social justice, social reconstructionism, and critical pedagogy. We will focus first on the definitions linking multicultural education to freedom.

Definitions Emphasizing Freedom

As noted earlier, James Banks, in defining the concept of multicultural education, has linked it to educational reform and educational equity. In more recent works, he has connected it to transformational change, cross-cultural competence, and freedom.[102] Here we will review the remarks that pertain to freedom. In an interview with Ann T. Lockwood, Banks observed that "the goal of multicultural education in the broader sense is an education for freedom," and we take that to mean providing an education for freedom. He clarifies his definition by stating that multicultural education (1) "should help students to develop the knowledge, attitude, and skills to participate in a democratic and free society," (2) that it "promotes the freedom, abilities, and skills to cross ethnic and cultural boundaries to participate in other cultures and groups"; and (3) that it encourages freedom by providing students with the skills "to participate in social and civic action to make the nation more democratic and free."[103] With the latter set of skills, students help their country achieve what Banks identifies as the major goal of multicultural education: "to create a nation-state that actualizes the democratic ideals for all that the founding fathers intended for an elite few."[104]

James Banks is not alone in linking multicultural education and freedom. For example, B. Parekh, in remarks quite similar to Banks's, stated that "multicultural education is an education for freedom that is essential in today's ethnically polarized and troubled world."[105] And Henry Trueba makes this connection as well in his discussion of the meaning and significance of multicultural education in modern America. In 1992 he wrote:

> In other societies, such as the United States and Britain, there is a more precise and encompassing notion of multicultural education. It is the preparation of all persons to live productively in a single, plural and democratic society, sharing the same rights and obligations.[106]

Finally, while they do not explicitly link multicultural education and freedom, we think you will see similarities between the freedom-oriented definitions just expressed and at least two of the multicultural-education-plus conceptions discussed next. To these we now turn.

Multicultural-Education-Plus Definitions

The fifth type of definition of *multicultural education* derives from the work of Carl Grant and Christine Sleeter, James Banks, Asa Hilliard III, Christine Bennett, and Sonia Nieto, among others. Both Banks and Grant, and to a lesser extent Hilliard and Bennett, have been leaders in defining and redefining the field of multicultural education. For example, in this chapter we see Grant associated with the 1977 ASCD document that almost equated multicultural education with cultural pluralism, and find Banks disseminating definitions that tightly linked multicultural education to educational equity and freedom, and the idea that multicultural education is a field of study and an emerging discipline. It is noteworthy, therefore, that in their writings in the 1970s and 1980s, both of these African-American educators connected multicultural education to a broader conception of education to make it, in their eyes, a more complete and meaningful approach. Perhaps this was because their own ethnic perspectives and experiences persuaded them that multicultural education was only a partial response to the curriculum needs of students of color, particularly those who have experienced the greatest amount of oppression. In Banks's case it was *multiethnic education,* and for Grant and his collaborator, Sleeter, it was *social reconstructionism.* Other educators such as Hilliard, Nieto, and Bennett also forged new connections; for Hilliard it was Afrocentric education (sometimes referred to as Africentric education), for Nieto it was critical pedagogy, and for Bennett it was global education. Next we briefly discuss Grant and Sleeter's conception of education that is multicultural and social reconstructionist, Banks's view of multicultural/multiethnic education, Nieto's synthesis conception of multicultural education, and last, Afrocentric education. Readers are encouraged to seek out original sources to gain a deeper understanding of these synthesis conceptions.

Multicultural-Education-Plus Social Reconstructionism.   Sleeter and Grant, in their book *Making Choices for Multicultural Education: Five Approaches to Race, Class and Gender.*[107] describe multicultural education as an approach that seeks to "reform the entire process of schooling for all children," "improve society for all," and "develop skills and a knowledge base that will support multiculturalism."[108] In contrasting multicultural education with education that is multicultural and social reconstructionist, Sleeter and Grant write that the latter "deals more directly than the other approaches have with oppression and social structural inequality based on race, social class, gender, and disability . . . [and] prepares future citizens to reconstruct society so that it better serves the interests of all groups of people and especially those who are of color, poor, female, and/or disabled."[109]

Multicultural/Multiethnic Education.   Although Banks, and Grant and Sleeter, utilize different concepts when they discuss multicultural education, it is our impression that Banks's overall conception of multicultural education is similar to Grant and Sleeter's conception of education that is multicultural and social reconstructionist. There are differences, but they are in degree rather than in kind.

One of the differences alluded to above concerns ethnic studies and/or multiethnic education. At the same time that Banks has provided lucid and valuable equity-oriented and freedom-focused definitions of multicultural education, he has also developed a rationale for multiethnic education, a form of education that would complement and strengthen multicultural education. For example, in 1981 he wrote:

> A generic focus within a school reform effort, such as multicultural education, can make a substantial contribution to the liberal education of students. However, school reform efforts should go beyond the level of generic multicultural education and focus on the unique problems that women, Blacks, youth and other cultural groups experience in American society. Many of the problems these groups have are unique and require specialized analyses and strategies. . . . Multicultural education is a politically popular concept because it is often interpreted to mean lumping the problems of ethnic minorities, women, and other groups together. Public and school policies that are based primarily on lumping the problems of diverse groups together will prove ineffective and perhaps detrimental to all of the groups concerned. Because of the unique problems some ethnic and racial groups have in American society, school districts should implement *multiethnic* education to complement and strengthen *multicultural* education. These concepts are complementary but not interchangeable.[110]

Geneva Gay, another leading advocate of multiethnic education, in discussing what she believes should be the central focus of multicultural education, notes that socioeconomic status, gender, and religion are legitimate areas of study and clearly intertwined with ethnicity. However, she cautions that "including them under the conceptual rubric of multiethnic or multicultural education may tend to divert attention away from ethnicity."[111] Thus we see that for Gay, the conception of multicultural education that asks teachers to consider ethnicity along with other variables (religion, gender, etc.) as they work to achieve educational equity is problematical; unless carefully monitored, the effort to implement the wider-ranging multicultural curriculum could dilute attempts to create and deliver multiethnic education. Finally, while we believe that the multicultural/multiethnic education distinction is useful in helping to interpret and understand the different content which teachers and teacher educators select for their courses, we note that James Banks recently (1999) described multiethnic education as a term that "was used frequently in the 1970s but is rarely used in educational discourse today."[112]

Multicultural-Education-Plus Critical Pedagogy.   The multicultural education theorist who most clearly connects multicultural education to critical pedagogy is Sonia Nieto. In 1992, in the first edition of her text, Nieto shared a well-rounded, thought-provoking conception of multicultural education, one that is similar to those presented by Sleeter and Grant and James Banks but one that introduces new terminology worthy of study. In her text *Affirming Diversity: The Sociopolitical Context of Multicultural Education,* Nieto presents an elaborate definition, as well as seven basic characteristics, of *multicultural education.*[113] One of these characteristics, *critical pedagogy,* is identified as the "underlying philosophy" of multicultural education, and this statement all by itself is intriguing because another influential theorist of multicultural education, James A. Banks, doesn't even mention that term in the glossary and index of his text *An Introduction to Multicultural Education.*[114] On the other hand, G. Pritchy Smith in discussing the knowledge bases for diversity states that if they:

> are not treated within the context of a critical pedagogy that challenges the status quo of inequities, includes critical dialogue, utilizes multiple perspectives, and ultimately empowers teachers to take social action in their personal and classroom lives to correct social injustices, impact will likely be minimal.[115]

While we would hesitate to describe critical pedagogy as the underlying philosophy of multicultural education, we think it is a way of thinking and teaching that educators should learn more about. With this in mind, we enumerate Sonia Nieto's definition and characteristics of multicultural education, as well as key elements in her conception of critical pedagogy. In addition, in a brief and speculative manner we discuss the idea of guilt in relation to antiracist teaching.

To begin with, Nieto provides the following definition of multicultural education:

> Multicultural education is a process of comprehensive school reform and basic education for all students. It challenges and rejects racism and other forms of discrimination in schools and society and accepts and affirms the pluralism (ethnic, racial, linguistic, religious, economic, and gender, among others) that students, their communities, and teachers represent. Multicultural education permeates the curriculum and instructional strategies used in schools, as well as the interactions among teachers, students, and parents, and the very way that schools conceptualize the nature of teaching and learning. Because it uses critical pedagogy as its underlying philosophy and focuses on knowledge, reflection, and action (praxis) as the basis for social change, multicultural education furthers the democratic principles of social justice.[116]

In addition, Nieto introduces and then discusses the following as the seven basic characteristics of multicultural education:

Multicultural education is *antiracist education.*

Multicultural education is *basic education.*

Multicultural education is *important* for all students.

Multicultural education is *pervasive.*

Multicultural education is *education for social justice.*

Multicultural education is a *process.*

Multicultural education is *critical pedagogy.*[117]

Antiracism Education and Students' Identities. Before discussing critical pedagogy, we should note that antiracism education plays a pivotal role in Nieto's model. She writes, for example, that "antiracism, and antidiscrimination in general, is at the very core of a multicultural perspective."[118] and further that "to be more inclusive and balanced, [a] multicultural curriculum must by definition be antiracist."[119] Beyond this, in her narrative on antiracist education, Nieto shares a number of ideas worthy of critical analysis. She notes, for example, that in studying racism, "teachers and students need to move beyond the guilt stage to one of energy and confidence, where they take action rather than hide behind feelings of remorse." She reinforces this thought by noting that "although everybody is not guilty of racism and discrimination, we are all responsible for it . . . and teachers [therefore] can focus on discrimination as something everyone has a responsibility to confront." Finally, concerning the guilt that may result from studying racism in American schools and society, Nieto writes that:

> being antiracist does not mean flailing out in guilt or remorse. One of the reasons that schools are reluctant to deal with racism and discrimination is because they are uncomfortable. They often place people in the role of either the victimizer or the victimized. An initial and quite understandable reaction of European American teachers and students is to feel guilty. Such a reaction, however, although probably serving an initial useful purpose, needs to be understood as only one step in the process of becoming multiculturally literate and empowered. If it remains at this level, guilt only immobilizes.[120]

While we agree with Nieto's final observation about moving beyond guilt, we do not consider it understandable or necessarily positive that European-American teachers and students have guilt feelings (as European-Americans) when they are presented with the facts about historical and contemporary racism in American culture. Embedded in Nieto's comments about guilt lies a pedagogical and ethical issue that goes to the core of much contemporary confusion about what it means for teachers and students to think, learn, and teach with a multicultural perspective.

The essence of this issue concerns the way teachers perceive, label, categorize, and develop expectations about students in their classroom and school. Should teachers, for example, view individuals—let us say Akila, Harry, and José—as individuals with complex, idiosyncratic, emergent ethnocultural identities? Or should they perceive, address, and expect Akila, José, and Harry to view themselves as members of distinct ethnocultural (or racial) groups—such as African American, European American, Asian American, Latino American—members who should have, or are entitled to have, specific emotional responses to historical and contemporary events, such as guilt, because of their teacher-perceived, socially constructed *group identity?* Or should the teachers somehow, wisely, attempt to do both?

We don't want to suggest that there is one clear, definitive answer to this question for every teacher in every school in the 15,000 plus school districts in the United States. Nor do we wish to suggest that teachers alone determine, or even strongly influence, the social identity of each of their students, or that it is clear where Professor Nieto stands on this issue. But we do believe that students and advocates of multicultural education will have to grapple with this question.

As the issue is confronted, we should remember that the multicultural education movement in the United States was created to protect the interests of groups of students who were excluded, underserved, miseducated, and oppressed because of their group identity, and therefore it is natural for multicultural education advocates to think in terms of groups as well as individuals. We should also remember that, no matter how noble the purpose, it is essentially undemocratic to define and limit an individual because of a purported or suspected group identity. James Banks catches this tension well as he defines multicultural education for freedom, and a review of his comments regarding freedom for individual students would be appropriate at this point. As for the authors, we lean heavily toward understanding and teaching individuals as individuals, but this does not preclude individuals from having strong group affiliations and identities to which we and other professionals must pay attention. As we noted in the preface:

> . . . we must ignite in our teachers a desire to study their students in the students' full cultural context, to see them clearly as individuals whose school behavior is influenced in different ways by the family, community, and ethnocultural groups of which they are part. Our teachers will need to understand that to treat their students respectfully as individuals, they must learn about the relevant social groups in their students' lives, in both the community and the classroom. This more sophisticated perspective on individuality is an integral part of the multicultural education we espouse and a key element in the implementation process we call "teaching with a multicultural perspective."

More specifically, to return to the issue of guilt, we think it wise not to assign historical or contemporary guilt to individuals on the basis of a group identity. When a student says that he or she feels guilt for what Germans or Christians have done to Jews, or Jews to Palestinians, or Muslims to Christians, or Hindus to Buddhists, or Japanese to Chinese, or Whites to Blacks, and so on, we think the proper response is: What have you personally done to warrant a feeling of guilt? Should all American men feel guilty for the ongoing brutality that individual men manifest toward women in society, or should men's feelings be a function of their personal actions toward women? We think the latter. But individuals who are men, or White, or of Asian descent, or African American, or women should as citizens take individual or collective action to set right the things that are wrong in our society because they are wrong. In other words, the actions that a citizen, let us say citizen Rachel, takes to correct unjust practices and conditions in her community and society should stem from her values and not from guilt related to actions taken by individuals who, in the eyes of someone, shares an ethnic or cultural group identity with Rachel. Of course, Rachel may have done bad things to good people, and in that case her corrective actions ought to

be provoked by guilt as well as by her values. Or in her own eyes her individual and group identity may be so closely intertwined that the issue of individual versus group guilt may be moot.

Key Elements in Critical Pedagogy.   Nieto's inclusion of critical pedagogy
in her model, and her explication of this concept, relate nicely to the perceptual issue discussed previously. While Nieto introduces critical pedagogy as the
underlying philosophy of multicultural education, her presentation suggests
that it can also be viewed as a set of ideas about a preferred way of teaching.
Thus, based on Nieto's remarks,[121] we understand that *pedagogy* will be considered *critical* when it creates a curriculum and pattern of instruction that:

1. is based on the experiences and viewpoints of students rather than an
   imposed culture;
2. explodes myths;
3. encourages a learning process that ideally moves from knowledge to
   reflection to action—in a flexible, nonlinear manner;
4. encourages the development, in students and teachers, of an active
   multicultural perspective, a pattern of seeing and thinking informed
   by the belief that to more fully understand reality, one must develop
   the habit of reflecting on multiple and contradictory perspectives;
5. ensures that cultural and linguistic diversity is acknowledged and supported rather than suppressed; and
6. reminds teachers that knowledge is neither neutral nor apolitical and,
   in doing so, draws attention to Paulo Freire's distinction between
   domesticating education—education that emphasizes passivity, acceptance, and submissiveness—and *liberating education*—education that
   encourages students to take risks, be curious, and ask questions.

How does critical pedagogy illuminate the perceptual tug-of-war about
identity just discussed? It sheds light primarily by advocating a curriculum and
pedagogy that emphasizes the experiences and viewpoints of students rather
than an "imposed culture." We believe that a pattern of perception that mech-
anistically divides students into geocultural groups—African American, European American, Latino American, Asian American, American Indian—
represents an imposed culture, unless that perception is deeply and consistently informed by the expressed viewpoints of the teacher's clients, that is,
his or her students and their parents or caretakers.

The methodology of critical pedagogy can also serve to clarify another key
element in Nieto's conception of multicultural education. Nieto states that
multicultural education is education for social justice, and in explaining
what teaching for social justice might look like, she mentions community
improvement projects at senior centers and waste treatment plants, and discussions which pertain to justice-related realities students experience in their
communities (e.g., police brutality, language discrimination, and homelessness).[122] In addition, she suggests that justice-oriented teaching will involve

teachers and students in discussions and action pertaining to inequality and other significant structural issues in our society. She notes, for example, that:

> To admit that inequality exists and is even perpetuated by the very institutions charged with doing away with it are topics too dangerous to discuss. Nevertheless, such issues are at the heart of a broadly conceptualized multicultural perspective because the subject matter of schooling is society, with all its wrinkles, warts, and contradictions. And because society is concerned with ethics and with the distribution of power, status, and rewards, education must focus on these concerns as well.[123]

These comments are quite helpful in identifying topics for discussion and social conditions to be ameliorated when teaching for social justice. Nevertheless, social justice remains an abstruse concept. Therefore, from Nieto and others we would welcome more detailed descriptions of the programs that would lead to, or the social conditions that would constitute, a society in which social justice has been achieved or approximated. After all, politicians and theoreticians from every point on the left-to-right continuum think their policies will create more justice in our society, and without more specificity regarding policies and societal conditions it will be difficult for individual teachers and faculties to embrace and develop social justice–oriented curricula.

With such specificity in mind, we now share part of the definition of social justice found in the *Dictionary of Multicultural Education:*

> Social justice and social responsibility can be treated as synonymous concepts . . . Social responsibility requires that human needs take priority over claims that derive from a system of role distribution in society. Justice demands equality and fairness in all private transactions, wages, and property ownership, as well as equal opportunity for all to participate in the public benefits generated by society, such as social security, health care, and education.[124]

This is not the social justice agenda the authors could easily rally behind, but it is starting to get to the kind of specificity that helps one decide. We would need to know more about the precise or approximate meaning of "... equality and fairness in all private transactions, wages, and property ownership," and equal opportunity in areas such as health care and education. Without the additional specificity it is hard to know if this is the social justice of a socialistic democracy or a progressive capitalistic constitutional democracy. While we would prefer the latter, it is perhaps more important to note that a conception of social justice which equates *real* or *complete equality* in *all* wages, private transactions, and property ownership with fairness is worthy of critical review. While extreme, rigid, exploitative, race-based, discriminatory inequality cries out for social justice, complete or even substantial numerical equality in these and other areas (wages, property ownership, etc.) would require a politically oppressive government and society; in short, another form of social injustice. Therefore, it appears to us that the achievement of social justice in the United States and elsewhere has more to do with defining humane and decent levels of inequality, as opposed to seeking full numerical equality in the areas mentioned previously. But, as alluded to earlier, as educators in various schools and school districts try to achieve educational equity they must strive for full numerical equality of resources and more. From this one can easily see that teaching about and striving for social justice and educational equity is complex and occasionally paradoxical.[125] As such it benefits from the component of critical pedagogy that encourages educators to reflect on multiple and contradictory perspectives. Indeed, such reflection may help us understand another complicated idea, *Afrocentric education,* and the efforts of some educators to link it to multicultural education.

Afrocentric Education.   Afrocentric education is based on the philosophy of Afrocentricity, which Molefi Asante defined as "placing African ideals at the center of any analysis that involves African culture and behavior."[126] Given this definition, one can define Afrocentric education as an educational approach which places African history, knowledge, and values at the center of the curriculum, and note that the degree to which an Afrocentric program will be compatible with multicultural education will depend on the way Asante's definition is interpreted and implemented in a specific curriculum. James Banks, for example, states that Afrocentricity can be interpreted as "the addition of an African American perspective to the school and university curriculum," and "when understood this way, it is consistent with multicultural curriculum because a multicultural curriculum helps students to view behavior, concepts, and issues from different ethnic and cultural perspectives."[127] On the other hand, as Alan Weider reports, there are different versions of Afrocentrism and Afrocentric education and our impression is that some Afrocentric schools are implementing programs which are not multicultural in vision and scope.[128] Unfortunately, multicultural education as a movement and philosophy has suffered because it has been erroneously associated with specific remarks made by individual Afrocentrists as well as an imaginary American social phenomenon—*the cult of ethnicity*—invented, or at least popularized, by the historian Arthur M. Schlesinger in his book *The Disuniting of America: Reflections on a Multicultural Society.*[129] Regarding this cult, in a misguided and remarkable fashion, Schlesinger wrote: "The cult of ethnicity exaggerates differences, intensifies resentments and antagonisms, [and] drives even deeper the wedges between races and nationalities,"[130] and "The attack on the common American identity is the culmination of the cult of ethnicity,"[131] and finally:

> The ethnicity rage in general and Afrocentricity in particular not only divert attention from the real needs but exacerbates the problems. The recent apotheosis [glorification] of ethnicity, black, brown, red, yellow, white, has revived the dismal prospect that in happy melting pot days Americans thought the republic was moving safely beyond—that is, a society fragmented into separate ethnic communities.[132]

In the last quote above Schlesinger is likely referring to Whites who in the 1787-1967 period were intermarrying and melting into one nationality and people. Still, it is shocking to see these words—*happy melting pot days*—employed to describe an era which was filled with tragedy and disappointments for the people who were not allowed to melt, the people of color.

In contrast to the type of unscholarly slanted critique found in Schlesinger's book, and other recent works, and despite the odd historical claims and racist remarks made by some Afrocentrists, our reading of selected articles clearly suggests that serious, worthwhile educational work is being carried out by Afrocentric-oriented teachers and counselors in both public and private settings. Although this work doesn't consistently reflect an integration of Afrocentric and multicultural education, the work is illuminating, thought provoking, and noteworthy. Therefore, after making a few speculative remarks about the genesis of Afrocentric education and its relation to multicultural education, we briefly describe some positive examples of private and public Afrocentric-influenced education.

Regarding the genesis of Afrocentric education, it is noteworthy that it evolved primarily within the context of American society as a part of the struggle which African Americans have waged to improve the quality of their education, their lives, and America's overall culture. Identifying the United States as the main context for the emergence and evolution of Afrocentric education is helpful because it allows us to see some connections between Afrocentric education and multicultural education on the one hand, and the condition of Black America in the 1960s, 1970s, and 1980s on the other. For example, we believe that:

1. both multicultural education and Afrocentric education are historically and strongly connected to the failure of the U.S. political and educational system to broadly embrace the African-American community with concern, respect, and support;

2. the tension between multicultural education and Afrocentric education is part of the ongoing historical debate within the African-American community about how African Americans can best prosper in the larger American community; the former is more closely associated with integration, and the latter with separate African-American institutions. To a certain extent, the positions taken by late twentieth-century writers and leaders like Molefi Asante, Louis Farrakhan, Asa Hilliard, Geneva Gay, Carl Grant, and James Banks can be understood as a continuation of the debate between W. E. B. Dubois, Ida B. Wells, Booker T. Washington, and Marcus Garvey, among others; and

3. the emergence of Afrocentric education as one alternative for African-American students is linked to the isolation of large segments of the Black population, and the failure of some African-American youth to locate a competing philosophy of life to countervail the experiential education they have received on the streets of America's urban centers.

Why was there a perceived need for a new philosophy of education, aimed at African Americans, in the closing decades of the twentieth century? As alluded to, the answer is tightly connected to the type of problems that plagued, and still remain a corrosive factor in, urban African-American communities. In some large urban school districts, demographic trends like hypersegregation and the increasingly high percentages of infants born within single-parent families, along with the social and economic distress caused by what William J. Wilson calls the *disappearance of work,*[133] have created a need or opportunity for what might be called a monoethnic or race-focused curriculum. Because the dropout rate, prison rate, and death rate of African-American males, and others, have reached alarming proportions in various urban centers, some educators are developing school and counseling programs that resemble the nineteenth- and twentieth-century "solutions" of selected ethnic and cultural groups; private Catholic and Jewish schools and military academies come to mind. Alan Singer's comments about Afrocentrism are pertinent here. After recognizing Afrocentrism's contributions to historical debate and his own ongoing education, Singer asserts that "Afrocentrism is not a study of history or an approach to historical understanding. It is a political and religious movement that uses historical information for the creation of unifying cultural symbols."[134] We would add that the cultural symbols and ideas are part of a variegated educational movement, and that the movement has scholarly as well as religious and political elements.[135] Several of the following examples will help to clarify this point, particularly the ones which make consistent use of the Nguzo Saba, or seven principles. These principles are "a comprehensive yet concise set of African-centered family and community values delineated and systematized by Maulena Karenga," a professor in the Black Studies Department at California State University, Long Beach.[136] The seven principles, which parenthetically are key elements in the Kwanzaa holiday celebration, are:

1. **Umoja** (Unity) To strive for and maintain unity in the family, community, nation, and race.

2. **Kujichagulia** (Self-Determination) To define ourselves, name ourselves, create for ourselves, and speak for ourselves instead of being defined, named, created for, and spoken for by others.

3. **Ujima** (Collective Work and Responsibility) To build and maintain our community together and make our brother's and sister's problems our problems and to solve them together.

4. **Ujamaa** (Cooperative Economics) To build and maintain our own stores, shops, and other businesses and to profit from them together.

5. **Nia** (Purpose) To make our collective vocation the building and developing of our community in order to restore our people to their traditional greatness.

6. **Kuumba** (Creativity) To do always as much as we can, in the way we can, in order to leave our community more beautiful and beneficial than we inherited it.

7. **Imani** (Faith) To believe with all our heart in our people, our parents, our teachers, our leaders, and the righteousness and victory of our struggle.[137]

Afrocentric Examples. The first example stems from work conducted at the Mary McLeod Bethune Institute (MMBI), an independent weekend (Saturdays) program in Los Angeles, California. Our brief summary is based on an article written by Subira Kifano in 1996.[138] Kifano points out that the MMBI has been offering a cultural enrichment program for African-American learners, from 3 to 11 years old, for 17 years (in September 1999 the school began its twentieth year of operation), and that during this period the MMBI staff developed a comprehensive model for Afrocentric education as well as a philosophy. Key elements in this philosophy include:

1. a definition and interpretation of reality from an Afrocentric perspective;
2. an emphasis on the acquisition of primary and higher-order thinking skills of critical, analytical, and creative thought;
3. the promotion of a strong desire among African-American youth to serve their people and communities;
4. an emphasis on value orientation and the development of a positive and proactive concept of the self, society, and the world; and
5. the inculcation of a respect for human diversity.[139]

The MMBI curriculum revolves around these key elements. Relatedly, Kifano reports that "The two most critical aspects of this curriculum are its emphases on historical grounding and ethical development," and the fact that "students are exposed to a profusion of information and lessons about heroic men and women from throughout the African Diaspora" and "encouraged to emulate the characters of these examples in their daily lives as part of a moral obligation to remember the legacies of their forebears."[140] To further illustrate the MMBI curriculum Kifano provides excerpts of lessons based on the lives of Malcolm X, Mary McLeod Bethune, and Fannie Lou Hamer, and notes that students are exposed to African languages, encouraged to develop a positive attitude toward using African-American language (also known as Black English and Ebonics), and "taught to first center themselves in their own culture before they are guided to move from that cultural core to find common ground with persons from other cultures."[141] Significantly, we learn that the MMBI students engage in several exercises which show them how to get along with diverse individuals "in ways that might help bring about a truly multicultural society in which all people are recognized and respected."[142]

From our second example we learn that African-American counselors and social workers are also developing and implementing programs which revolve around the seven principles. More specifically our second example is based on work carried out at the MAAT Center, an African-American-operated, nonprofit agency located in Washington, D.C., and founded in 1986. (Ma'at is an ancient Egyptian word which means an ethical way of life.) The Center serves African-American youth from ages 11 to 19 who are referred by the courts, and emotionally and behaviorally disturbed African-American youth of the same age who are referred by the mental health and school system. The Center utilizes an Afrocentric orientation as it develops and implements its counseling strategies.

The information provided above and below is based on two articles written by Aminifu Harvey and coauthors,[143] but we draw mainly on the article entitled "An Afrocentric Program for African American Males in the Juvenile Justice

System." In this article the authors report on a *Rites of Passage* program which serves at-risk African-American youth and their families. The program, which consists of in-home family therapy and individual adolescent counseling, adolescent after-school groups, and family enhancement and empowerment interventions, utilizes an Afrocentric orientation to teach their clients "how to build character, self-esteem, and unity among themselves as a family, community, and race of people—African Americans."[144] It is noteworthy, first, that in the once-a-week, two-hour, after-school group sessions the seven principles are used "to teach youths the principles of spirituality, culture, family, education, economics, and community . . . to help them understand themselves, others, and the world in which they live,"[145] and second that the two-hour sessions cover topics such as African-American culture and heritage, oppression and racism, principles and guides for living, male and female physical development and birth control, fatherhood and marriage, diet and exercise, and entrepreneurial development, among others. The authors report that many of the youth they work with "develop an increased sense of unity, identity, and purpose as they understand and begin to incorporate the principles of Nguzo Saba into their world view."[146] Parenthetically, educators interested in the use of an Afrocentric approach to counseling specific groups of African Americans will find the article "A Rite of Passage Approach Designed to Preserve the Families of Substance-Abusing African American Women" quite interesting.[147]

Finally, with our last examples we turn to expressions of Afrocentrism within public school systems, but we make no claims that these examples accurately reflect the status of Afrocentric-influenced curricula in contemporary urban public schools with high concentrations of African-American students. In earlier editions, we reported that two African-American immersion schools in Milwaukee, Wisconsin, Dr. Martin Luther King Jr. African-American Immersion Elementary School (referred to as "MLK Jr." below) and Robert I. Fulton Middle School (now called Malcolm X Academy), were opened in 1991. An initial major focus for these schools was the education and human development (survival) of Black males, but meeting the needs of young African-American females was also a major priority in these coeducational schools.[148] In July 1999, we interviewed Mrs. Josephine Mosley, who has been MLK Jr.'s principal for the last ten years.[149] She reported that her school was and has been 100 percent African American and that her 504 students were almost equally divided between boys and girls. Regarding MLK Jr.'s overall curriculum, Mrs. Mosley told us that in each grade, kindergarten through fifth, students learn about their African and African-American heritage. In addition, the school has a strong family orientation, and its students wear uniforms, receive weekly report cards and a strong self-esteem program, and learn about the seven principles. "By the third grade" Mrs. Mosley reported "most students can recite and explain the seven principles." The principles are included in announcements each day, and each principle becomes a curriculum theme for an entire month.

Mrs. Mosley also reported that her students have very good test scores compared to schools with similar demographics, and she attributed this to MLK Jr.'s focus on the seven principles and the other curriculum characteristics mentioned previously. However, despite this achievement, Mrs. Mosley indicated that in Milwaukee, at least, Afrocentric-oriented schools were not a growing phenomenon. "We are allowed to be who we are," and "we have stayed alive because we believe in what we're doing." But, and we paraphrase here, we are not the model for other Milwaukee schools with similar demographics. In 1991 we had school board support and a one-time $150,000 grant, but today there is much less districtwide support and interest.

Our final example of an Afrocentric-oriented educational program in the public schools is found in the curriculum created by the Malcolm X Academy in Detroit, Michigan. The brief description of this program is based on information shared by Clifford Watson and Geneva Smitherman in their book *Educating African-American Males: Detroit's Malcolm X Academy Solution.*[150] Smitherman and the late Clifford Watson were key players in the political and educational work which led to the creation of Afrocentric schools within the Detroit school system.

In 1991 Malcolm X Academy and two other African-centered K–5 elementary schools, Marcus Garvey and Paul Robeson, were opened with the understanding that each would add a grade a year so that by 1994 each would be a K–8 school. Initially, these schools were intended to be exclusively male but a lawsuit brought by the National Organization of Women forced Detroit's administrative leaders to open the schools to boys and girls. As a result the three schools were called African-centered rather than Male Academies, but the authors note that in the 1991–1994 period each school had a student population that was 90 percent or more Black male.[151] Relatedly, the authors point out that the creation of these schools was a response to the political, economic, and educational crisis facing Black males in the Detroit schools and surrounding communities. As if to underline this reality, the 1990 conference which led to their creation was entitled 'Improving Self Concept for At Risk Black Students, with Emphasis on Saving the Black Male.'[152]

While Watson and Smitherman tell a very interesting story about the chain of events leading up to the creation and naming of Malcolm X Academy, and the manner in which its students would be selected (random selection based on three categories of risk defined by application content), we will limit our remarks to the mission, curriculum, and early evaluation of Malcolm X Academy. To begin with, the authors note that the mission of Malcolm X grew out of its grounding in the pedagogy known as African Immersion or Afrocentricity, and that "while focus is on African and African American culture, the pedagogy is multicultural and includes study of all groups in the historical and cultural presence of the United States and the world."[153] In addition, Malcolm X's curriculum stresses multicultural, humanistic, and futuristic education, and "seeks to create students who will achieve academic excellence, while developing ethnic awareness, pride, and high self-esteem."[154] To help accomplish these goals students will start the reading process in preschool; learn Kiswahili, Spanish, and French; participate in vocational education and develop computer skills; be placed in accelerated programs; and will not experience failure.[155] Additional intriguing elements in Malcolm X's overall curriculum include the study of African and African-American literature, history, and culture; the study of Black contributions to math and science as math and science is taught; the utilization of a school uniform and strict dress code; an extended school day, school year (11 months), and a Saturday program; an emphasis on personal discipline, social adjustment, and self-control; and the involvement of all parents in the school program. For example, parents pledge a minimum of three hours a month to the Academy and sign a covenant to support the Malcolm X program.[156] Other elements include peer tutoring and counseling, the teaching of community and civic responsibility, and a nine-month rites of passage program for seventh graders. The latter, which calls for extra work during the week and three hours on Saturdays, is conducted by an independent community organization. This special yearlong cultural ritual, culminating in a well-attended "Rites of Passage" ceremony, provides students with the opportunity to learn many valuable things. This includes learning the principles of the Nguzo Saba, and writing a paper wherein students demonstrate that they know how to use the seven principles in their community.[157]

Most significantly, from 1991–1993, in terms of academic achievement in reading and math on standardized state exams, and in discipline and attendance, utilizing district parameters, Malcolm X's students were doing quite well. As one example of this success, in 1993–1994 on the state's standardized math test 93.4 percent of Malcolm X's seventh graders (N = 61) scored in the top grouping. This meant that the seventh graders had received the second highest math scores in the state of Michigan.[158]

Furthermore, an August 1999 phone call to Mrs. Dawson, Malcolm X's current acting principal, and a staff member since 1991, revealed, first, that the school is still a popular alternative for Detroit families, and second, that its achievement scores have been satisfactory in terms of school district standards. Given this information about Malcolm X Academy, and the paucity of data regarding Afrocentric-oriented programs in the mainstream press and many teacher education programs, we believe that Malcolm X Academy and its sister institutions in Detroit and beyond are worthy of continued and deeper analysis.[159]

MULTICULTURAL EDUCATION: CONTROVERSIES AND OPPORTUNITIES

The diverse set of conceptions delineated previously should suggest why multicultural education, specifically, and the broader idea of multiculturalism remain complex and controversial. In addition, a review of the factors contributing to the complexity may prove helpful, particularly for individuals whose prior reading about multicultural education, or prior related experiences, may have left them with a negative impression. So, what is it about multicultural education that provokes so much heated discussion? Why does it produce discomfort?

We see at least eight related factors contributing to the complexity and controversy, and these factors help to define issues that need to be addressed as advocates make the case for multicultural education in various settings. To begin with, leading supporters of multicultural education have stressed that it was and is a reform movement. From the emergence of multicultural education as a curriculum movement, its advocates have set out to shake the status quo at all levels of school district and university operation. For example, multicultural education has always been seen as a revisionist approach to U.S. and world history. Thus, it has been accurately associated with historical research and opinion that tends to puncture theories and myths dearly held by individuals comfortable with the way things are. It would be in courses influenced by multicultural education, for example, that students would have the opportunity to analyze and discuss evidence linking Columbus to brutal crimes as well as entrepreneurial endeavors, or be exposed to a more complex understanding of Lincoln's attitudes about Black Americans prior to and during the Civil War.

Second, the United States is a nation in which *individualism,* including the related idea of reward and recognition based on individual merit, is a core value. In contrast, multicultural education, in addition to being a multifaceted strategy which seeks to improve the education *all* students receive, was and is a reform movement which aims to protect and improve the situation of *groups* of individuals who have been disenfranchised and/or educationally underserved *because of* their group identity. Within the traditional educational arena, this representation has led to a focus on educational equity, and this focus, in turn, has led to an association with affirmative action. Typically, as a result of affirmative action policies, people receive opportunities and rewards because of their individual accomplishments *and* their group identity. In other words, as a part of race-, gender-, ethnic group-, or handicap-conscious selection practices, a specific dimension of a person's identity is considered a strength and becomes part of that individual's merit or value to the selecting program or hiring organization. No matter how strong and logical the rationale for affirmative action in a specific setting is because of demonstrated historical patterns of discrimination, the association between multicultural education and affirmative action contributes to the controversy surrounding multicultural education. And the public's lack of information about the positive results of affirmative action remedies makes the situation worse. Parenthetically, one significant source of information about the positive effects of affirmative action in the admissions process of African-American students at 28 very selective colleges and universities is presented in *The Shape of the River,* a book by Derek Bok, the former president of Harvard University, and William Bowen, the former president of Princeton University.[160]

Multicultural education's linkage to cultural pluralism and support for what might be called a hyphenated form of American identity provides the third source of controversy. As Horace Kallen, Milton Gordon, and others remind us, schools have been and remain sites where programs of Americanization are implicitly or explicitly implemented. In this arena, advocates of multicultural education have articulated a new vision of what it means to be an American. As distinct from the melted-down, fully assimilated, unidimensional Anglo-Saxon model of the true American, multiculturalists have developed a multidimensional, pluralist, rainbow image of the model American. Multicultural-ists envision an America in which differences as well as the common ground can be celebrated. In contrast, some of their opponents want an America in which cultural differences are reduced and the common ground expanded and emphasized. The rainbow image, because it embraces hyphenated identities, bilingualism, and other cultural maintenance strategies, frightens those who believe that the celebration of cultural differences could lead to a more divisive and vulnerable nation. The fact that most advocates of multicultural education are concerned with building a unifying American identity, as well as a culture that supports diversity, is not well understood by those who perceive diversity as a threat that will ultimately weaken the fabric of American society.

A fourth source of controversy stems from recent citizen-led efforts to curtail policies and programs associated with multicultural education. More specifically, multicultural education, as a national movement, is made more vulnerable and controversial when the legality of strategies associated with it are incompletely discussed and debated in the context of a political campaign, via a proposition process which bypasses discussion and analysis by elected statewide representatives. And this is exactly what has happened in California, the nation's largest and most ethnically diverse state. In 1996 California citizens passed Proposition 209, which abolished state-sponsored affirmative action, and in 1998 California voters passed Proposition 227, a law which made it *much more difficult* for K–12 schools to design and implement well-conceived bilingual education programs. While not illegal, bilingual education, in general, is on the defensive in the state of California.

Fifth, multicultural education creates discomfort and controversy because it interferes with the way some educators want to view and name the world. Advocates of multicultural education encourage future educators to be selectively aware of and react positively to the cultural, ethnic, racial, gender, and socioeconomic diversity in their school and in society. However, some educators and future educators believe that continued attention to labels that highlight differences will ultimately create a more divided, racist, sexist, and economically segregated world. Some of these educators oppose the multicultural view of the world because of its link to affirmative action and group rights; others oppose it because, in their view, the world should ideally be color-blind, with little or no emphasis placed on labels. These individuals tell us they want to see past the differences in color, language, SES, and the like, to discover and cultivate the common humanity that is important to them, as well as to advocates of multicultural education.

Multicultural education frustrates such individuals because it explicitly suggests that a consistent, inflexible, universalistic, no-color, one-humanity perception of the world is problematic. In turn, individuals who refuse to acknowledge the presence of diversity threaten individuals who are a part of various cultural groups. By refusing to see and acknowledge the potential significance of the color, culture, ethnicity, and gender of others, individuals whom we will call *humanitarian monoculturalists* diminish the right of others to define themselves. This stand, which refuses to acknowledge the existence of people as they are or want to become, tends to make some individuals and groups more invisible than they already are (e.g., the gay community). The act of rendering people invisible might make them, during a crisis, more vulnerable or disposable. To sum up, in this case multicultural education is controversial because it challenges the way some individuals want to see and name the world, and themselves in relation to the world; it cuts deeply into one dimension of their value system as it prods them to see and partially accept the peoples of the world in their rich complexity.

The sixth area of controversy stems from multicultural education's focus on equity and social justice. Fundamentally, educational equity costs money. Equity, for example, means that school and transportation facilities will be transformed to provide access for the physically challenged, and new training programs will be developed for teachers who work with second-language learners. The idea that all Americans should have a real and fair opportunity to learn in school has always met resistance from some educational administrators and taxpayers, who saw this egalitarian emphasis reducing the amount of money available for other programs, such as programs for the gifted and talented, which in the eyes of some are linked to national security. And an emphasis on social justice will surely raise some eyebrows, as teachers, counselors, or administrators in the name of stewardship or social justice, or simply citizenship education, assume a more activist role in school or community politics in a manner which engages their students in real-world political activities.

The seventh reason for the controversy surrounding multicultural education is that it emphasizes antiracism and antisexism education. Ultimately, multicultural curricula will have to confront the forces that have made society and school unequal for students of color and women. In short, racism and sexism, and perhaps capitalism, and inevitably other -isms, will be discussed; in some courses, antiracism education will be a major topic of study, with the instructor engaging students in critical thinking and reflection about racism and about actions designed to oppose racism and sexism. Because antiracism activities can result in dialogue marked by guilt, anger, and blame, educating Americans about racism has been difficult.[161] Furthermore, a review of some of the antiracism literature produced by advocates of multicultural education suggests that multicultural education, as it is construed and implemented in some universities, will remain controversial because the depiction of *White racism*—past and present—is sometimes excessive.[162] But excessive or not, the mission of multicultural education requires that racism, sexism, handicappism, linguicism, and similar topics be discussed and confronted, and this ensures that discomfort, conflict, controversy, and commitment will be a part of the multicultural education conversation.

The eighth factor contributing to controversy is the multifaceted evolutionary nature of the concept of multicultural education. Several diverse conceptions are associated with multicultural education, and sometimes advocates of one kind of multicultural education argue with advocates of another. This type of debate is what one would expect in a reform movement which is also establishing itself as a special type of academic discipline. For you, who may be new to multicultural education, the key point to remember is that multicultural education is not a monolithic entity. When you encounter praise or criticism of multicultural education, you should ascertain which conception of multicultural education the critic is comfortable with, if any.

And readers should not be dismayed by the complexity and diversity enumerated within this chapter. Indeed, in 1991 the complexity and richness of multicultural education led advocates of multicultural education, with all their commonalities and differences, to create a national organization, the National Association for Multicultural Education (NAME), and NAME has created new resources and opportunities for current and future educators and advocates. In less than a decade NAME has created a national office,[163] a magazine (first *Multicultural Education* and now *Multicultural Perspectives*), a website www.inform.umd.edu/NAME, and a ten-region infrastructure facilitated by regional officers and state affiliates. In addition, to help achieve its goals and advance the field of multicultural education, NAME sponsors an annual conference and supports regional conferences throughout the nation. NAME's goals are to:

1. respect and appreciate cultural diversity;
2. promote the understanding of unique cultural and ethnic heritages;
3. promote the development of culturally responsible and responsive curricula;
4. facilitate acquisition of the attitudes, skills, and knowledge to function in various cultures;
5. eliminate racism and discrimination in society; and
6. achieve social, political, economic, and educational equity.

While NAME and its goals and resources are clearly worthy of attention, current and future teachers can and should forge their own approach to multicultural education by adapting the synthesis conception outlined earlier. And, as they do so, they should remember three things. First, multicultural education is not only for all students, it is for teachers at *all* levels and in *all* content areas. Second, teachers' decisions about instruction, content, and classroom management help to create a multicultural curriculum and learning environment. In other words, teachers are practicing multicultural education when they (a) seek out and utilize teaching strategies which effectively promote learning for a wide range of students; (b) modify their content to make it more accurate, relevant, and motivating; and (c) organize the physical environment so that it promotes positive cross-cultural, cross-ethnic, and cross-gender contact and understanding. A seating arrangement, for example, can enhance or cut off cross-cultural dialogue. Third, the playing field for multicultural education extends beyond the classroom into the broader school environment and the surrounding community. For example, much good multicultural work can be done in the network of clubs and sports activities which form the significant extracurricular school program. In the chapter which follows where the focus is on creating equitable and democratic practices in school settings, we will get more specific about teaching that is multicultural in nature.

DISCUSSION QUESTIONS

1. The conception of multicultural education recommended in this chapter includes educational equity as one of its significant goals. In aiming at this goal, teachers are encouraged to examine the participation and achievement of their students from a dual perspective. Essentially, this means that teachers would monitor the participation and achievement rates and interaction styles of both individuals and socially relevant groups in their classrooms; these groups include African Americans, Latino Americans, American Indians, and girls and boys. In your opinion, should this dual observation be the responsibility of classroom teachers, or should their observational and evaluative focus remain exclusively on individual students? What are the pros and cons of dual assessment at the classroom, school site, and school district level of operation? How could secondary students help the teacher carry out specific group assessment activities?

2. When we assert that classroom instruction, to be considered effective, must occur within the context of a multicultural curriculum, we are really saying that classroom teachers (and, by implication, entire schools) who do not actively pursue several of the goals of multicultural education should not be considered effective, even if their students are learning how to write, compute, read, draw, and carry out science experiments. In your opinion, is our assertion logical, or do you think we have gone too far in advocating the importance of multicultural education? Provide several reasons for your response, and, if time permits, argue both sides of the question.

3. We make the following assumption: In the classroom, multicultural education can and should be implemented in different ways and with different emphases at the elementary, middle school, high school, and other levels of education. Assuming that this is a valid idea, at approximately what grade level would it be appropriate to read and discuss literature (fiction and nonfiction) that explicitly discusses racism and sexism in American culture? in other nations? Provide one or two reasons to explain your choices, and, if possible, identify specific curriculum materials appropriate for introducing these concepts to a specific age group.

4. We believe that it is wise to distinguish multicultural education from other, related curriculum topics such as self-esteem education, global education, futures education, and environmental education. Do you think that any of these related curriculum topics should be considered an integral component of multicultural education? If yes, please identify the curriculum topic(s) and your reasons. If not, please explain.

5. We believe that the goals of multicultural education are intertwined with the goals of citizenship education. Based on your growing knowledge of multicultural and citizenship education, where do you see the overlap between these two important areas of education?

6. Why might it be appropriate to conceptualize and discuss global education, environmental education, futures education, and citizenship education as content areas

to be presented from a multicultural perspective, rather than conceptualizing one or more of these curriculum areas as a major goal of multicultural education?

7. We assert that our conception of multicultural education provides an integrated conception of curriculum and instruction and that such integrated models are valuable places for prospective educators to begin their study of effective schools and instruction. What is the difference between a model of instruction and an integrated model of curriculum and instruction? Can you give examples of the former? If yes, contrast the elements of one with the other.

8. In our conception of multicultural education and effective teaching, we underline the importance of establishing positive, collaborative relationships among parents, teachers, and students. In terms of achieving other goals of multicultural education—educational equity and positive intergroup relations, for example—what programs and research suggest that such collaboration is a sound idea? In responding to this question, the following resources should prove helpful:

Amy R. Anson, Thomas D. Cook, et al., "The Comer School Development Program: A Theoretical Analysis," *Urban Education* 26, no. 1 (April 1991): 56–82.

James P. Comer, "Educating Poor Minority Children," *Scientific American* 259, no. 5 (November 1988): 42–48; James P. Comer, *School Power* (New York: Free Press, 1980).

J. Epstein, "Parent Involvement: What Research Says to Administrators," *Education and Urban Society* 19, no. 2 (February 1987): 119–136.

Charles Payne, "The Comer Intervention Model and School Reform in Chicago: Implications of Two Models of Change," *Urban Education* 26, no. 1 (April 1991): 8–24.

C. Snow, W. S. Barnes, J. Chandler, I. Goodman, and I. Hemphill, *Families and Schools: Effects on Literacy* (Cambridge, Mass.: Harvard University Press, 1989).

"Strengthening Partnerships with Parents and Community," *Educational Leadership* 47, no. 2 (October 1989), 4–67.

9. What do you think were the four most important points made in this chapter? Why were these your choices?

10. In your opinion, which specific beliefs among educators will change as they shift from a monocultural to a multicultural perspective?

11. Which idea or ideas in this chapter appear to be questionable? Explain your reasoning.

12. If our conception of multicultural education differs from one you brought to class, how does it differ?

13. We believe that children at any grade level and that content from any part of the curriculum can be taught with a multicultural perspective. In your opinion, how would this apply to science and/or mathematics? As you respond, consider (a) the specific contributions that mathematicians working in various non-Western cultures have made throughout history and (b) the contributions of outstanding mathematics educators such as Jaime Escalante, Uri Treisman, and Abdulalim Shabazz of Clark Atlanta University. For information about Shabazz and more regarding Jaime Escalante, see "Do We Have the Will to Educate All Children," by Asa Hilliard III, in *Educational Leadership* 49, no. 1 (September 1991), 31–36. Other useful resources include:

M. Frankenstein's essay "Incorporating Race, Class, and Gender Issues into a Critical Math Literacy Curriculum," *Journal of Negro Education* 59, no. 3 (1990): 336–347.

J. Keating's essay "Designing Multicultural Science Curricula for American Indian High School Students," *Multicultural Education* 4, no. 1 (Fall 1996): 24–26.

W. G. Secada's chapter "Race, Ethnicity, Social Class, Language, and Achievement in Mathematics," in D. A. Grovers, ed., *Handbook of Research on Mathematics Teaching and Learning* (New York: Macmillan, 1992), 623–660.

W. F. Tate's essay "Race, Retrenchment, and the Reform of School Mathematics," *Phi Delta Kappan* 75, no. 6 (1994): 477–485.

M. Ogawa's essay "Science Education in a Multiscience Perspective," *Science Education* 79, no. 5 (1995): 583–593.

W. B. Stanley and N. W. Brickhouse's essay "Multiculturalism, Universalism, and Science Education," Science Education 78, no. 4 (1994): 387–399; see also a series of thought-provoking responses to this essay in *Science Education* 79, no. 3 (June 1, 1995): 354–355.

H. Selin's two-part essay "Science Across Cultures," *The Science Teacher* 60, nos. 3/4 (March/April 1993): 38–42 and 32–36.

H. Selin, ed., *The Encyclopedia of Science, Technology and Medicine in Non-Western Cultures* (New York: Garland Press, 1996).

J. Weinglass's essay "Changing the Culture of Mathematics Instruction," *Journal of Mathematical Behavior* 11, no. 2 (June 1992): 195–203.

C. Zaslavsky's book *The Multicultural Classroom: Bringing in the World* (Portsmouth, N.H.: Heinemann, 1996).

J. Bianchini's essay "From Here to Equity: The Influence of Status on Student Access to and Understanding of Science," *Science Education* 83, no. 5, (September 1999): 577–601.

14. We suggest that teachers who work with a multicultural perspective will be inclined to study the ideas of educators (and philosophers, management experts, etc.) who work in cultures other than their own. What are some of the positive attributes and potential pitfalls in such an inherently practical approach to professional growth? As you develop or refine your point of view, consider reading one or more of the following essays or books:

Janice E. Hale-Benson, *Black Children:Their Roots, Culture, and Learning Styles* (Baltimore: Johns Hopkins University Press, 1982).

Jerry I. Milligan, "Learning to Read in New Zealand," *Teaching* K-8 21, no. 1 (August/September 1990): 62–65.

Gay Su Pinnell, Mary D. Fried, and Rose Mary Estice, "Reading Recovery: Learning How to Make a Difference," *The Reading Teacher* 43, no. 4 (January 1990): 282–295.

James W. Stigler and Harold W. Stevenson, "How Asian Teachers Polish Each Lesson to Perfection," *American Educator* 15, no. 1 (Spring 1991): 12–20, 43–47.

15. We believe that our conception of multicultural education is conservative. Why do you think we have this perception, and do you agree with our assessment? Explain your answer.

16. In this chapter we discuss the perspective of those we have called humanitarian monoculturalists, individuals who believe that teachers should not see and react to various types of classroom diversity, such as color, gender, socioeconomic status, immigrant status, language, and so on. What part of this vision contains wisdom? Do you share any part of this perspective; if so, describe your views. Also, can you see a way to integrate this perspective with the multicultural perspective recommended in this text? If so, elaborate with as much specificity as possible.

17. What questions would you like to ask us? Try to answer one of these yourself. If time permits, consider sharing your answer and/or your question with us via E-mail. We

will do our best to respond in a prompt fashion. See the preface for our E-mail addresses, and please note that we may list your question and all or part of your answer (but not your name) on our World Wide Web homepage.

18. The authors suggest that there is a tension, perhaps a productive tension, between the core value of individualism and the group orientation of multicultural education. Based on your personal experience with, and readings about, multicultural education, do you think such a tension exists? Explain your response, and, if you agree, share your thoughts about this tension.

19. The authors briefly discuss several conceptions that link multicultural education to a related philosophy—namely, multiethnic education (James Banks), social reconstructionism (Carl Grant and Christine Sleeter), critical pedagogy (Sonia Nieto), and Afrocentrism (Asa Hilliard and Molefi Asante). Based on your prior reading and experience, do any of these integrated conceptions appear to have particular merit? If yes, explain your reasoning. Do any appear to be particularly flawed? If yes, explain your reasoning.

20. In the final section of the chapter, we briefly discuss the connection between multicultural education and the practice of affirmative action, and write: "No matter how strong and logical the rationale for affirmative action in a specific setting is because of demonstrated patterns of discrimination, the association between multicultural education and affirmative action contributes to the controversy surrounding multicultural education."

    a. In your own words, what is affirmative action, and what, in all its rich complexity or simplicity, is your position on affirmative action?

    b. In your opinion, how is affirmative action making a positive contribution to the contemporary American political and economic system? What are the negative repercussions?

    c. Are there affirmative-action-like programs in your school district, university, or local community that you believe are worthy of support and/or modification? If so, please describe. If there are none, describe some programs you would like to see implemented.

21. At the beginning of *"The Social Construction of Knowledge"* section of this chapter, we imply that teachers should develop a moral vision and voice as they strive to be more effective in their multicultural teaching. The mind-set of future and current teachers ought to shift when they view their work as a moral endeavor. We use this language because we consider teaching to be a moral activity, and are guided in this conviction by the work of Gary Fenstermacher, among others. Fenstermacher, for example, in his essay "Some Moral Considerations on Teaching as a Profession,"[164] has written:

    a. *The teacher's conduct at all times, and in all ways, is a moral matter. For that reason alone, teaching is a profoundly moral activity . . . The teacher is a model for the students, such that the particular and concrete meaning of such traits as honesty, fair play, consideration of others, tolerance and sharing are "picked up," as it were, by observing, imitating, and discussing what teachers do in classrooms.* (p. 133)

    b. *Nearly everything a teacher does while in contact with students carries moral weight. Every response to a question, every assignment handed out, every discussion on issues, every resolution of a dispute, every grade given to a student carries with it the moral character of the teacher. This moral character can be thought of as the manner of the teacher.* (p. 134)

    c. *Teachers who understand their impact as moral educators take their manner quite seriously. They understand that they cannot expect honesty with-*

out being honest or generosity without being generous . . . [Furthermore,] just as teachers possess a manner that defines the moral character of their teaching, so learners have a manner that identifies their moral development . . . Teaching is a moral activity not simply because teachers exercise authority and control over those in their care . . . it's a moral activity because teachers have a specific responsibility for the proper and moral development of their students. (p. 135)

22. What are your general thoughts regarding these quotes? More specifically, do you agree with this description of the work of teachers? Why or why not?

23. Fenstermacher tells us that one major goal of the National Network for Educational Renewal (NNER) is to stimulate the renewal of a common and collective commitment to public education in the United States.
    a. From your vantage point is this a worthy and/or important goal? Why or why not?
    b. If your answer to the above is yes, what are some things you could do to contribute to this renewal?

24. Do you think the four guiding themes (of the NNER) provide an adequate mission for public school educators and public education? Or, do you feel that some important theme is missing? If so, please specify.

25. Fenstermacher asserts that "the task of readying the young for democratic life is the business of all educators."[165]
    a. Do you agree with this statement? Why? Why not?
    b. Considering the role you play in public or private education, what specific things do you do to prepare your students for democratic life?
    c. With the four guiding themes in mind, could you do more? If yes, please specify.

26. Beyond the connections outlined by the Davidmans, do you see other connections between the NNER guiding themes and the goals of multicultural education?

NOTES

1. Mary Kay Thompson Tetreault, "Classrooms for Diversity: Rethinking Curriculum and Pedagogy," chap. 7 in *Multicultural Education: Issues and Perspectives,* 2nd ed., ed. James A. Banks and Cherry A. McGee Banks (Boston: Allyn and Bacon, 1993), 130.

2. E. Paul Torrance, "Lessons About Giftedness and Creativity from a Nation of 115 Million Overachievers," *Gifted Child Quarterly* 24, no. 1 (Winter 1980): 10–14.

3. Peter Drucker, "Infoliteracy," *Forbes,* August 29, 1994, 104–109.

4. Brian M. Bullivant, "Culture: Its Nature and Meaning for Educators," chap. 2 in *Multicultural Education: Issues and Perspectives,* 2nd ed., ed. James A. Banks and Cherry A. McGee Banks (Boston: Allyn and Bacon, 1993), 29.

5. Ibid., 29.

6. James A. Banks, "African American Scholarship and the Evolution of Multicultural Education," *Journal of Negro Education* 61, no. 3 (Summer 1992): 273–286.

7. James A. Banks, *Multiethnic Education: Theory and Practice* (Boston: Allyn and Bacon, 1981), 32.

8. Carlos E. Cortés, "The Societal Curriculum: Implications for Multiethnic Education," in *Education in the 80's: Multiethnic Education,* ed. James A. Banks

(Washington: National Education Association, 1981), 24–32; see also Carlos E. Cortés, "Knowledge Construction and Popular Culture: The Media as Mutilcultural Educator," in *The Handbook of Research on Multicultural Education*, ed. James A. Banks and Cherry A. McGee Banks (New York: Macmillan, 1995).

9. Carlos E. Cortés, "Mass Media as Multicultural Curriculum: Public Competitor to School Education," *Multicultural Education* 2, no. 3 (Spring 1995): 4.

10. Ronald Edmonds, "Effective Schools for the Urban Poor," *Educational Leadership* 36, no. 2 (October 1979): 15.

11. Rebecca Powell, "Achieving Equity in Classrooms: Guidelines for Educators," Paper presented at the annual conference of the National Association for Multicultural Education, St. Louis, Missouri (October 1998), 1.

12. Beth Blue Swadener, "Educational Equity" in the *Dictionary of Multicultural Education*, ed. Carl A. Grant and Gloria Ladson-Billings (Phoenix, Ariz.: The Oryx Press, 1997), 101–103.

13. Ibid.

14. David E. Washburn, "Let's Take a Hard Look at Multicultural Education," *Multicultural Education* 2, no. 2 (Winter 1994): 20–23.

15. Milton M. Gordon, *Assimilation in American Life: The Role of Race, Religion, and National Origins* (New York: Oxford University Press, 1964), 85–86.

16. Perry A. Zirkel and Sharon N. Richardson, Summary of *Pierce v. Society of Sisters,* 268 U.S. 510 (1925) in *A Digest of Supreme Court Decisions Affecting Education,* 2nd ed. (Bloomington, Ind.: Phi Delta Kappa Foundation, 1988), 17.

17. Horace M. Kallen, "Democracy Versus the Melting Pot: A Study in American Nationality," *The Nation,* February 25, 1915, 218–220; this essay is reprinted in Kallen's *Culture and Democracy* (New York: Boni and Liveright, 1924).

18. Joyce Epstein, "Parent Involvement: What Research Says to Administrators," *Education and Urban Society* 19, no. 2 (February 1987): 119–136; see also Anne Ensle, "Critical Elements in Parental Involvement of Culturally and Linguistically Diverse Parents," *Bilingual Research Journal* 16, nos. 3/4 (Summer 1994): 141–143.

19. Gene L. Maeroff, "A Blueprint for Empowering Teachers," *Phi Delta Kappan* 60, no. 7 (March 1988): 473.

20. Richard Vega, "Hate Crimes on the Rise," *USA Weekend* (January 8–10, 1993): 5.

21. James A. Banks, *An Introduction to Multicultural Education,* 2nd ed. (Needham Heights, Mass.: Allyn and Bacon, 1999), 83.

22. W. C. Parker, "Multicultural Education in Democratic Societies," paper presented at the annual meeting of the American Educational Research Association, Chicago, 1991.

23. Michael R. Olneck, "Terms of Inclusion: Has Multiculturalism Redefined Equality in American Education?" *American Journal of Education* 101, no. 3 (May 1993): 234. Published by the University of Chicago. ©1993 by the University of Chicago. All rights reserved.

24. Ibid., 253.

25. John Higham, "Multiculturalism and Universalism: A History and Critique," *American Quarterly* 45, no. 2 (June 1993): 204.

26. An example of an essay that sheds little light on multiculturalism or multicultural education is George F. Will, "A Kind of Compulsory Chapel: Multiculturalism Is a Campaign to Lower America's Moral Status," *Newsweek,* November 14, 1994, 84.

27. Ann T. Lockwood, "Ann Turnbaugh Lockwood Interviews James A. Banks," chap. 6 in *An Introduction to Multicultural Education,* ed. James A. Banks (Boston: Allyn and Bacon, 1994), 81–82.

28. Ibid., 82.
29. Ibid., 81.
30. Beverly M. Gordon, "African-American Cultural Knowledge and Liberatory Education: Dilemmas, Problems, and Potentials in a Postmodern American Society," *Urban Education* 27, no. 4 (January 1993): 466.
31. Ibid.
32. See John U. Ogbu, "Immigrant and Involuntary Minorities in Comparative Perspective," in *Minority Status and Schooling: A Comparative Study of Immigrant and Involuntary Minorities,* ed. Margaret A. Gibson and John U. Ogbu (New York: Garland, 1991), for more information about the cultural models of selected immigrant and nonimmigrant groups.
33. John U. Ogbu and Herbert D. Simons, "Voluntary and Involuntary Minorities: A Cultural-Ecological Theory of School Performance with Some Implications for Education," *Anthropology and Education Quarterly* 29, no. 2 (June 1998): 155-188.
34. Imogene C. Brower, "Counseling Vietnamese," in *Counseling American Minorities: A Cross-Cultural Perspective,* ed. Donald R. Atkinson, George Morton, and Derald Wing Sue (Dubuque, Iowa: William C. Brown, 1983), 110.
35. Michele McCalope, "Blacks Furious over Exclusion from New Great Books of the Western World," *Jet,* December 1990, 14-18.
36. Beverly T. Watkins, "Many Campuses Now Challenging Minority Students to Excel in Math and Science," and "Berkeley Mathematician Strives to Help People Get Moving," *Chronicle of Higher Education* 35, no. 40 (June 1989): A-13.
37. Uri Treisman, "Studying Students Studying Calculus: A Look at the Lives of Minority Mathematics Students in College," *The College Mathematics Journal* 23, no. 5 (November 1992): 369.
38. Rose Asera and Uri Treisman, "Routes to Mathematics for African-American, Latino, and Native-American Students in the 1990s: The Educational Trajectories of Summer Mathematics Institute Participants," *Issues in Mathematics Education* 5 (Summer 1995): 28.
39. Ibid.
40. James P. Comer, "Educating Poor Minority Children," *Scientific American* 259, no. 5 (November 1988): 44.
41. Ibid., 48.
42. Ibid., 44.
43. As of May 1999 the phone number of the School Development Program (SDP) was 203-737-1020 and its fax number was 203-737-4001. On the World Wide Web, the SDP is located at http://info.med.yale.edu/comer. More information about the SDP or the Comer Website is available by contacting Joanne Corbin at 203-737-1012 or by E-mail at Joanne.corbin@yale.edu.
44. Bruce C. Davis, "A Successful Parent Involvement Program," *Educational Leadership* 47, no. 2 (October 1989): 21-23.
45. Jay Matthews, *Escalante, the Best Teacher in America* (New York: Holt, Rinehart and Winston, 1988).
46. Jaime Escalante and Jack Dirmann, "The Jaime Escalante Math Program," *Journal of Negro Education* 59, no. 3 (Summer 1990): 407-423.
47. Matthews, *Escalante, the Best Teacher in America,* 13.
48. Ibid., 130.
49. Ibid., 14.
50. Escalante and Dirmann, "The Jaime Escalante Math Program," 415.
51. Ibid., 414 and 417.

52. Susan K. Sherwood, "Portrait of an Integration: A Child with Severe Multiple Disabilities Integrated into a Regular First Grade Classroom." Unpublished manuscript. Sherwood is now a professor and teacher educator at Wartburg College in Waverly, Iowa.

53. Susan K. Sherwood, "A Circle of Friends in a First Grade Classroom," *Educational Leadership* 48, no. 3 (November 1990): 41. This article is a brief version of the manuscript cited above.

54. Sherwood, "Portrait of an Integration," 8.

55. See the provisions of PL 101-336—the Americans with Disabilities Act of 1990— which gives civil rights protection to individuals with disabilities in private sector employment, all public services, public accommodations, transportation, and telecommunications, and PL 101-476, the Individuals with Disabilities Education Act of 1990, which updates and extends PL 94-142, the Education for All Handicapped Children Act of 1975.

56. The following resource will prove helpful for teachers interested in learning more about the full inclusion of students with severe disabilities: A. Halvorsen and W. Sailor, "Integration of Students with Severe and Profound Disabilities: A Review of Research," in R. Gaylord-Ross, ed., *Issues and Research in Special Education* (New York: Teachers College Press, 1990), 100–172.

57. Mary Catherine Swanson, "The AVID Story: Advancement via Individual Determination," *Thrust for Educational Leadership* 22, no. 6 (April 1993): 9.

58. Ibid.

59. Ibid., 9–10.

60. Ibid., 9.

61. Ibid.

62. Hugh Mehan and Irene Villanueva, "Showcasing Center Projects: Untracking and College Enrollment," *Focus on Diversity* 1, no. 2 (Spring/Summer 1992): 1. (*Focus on Diversity* is a publication of the National Center for Research on Cultural Diversity and Second Language Learning at the University of California, Santa Cruz.) See also "The AVID Classroom: A System of Academic and Social Supports for Low-Achieving Students," by Mary Catherine Swanson, Hugh Mehan, and Lea Hubbard, in *Creating New Educational Communities: Schools and Classrooms Where All Children Can Be Smart,* ed. Jeannie Oakes and Karen Hunter Quartz, vol. 94, The National Society for the Study of Education (University of Chicago Press, 1995), 53–69.

63. "AVID Data Collection Process and Results—1997-98," *ACCESS* 5, no. 2 (Winter/Spring 1998-99): 10.

64. "Gene I. Maeroff: Altered Destinies," *ACCESS* 5, no. 2 (Winter/Spring 1998-99): 6.

65. Personal interview with Charles Vidal.

66. George Leonard, "The End of School," *The Atlantic*, May 1992, 32.

67. Ibid.

68. Diane Flores, "Hanshaw: Model Middle School Opens in South Modesto," *Modesto Bee,* September 3, 1991, A-1 and A-12.

69. Daniel Gursky, "Personal Best: Charles Vidal," chap. 6 in *Classroom Crusaders: Twelve Teachers Who Are Trying to Change the System,* ed. Ronald A. Wolk and Blake Hume Rodman (San Francisco: Jossey-Bass, 1994), 88. This chapter originally appeared as an article in the October 1992 issue of *Teacher* magazine.

70. Ibid., 88.

71. Ibid., 89.

72. The current principal of Hanshaw is Ed Miller. The school phone number is 209-576-4847, its address is Hanshaw Middle School, 1725 Las Vegas Street, Modesto, CA 95354; its fax number is 209-576-4723.

73. Mark F. Goldberg, "A Portrait of John Goodlad," *Educational Leadership* 53, no. 6 (March 1995): 82.
74. Kenneth A. Sirotnick, "On Inquiry and Education," chap. 1 in *The Beat of a Different Drummer: Essays on Educational Renewal in Honor of John I. Goodlad,* ed. Kenneth A. Sirotnick and Roger Soder (New York: Peter Lang, 1999), 1–16.
75. Ibid., 6.
76. Directory of Settings: National Network for Educational Renewal (Seattle: Institute for Educational Inquiry, 1998). Phone number is 206–325–3010.
77. Gary D. Fenstermacher, "Agenda for Education in a Democracy," chap. 1 in *Leadership for Educational Renewal: Developing a Cadre of Leaders,* ed. Wilma F. Smith and Gary D. Fenstermacher (San Francisco: Jossey-Bass, 1999), 4.
78. Ibid., 6.
79. John I. Goodlad, *A Place Called School* (New York: McGraw Hill, 1984).
80. John I. Goodlad, *Teachers for Our Nation's Schools* (San Francisco: Jossey-Bass, 1990).
81. John I. Goodlad, *Educational Renewal: Better Teachers Better Schools* (San Francisco: Jossey-Bass, 1994).
82. Fenstermacher, "Agenda for Education in a Democracy," 11.
83. Ibid.
84. Ibid., 13.
85. Ibid.
86. Ibid., 14.
87. Peter Block, *Stewardship: Choosing Service Over Self-Interest* (San Francisco: Berrett-Koehler, 1993), xx.
88. Wilma F. Smith, "Serving as Moral Stewards of the Schools," chap. 7 in *Leadership for Educational Renewal: Developing a Cadre of Leaders,* ed. Wilma F. Smith and Gary D. Fenstermacher (San Francisco: Jossey-Bass, 1999), 180.
89. Carl A. Grant, ed., *Multicultural Education: Commitments, Issues, and Applications* (Washington, D.C.: Association for Supervision and Curriculum Development, 1977), 2.
90. Mira L. Baptiste and H. Prentice Baptiste, "Competencies Toward Multiculturalism," in *Multicultural Teacher Education: Preparing Educators to Provide Educational Equity* 1 (Washington, D.C.: American Association of Colleges of Teacher Education, 1979), 44.
91. James A. Banks, *Multiethnic Education: Theory and Practice*, 32.
92. Donna M. Gollnick and Philip C. Chinn, *Multicultural Education in a Pluralistic Society,* 2nd ed. (Columbus, Ohio: Merrill, 1986), 5.
93. James A. Banks, "Multicultural Education: Characteristics and Goals," chap. 1 in *Multicultural Education: Issues and Perspectives,* ed. James A. Banks and Cherry A. McGee Banks (Boston: Allyn & Bacon, 1989), 3.
94. James A. Banks and Cherry A. McGee Banks, in the Introduction to the *Handbook of Research on Multicultural Education,* ed. James A. Banks and Cherry A. McGee Banks (New York: Macmillan, 1995), xi.
95. Ibid., xii.
96. G. Pritchy Smith, *Common Sense about Uncommon Knowledge: The Knowledge Bases for Diversity* (Washington, D.C.: American Association of Colleges of Teacher Education, 1998).
97. Mark J. Drozowski, *Insider's Guide to Graduate Programs in Education* (Boston: Allyn and Bacon, 1997).
98. It is noteworthy that some definitions, like the Banks and Banks definition, are part of an elaborate conceptualization of multicultural education while others are not. For example, to help explain his conception James Banks has constructed

and explained the "dimensions of multicultural education" (content integration; the knowledge construction process; prejudice reduction; equity pedagogy; and an empowering school culture and social structure). See pp. 3-24 in the *Handbook of Research on Multicultural Education* for a detailed explanation.

99. Standard 2.1 is included in its totality in *Multicultural Teacher Education: Case Studies of Thirteen Programs,* vol. 2 (Washington, D.C.: American Association of Colleges of Teacher Education, 1980, 1-2. In the new Standards of the National Council for the Accreditation of Teacher Education (NCATE), disseminated in 1986, the glossary includes *multicultural perspective* but not *multicultural education.*

100. Ann Morey, ed., *Excellence in Professional Education* (Long Beach: Office of the Chancellor, California State University System, 1983), 85-86.

101. This definition appears in a survey entitled *Questionnaire on Multicultural Teacher Education.* For further information, contact Professor Eugene Kim at the School of Education, California State University, 6000 J Street, Sacramento, CA 95819.

102. James A. Banks, *An Introduction to Multicultural Education* (Needham Heights, Mass.: Allyn and Bacon, 1994), 16-17.

103. Ibid., 81-82.

104. Ibid., 6.

105. B. Parekh, "The Concept of Multicultural Education," in S. Modgil, G. K. Verna, K. Mallick, and C. Modgil, ed., *Multicultural Education: The Interminable Debate* (Philadelphia: Falmer Press, 1986), 19-31.

106. Henry Trueba, "Many Groups, One People: The Meaning and Significance of Multicultural Education in Modern America," *Bilingual Research Journal* 16, nos. 3/4 (Summer/Fall 1992): 92.

107. Christine E. Sleeter and Carl A. Grant, *Making Choices for Multicultural Education: Five Approaches to Race, Class, and Gender* (Columbus, Ohio: Merrill, 1988), 137-173.

108. Ibid., 153.

109. Ibid., 176.

110. Banks, *Multiethnic Education: Theory and Practice,* 52-53.

111. Geneva Gay, "Multiethnic Education: Historical Development and Future Prospects," *Phi Delta Kappan* 65, no. 8 (April 1983): 560-563.

112. Banks, *An Introduction to Multicultural Education,* 117.

113. Sonia Nieto, *Affirming Diversity: The Sociopolitical Context of Multicultural Education,* 2nd ed. (White Plains, N.Y.: Longman Publishing Group, 1996), 205.

114. Banks, *An Introduction to Multicultural Education,* 115 and 143.

115. Smith, *Common Sense about Uncommon Knowledge: The Knowledge Bases for Diversity,* 99.

116. Nieto, *Affirming Diversity: The Sociopolitical Context of Multicultural Education,* 307.

117. Ibid., 308.

118. Ibid.

119. Ibid.

120. Ibid., 310.

121. Ibid., 318-322.

122. Ibid., 317.

123. Ibid.

124. Sara S. Garcia, "Social Justice" in the *Dictionary of Multicultural Education,* ed. Carl A. Grant and Gloria Ladson-Billings (Phoenix, Arizona: The Oryx Press, 1997), 247-248.

125. Patricia T. Davidman and Leonard Davidman, "On the Teaching and Personal Construction of Educational Equity," *Multicultural Education* 5, no. 3 (Spring 1998): 18–22.

126. Molefi K. Asante, *The Afrocentric Idea* (Philadelphia, P.A.: Temple University Press, 1987), 6.

127. Banks, *An Introduction to Multicultural Education*, 27.

128. Alan Weider, "Afrocentrisms: Capitalist, Democratic, and Liberationist Portraits," *Educational Foundations* 6, no. 2 (Spring 1992): 33–43.

129. Arthur M. Schlesinger, Jr., The Disuniting of America: *Reflections on a Multicultural Society* (New York: W.W. Norton, 1992).

130. Ibid., 102.

131. Ibid., 119.

132. Ibid., 102.

133. William Julius Wilson, "When Work Disappears: New Implications for Race and Urban Poverty in the Global Economy," *Ethnic and Racial Studies* 22, no. 3 (May 1999): 479–499.

134. Alan Singer, "Multiculturalism and Afrocentricity: How They Influence Teaching U.S. History," *Social Education* 57, no. 6 (October 1993): 284.

135. Carol D. Lee and Diana T. Slaughter-Defoe, "Historical and Sociocultural Influences on African American Education," chap. 20 in the *Handbook of Research on Multicultural Education,* ibid. See especially their section on "Black Studies, Afrocentricity, and Multicultural Education: Foundations": 355–56.

136. Subira Kifano, "Afrocentric Education in Supplementary Schools: Paradigm and Practice at the Mary McLeod Bethune Institute," *Journal of Negro Education* 65, no. 2 (Spring 1996): 209–218.

137. M. Ron Karenga, *Kwanzaa: Origin, Concepts, and Practice* (San Diego, Calif.: Kawaida Publications, 1977), 9.

138. Kifano, "Afrocentric Education in Supplementary Schools: Paradigm and Practice at the Mary McLeod Bethune Institute," 209–218.

139. Ibid., 212.

140. Ibid.

141. Ibid., 215.

142. Ibid.

143. Aminifu R. Harvey and Antoinette A. Coleman, "An Afrocentric Program for African American Males in the Juvenile Justice System," *Child Welfare* 76, no. 1 (January/February 1997): 197–211; Aminifu R. Harvey and Julia B. Rauch, "A Comprehensive Afrocentric Rites of Passage Program for Black Male Adolescents," *Health and Social Work* 22, no. 1 (February 1997): 30–37.

144. Ibid., 199 ("An Afrocentric Program . . .").

145. Ibid., 203.

146. Ibid.

147. Vanesta L. Poitier, Makini Niliwaambieni, and Cyprian Lamar Rowe, "A Rite of Passage Approach Designed to Preserve the Families of Substance-Abusing African American Women," *Child Welfare* 76, no. 1 (January/February 1997): 197–211.

148. Donald Leake and Brenda Leake, "African-American Immersion Schools in Milwaukee: A View from the Inside," *Phi Delta Kappan* 73, no. 10 (June 1992): 783–795; Carole Ascher, "School Programs for African-American Males . . . and Females," *Phi Delta Kappan* 73, no. 10 (June 1992): 777–782.

149. The phone number of Dr. Martin Luther King Jr. African-American Immersion Elementary School is 414-562-4174. Its fax is 414-267-2766.

150. Clifford Watson and Geneva Smitherman, *Educating African American Males: Detroit's Malcolm X Academy Solution* (Chicago, Ill.: Third World Press, 1996).
151. Ibid., 24.
152. Ibid., 36.
153. Ibid., 55.
154. Ibid., 58.
155. Ibid., 59.
156. Ibid., 59–60.
157. Ibid., 75–76.
158. Ibid., 86.
159. The phone number of Malcolm X Academy is 313–873–0081.
160. William G. Bowen and Derek Bok, *The Shape of the River: Long-Term Consequences of Considering Race in College and University Admissions* (Princeton, N.J.: Princeton University Press, 1998).
161. Beverly D. Tatum, "Talking About Race, Learning About Racism: The Application of Racial Identity Development Theory in the Classroom," *Harvard Educational Review* 62, no. 1 (Spring 1992): 1–24.
162. Christine Sleeter, "White Racism," *Multicultural Education* 1, no. 4 (Spring 1994): 5–8 and 39.
163. For general or membership information about NAME, contact Jill Moss Greenberg at 202–628–8263 or at name@nicom.com, or write to 733 15th St. NW, Suite 430, Washington, DC 20005. As of June 2000, regular membership dues were $75.00 and dues for students and community activists were $35.00. All memberships include subscription to *Multicultural Perspectives*, the quarterly journal which is NAME's official publication.
164. Chap. 4 in *The Moral Dimensions of Teaching,* ed. John I. Goodlad, Roger Soder, and Kenneth A. Sirotnick (San Francisco: Jossey-Bass, 1991).
165. Fenstermacher, "Agenda for Education in a Democracy," 13.

CHAPTER 2

Creating Equity Conditions and Democratic Practice in School Settings

Never doubt that a small group of committed people can change the world.

Margaret Mead

CHAPTER OVERVIEW

The march toward educational equity and related political and economic rights for disenfranchised and oppressed groups has been a centuries-long struggle in the United States. In this effort the *Brown v. Board of Education* (1954) Supreme Court decision was a significant victory and turning point in the twentieth century struggle for civil rights. This decision, which stemmed from several decades of pioneering litigation led by National Association for the Advancement of Colored People (NAACP) civil rights leader Charles Hamilton Houston, created a climate of opinion that led individuals from other ethnic and cultural groups to use the courts more vigorously to seek redress for limitations on their educational and civil rights.[1] The *Serrano v. Priest* case, decided in 1973, is an example. In this case, the plaintiffs argued that the school funding procedures prevailing up to 1971 resulted in a pattern of rich and poor school districts and that this pattern in effect denied equal opportunity for significant numbers of California students. In addition, other California-based lawsuits, such as *López v. Seccombe* (1943) and *Méndez v. Westminster* (1946), illustrate that other lesser-known civil rights organizations, such as California's Unity Leagues, were successfully fighting for the rights of American citizens, in these cases Mexican Americans, during and after World War II.

The struggle to create equality of opportunity, or at least some form of measurable and tolerable equivalency, in America's schools continues to this day. Since 1954 there have been prominent legal victories, notable setbacks, and persistent negative trends related to school desegregation and the equalization of school funding. While teachers should be aware of these victories and setbacks, the following points are critical for contemporary educators to grasp:

1. dramatic inequality of educational opportunity still prevails in many schools, school districts, and states;
2. this inequality is accepted as the natural order of things by a major segment of the American population; and
3. to a certain extent, persistent structural inequality is an inevitable result of present-day liberal capitalistic democracy.

In short, it is difficult to diminish significantly the inequality in our schools because the system we have—a system that may be the best form of democracy extant—is designed in part to create and maintain inequality of wealth, status, and political influence. As a result of this persistent and, in some areas, increasing inequality, the language used to direct the equity struggle has changed. In the 1990s, equity advocates placed stronger emphasis on *equality of results,* as well as equality of opportunity, and more multicultural education advocates linked educational equity to the larger, more complex issue of *social justice*. In this vein, we sometimes hear affirmative action policies in schools and beyond discussed as a form of reparations for past injustice.

The new emphasis on equality of results derives from a variety of sources and conditions. These include (1) the realization that extensive, enduring de facto segregation caused by housing patterns and middle-class flight from inner cities has made equality of opportunity in schools through integration virtually impossible for millions of minority students (who are now part of the majority, "students of color" population in numerous American cities) and (2) the belief that at various levels of American society there is more support for inequality than for equality of opportunity. Thus, in those communities in which students are so racially and ethnically isolated as to make integration unrealizable, advocates of equity have created their own version of separate but equal. It has much to do with equality of resources, or more equality of results, and curricula geared to the psychosocial and political needs of students of color, students living in poverty, and students whose gender, linguistic background, or sexual orientation places them at risk in school and society.

When striving for equitable conditions in schools and social justice in schools and society, administrators, counselors, parents, students, politicians, and other concerned citizens, corporations, and teachers all have roles to play, and these roles vary from setting to setting. In this chapter we focus on the responsibilities of teachers as educators and citizens in a democracy, and we delineate strategies K–12 teachers can use to start off the school year (or semester) positively in terms of equity. Toward this end we discuss:

1. visits to the surrounding community;

2. examination of student files and portfolios, if available;

3. development of a plan for communicating with, and involving, parents (introductory letters, parent interviews, class newsletters);

4. selection of content that aims at specific goals of multicultural education;

5. creation of a democratic and collaborative learning environment through class- and team-building activities;

6. utilization of a typology of multicultural teaching.

In the context of the typology, we enumerate 37 strategies teachers can use to create more equity in their classrooms at the beginning of, and throughout, the school year.

INTRODUCTION

In chapter 1, we explored the idea of teaching with a multicultural perspective by describing the work of eight imaginative educators, and we hope that you now have a clearer grasp of the type of teaching and research that is congruent with this approach to education. In this chapter we further clarify the meaning of teaching with a multicultural perspective and the meaning of educational equity, the latter being a preeminent goal for most advocates of multicultural education. To accomplish this end, the chapter begins with remarks about the contemporary meaning of educational equity, and then progresses to a discussion of teaching with a multicultural perspective from the point of view of in-service and student teachers. In these sections we will show how strategies associated with a multicultural teaching perspective combine to create equitable and democratic learning conditions, and we will demonstrate that this comprehensive approach to teaching is practical for experienced K–12 teachers and student teachers. However, before turning to the strategies, we present a brief historical review that provides a useful context for understanding the current debate regarding educational equity. We urge our readers to go beyond our brief treatment. A detailed understanding of the patterns of exclusion and discrimination in U.S. history helps to inform one's advocacy for learners whose place in society is linked to that long history of oppression.[2]

Educational Equity: A Contemporary Perspective

Summarizing the history of public education in the United States between 1926 and 1976, historian R. Freeman Butts discussed this 50-year period in terms of the search for equality and the search for community.[3] These two quests have continued unabated through the 1990s, but have been overshadowed in some quarters by the quest for excellence and higher so-called "world-class" standards. Taken together, these endeavors can be viewed as part of the ongoing struggle to create a more egalitarian *and* economically competitive democracy. Whether or not these quests have led to desirable ends, they have modified the face of public education in the United States, and the shift has led to changes in the basic responsibilities of public school teachers.

This struggle, and the protests, lawsuits, and legislation that figured prominently in the century-long battle against segregation, poverty, and unequal access to learning, created the legal conditions under which teachers all over the United States were increasingly expected to instruct students who were in one way or another different from the teachers themselves.[4] More specifically, as a result of *Brown v. Board of Education* and later decisions such as *Cooper v. Aaron*[5] and *Alexander et al. v. Holmes County (Mississippi) School Board*[6] and rapidly unfolding demographic shifts, teachers all across the country were assigned to work with students whom the government considered racially different from them. No longer would White teachers be restricted to White students and Black teachers to Black students; these decisions have affected patterns of employment for Latino-American, Asian-American, and Native-American teachers as well.

Quite significantly, the success of the Reverend Oliver Brown and a dozen other Black parents in *Brown v. Board of Education* encouraged other educationally disenfranchised groups to seek, or continue to seek, "equal protection of the laws" as guaranteed by the Fourteenth Amendment to the U.S. Constitution. For example, in 1970 a federal judge ruled that Corpus Christi, Texas, was operating a dual school system for White Americans and Mexican Americans and ordered the Board of Education to submit a plan for desegregation as provided in the *Brown* case.[7] In 1971, in a related case argued on behalf of Mexican-American children in East Los Angeles, the California Supreme Court in *Serrano v. Priest* ruled that the state's system of financing public schools exclusively through local property taxes invidiously discriminated against poor children; the court held that this system made the quality of education dependent on the wealth of the school district in which students happened to live.[8]

While *Brown v. Board of Education* was a case of national import which stimulated a broad range of civil rights advocacy which continues to this day, it is likely that a 1946 decision, *Méndez v. Westminster,* was a factor in shaping the opinion Chief Justice Earl Warren would write in 1954. In 1945 Gonzalo Méndez and other Mexican-American parents in Orange County, California, took Westminster, Garden Grove, Santa Ana, and El Modeno School Districts to court to protest the segregation of their children and other Mexican-American students. In 1946 Judge Paul J. McCormick, writing for the U.S. Ninth Federal Court, ruled that the segregation was illegal because the segregation of Mexican-American students was not specifically mentioned in California's Education Code.[9] In 1947 the U.S. Circuit Court of Appeals upheld Judge McCormick's opinion, and Albert Camarillo reports that the 1947 decision "prompted Governor Earl Warren to ask the legislature to abolish the last statutes in California's Education Code that permitted segregation."[10] From Camarillo and Charles Wollenberg we learn that approximately eight years prior to his monumental *Brown v. Board of Education* decision, Earl Warren had the opportunity to consider the perspective of Judge McCormick who wrote that segregation "fosters antagonisms in the children and suggests inferiority among them where none exists."[11]

Also noteworthy is the parallel language employed by Earl Warren in *Brown v. Board of Education,* and the language utilized in California's 1971 *Serrano* decision and New Jersey's 1997 *Abbott v. Burke IV* decision.[12] In 1954, expressing the unanimous decision of the U.S. Supreme Court, Chief Justice Earl Warren wrote:

> In these days, it is doubtful that any child may reasonably be expected to succeed in life if he is denied the opportunity of an education. Such an opportunity, where the state has undertaken to provide it, is a right which must be made available to all on equal terms.[13]

Utilizing a similar theme 17 years later in the *Serrano* decision, the California Supreme Court said:

> By our holding today we further the cherished idea of American education that in a democratic society free public schools shall make available to all children equally the abundant gifts of learning. This was the credo of Horace Mann, which has been the heritage and the inspiration of this country.[14]

In New Jersey in 1997 equality of opportunity was once again an influential theme as Justice Alan B. Handler writing for five of the seven judges on New Jersey's State Supreme Court wrote:

> Our [New Jersey] Constitution requires that public school children be given the opportunity to receive a thorough and efficient education. That constitutional vision irrefutably presumes that every child is potentially capable of attaining his or her own place as a contributing member in society with the ability to compete effectively with other citizens and to succeed in the economy. . . . Our constitution demands that every child be given an equal opportunity to meet his or her promise.[15]

In the 1970s, 1980s, and 1990s the belief that equality of opportunity should prevail for all students in public schools led to a number of important judicial decisions. In 1974 in *Lau v. Nichols,* a class-action suit on behalf of Chinese-speaking students who attended the San Francisco schools, the U.S. Supreme Court ruled that schools must provide special language programs for students who do not understand or speak English.[16] In 1975, in a decision that affected every school and school district in the nation, Congress broadened the concept of equal educational opportunity to include the physically and mentally handicapped. The occasion was passage of Public Law 94–142, the Education for All Handicapped Children Act. This law stipulated that handicapped children must be educated in the environment that is least restrictive to their learning. Thus, handicapped students would be educated in regular classrooms (mainstreamed), in special classes, or some combination thereof, and it would be the responsibility of the school site administrator to ensure that an individual educational plan (IEP) was written and followed for such students. Other acts of Congress in 1965, 1972, 1973, and 1974 created more educational opportunity for children of low-income families, for Native Americans, and for women.[17]

In addition, numerous court decisions in various states attempted to promote equal opportunity, or some form of tolerable equivalence, by requiring state legislatures to create plans for fairly allocating financial resources to school districts. For example, in its June 1989 decision in *Rose v. Council for Better Education, Inc.* (a consortium of 60 of Kentucky's poorer school districts), the state Supreme Court declared the *entire* school system of Kentucky to be unconstitutional and ordered sweeping changes to ensure financial and educational equity for the state's 176 school districts.[18] It is instructive that Kentucky Chief Justice Robert Stephens, in the majority opinion that declared the public school system unconstitutional, described the *Brown* decision as "the polestar of this opinion."[19]

Kentucky was not alone in 1989. In that year, lawyers for plaintiffs in Texas, Montana, New Jersey, and Wisconsin were successful in persuading their supreme courts to declare the school finance systems in these states unconstitutional.[20] Significantly, the decisions broke legal ground in the judiciary's efforts to pressure state legislatures to provide equitable public school education. Thus, in Kentucky the sweeping changes pertained to teacher certification; regulations governing the creation of school districts, school boards, and the department of education; the construction and maintenance of schools; and the statewide school finance plan.[21] And the pattern of state Supreme Courts finding school funding programs unconstitutional continued in the 1990s as the systems in Wyoming (1995) and Alabama, Vermont, and Ohio (all in 1997) were declared unconstitutional.[22] Within this set of decisions the 1990 New Jersey Supreme Court *Abbott v. Burke* decision was unique because it declared the "state finance system unconstitutional only for a specific class of districts—namely, poorer urban districts."[23] Deborah Verstegen points out that the New Jersey decision was historic "because the court called for more than equity between rich and poor districts. Poor urban children and youths need more programs and services the court opined, and funding imbalances must favor the least advantaged."[24]

This 1990 decision—*Abbott v. Burke II*—was second in a series of five Abbott decisions, and the series was notable in several ways. To begin with, the last decision, *Abbott v. Burke V* in May 1998, represented a major victory for the 260,000 students in the 28 Abbott low-income school districts, as well as the lawyers associated with the Newark-based Education Law Center, (www.edlawcenter.org), the nonprofit law firm which waged the 28-year battle (1970–1998) on behalf of needy students in the Abbott school districts. In *Abbott v. Burke V* the state legislature and Department of Education were once again ordered to provide a constitutionally thorough and efficient education for the "Abbott" students. Among other things, this meant equalizing spending between New Jersey's wealthiest suburbs and the 28 Abbott districts and providing, on top of this, additional funds to pay for supplemental educational, health, and school construction programs needed by the "Abbott" students.[25] While prior Abbott decisions had channeled hundreds of millions of dollars into the Abbott districts, *Abbott v. Burke V* led to a fundamentally different distribution of the state's education funds. For example, in the 1999–2000 budget 2.4 billion dollars, 44 percent of the state's $5.4 billion education budget, were earmarked for the 28 Abbott districts, districts which educated 21 percent of the state's students.[26]

Beyond the critical tenacity displayed by the Education Law Center, most notably the late Marilyn J. Morheuser and David G. Sciarra, the current Executive Director, and the New Jersey State Supreme Court, *Abbott v. Burke V* is distinctive in contemporary equity legislation because in addition to a healthy budget it links educational standards and a systematic assessment program to *whole school* reform models. By the year 2001 each of the elementary schools in the 28 Abbott districts is required to adopt one of five recommended reform models, unless they can clearly demonstrate that they have a successful program already in place; secondary schools are expected to study, but not necessarily adopt, various models of instruction identified by the New Jersey Department of Education. The five elementary models are Robert Slavin's *Success for All/Roots and Wings,* James Comer's *School Development Program,* Henry Levin's *Accelerated Schools* model, the *Modern Red Schoolhouse Design* (linked to E. D. Hirsch's Core Curriculum), and the *Community for Learning/Adaptive Learning Environments* model (developed by Margaret C. Wang at Temple University). Website addresses and summaries for each of these models and the secondary models are available at (www.state.nj.us).[27] Summaries of, and evaluative remarks regarding, most of these models are also available in *Show Me the Evidence! Proven and Promising Programs for America's Schools* by Robert E. Slavin and Olatokumbo S. Fashola.[28] Parenthetically, in 1998–1999 in the cohort of 55 elementary schools adopting a whole school model, 27 adopted Success for All, 13 adopted the School Development Program (as did two middle schools), 11 adopted the Community for Learning, and the remaining models had one or two each. Approximately 100 schools are expected to adopt one of the models in 1999–2000 (cohort two).[29]

As influential as the *Abbott v. Burke V* approach may become in the 2000–2005 period, as we see the effects of linking substantial equity-plus funding, curriculum standards and assessment (imposed by the State), and whole school reform models (imposed by the State Supreme Court), the reader should be aware of the discontinuity between historic decisions like *Brown v. Board of Education* and *Abbott v. Burke V,* on the one hand, and significant positive change in schools and school districts on the other. For example, 10 years after *Brown,* the public schools in the south were more segregated than they had been in 1954, and a 1993 study by the National School Boards Association reported that "66 percent of the nation's black children attend schools with mostly minority students."[30] In addition, a 1999 report from the Harvard University Civil Rights Project entitled *Resegregation in American Schools,*[31] revealed that:

a. there is rapidly increasing segregation in the southern United States (e.g., the percentage of black students in majority white schools in the South fell from a peak of 43.5 percent in 1988 to 34.7 percent in 1996);

b. there is increasing segregation in states with substantial black enrollments (e.g., virtually all states with substantial black enrollments
increased integration in the 1970s but showed a rise in segregation
between 1980 and 1996);

c. Latinos attend the most severely segregated schools (e.g., data from
1996–1997 shows that 35.4 percent of Latinos attend schools with
over 90 percent minority student population compared with 23.1 percent in 1968–69, and nearly 75 percent of Latinos attend schools with
over 50 percent minority student population, up from 64.3 percent in
1968–69); and

d. on the average white students attend schools with classmates who are
81 percent white, and they are, therefore, the group which is most isolated from other racial groups.[32]

More significantly, Gary Orfield and John T. Yun, the report's authors,
demonstrate that there is a substantial link between segregation by race and
poverty. They write, for example, that: (a) "Racially segregated schools for all
groups except whites are almost always schools with high concentrations of
poverty," (b) "Almost nine-tenths of segregated African American and Latino
schools experience concentrated poverty," and (c) "Students in segregated
minority schools were 11 times more likely to be in schools with concentrated
poverty than their peers in predominantly white schools."[33]

The general pattern of de facto segregation which existed in 1999, and
which appears to be increasing in American schools, as well as the 28-year
battle to create a setting in which equitable education for New Jersey's low
socioeconomic status students could be imagined, underlines the need for
ongoing vigilance and bold efforts by advocates of multicultural education.
Abbott v. Burke, in particular, reveals the tenacity and patience that is needed
to achieve equitable funding for public schools in our market-driven economic system. Our system, to a great extent, revolves around a central belief,
namely that it is the opportunity to attain and maintain unequal wealth
among individuals, and thus communities, which drives economic progress
in general and job creation specifically. The reality of numerous separate and
unequal communities has led some educators, judges, and legislators to reluc-
tantly return to the concept of separate but equal, at the same time that they
and others strove to create and maintain opportunities for integrated learning opportunities across the K through higher education continuum.[34]

Separate but Equal Revisited

As noted previously, the direction was not always forward. One can easily point
to contemporary realities across the nation that suggest the legal victories of
the 1950s, 1960s, and 1970s fell severely short of the mark in creating equal
educational opportunity for millions of students.[35] For example in 1997, in one
of the most comprehensive school finance studies ever conducted the General Accounting Office of the federal government analyzed 1991–1992 data
and reported that nationwide (a) "high-income districts outspent low-income

districts by an average of 24 percent more per student," and (b) in the period between 1991 and 1997 "24 states had changed their [school] funding systems."[36] All of these changes and the above-mentioned court decisions make clear that the quest for greater and fairer access to learning, which began before *Brown v. Board of Education,* continued into the 1990s and will continue beyond. But the emphasis today is no longer on integrated schooling. As indicated earlier the legislative agenda in many states is a combination of high and specific curriculum standards, strong accountability programs, and efforts to make state funding formulas less unequal. This approach arises from a number of factors; significant among them is the projection that by the year 2020, White students will be a minority, or nearly so, in the nation's schools.[37] In the 2000–2005 period and beyond, large numbers of Latinos and African Americans, and other minority ethnic groups, concentrated in large urban centers, will inevitably experience a form of de facto segregated schooling because of housing and immigration patterns, White flight, escalating violence, and past decisions of the U.S. Supreme Court.[38]

Given these factors, meaningful face-to-face integration, as it was conceived and defined in the 1950s, 1960s, and 1970s, which focused on bringing Whites and Blacks together, no longer seems to be a viable strategy for equalizing education for millions of students of various colors and ethnicities, even though in 1999 chapters of the National Association for the Advancement of Colored People struggled to maintain expensive busing programs designed to promote integration.[39] Furthermore, the nation has other serious problems to solve. In 1997 with 14.1 percent of the nation's 18–24-year-olds lacking a high school diploma, 18 percent of the African Americans and 33.3 percent of the Hispanics in this age group without a high school diploma,[40] dropout rates reaching 50 percent in some of the nation's urban centers, and problems such as teenage violence, drug abuse, and hate crimes still a serious concern, the nation's legislators and educators sought new solutions, and as they did so they took a new look at educational equity.

When Chief Justice Earl Warren concluded, in 1954, that "in the field of public education 'separate but equal' has no place," no one could have foreseen that educational leaders and politicians in the 1980s and 1990s, faced with the harsh realities of de facto segregation, would revisit the idea of separate but equal. These leaders realized, first, that large numbers of children would continue to be educated in settings that were unequal in terms of Black/White integration, dollars spent per child, school morale, age of school facilities, safety, amount of support provided by school volunteers, teacher experience, and so on; and, second, that the leaders were helpless to change this de facto reality. Thus, they opted for the next best thing: to aim for equality of outcomes in settings that were far from integrated. An early example of this reality-based approach to educational equity (an approach that rejects busing as a solution and accepts the inevitability of some racial isolation) is evident in the desegregation case *Carlin v. San Diego Unified School District,* decided in 1977. Judge Lewis Welsh, the presiding judge, ordered the school district to devise a program that would raise achievement test scores in the racially isolated minority schools identified by the court. Specifically, he required 50 percent of the students in grades K–11 to achieve at or above the national norm on the California Test of Basic Skills (CTBS) Total Reading, Language, and Mathematics subtests within five years.[41]

The new logic seemed to go like this: if it is inevitable that large numbers of students will study in quasi-segregated and unequal facilities, then let us assure that the education these students receive will be powerful enough to propel large numbers of them through high school and into postsecondary institutions. In this new era and interpretation of equity a diverse set of strategies is recommended and employed. These include the already mentioned curriculum standards, high stakes testing, equitable funding patterns, and whole-school reform models, as well as wider state support for Title IX compliance in athletic programs and beyond, greater and deeper levels of parent participation, higher standards for teacher preparation, and more testing of teachers to ensure their academic competence. In addition, in the name of equity, we also hear more about voucher plans, charter schools, reconstituted schools (schools which receive an entire new faculty and administration in an attempt to break out of the cycle of failure),[42] simultaneous renewal, large school districts which have been taken over and run by state departments of education for as long as a decade,[43] and school districts which hire private corporations to run their entire program (privatization).[44]

The wide range of strategies carried out in the name of equity helps us understand why the concept of equity is difficult for teachers and administrators to fully understand and utilize in their day-to-day educational affairs. Indeed, given the varying interpretations the concept has received, some confusion is understandable. But ultimately the ambiguity need not be a hindrance to constructive action and advocacy, as we shall see. As we shed light on the concept of equity, the reader will realize, or be reminded, that *equity,* like *multicultural education* and other social science concepts, exists in the eye, and is created in the mind, of the beholder. In addition, any confusion which readers have regarding equity should diminish as they realize four things. First, it is logical and inevitable to have differing interpretations of equity. Second, it is their responsibility to construct the meaning of equity that will guide their work. Third, their interpretation may incorporate competing conceptions of educational equity, and finally their conception may vary across settings. To facilitate the reader's analytical process, we will draw on the theorizing of Kenneth Sirotnick, Elliot Eisner, Patrice LeBlanc Kohl, Elaine Witty, Christine Bennett, and Geneva Gay. The work of Sirotnick and Eisner, to which we now turn, is instructive because their perspectives are quite different.

Competing Conceptions of Equity: Kenneth Sirotnick

For Sirotnick, equity is concerned with the allocation of resources to groups, is assessed quantitatively, and is conceptually linked to the idea of excellence. For example, Sirotnick writes that "excellence is indicated by conditions, practices, and outcomes in school that are associated with high levels of learning for most students in all valued goal areas of the common curriculum."[45] Based on this definition, he states:

Equity is indicated when there are no systematic differences in the distributions of these conditions, practices, and outcomes based upon race, ethnicity, economic status, or any other irrelevant grouping characteristic.[46]

When Sirotnick refers to race, ethnicity, and economic status as an "irrelevant grouping characteristic," he is not saying that these concepts are irrelevant in the real world of school districts and society; rather, he implies that for the purpose of providing education that is equitable and excellent, these factors should be irrelevant—they ought not count for as much as they do in the minds of educators and legislators. In addition, it is noteworthy that to operationalize Sirotnick's conception, practitioners must precisely establish what the phrase "*no systematic differences*" will mean in their educational organization. Because educators in different organizations may associate different "conditions, practices, and outcomes" with excellence, and develop different numerical parameters to identify when "*no systematic differences in the distributions*" exist, Sirotnick's conceptual clarity may not necessarily yield continuity of meaning across schools, school districts, and states. Indeed, it may prove difficult to locate schools, school districts, or states that have put in the hard analytical work required to assess excellence and equity as defined by Sirotnick. But whether or not these observations prove accurate, Sirotnick's work provides a set of clear definitions and an opening game plan for educators who want to create and deliver excellent curricula to a wide range of students.[47]

Competing Conceptions of Equity: Elliot Eisner

In contrast to Sirotnick, Eisner's equity theorizing focuses on the education that *individuals* receive, and his perception of what is fair and good in schooling dramatically differs from Sirotnick's conception. Eisner wrote that "equity is achieved in education not only by giving students an opportunity to come to school, it is also influenced by what they find when they arrive. School programs that create a very narrow eye of the needle through which all children must pass diminish educational equity."[48] Eisner continues:

> The genuinely good school does not diminish individual differences, it expands them. Virtue in the context of education is not achieved by bringing all children to the same destination; it is achieved by helping them learn how to become who they are.[49]

When Eisner says that differences between individuals should be expanded, he does not mean that a genuinely good school should set out to increase the preschooling differences between various ethnic, racial, and socioeconomic groups. What his statement makes clear is that our perspective on what is real and important influences our interpretation of fairness and goodness. Sirotnick creates a conception aimed at reducing differences in test scores and graduation rates, between *groups,* primarily because he believes these group differences are problematic and not inherently real or immutable. They are, to a great extent, created by societal conditions; and society, through its investment in schools, can significantly reduce these *group* differences. However, if Sirotnick had focused on what is good and fair for individuals, he might have written Eisner's essay. Schools, after all, are not formed to stamp out hubcaps. They are, we hope, involved in the design and implementation of curricula to develop creative individuals and thoughtful citizens, citizens who enhance their democratic legacy, in part, by maintaining and expanding upon their individual differences.

But school practitioners, as we indicated in chapter 1, do not deal only with real individuals. They also deal, directly and indirectly, with real social groups. These groups include students who are severely handicapped, or homeless, or Latino American, or African American, or female, or learning English as a second language, or some combination of these. Furthermore, with regard to these groups, classroom teachers and administrators have overlapping and different responsibilities vis-à-vis teaching, schoolwide evaluation, and policy making. And, to fulfill these responsibilities professionally, they need more than an either-or conception of equity. They need a conception that helps them to work wisely and fairly with both individuals and groups, and a philosophy that enables them to do this without trampling on the constitutional rights of individuals or groups. In short, they need to develop a conception of equity that wisely and flexibly integrates the perspective of Sirotnick and Eisner, and the insights of Kohl, Witty, and Bennett.

Competing Conceptions of Equity: Patrice LeBlanc Kohl, Elaine Witty, and Christine Bennett

To achieve the wise balanced perspective alluded to previously, educators will need teaching and administrative strategies which help to build classroom and schoolwide unity in settings where respect for individual and group diversity is manifest. With this unity in mind, one of the positive features in the work of Eisner and Sirotnick is their avoidance of creating an explicit us/them distinction in their equity theorizing. For Eisner equity aims at unleashing the potential of all children, and for Sirotnick equity is realizable for all children if differences in group achievement rates, and so on are diminished. For Kohl, Witty, and Bennett, equity is also for all children, but with Bennett there is a slight difference, which we highlight next for heuristic purposes.

The slight difference pertains to the degree to which ethnicity is emphasized in discussions of equity and excellence. For example, Bennett states that: "Equity in education means equal opportunities for all students to develop to their fullest potential,"[50] and, further, that "The movement toward equity aims at achieving fair and equal educational opportunities for all of the nation's youth, particularly ethnic minorities and the economically disadvantaged."[51] In addition, she notes:

> Although one's ethnic identity is just one of a number of identity sources available, ethnicity is the heart of the equity problem in this society. Therefore, discussions about achieving educational excellence require concern about those ethnic groups that have been consistently cut off from equal access to a good education.[52]

While we agree with part of this statement, we believe that as teachers develop and enforce equity initiatives for their students they should not automatically place the needs of students who are poor or members of ethnic and racial groups above the needs of students who are being treated unfairly because of learning disabilities, gender, or sexual orientation. If educational equity is for all children then educators should keep their minds fully open to all of the potentially unfair conditions in their schools.

In this regard the work of Kohl and Witty is helpful because in their review of the equity literature they chose to focus on four equity areas: disabilities; ethnicity/race; socioeconomic status; and gender, and noted that their selection of these groups "was not meant to slight any other equity groups; it was a decision based on the authors' areas of expertise and the reality of space constraints."[53] Kohl and Witty go on to say that "Equity addresses the primary goal of education in the United States—educating all children,"[54] and from this, and other remarks, we infer that for these authors equity is a condition to be created for various groups, and, further, that educators should strive to create equity for all groups and individuals in their population of learners who are being treated unfairly.

While they appear to slightly diverge on which group or groups should be the focus of equity initiatives, both Kohl and Witty and Bennett make a clear distinction between equity and equality. Kohl and Witty state that "Equity should not be confused with equality,"[55] and clarify this remark by stating:

> State equalization formulas for distribution of finances are an example; all children receive equal amounts of funding for schooling. However, equity focuses on the redistribution of funds to those who need it the most.[56]

In a similar vein, Bennett wrote that "Equity in education must not be confused with equality or sameness of result or even identical experiences. Potentials may differ, and at times equity requires different treatment according to relevant differences."[57] Working the same theme, Carl Grant states that multicultural education is a philosophical concept and educational process that recognizes "that equality and equity are not the same thing: equal access does not necessarily guarantee fairness."[58] And Robert Slavin reinforces this point as he discusses *overburdened low-SES schools,* schools which deserve more than equal funding per student because a greater amount of their budget is channeled into their security and special education programs, leaving less than equal funding available for the schools' regular education programs.[59]

While we agree that equity will often mean more than equal, this will not always be the case. For example, in the area of high school graduation rates or participation of females in university-level athletic programs, equity would be achieved if equality were achieved. Indeed, in rare circumstances something less than equality will serve to establish lack of discrimination, fairness, or what we call equity. The case of equity for females in sports activities at National Collegiate Athletic Association (NCAA) Division One campuses is an example of the latter. Presently, to determine if a university's program is in compliance with Title IX of the Education Amendments of 1972, the U.S. Department of Education's Office of Civil Rights utilizes three criteria, one of which is the *substantial proportionality* test.[60] J. Naughton points out that "Although the phrase has never been legally defined, colleges at which the proportion of female athletes is no more than five percentage points less than the proportion of female undergraduates are generally considered to have met the test."[61] We interpret this to mean that a university with 40 percent female undergraduates can be in compliance if 35 percent of the university's athletes are women. While it may be confusing to learn that equity will (a) often mean more than equality, and (b) sometimes be accomplished by achieving equality, and (c) occasionally, but rarely, be accomplished by less than equal resources, we believe that an awareness of this complexity is helpful because the truth is often complicated and situational; what holds true in one context for one group may not work for another group in the same or different context. This realization is part of Geneva Gay's perspective on equality of opportunity and excellence for ethnic minority students, a perspective to which we now turn.

Competing Conceptions of Equity: Geneva Gay

Geneva Gay, in developing her views on equality of opportunity and excellence, never loses sight of the inequality that is persistently a part of the lives of many students of color, or the experiential discontinuities existing between these students and many of their teachers. "How," she asks, "can teachers who have grown up in ethnically isolated communities and in a racist society teach ethnic minorities as well as they can Anglos?"[62] Although Gay has much wisdom to share about how teachers might be better educated to serve ethnic minority students, her contributions to this equity discussion go beyond advice on teacher training. First, she reminds us that the equity debate is highly pertinent because of the extent of inequality still prevalent in our education system. She writes, for example, that "educational equality for ethnic minority students cannot be achieved without massive, schoolwide, institutional reform," and that such efforts "should begin with a redefinition of equality as equal access to the best-quality substance of schooling for all students."[63] Second, she emphasizes that numerical equality in educational inputs, while desirable, is not sufficient. It is not enough to ensure that per pupil spending will be equal for all students in a given state. As wonderful as this might be, for Gay it is a starting point.[64] Beyond numerical equality, she urges educators to examine the *quality* and *nature* of the schoolwide curriculum to see if it (1) wisely responds to the ethnic and cultural diversity in the student body and (2) provides access to high-quality programs for *all* students. Thus Gay would have educators employ a group-oriented numerical model to establish what might be called preliminary numerical equality, and then, unlike Sirotnick, she would have educators perceive racial, cultural, and socioeconomic diversity as highly relevant for the task of selecting appropriate curricula to help create educational equity in the curriculum area for ethnic minority students. Finally, Gay highlights the important role that classroom teachers play in providing educational equality, and suggests four areas worthy of inquiry. These are self-knowledge, knowledge of the cultural values and behavioral codes of students, knowledge of learning and teaching styles, and cross-cultural communication knowledge and skills. Such skills will leave teachers better prepared to communicate with parents and other community members.[65]

The aforementioned perspectives on equity remind us that most words in the English language have more than one meaning and that aspects of the definition may change when the word is used in a new context. The meaning of educational equity, for example, will vary somewhat according to the level of education under discussion. When we ask whether educational equity exists at the national, state, school district, school site, or classroom level of operation, different types of evidence will come into play. In an attempt to examine, specifically, the responsibilities and concerns of classroom teachers, we will confine our discussion to the school district level of operation, even though this level of analysis allows for only partial insight into educational equity.[66]

Educational Equity: The School District Perspective

Educational equity, as a characteristic of a school district, exists when certain conditions are met. In this section we discuss three types of equity conditions: physical and financial conditions, educational outcomes, and opportunity to learn. For a district to meet the first of these conditions, the students should have the opportunity to study in schools that are roughly equivalent in terms of physical dimensions, attractiveness, educational equipment, and safety. Inevitably, school districts will have newer and older schools; to keep the older schools as attractive and safe as the newer ones, more money will have to be spent on the older buildings. Further, the students in each school in the district should have an equivalent amount of money spent on their education. If district policy allows the more experienced and better-paid teachers to gravitate to one set of schools—those serving middle- and higher-socioeconomic students—and assigns newer teachers to staff the more challenging, lower-socioeconomic schools, then, in terms of dollars and experience, the district is not providing equitable conditions for its students.

The second window on educational equity pertains to educational outcomes. To study this variable, we examine educational results in terms of pertinent culturally defined social groups. To illustrate the relationship between excellence and equity, we can look at one critical outcome variable: rates of graduation from high school. Let us consider a hypothetical district, the APT Unified School District, in which 60 percent of all students who enter school in kindergarten continue through to the high school years, 20 percent transfer into the district during the junior high school years, and another 20 percent come in during high school. How many of the students who started kindergarten in the district would need to graduate—70 percent, 80 percent, 90 percent, 95 percent, or 98 percent—for *you* to consider this district excellent? Let us assume that both you and the school district's parents, school board, and administrators believe that 90 percent is a suitable criterion for excellence. Because we favor a society that is equitable in terms of educational outcomes, we can also assume that both you and the school board want pertinent social groups—girls and boys; Hispanics, Asians, Native Americans, Whites, and Blacks; and low-, medium-, and high-SES students—all to achieve a 90 percent graduation rate. Finally, if one or two of these groups had a graduation rate of 40 percent while other groups were achieving 90 to 100 percent, and the lower-achieving groups typically earned less money per family than the other groups, neither you nor the school board would likely describe APT Unified as excellent.

This group-oriented, quantitative-outcomes basis for assessing quality is what some educators have in mind when they say there can be no excellence in education without equity. Increasingly since the 1970s, educational equity and educational excellence have become intertwined concepts. Because of this integration of meaning, when we evaluate the quality of a K–12 educational organization, we no longer look only at overall graduation rates, overall participation in sports programs, overall admittance to community colleges, overall anything; excellence is now closely related to the organization's success with the varied ethnic and cultural groups that make up its student body. Educational leaders are becoming aware that it will be members of these varied groups— people of color and women—who will constitute a significant part of the labor force in the twenty-first century. For example, Robert Reich reported that in 1990 60 percent of the net additions to the American workforce were women, 2 percent were minorities, and 15 percent were White males, and speculated that by 2020 66 percent of American workers will be female and minority.[67] It is clear from this, and other data, that as we enter the twenty-first century the fate of America rests on all of its students. Furthermore, despite challenges to affirmative action in several states, it is also true that educational success of students of color, women, and economically disadvantaged students is of special importance to many political and educational leaders.

The third window on educational equity pertains to equal opportunity to learn at the school and classroom level of operation, and it is through this window that teachers, counselors, and principals will see the equity condition they can influence most directly. For educational equity to exist at this level, in every classroom and school in the district each student and each culturally pertinent group must have the following:

1. open and ample access to learning across a wide range of content areas;
2. the opportunity and resources for all students to grow, academically and emotionally, to their fullest potential;
3. a successful experience in learning;
4. the opportunity to develop knowledge, skills, and attitudes associated with active citizenship.

Gender Equity As we encourage teachers, counselors, and principals to diligently and creatively peer through this third window, we encourage these educators and you, the reader, to keep the important and complicated area of gender equity in mind. Current and future teachers should have the opportunity to study Title IX and educational results stemming from its passage, as well as current implications and controversies pertaining to gender equity. Hopefully, our following brief remarks will trigger such study and discussion.

Although the struggle for gender equity in educational settings antedates 1972, the passage by Congress of Title IX of the Education Amendments of 1972, an amendment sponsored by Senator Birch Bayh and Representative Edith Green, was a landmark event. Notably, the preamble of this title states that: "No person in the United States shall, on the basis of sex, be excluded from participation in, be denied the benefits of, or be subjected to discrimination under any program or activity receiving Federal Financial assistance."[68] This language has been the basis of many court cases seeking parity for girls and women, and is widely assumed to be associated with increasingly positive statistics for women in American education. For example, in a 1997 article Iram Valentin pointed out that:

1. in 1995, women were 37 percent of college athletes compared to 15 percent in 1972;

2. in 1996, girls were 39 percent of high school athletes compared to 7.5 percent in 1971;

3. in 1994, 63 percent of female high school graduates from 16–24 years of age were enrolled in college compared to 43 percent in 1973; and

4. in 1994, women received 38 percent of medical degrees compared to 9 percent in 1972, 43 percent of law degrees compared to 7 percent in 1972, and 44 percent of all doctoral degrees compared to 25 percent in 1977.[69]

Relatedly, in its 1997 assessment of Title IX, the National Coalition for Women and Girls in Education (NCWGE) reported that prior to Title IX (a) athletic scholarships for women were virtually nonexistent but in 1997 23 percent of athletic scholarship dollars went to women, and (b) many colleges and universities set quotas limiting women's admission and subjected women to tougher admissions criteria, but in 1995 women earned more than half of the associate's, bachelor's, and master's degrees, and 39 percent of doctoral degrees.[70] Furthermore, lest anyone think that gender equity in general, or Title IX in particular, was dominantly focused on access to K–16 athletic programs, it is noteworthy that the NCWGE's *Report Card on Gender Equity* made separate assessments in the following areas: access to higher education; athletics; career education; employment; learning environment; math and science; sexual harassment; standardized testing; and treatment of pregnant and parenting students.

This evaluation was consistent with the intent of Title IX. The statute prohibits discrimination on the basis of gender in public and private educational institutions which receive federal financial assistance, and includes protection against sexual harassment and discrimination on the basis of marital and parental status. Valentin further notes that:

The act applies . . . from kindergarten through graduate schools, and covers admissions, recruitment, educational programs and activities, course offerings and access, counseling, financial aid, employment assistance, facilities and housing, health and insurance benefits and services, scholarships and athletics.[71]

This is quite a broad sweep, and this breadth, as well as the successes of the women's movement in general, and Title IX specifically may help to explain why the gender equity movement has attracted some thought-provoking critics. While we believe that there is much room for improvement on the road to parity and fairness for women in education, particularly in the areas of science, math, and technology, we would like to call one critic, Judith Kleinfeld, to your attention. Among other claims that we consider worthy of analysis, Kleinfeld asserts that in the 1990s (a) male and female academic achievement is pretty much a draw and (b) the most significantly shortchanged group in American education (and society) is African-American males. In short, Kleinfeld suggests that the emphasis placed on discrimination against women is now, at the beginning of a new century, exaggerated and misguided because it distracts educators from more serious problems.[72]

We believe that discrimination against women and African-American males persists, and that attention needs to be paid to discrimination against both groups. To facilitate the further study of gender equity organizations and documents, we share the following websites:

1. the Women's Education Equity Act (WEEA) Resource Center www.edc.org/WomensEquity/;
2. the American Association of University Women www.aauw.org;
3. the Center for Research on Women at Wellesley College www.wellesley.edu/WCW/index.html;
4. the Legal Defense and Education Fund of the National Organization of Women www.nowldef.org; and
5. the gender equity component of Education Week's website www.edweek.org/context/topics/gender/htm.

Finally, we touch back to the four conditions listed on page 108. We believe that these conditions can be translated into a set of equity-oriented questions that all teachers can utilize. As we outline these possibilities, we will move from the goals and outcomes associated with educational equity to specific behaviors that teachers can manifest if they aim at one or more of the goals of multicultural education.

First Steps Toward Educational Equity and Democratic Practice

Like others who believe they have articulated a more complete model of effective teaching and say, "Behold, we have a good and logical thing," we have the additional responsibility of posing some basic operational questions about that model—in this case, multicultural education: If I teach with a multicultural perspective, what do I do that is different? Or more fundamentally, how do I begin? We will address these questions by examining decisions that can be made during the early phases of the school year or the student teaching assignment.

Before we begin our discussion, however, it is important to note several things. First, what we discuss here is just one interpretation of how classroom teachers can apply a multicultural perspective in student teaching or in the beginning years of their career. There is no single recipe that specifies how all teachers at all grade levels in all settings should implement multicultural education, but there is one common ingredient—the seven goals of multicultural education—that provides a framework for thinking about the topic. Although we must ultimately explore a variety of teaching decisions and strategies to familiarize you with potential building blocks for multicultural education, there is a good response to the question "What do I do that is different?", that is, when you work with a multicultural perspective, you aim at all, or most, of the goals of multicultural education. Second, your strategies will change from grade level to grade level and decade to decade, but your goals, for the most part, will remain the same. Third, we say "for the most part" here because it is logical to assume that educational conditions or personal philosophy will point some of you toward new goals or heightened versions of the ones we include. For example, teachers who are convinced that the political and social structure of a state or nation oppresses their students should engage in some form of liberation or emancipatory education. The form such education will take will be influenced by the nature and degree of oppression. It is, to be sure, a long way from Baghdad, Iraq, to Detroit, Michigan, and emancipation education in Havana, Cuba, will certainly be handled differently from such education in Mexico City or Los Angeles, if only for reasons of job security and teacher safety.

Multicultural Planning Questions

To help you weave these goals into your short- and long-term lesson and unit planning, we have developed a preliminary set of goal-focused planning questions:

1. Do the lesson content and strategies promote educational equity? For example, does the lesson content help to create an inclusive curriculum, one that attempts to maximize student participation in the everyday and overall class curriculum? Are boys and girls given equal opportunity to participate in the lesson or activity?

2. Do the lesson content and strategies make use of, or help to develop, collaborative empowering relationships among parents, students, and teacher?

3. Do the lesson content and strategies promote cultural pluralism in society or intergroup harmony in the classroom?

4. Does the lesson content help to increase the students' knowledge of various cultural and ethnic groups, including their own?

5. Do the lesson content and strategies increase students' proclivity and ability to see and think with a multicultural perspective?

6. Does the lesson content help to correct distortions in the historical, literary, or scientific record that may stem from historical racism or from other forces related to the oppression and exploitation of

specific ethnic and cultural groups? Does it present material in a manner that suggests that racism-related distortions are or may be part of the historical and scientific record the class is studying?

7. Does the lesson content provide knowledge or skills, or promote attitudinal development, that will leave the students better equipped and more inclined to participate in, and help improve, the democratic institutions of their society?

8. Does the lesson content contribute to the students' willingness to cross ethnic and cultural boundaries to participate in and/or learn about different cultural and ethnic groups?

To illustrate further the kinds of teacher decisions and behaviors that will logically result from planning with a multicultural perspective, we will identify several decisions teachers can make before the beginning of the school year, and then several that can be made during the first months of the semester. Together, these decisions will establish a strong foundation for multicultural teaching throughout the entire semester. Following this discussion, we will address related questions from the unique perspective of the student teacher.

BEFORE THE SCHOOL YEAR BEGINS

Prior to the beginning of the school year, you can develop an equity-oriented learning environment by discovering as much as possible about your students, their families, and the communities they reside in. This can be accomplished by visiting the local community to learn about its special resources and characteristics, by speaking with your school principal and counselor, and, most important, by reading your students' files and portfolios. The purpose is to learn about students' health problems, past academic performance, and attendance, and to discover pertinent family and student-related data such as the following:

1. Was the student ever in a "special learner" category (learning disabled, learning handicapped, limited English proficient), and is the student still in one of these categories?

2. Who is the child's primary caretaker?

3. Is English or Spanish or some other language spoken at home (to place you in a better position to communicate orally or in writing with your students' parents/caretakers)?

4. Does it appear, from the child's name, such as Nguyen Hung Dung, that the student is a member of an ethnic, immigrant, or refugee group with which you are relatively unfamiliar?

Examination of Student Records

As we enter the twenty-first century, more elementary and middle schools—in which teachers have fewer students to interact with and in which teachers stay with the same set of students across the school year—are likely to augment the school file. Traditionally it has contained health, attendance, and test score data and in some cases a record of parent-teacher conferences; in many schools it will be expanded to include a portfolio to allow representative student work in writing and art, for instance, to be passed on to all of the student's new teachers so they can examine concrete examples of student progress during the last six or twelve months. This augmented information will place you in a better position to develop trust, respect, and rapport with your students and parents at the beginning of the school year. In a variety of settings during the first days of school, you can allude to your examination of student's prior work as you predict the type of progress you think students will make in your class that year. This subtle display of professional knowledge gained from files and portfolios should reassure and encourage parents and students.

You will probably discover, or already know of, experienced teachers who do not look at files until the second or third *month* of the school year, so they can form their *own* opinions about each student without being influenced by the opinions of past teachers and past academic performance. We strongly encourage you to examine the files and portfolios beforehand so that you can begin to see the students in their full family, community, and developmental context, and thus be better prepared to develop your own tentative views regarding your students. We consider the examination of these files to be the professional responsibility of a multicultural educator and encourage you to pay attention to the information shared by your colleagues as well as your own professional instincts about this database. Teachers need to know as much as possible about their clients as decisions and recommendations are made concerning educational growth and development. This was true a decade ago but is even more important today, when so many of our students' parents are hard pressed just to take care of their family's health and financial needs.

High school teachers who work with 120–150 students per semester may balk at examining so many files, but findings from a large national inquiry carried out under the auspices of Phi Delta Kappa strongly support the idea that all K–12 teachers should review student records prior to the first day of classes, if only to examine each student's pattern of attendance.[73] In one section of the study, students with excessive absences of more than 20 per year (group 1/N = 1,497 students) were compared with students who were not absent excessively) group 2/N = 20,209 students). The comparison was sobering. Group 1 students were:

5 times more likely to be suspended from school;

6 times more likely to use drugs;

3 times more likely to use alcohol;

4 times more likely to have low grades;

6 times more likely to have failed courses; and

2 times more likely to have low reading scores.[74]

Indeed, a pattern of persistent absence places students at such risk that we expect, in the information era, to see more schools immediately providing teachers with an attendance summary when the level of absence approaches or exceeds the danger zone.

Developing a Collaborative Plan

We believe that you should have a professional, and therefore respectful and collaborative, relationship with your clients—your students and their parents. This means that you and they will have rights and responsibilities vis-à-vis the learning process that you both will initiate and participate in within the confines of the public school classroom. We emphasize the word public to stress that the class you will teach is not exclusively your class, or the students', or even the local community's. It belongs to the larger public, and in a broader sense to the American people and their culture. Although you work or will soon be hired to work in one of America's 15,000 school districts, in a very real sense you are there as a representative and transmitter of U.S. history and culture, helping to build continuity between the nation's past and present, and hopefully justice in its future. This is a significant moral responsibility and one worthy of your consideration as you carry out your civic duties as a teacher.[75] Equally significant is the fact that you will play out this general cultural transmission role in a specific community, one that may have its own concept of what your classroom curriculum should look like and what the community's responsibilities for the education of its students ought to involve. These concepts will vary across regions and ethnic communities, and you will need to learn the specific cultural facts about your local community, particularly if it is one in which school boards or state legislatures have increased parental influence over the governance of local schools.

To fulfill this responsibility and to prepare yourself to go beyond the data in the student files, you should develop a plan for implementing ongoing, two-way communication between yourself and your students' parents. If you are new to this idea or new to a particular school, you should have an early discussion about parent communication and parent involvement with your principal to learn (1) what already exists in the school program, (2) what your minimal responsibilities in this area are, and (3) whether some of the things you would like to try seem reasonable, given school and district written and unofficial policies regarding parent involvement and the cultural climate in the community. To assist you in developing your own ideas regarding parent communication and parent involvement in your classroom, several resources are briefly described in Appendix 6. Research demonstrates that many different approaches to parent involvement work,[76] but some, such as the one initiated by Madeline Hunter in her UCLA Lab School in the 1970s, will make a greater contribution than others to multicultural education. Among other things, parents at Hunter's Lab School were asked to share their special expertise regarding the culture of a particular country, people, or region, and they were invited to do this as part of a small cadre of parents.[77] We will return to this use of parents' expertise in the next section when we discuss other strategies that should be employed at the beginning of the school year or semester.

Planning to Use Cooperative Learning

With equity, empowerment, and collaboration in mind, it is our opinion, based on research, that you should decide as early as possible that (1) cooperative learning will play an important role in the instructional and organizational format you will employ and that (2) you will develop a plan for introducing and utilizing cooperative learning groups in your classroom. Because cooperative learning is a major teaching strategy for multicultural education, we recommend that you carefully lay out the ideas you will use to introduce it and then deliver your remarks extemporaneously. For example, in a third-grade or tenth-grade class, you might say something like this:

> Although I will be the main teacher in this class, I want you to know that we will all be teachers and learners in this classroom, and we'll be responsible for helping each other teach and learn. Furthermore, we'll fulfill our responsibilities as a community of learners in a variety of ways. For example, we will also engage in several different forms of cooperative learning. Raise your hand if you have had some experience in cooperative learning. Good. Let's hear about some of those experiences, and then you'll all have a chance to share some of your thoughts about cooperative learning in writing.

You may well be wondering, What is so special about cooperative learning? If the goals of multicultural education are preeminently important, why is cooperative learning singled out as a major strategy?

Although the goals are preeminent, it is also true that cooperative learning has earned a special position in the universe of possible strategies. Research data accumulated over three decades suggest strongly that cooperative learning is a powerful cross-content, cross-grade-level strategy for simultaneously accomplishing four of the goals of multicultural education—namely, educational equity, maintenance and expansion of freedom and democracy, intergroup understanding and harmony, and the establishment of positive, collaborative, empowering relationships among students, teachers, and parents. In his well-researched, illuminating text on cooperative learning[78] Robert Slavin provides convincing evidence to support this thesis. For example, regarding academic achievement in K–12 settings Slavin wrote "Overall, the effects of cooperative learning on achievement are clearly positive. Sixty-three (64%) of the ninety-nine experimental-control comparisons significantly favored cooperative learning. Only five (5%) significantly favored control groups."[79] Furthermore, when discussing one specific cooperative learning strategy, namely student team achievement divisions (STAD), which accounted for 25 percent of the above-mentioned comparisons, he pointed out that the "Effects of STAD have been consistently positive in all subjects with the surprising exception of spelling" and ". . . have been equally positive with younger and older students, and with students in different types of schools."[80] In addition, Slavin has suggested that increased academic achievement is more likely when two conditions are in place. He wrote "First, groups must be working toward a common goal, such as the opportunity to earn recognition or rewards based on group performance. Second, the success of the groups must depend on the individual learning of all group members, not on a single group project."[81] On a related topic, namely the potential of cooperative learning to improve race relations, Slavin noted that when the proper conditions are in place, such as the opportunity for interracial cooperation and equal-status roles for students of different races, research has demonstrated that "students are more likely to have friends outside their own race group than they would in traditional classrooms."[82] Also, it is instructive to note, first, that numerous university professors are making use of cooperative learning strategies, and second, that the collaborative approach developed by Uri Treisman to support calculus students at the University California at Berkeley (see chapter 1) has spread to approximately 100 campuses nationwide and has received the ongoing support of the Charles A. Dana Foundation. Although several components are important in Treisman's model, including special attention to the type of problems presented in the calculus course, collaborative learning is critical in this approach because it helps to build a community of learners and support network in a course well-known for its failure rate.[83]

Beyond the research results summarized by Slavin, there is another vital contribution that cooperative learning makes when the groups that are formed are heterogeneous in terms of ethnicity, gender, *and* current academic performance. In working with such classes, teachers and schools are making a critical move away from the deleterious effects, which Jeannie Oakes and others have persuasively documented, of tracking and ability grouping.[84] Overall, for K-12 equity-oriented instructors, an extensive literature suggests that they ought to become expert users of cooperative learning. To facilitate your planning in this area, a list of resources is included in Appendix 6, and an activity at the end of the chapter provides you with guidelines for observing and interviewing a teacher who makes effective use of cooperative learning.

Planning a Curriculum of Inclusion

Now that you have chosen to study, or are considering the study of, your community, students, and parents and have begun to think about the ways in which you will incorporate cooperative learning into your curriculum, it would be appropriate to identify and review the content you will be teaching during the first months of school, to make sure you understand the concepts you will be teaching. When this review is completed, you will be ready to carry out a critical task pertaining to educational equity. More specifically, after examining the content you will be teaching, you should be able to list ways this content can be used to demonstrate the following:

1. the art, music, language, history, ethics, politics, sports, literature, and technology of the United States has been positively influenced by a wide range of individuals, cultures, and ethnic groups; and

2. in contemporary American society, women and men of all colors and ethnic groups are succeeding in a wide range of occupations.

Thus, no matter what your grade level or content area, you should be well prepared to show your students, from day one, that men and women of all colors and ethnic backgrounds have created and are continuing to create America. In your class, students should learn that there is opportunity for all to succeed throughout American society (or Canadian society, etc.), and it is your responsibility to give your students convincing reasons to believe that they will be able to use their education—both to succeed in society as it exists and to help transform it into a more democratic and equitable society. The convincing reasons you provide—the names, faces, and accomplishments (the stories) of diverse Americans who are using their education for the public good and/or personal advancement—can be taught directly and indirectly. For example, the stories can be part of specific lessons in history, science, math, English, etc., or they can be made part of classroom and school bulletin boards. They can be part of a teacher's optional reading assignments, or they can simply be rewards for a job well done. In short, the teaching which helps children see themselves as part of America's democratic legacy and future can be both explicit and subtle, and will often be both.

We believe that such direct and indirect teaching can have a positive influence on the retention rate in the nation's high schools, and we further believe that all teachers should become a part of the effort to reduce the tremendous dropout rate that saps the strength of U.S. education, and helping students see the long- and short-term practical benefits of their education is an important element in this struggle. If, in doing this, you can let all your students know that there is a challenging future for them in the field of education, you will also be serving the profession well. In addition, if you point out that your school district and the nation has a great need for teachers of color and bilingual teachers specifically and dedicated teachers in general, you would also be making a positive contribution to educational equity and excellence. Our analysis of data provided by the National Center for Education Statistics pertaining to racial/ethnic background of K–12 public school teachers between 1971 and 1996 is sobering.[85] Between 1971 and 1996 the percentage of White teachers in the overall K–12 public school teacher population went from 88.3 to 90.7 percent, a 2.7 percent increase. In the same period and population the percentage of Black teachers went from 8.1 to 7.3 percent, while the "other" population declined from 3.6 to 2.0 percent.[86] If the 1971–1996 trends continue, the data suggests that 90 to 95 percent of K–12 public school teachers in the 2000–2005 period will be White. In contrast, other data suggests that during this period the K–12 population of students will become increasingly diverse with students of color continuing to become the majority population in various cities, states, and school districts.[87] For example, between Fall 1986 and Fall 1995 the percentage of White students in K–12 public schools dropped from 70.4 to 64.8 percent. In addition, in 1995 students of color were the majority in the District of Columbia and five states (California, Hawaii, Mississippi, New Mexico, and Texas), more than 40 percent of the population in seven other states (Arizona, Florida, Georgia, Louisiana, Maryland, New York, and South Carolina), and more than 33.3 percent in eight other states (Alabama, Alaska, Delaware, Illinois, Nevada, New Jersey, North Carolina, and Virginia).[88]

While White teachers can certainly be effective teachers for students of color and vice-versa, the 1971–1996 decrease in the overall percentage of teachers of color does not bode well for educational equity. But, classroom teachers, aware of such trends, via their informal and personal encouragement in class, and their support of teacher clubs and other special programs and teacher recruitment efforts, can be instrumental in creating a more diverse, representative teaching faculty for the twenty-first century. Teachers who engage in such recruitment will also be helping to implement an empowering curriculum, an idea to which we shall now turn.

Planning a Curriculum of Empowerment

The most vital step a faculty or an individual teacher can take toward the creation of an empowering curriculum is to identify empowerment as an important goal in the official schoolwide curriculum. The official curriculum exists alongside the informal, hidden, and intermittent curriculum—the "this teacher does it and that teacher doesn't and that's okay" curriculum. But curriculum goals and objectives become part of the official curriculum slowly, and the change process often involves the effort of an individual teacher or team of teachers who pilot and evaluate the strategy in a more limited setting—one classroom or a cluster of classrooms. So it is appropriate here to look back at our chapter 1 empowerment remarks to consider certain questions—more specifically, the kinds of questions that will help teachers develop a curriculum that will more efficiently and consistently help students to become inner-directed, self-actualizing, confident, competent *citizens* in the various settings they will occupy across a K–12 career: clubs, student councils, community service organizations, athletic and academic teams, a variety of classrooms, and so on.

Recall that the empowerment equation outlined in chapter 1 consisted of knowledge, confidence, multiple opportunities for self-direction, communication skills, week-by-week teacher modeling, validation, advocacy, and programs that empower parents, teachers, and related caretakers. We shall now comment on most of these elements.

To help you step forward in the confidence, self-direction, modeling, and knowledge components of empowerment, you will find the following questions—and the actions that follow from them—worthy of your consideration.

1. In what different ways can my students help to define, or shape, the curriculum in this class?

2. How can I arrange the curriculum—lessons, homework, exams, and ongoing formative assessment—so that students can make meaningful *choices* about how they will use their learning time?

3. In what different ways can I make my classroom more of a democratic learning community, a community wherein students play various roles to help the community function more creatively, efficiently, and democratically?

4. How can I restructure the curriculum and make greater use of technology and other resources (for instance, the library) to enlarge the range of choices alluded to previously?

5. What can I, as the leader and authority figure in the class, do and say to establish the norm that it is wise, good, and necessary for students in this class, and other classes, to learn how to question authority figures (within the academic discipline, the school hierarchy, local and regional government, and so on)?

6. How can I simultaneously deliver a curriculum that is challenging to each learner and success oriented?

7. What specific content (readings, videos, audios, websites, etc.) can I provide in order to underline the message that progress in all areas of intellectual, political, and economic endeavor depends on individuals who know how to, first, question the status quo, and, second, provide creative alternatives?

Learning how to question the status quo wisely is a complex communication skill. Thus it is timely to turn now to the communication element of empowerment.

Communication Skills, Advocacy, and Empowerment

When you ask yourself what communication skills are pertinent to an empowerment curriculum, the first thought is that they all are. So perhaps we should ask another question. For example, which skills not now widely included in the standard K–12 language arts curriculum are critical to empowerment? Beyond the important skill of learning how to question sources of authority tactfully and effectively when you disagree with an idea, assertion, or policy they are responsible for, we would include the following:

1. skill in debating an issue from several points of view;

2. skill in writing letters to political representatives via standard techniques as well as E-mail to request information and share opinions about specific issues;

3. skill in developing and disseminating petitions and other forms of political expression, such as political campaign advertisements in which citizens show their support for specific ideas or candidates;

4. skill in using organizations such as the American Civil Liberties Union (ACLU) and the Mexican American Legal Defense and Education Fund (MALDEF) to defend one's constitutional rights;

5. skill in conducting research via survey and interview to find out what fellow students and others believe about specific issues; and

6. skill in using the Internet to locate information and human resources for problem-solving and self-teaching efforts.

No doubt you can think of several other pertinent skills, and some of these may be a part of the standard K–12 curriculum in your district. But the content and skills enumerated have probably raised some concerns. Will administrators and parents and school board members uniformly welcome a curriculum of empowerment? Will they be supportive when students engaged in a class project conduct a scientific survey calling into question some local school or community policy? These questions bring us to the element of advocacy, but also touch back to the issue of teacher empowerment.

Clearly, one can be an advocate or supporter of many things: a student or group of students, one's own interests, a teacher's organization, or a curriculum. Here, when we link advocacy to an empowering curriculum, we have in mind the reality that many school populations include students who, for reasons of poverty, handicap, linguistic background, gender or sexual orientation, culture, and ethnicity, need special support to survive and thrive. In addition, as we implied previously, a curriculum of empowerment needs advocates because it inevitably challenges someone's status quo. Teachers who take seriously the idea of empowerment and advocacy must create allies within the school faculty and administration and in the general community. This is not a task for Don Quixote and Sancho Panza.

The good news here is that the act of finding allies to help you advocate for students more effectively will increase your influence as a teacher. Furthermore, the very act of validating students in your classroom curriculum, and standing up for students in the schoolwide dialogue about cultural pluralism and bilingualism, will help your future allies find you. In addition, as time permits, teachers should consider developing a wider range of support, and professional organizations and the Internet should be helpful. Indeed, as we will discover in the next section, the Internet will quickly lead you to many professional organizations and much more. However, as with information provided in telephone directories, and other publications, the reader should be aware that what was an accurate URL (website address) in February 2000 may be inaccurate in later years, and so on. But, the extraordinary wealth of information now available on the Internet is well worth this occasional inconvenience.

Developing a Network of Support

Your ability to provide productive opportunities for student empowerment will be enhanced by your efforts to link up with equity-oriented educators in your school district and region. Beyond your region there are organizations like the National Association for Multicultural Education (NAME) (www.inform.umd.edu/NAME) which has many state chapters and ten regional directors with phone numbers and other information listed on the homepage. Other organizations of potential interest include the Southern Law Poverty Center (www.splcenter.org/) which, among other things, distributes the magazine *Teaching Tolerance* and other excellent curriculum materials/videos to thousands of schools across the nation free of charge and also provides grants of up to $2,000 to K–12 teachers to implement tolerance projects in their schools and communities; the National Association for Bilingual Education (NABE) (www.nabe.org); the National Coalition of Education Activists (NCEA) (Members.aol.com/nceaweb); and a variety of professional organizations like the National Council of Teachers of English which provide a variety of resources for teachers of English, social studies, science, mathematics, and so on. One can locate the homepages of these professional organizations via your favorite search engine, or go directly to an outstanding, award-winning, multicultural education-focused website which, among other valuable things, provides links to these professional organizations and many other interesting organizations. The website we refer to is called the Multicultural Pavilion (curry.edschool.virginia.edu/go/multicultural/) and it was created and is maintained by Paul Gorski. After reaching the homepage click on 'Research and Inquiry' and then 'Progressive Education Organizations' to come to a fascinating, partially annotated, partially hyperlinked set of organizations. And, if time permits return to the homepage to browse through other valuable components of the Multicultural Pavilion including (as of February 2000):

1. *Teacher's Corner* which leads to teaching tools for multicultural curriculum transformation;
2. *Research and Inquiry* which leads to various statistical databases, journals and magazines, articles and interviews, libraries and information archives, and progressive education and research organizations;
3. a listserv and online discussion board;
4. *Multiculturalism and the Arts* which leads to art resources, exhibits, the multicultural song index, and links; and
5. an illuminating essay by Paul Gorski entitled "Multicultural Education and the Internet: Online Resource Guide." This essay provides good advice regarding utilization of the Internet, a briefly annotated, mind-expanding set of diversity websites, and an interesting set of E-mail forums (also known as listserv or mailing lists).

The Women's Educational Equity Act (WEEA) Resource Center, a project funded by the U.S. Department of Education, also maintains a very interesting and informative website (www.edc.org/WomensEquity/). Among other things this homepage provides links to the Resource Center's:

1. top ten websites;
2. favorite 200 websites; and
3. an extensive list of women's history websites (including biographies of famous women, suffragists, mathematicians, scientists, athletes, and more).

In addition, the Resource Center also maintains EDEQUITY Online, an electronic discussion group (listserv), which we have found quite informative. The Resource Center describes EDEQUITY as "an international ongoing electronic discussion about all aspects of educational equity in a multicultural context," a site which "gives people an opportunity to ask questions and exchange information about teaching strategies, useful texts and film; innovative programs, current research, and funding sources."[89] EDEQUITY Online also allows you to receive guest privileges to read through recent or archived material without joining the list. To subscribe to EDEQUITY send the message "subscribe edequity" (no quotes and no subject line) to (Majordomo@mail.edc.org). If you have questions about signing up, send an E-mail message to (weeactr@edc.org).

Another listserv discussion group that might be of interest focuses on bilingual education. To subscribe via E-mail, send a message to listserv@Reynolds. K12.or.us and in the body of your message type:

SUBSCRIBE BILINGUE-L _____   _____
                     Your First Name   Your Last Name

THE FIRST FOUR WEEKS AND BEYOND

Cross-Cultural Parent–Teacher Communication

In the initial month of the school year, you should activate your plan to communicate with parents. Your career in teaching will be more successful if you and as many parents as possible are working together toward common goals. We therefore recommend that you make a strong, culturally sensitive attempt to communicate with all your parents. Setting this goal implies that you will use multiple means of communication, and your repertoire of strategies will probably extend beyond your school's planned events.

Some of your students and their families may be recent arrivals who have been in the United States fewer than five years. They may be immigrants who chose to come or refugees who were forced from their homeland. Many of these families may have come from a culture with no tradition of parents playing an active role in their children's education.[90] When you attempt to communicate and establish collaborative relationships with these parents you will need to modify goals, expectations, and strategies; you may have to change some of your face-to-face communication patterns as well. Communicating with immigrant parents and some nonimmigrant parents, particularly those who constitute the entrenched and isolated "poor" in America, can be a cross-cultural experience depending upon your personal background and prior experience, and with the former you may need a translator. Furthermore, it is helpful to assume that there may be pertinent differences between the culture of your school and the culture and language of the home. We suggest that these differences, when they exist, should influence the way you engage in verbal and nonverbal communication with parents, students, and instructional aides.

Research has demonstrated that cultural differences do exist and that they are significant.[91] Vietnamese parents, Punjabi Sikh parents (from the Punjab, in northwestern India), and Hmong parents from Laos, when they arrive in America, are unfamiliar with the idea of being active, collaborative parents who visit school on several occasions a year. If their child is well behaved and doing well in school, they see no reason to visit. Traditional Vietnamese parents are made ill at ease by a teacher who constantly tries to look them in the eye while talking, is loud and informal, and is unaware of the superior position of the male in the Vietnamese family structure. Also, traditional Vietnamese and Punjabi Sikh parents, as well as some American parents, may be uncomfortable if asked to discuss the relationships they have with their children at home. (An example of such a question might be, How do you discipline your child at home?) In their mind and former culture, home is the parent's business, and school is the teacher's business; they have not yet learned, or simply do not value, the American propensity, embodied by national television and radio talk-show hosts, to ask relative strangers the most intimate questions, and to do so in public settings.

Establishing collaborative relationships with parents, teachers, and students will likely prove difficult when the home culture that values education does not value collaboration or has a centuries-old, and different, conception of collaboration between teachers and parents. In addition, the likelihood for cultural discontinuity and conflict, or at least misunderstanding, is heightened when immigrant or minority cultures do not value *equal* educational opportunity, or results, for males and females, as we understand these terms in the United States. This is the case with many Punjabi Sikhs, who want their young men to go to four-year colleges but their young women to agree to arranged marriages before decisions about advanced education are made. Typically, in this immigrant culture the husband has final say over whether a child or wife will attend college. When there is a clash between a basic value in the home culture—arranged marriages help to ensure the continuity and survival of traditional Sikh culture in the United States—and an important value of the school culture, like gender equity, the teacher working within a framework of multicultural education must make personal choices between various goals in the model. For example, the teacher working with Punjabi Sikh students is faced with the challenge of modeling cultural pluralism (understanding and valuing the internal logic of many cultures) and simultaneously presenting the promise of American culture, which includes equal opportunity for men and women. Teachers should be aware that in subtly advocating equal opportunity and independence for Sikh students, they are inviting these students to separate from the traditional culture of the family, and perhaps the family itself. And they should also remember that some Punjabi Sikh-American families may have already begun to value equal opportunity for men and women. In such contexts multicultural education can become complicated, particularly if the teacher attempts to create a multicultural curriculum without gathering data about specific family dynamics.

Interviewing School Leaders

Even with incomplete knowledge of the various cultures one is working with, however, it is possible to attempt to establish educational equity and a collaborative parent–teacher relationship and to teach students to understand and appreciate the internal logic of specific cultures and the commonalities and differences between disparate cultures, like the Sikh and mainstream American cultures. To achieve this delicate balance, teachers will benefit from dialogue with the principal, the school psychologist, and other knowledgeable educators. Such dialogue will help teachers gain insight into the *local wisdom of practitioners* as teachers develop their own perspective on what is appropriate multicultural education. Questions that might prove helpful when discussing this issue with the principal or school psychologist include the following:

1. Will students from (name of culture or ethnic group) _____ tend to communicate explicitly (verbally) or implicitly (nonverbally) in a manner that (a) differs from mainstream American patterns of communication or (b) conflicts with most schools' or teachers' expectations for appropriate student behavior?

2. Are there patterns of explicit and implicit communication that teachers should utilize or avoid when interacting with students or parents?

3. In terms of sex-role socialization in a particular cultural group, are there cultural facts I should know as I
   a. implement my curriculum in general?
   b. form heterogeneous cooperative learning groups?
   c. carry out physical education (P.E.) activities?

4. Regarding the (name of group) _____ students in my class, are there generalizations about their learning style or the instructional style of teachers in their former country that would provide useful background knowledge?

5. Are you aware of books, articles, and videotapes that would provide me with useful background knowledge about _____ culture and language, recommended teaching strategies, and other information?

6. Are there educators or community members, in our school or in the region, who are knowledgeable about _____ culture and language and/or recommended teaching strategies?

We have focused here on cultural differences between immigrant parents and teachers, but teachers should be aware that socioeconomic differences between parents and teachers can also lead to communication breakdowns. This situation is likely to occur when the parents belong to the group considered to be the "poor" in America. With this in mind, teachers are strongly encouraged to examine the parent–teacher communication resources listed in Appendix 6 as well as the resources pertaining to selected immigrant and language minority groups.

Special Communication Strategies

Now that you are better prepared for cross-cultural encounters, it is helpful to examine the planned events referred to earlier; for example, your school will probably organize a Back-to-School night within the first four to six weeks of school, and parent-teacher conferences may follow. However, if you rely on these events alone to meet parents, you may fall short of your goal of communicating with all of them, and you will certainly fail to make contact with many of the parents whose children would benefit most from ongoing parent–teacher dialogue.

Knowing this and keeping the goal of equity in mind, you should be proactive. Start the school year ready to implement a set of communication strategies; some teachers even begin their communication with parents and future students several weeks before the first day of school. To facilitate your work in this area, we have listed some recommended strategies that K–12 teachers can adapt to their specific circumstances.

During the first week of school, send home a polite, positive letter to parents in the appropriate languages. We developed a letter as a model for K–8 teachers who were sending home abrupt, culturally uninformed letters to parents after attending a brief workshop called "Assertive Discipline." Teachers should adopt a professional and respectful tone when addressing parents. It is your responsibility to request, encourage, and invite parents to get involved in their child's education, but you cannot demand it. What may seem reasonable to you—expecting parents to check their child's homework each night and sign off on it—can prove stressful to some parents who do not want to sign off on material they do not understand and may be confusing to some parents who come from cultures in which parents are not asked to do the teacher's work; in addition, it can be burdensome to a single parent who comes home late and has several children. However, an invitation to check homework periodically for neatness and legibility, expressed in language that dignifies parents, can be constructive for all concerned. If your principal agrees, she or he, a mentor teacher, or possibly a teacher aide who is also a parent in the community could check your letters for content and tone before you send them out. We have included two letters (Figures 2.1 and 2.2); the first, which has been employed in our region and which a number of our preservice candidates like, is too rigid and assertive for us. We composed the second letter to illustrate how rules can be discussed with parents in a positive tone and spirit.

Follow up this first letter with a call inviting parents to visit with you during Back-to-School night; prepare your material carefully for that evening. If your school has facilities to generate computer-assisted automatic phone messages, use this technique to extend invitations to parents who are hard to reach. At the same time be aware that some new immigrant parents will be unfamiliar with telephones, and that something as logical to an American as an invitation by phone may be perceived as frustrating and intrusive by some of these parents.

Prior to Back-to-School night, arrange to have a 20- to 45-minute interview with the parents of each of your students. If you schedule meetings two to three afternoons a week, you should be able to meet with many of them within the first six weeks. Although some teachers prefer to meet parents in their homes or some other setting in which parents are comfortable, we recommend that you attempt to meet them in your classroom so that you can use your charts, wall space, and other teaching tools to help answer questions and make a good impression. If it proves impossible for parents to meet you at the school, however, by all means arrange to meet them at their home, a nearby restaurant, the library, or a skating rink. Let the parents know that it would be helpful to you if you could ask them a few questions about their concerns, the child's recent health history, and interests at home. Here are a few of the questions that

Dear Parents:

In order to guarantee your child, and all the students in my classroom, the excellent learning climate they deserve, I am utilizing the following discipline plan as of September 1.

MY PHILOSOPHY

I believe that all my students can behave appropriately in my classroom. I will tolerate no student stopping me from teaching and/or any student from learning.

CLASS RULES
1. Students will stay in seats unless given permission to get up.
2. Students will raise hands for help, questions, or group participation.
3. Students will keep hands, feet, and objects to self.
4. There will be no teasing of others.
5. All students will follow directions.
6. Students will walk in the class quietly and sit appropriately.

IF A STUDENT CHOOSES TO BREAK A RULE

1st Consequence—Verbal Warning
2nd Consequence—Name on the Board
3rd Consequence—Writing Assignment in the "You Blew It Book"
4th Consequence—Notice Sent Home
5th Consequence—Phone Call Home or Parent Conference
Severe Disruption—Sent to Principal or Immediate Jump to Consequence #3

STUDENTS WHO BEHAVE WILL EARN

Stars for the "Star Chart," Special Cooking Activities, Special Lunch, Walking Field Trips, Class Awards, School Awards, Other Special Activities, and Lots of Positive Reinforcement

It is in your child's best interest that we work together on his/her schooling. I will thus be in close contact with you regarding your child's progress in my classroom. Please sign the tear-off sheet below and have your child bring it with him/her to school tomorrow. If you have any questions or comments, please feel free to call, come by the classroom, or write me a note. I will be discussing this discipline plan during the upcoming Back-to-School night in October (date to be announced).

Sincerely,

I have read and understand the discipline plan for your classroom.

(Signature of Parent or Guardian) _____

Figure 2.1   Letter #1 (A Bit Too Assertive)

Dear Parents:

Welcome to a new school year. I have been getting to know your child this week and thus have a good reason to be excited about the coming school year.

In order to promote an enjoyable as well as academically productive year, I would like to share some ideas about my approach to classroom discipline. This year I will combine elements from several successful approaches to discipline to create an orderly classroom environment wherein your child can safely learn valuable content and simultaneously have the opportunity to grow in self-discipline, self-direction, and self-esteem.

During the first week of class, I will introduce several important rules. Then, with the class's help, a rationale and set of consequences will be developed for each rule. Some of the rules and a preliminary rationale (in parentheses) follow:

1. Students will raise their hand when they wish to ask a questions or share information. (Calling out is disruptive and discourteous.)

2. Students will walk, not run, jump, or skip in the classroom. (We want our classroom to be a safe learning environment.)

3. Problems will be discussed and analyzed during classroom meetings. (Trying to solve problems by fighting is disruptive, nonproductive, and dangerous.)

4. Students will be polite to each other and their teachers. (Polite students avoid problems better than impolite students and are quite pleasant to work with.)

By or before mid-October, I hope the class will be ready to share a document that lists its rules along with a rationale and list of consequences for each rule. The rules and consequences will be applied sensitively and flexibly and will be periodically reviewed.

This letter is written to you because you are part of our classroom community. I believe that the letter will place you in a better position to speak knowledgeably about this program with your child. If you have any comments or questions, please share them in a note or at our upcoming parent–teacher conference.

I appreciate the opportunity to work with your child and look forward to our time together.

Yours truly,

Figure 2.2   Letter #2 (A More Positive Tone)

elementary teachers in our region have found useful in initiating a culturally informed collaborative relationship with parents and their children.

1. Could you tell me how old Marquis is, and if he has any special interests or hobbies I can make use of as I'm working with him?

2. Does Marquis have any special chores or responsibilities at home and, if so, what are they?

3. A follow-up question could be, How long has he been taking trumpet lessons?

4. Are there any rules at home that Marquis is expected to follow and, if so, what are they?

5. If Marquis doesn't follow family rules, what kinds of discipline do you use?

6. Do your disciplinary techniques generally work?

7. What are your expectations for Marquis at school?

8. What kind of letter grades would you like him to get?

9. As Marquis's parents, do you have any special concerns, requests, or expectations that you'd like to share with me?

10. What has been Marquis's strongest area in school? Has he had any weak areas?

11. How does he get along with other children? Brothers and sisters?

12. Has Marquis had any recent health problems—over the summer?

13. Is he currently taking medication for any reason and, if so, for what purpose?

14. Do you think Marquis would be interested in tutoring younger children?

15. What does Marquis do on the weekends?

16. There are many ways parents can help out in my classroom for an hour a week or more. Would you be interested in serving in my class, or in the school, as a volunteer? You can try this for a period of one to three weeks to see whether you like it.

17. In the area of homework, have you worked with Marquis in earlier grades?

18. Are you comfortable with the idea of checking Marquis's homework on a weekly or daily basis for neatness?

19. Is there something else you'd like to discuss that I haven't addressed with my questions?

Note that prior to asking question 16, you should make some brief remarks that tell parents they can play a variety of supportive roles in your classroom. They can serve as part of an audience for the culminating presentation of a unit of instruction; they can be a tutor, presenter on a topic of special interest, fellow traveler on a field trip, or volunteer aide to generate supplies for craft activities; or they can play many other roles. Your message is that there are dozens of ways to support your classroom and school; if the parents cannot come to the school, there are ways to support the school program in their own home. Some handouts with simple ideas regarding homework support would be helpful here. Always remember, however, that some new immigrant as well as non-immigrant parents may be unaccustomed to playing the supportive role you are describing. Checking homework at home may be something they have never been asked to do before, and the idea of sharing their concerns and expectations with their child's teacher may be a wholly new experience. Thus patience, encouragement, and a pleasant demeanor will serve well here.

Finally, in this one-to-one meeting with parents, which occurs before the large-group Back-to-School night presentations, you can raise questions sensitively about concerns of your own, perhaps stemming from your analysis of student record cards. For example, the attendance pattern of individual students can fundamentally affect educational equity, and if your review of the cumulative file reveals that a student has had an uneven, or poor, rate of attendance during the past two years (over 20 absences per year), you could take several steps.

1. inquire further to learn whether other siblings have similar rates of attendance and absence;
2. wait two months to see whether the pattern of absences continues;
3. share the attendance data with the student's parents and ask them why Marquis had missed so much school in the past two years;
4. mention to the parents that by working together as a team, you could definitely improve Marquis's attendance.

If handled well, such questioning might lead to a productive, problem-solving dialogue between you and the parents. Handling it well means that you are careful not to throw the parents on the defensive but, rather, take a proactive posture with a student whose poor school attendance may be associated with other risk factors, such as those cited in the Phi Delta Kappa study mentioned earlier. As we make these comments, we are reminded of a local junior high school teacher who discovered that poor attendance patterns can be related to family pressure and cultures in conflict. In this case the parents were using the daughter's labor in the fields as an extra source of income. When asked about the excessive absences, an angry mother said, "At least we teach our daughter the value of hard work." The teacher, who now realized that the parents were breaking the compulsory attendance law, understood that she would have to report the parents to the local attendance board. But she wondered whether there was some kind of compromise she could help create that would protect her student's rights to a public school education but not pit the family against the school authorities. What could she say and do that might lead to a judicious compromise? In this instance we suggested that the teacher discuss the issue with the school district's migrant education coordinator and her principal. We further suggested that the family be reminded that when their daughter was sixteen she would be eligible to attend the school district's alternative high school and have a schedule which permitted her to attend school in the mornings and work in the afternoons. Conceivably, with a positive attitude and patience on both sides, both a job and a high school diploma were within reach.

While elementary teachers can try to meet with all or many of their parents for the structured interview discussed previously, it is not practical for most secondary school teachers. But secondary school teachers can adapt the strategy for use with a specific class or a specific set of parents whose children, in particular, would benefit from face-to-face contact between parent(s) and teacher.

Class-building Activities

Another major activity that begins during the first month of the year is class building. As an equity and democracy-oriented educator, you will try to create a total learning environment that promotes democratic practice and intergroup understanding and harmony. Your work will be greatly facilitated if your students recognize that they are part of a community of learners, a group that cares about each other's feelings, academic progress, and social development. Classroom teachers should understand that increasing numbers of students come to school ill-prepared to care, share, and help each other. Many factors have combined to create this dilemma, and schools cannot avoid filling what Spencer Kagan calls a "socialization void."[92] Your students will become either more competitive and individualistic or more cooperative and caring in your classroom, and the way you choose to structure the learning process will be the decisive factor. You can help fill the socialization void by building a "we're in this together" class norm, and you can promote a democratic and collaborative ethos by

1. providing class time at the beginning of the school year or semester for the students to get acquainted;

2. identifying a class project to which all individuals, through cooperative learning groups or other ways, will contribute—examples include a mural, a monthly or quarterly newsletter, a play, a beautification project for the class or the school, the development of a class song or logo, a partner system to help each other with homework, an upper-grade-class teaching or tutoring project for a lower grade, or an evaluation system in which students are rewarded for helping other students learn. For instance, in a partner study program, students could receive points when their partner's weekly test scores go up;

3. holding classroom meetings to develop and refine the rules and consequences (the justice system) for the class;

4. explicitly linking the classroom meeting process to the larger activity of establishing, across the semester (secondary) and school year (elementary), a *democratic* listening, thinking, questioning, and learning environment, and by explaining the special qualities of this type of learning environment;

5. providing one activity a week, during the first month, in which students will simultaneously discover more about each other and learn to be accepting of each other's opinions and values;

6. providing each student with a partner or partners to facilitate learning both within and outside the classroom; and

7. telling your students that you expect to learn a lot about and from each student, that you and they will be both teachers and learners in this classroom, and that in your class they will learn how to compete with themselves, cooperate with others, and create and maintain a democratic community.

In his compilation of resources for cooperative learning, Kagan describes a structure entitled "Corners," which can provide students with the opportunity to learn more about each other's commonalities and to develop an appreciation for their own point of view and the views of others.[93] In this activity the teacher picks four types of an item that students will have different opinions about or preferences for, such as four different foods, television shows, forms of entertainment, music, careers/professions, approaches to solving inflation, seasons, sports, characters in a novel, or pets. Students will be given time to make their choice and decide the reasons for this choice. After proceeding to the corner of the room designated for their chosen item, students will share the reasons for their preference with a partner and form groups of approximately four, in which each student will paraphrase the reasons their partner just presented.

Then a spokesperson from each corner will summarize all the reasons that were presented in that corner. After each spokesperson presents the group's reasons, the original pairs of partners will collaboratively paraphrase each spokesperson's ideas; when all spokespersons have been heard, the corner groups will come together as one group or in groups of four to make certain that everyone can identify reasons for each of the choices. This type of class-building activity can also lead to a creative writing activity or some other content-related lesson. A corner's session on seasons, for example, could serve as an introduction to a poetry-writing activity or a science unit on weather, and one on sports could serve as a lead into the introduction of a new physical education activity or as a piece of literature related to sports.

Team-building Activities

In addition to class-building activities, equity and democracy-oriented teachers will engage in team-building activities after they have learned more about the special strengths and growth areas of individual students. They will structure the small groups so that, over the course of the semester or year, each student will work closely with students of different ethnic and cultural backgrounds, academic potential, and gender.

Unless you inherit a group of students intact from a previous semester in which they have already had a number of team-building experiences, initially you should engage in a series of team-building activities. As Kagan has noted, "Teambuilding creates enthusiasm, trust, and mutual support which in the long run leads to more efficient academic work."[94] Team-building activities follow the same logic as class-building activities, so after forming your teams, you will provide them with activities that (1) allow them to get acquainted, (2) develop the team's identity and cohesiveness, (3) enable team members to experience mutual support, and (4) provide opportunities to value the unique personalities and perspectives of individual team members. some examples of team-building activities include:

1. For Getting Acquainted: As a part of class-building exercise, each student can develop a personal web (see Figure 2.3) that might contain some or all of the following information: hobbies; names of family

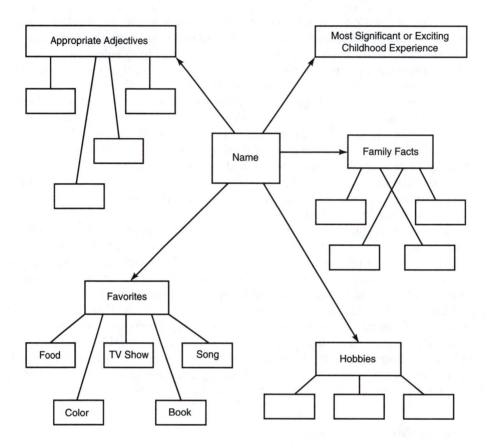

Figure 2.3 My Personal Web

members; favorite food, TV shows, sports, singers, songs, colors, athletes, and books. The students, working in pairs, can orally share their webs with their partners, and then each student can introduce her partner to the class, selecting one or two facts from each major category, using the visual web as a frame of reference if needed. After additional information is added to each category, or a new category is added, the web can be used for the same purpose when the first teams are formed. In this setting, the partners introduce each other to the other pair on their four-student team; next comes a team interview, in which each member asks at least one question. The partner being introduced can answer, pass, or invite the introducer to take a shot at the question. The expanded webs can be used again when teams are restructured, and each team, using the same rules for selecting a team name, can select a new category to be added to the personal web.

2. For Team Identity Building: Having students select names for their groups is an enjoyable team-building activity, provided certain rules are followed. Kagan identifies three rules to facilitate the process: (a) each team member must have a say; (b) no decision can be made unless everyone consents; and (c) no member consents to the group decision if he or she has a serious objection.[95] With a multicultural perspective in mind, we would suggest a fourth rule: (d) team names should be positive. The names should contribute to the class-building and team-building process and should not be exclusionary (the Four White Dudes) or self-derogatory (the Four Jerks or the Three Idiots) or suggestive of ill will (the Klan, or the name of any gang in the community). If you do not establish ground rules for your team names, you should be prepared to accept anything, and "anything" could easily undermine the goals you are attempting to achieve through multicultural and cooperative education. Collaborative art projects, such as designing and creating a team mural or team banner, are also excellent vehicles for building team identity, as are collaborative writing and oral presentations. However, in all team-building endeavors, the teacher should carefully structure the directions and the task to ensure that all team members are meaningfully involved.

3. For Appreciating Individual Differences: One approach is to establish brainstorming rules—for instance, that everyone participates, all ideas are accepted (No "Put-downs), zany ideas are welcome, connections can be encouraged. One idea builds on a previous idea or connects two other ideas. Then each team can use the brainstorming process to generate ideas for improving one area of the school community (the classroom, lunchroom, playground, bathrooms, indoor physical education facilities, library). After the teams have delineated and copied a long list of possibilities, each team member will

    a. pick the two ideas he considers the most important (the criterion could be practicality rather than importance)
    b. write down one or two reasons for each choice
    c. share his first choice and reasons with the group.

After each team member has presented her idea and reason to the group, the other team members can comment, on a quasi-voluntary basis, on why they liked the idea and reasons. The encourager in the group will make sure that everyone receives some positive feedback, and after the first round, team members can share their second choice and reasons. As the culminating step, the team, using a consensus process, can submit its six best ideas to the teacher or to the entire class; all team members will pick one of their own ideas for this list, and each student's name will be listed next to the idea. This activity can end with the submission of that list, or it can be developed into a group project with the students conducting research and then submitting their proposals for improvement to the appropriate individuals in the school.

Selection of Content

In the previous section we suggested that the way you communicate with parents and the way you structure your class for learning can promote educational equity to a greater or lesser degree. The main idea in this section is that the same premise holds true for curriculum content. Curriculum content is not neutral. What you choose to teach in history, current events, agricultural education, home economics, language arts, English, music, art, mathematics, science, physical education, and foreign languages can:

1. contribute to individual self-esteem and thereby to educational equity and related goals such as interethnic and intercultural harmony;

2. provide examples of individuals from different cultural and ethnic groups who are cooperating in normal as well as trying circumstances and thereby contribute to intergroup understanding and harmony;

3. allow students to see that people just like themselves have contributed, and are contributing, to American and world civilization in all its facets, and thereby contribute to educational equity by increasing the students' ethnic and cultural pride and belief that their education can lead to attainable, interesting careers;

4. provide students with intriguing, accurate information about specific cultural and ethnic groups at home and abroad and thereby increase the students' multicultural/multiethnic knowledge base, their ability to think from a multicultural perspective, and perhaps their potential for successful interaction with individuals of varying ethnic and cultural backgrounds;

5. create opportunities for students to articulate the various points of view on culturally laden issues and thereby contribute to the students' ability to think from a multicultural perspective, and perhaps interact with individuals of varying cultural backgrounds;

6. help students see history and current events through the eyes of the conquered as well as the conqueror, the slave as well as the plantation owner, the soldier as well as the general, the poor as well as the rich. Thus, with your content choices you can uncover and share a multiperspective or monoperspective (ethnocentric) view of American and world history, and your responsibility—with multicultural education in mind—is to the former;

7. reduce stereotypes, in a variety of ways and in a variety of content areas (see the unit on stereotypes in chapter 4);

8. reduce any propensity students might have for racist and sexist (to choose two serious -isms) attitudes and actions, and stimulate a positive attitude toward antiracist and antisexist behavior; and

9. contribute to your students' propensity to be constructively active in society by including stories and so on about *various* kinds of social activists whose efforts have improved American society, or other societies, on a local as well as a national level. Variety is the key here and the historical and contemporary activists we discuss

come from across the political spectrum. Some of the individuals we recommend for a yearlong unit on social activists include Morris Dees (civil rights lawyer and cofounder of the Southern Poverty Law Center), Millard Fuller (cofounder of Habitat for Humanity), Dolores Huerta and the late César Chávez (cofounders of the United Farm Workers), and the late Ida B. Wells (antilynching crusader, suffragist, investigative journalist, and more).

This list of curriculum possibilities should encourage you to keep the goals of multicultural education clearly in mind as you choose your content or decide what to emphasize in content you are required to teach. In Chapters 3, 4, and 5 we will return to the issue of curriculum content as we discuss lessons, lesson sequences, and units of instruction that in various ways—methods and content—incorporate a multicultural perspective. This material will illustrate how you can teach with a multicultural perspective throughout the school year and across the school curriculum.

Now that we have examined the manner in which in-service teachers can incorporate a multicultural perspective in their planning and teaching at the beginning of a semester or school year, we will delineate strategies that student teachers can adapt for their own classrooms, so that they too can plan and teach with a multicultural perspective. Teachers who serve or plan to serve as master teachers will also benefit from this discussion, particularly the parts that deal with the Classroom Demographic Profile and the Typology of Multicultural Teaching. These tools offer information you can provide future teachers to prepare them for the complexity of your classroom and beyond.

TEACHING WITH A MULTICULTURAL PERSPECTIVE DURING STUDENT TEACHING

It is critical for the prospective teacher to realize that student teaching is not just something to get through. Student teaching provides a series of experiences that will deeply influence your first years of teaching. The ideas you try out and evaluate during student teaching are those you will likely try again in modified form early in your teaching career. Other ideas that you read about in methods courses but elect not to put into practice because they do not fit your student teaching assignment may remain untried during your first teaching years. Some of your student teaching experiences may help you decide where to seek a teaching position, or even whether or not to become a teacher. Thus we encourage you to experiment with a variety of strategies during your student teaching assignment and to give the ideas discussed next serious consideration. Although they range in complexity, all of these tactics have been successfully implemented by K-12 student teachers in a variety of instructional programs.

Even though you are working in someone else's classroom, there are many ways for you to incorporate a multicultural perspective into your student teaching. Furthermore, besides the actual planning and teaching of lessons and lesson sequences, there are several important research activities that can guide your student teaching toward the seven goals in our conception of multicultural education. We will discuss some of these possibilities under the following head-ings: parent–teacher communication; interviewing and observing students, teachers, and community; developing and extending a classroom demographic profile; and using the Typology of Multicultural Teaching as you develop lessons, lesson sequences, units of instruction, and your total class curriculum.

Parent–Teacher Communication

How does parent–teacher communication contribute to multicultural education and, more specifically, educational equity? Clearly, effective, culturally sensitive communication can lead to greater cooperation and collaboration between par-ents, students, and teachers, a development that in turn can promote equity by creating more access to learning for your students. Schoolwork and homework become more rewarding when parents adopt strategies that support school goals. If you ask the right questions, parent–teacher communication can also provide you with additional insight into your students' interests, personalities, and cul-tural background, and this knowledge can create more opportunity for learning and culturally sensitive instruction in your classroom. In addition, by sending home introductory letters in the appropriate languages, by using interpreters when necessary, by showing interest in family concerns, and by providing cul-turally appropriate communication when interacting with students and parents, you are modeling a positive pluralistic attitude; in so doing, you are teaching cul-tural pluralism in a most meaningful and convincing manner.

Although you ought to be an active communicator with parents, you should appreciate that typically in student teaching, you are not trying to develop a full-blown collaborative relationship with parents (that is your mas-ter teacher's responsibility). You are simply practicing parent–teacher com-munication, and a logical place to begin is with a letter introducing yourself to the parents of your students. Most parents will hear about you regardless of whether you choose to send a letter, but what they hear may not be accurate. For example, students in a primary grade may announce that they have a new teacher, leading some parents to wonder what happened to their old teacher. For this and other reasons, we believe that it is polite and professional for you as a student teacher to let parents know exactly who you are. The letter you write should be checked by your master teacher and your principal, if your master teacher considers this appropriate. There is no one correct formula for an introductory letter. However, there are some recommended ingredients, including your name, the length of your stay, the name of the program you are part of, a statement about your personal goals, a special project you are plan-ning such as a unit of instruction, and a closing positive statement. A brief example is presented in Figure 2.4.

If you will be teaching a unit of instruction during your student teaching, it would be appropriate to send parents a newsletter that describes the con-tent of the unit and special activities their child will be involved in. In the newsletter you can also invite parents to participate as helpers on a field trip,

Dear Parents:

This letter is to inform you that for the next _____ weeks I will be working in your child's classroom. My name is Melinda Mendoza, and I am a student teacher in the Bowling Green Teacher Education Program. This is my second student teaching assignment, and I look forward to beginning my career in teaching this September.

I am grateful for the opportunity to teach and learn in Mrs. Chiarelott's class and for the chance to work with all of her students. Among other things this semester, I will be teaching a unit on twentieth-century inventors and will be sending you more information about this unit later in the semester. In the meantime, if you are in or near the school, please drop in to say "hello." I would like to meet as many parents as possible.

Sincerely,

Figure 2.4   Sample Student Teacher Letter

as guest speakers if they possess some special knowledge related to the unit or as a guest during a culminating unit activity. A follow-up newsletter composed by students and teacher, summarizing the unit's activities and learnings, could be one of the culminating activities.

As a student teacher, you should attend as many official parent-related meetings as possible (PTA, school site council, parent–teacher conferences, etc.). As you observe, take notes on how the teachers and administrators make a wide range of parents feel comfortable about participating in the school setting. In addition to attending these meetings, you should continue to expand your knowledge of parent-involvement strategies. One excellent resource for this purpose is *Communicating with Parents,* a manual designed to assist principals and teachers in involving parents at home and at school.[96] The teachers in your school and school district are another excellent source of parent-involvement strategies. Your master teacher and principal can help you identify, and then interview, teachers who have excelled in the area of parent involvement and parent partnerships. Teachers stimulate high parent involvement in a variety of ways. Some make extensive use of the phone; others use newsletters to entice parents to visit the classroom or may plan projects, exhibits, and evening workshops that parents will find intriguing; others are adept at meeting parents at home or in restaurants and other neutral settings. Interviews with such teachers will help you realize that student teaching can be a wide-ranging field experience that focuses on one or more classes but may also extend into classrooms with special populations, the school, and, most significantly, the community. Interviewing and observing are major strategies for developing the knowledge base that will allow you to see, plan, and teach with a multicultural perspective. In the next section, we will present tools to facilitate your use of these strategies during student teaching.

Interviewing and Observing During Student Teaching

Prospective and new teachers should understand that educators do not learn how to teach solely by reading, observing, and engaging in practice teaching. Much that is important in good teaching arises from an awareness of curriculum, community, and culture that is difficult to achieve from observation alone; some pertinent knowledge can be derived only from the multiple experiences of local practitioners (teachers, instructional aides, principals, counselors, and others). For example, the writer of an essay, or a special presenter in a methods course, may describe the discontinuity between an American citizen's response to certain nonverbal cues (smiling and nods) and the interpretation by a newly arrived Vietnamese immigrant of such cues. This knowledge about a specific immigrant group will be helpful in general, but the practitioners in your school district can give you insight into how teachers use such knowledge in distinguishing between new immigrants and those who are in the process of trying on "American" forms of nonverbal communication. Prospective and new teachers should regularly question teachers, university supervisors, parents, students, instructional aides, principals, and community leaders. In short, student teachers should become patient, well-organized, energetic interviewers and should always remember the individuality of their students and families. The risk of oversimplification and stereotyping is a constant problem as we attempt to apply cultural information about various groups.

Elementary and secondary student teachers will also benefit from adding as much diversity as possible to their student teaching experience; in some cases this will mean trying, politely, to break the mold of the traditional student teaching program. For example, in a typical secondary teacher education program, math majors will do their student teaching in a variety of math classes. This is logical, but not necessarily the most fruitful arrangement for every math major. Some math majors might benefit from a student teaching experience that, in addition to several sections of math daily, allowed them to help out in an English language development (ELD) class, or an Advancement via Individual Determination (AVID) class, or in a math class in which they could engage in some form of real-world, interdisciplinary teaching. Elementary teachers, on the other hand, might spend time in a "special day class," interacting with students who are not fully mainstreamed, or they could help out in a bilingual classroom. It is noteworthy that in our teacher education program, a considerable number of teacher candidates decide to increase their proficiency in Spanish after regularly helping out in an English language development class, or a bilingual class, or a class in which a content educator makes minor but consistent use of a second language. Actually being in bilingual settings provides a richer experience than a university-based discussion about bilingualism. No doubt a judicious mixture of the two is what is needed.

You should also note that in the busy student teaching environment, you may not be able to have extensive interviews with community and agency leaders and citizens; at the school site, however, many interviewees can enhance your potential for teaching with a multicultural perspective. Your primary sources of local information about the cultures of your students will be your master teacher, the principal, the school psychologist, and the students themselves; other valuable sources could be a migrant coordinator, migrant aide, bilingual teacher, or parent volunteer. Obviously, if you can arrange to do part of your student teaching in classrooms with second-language learners ("English learners"), you will have an advantage getting interviews with bilingual teachers. The next section discusses in detail your initial interviews with your principal and one of your master teachers.

INITIAL INTERVIEW WITH TEACHER

If possible, the first interview with the master teacher should occur several weeks prior to your student teaching, and it would be helpful if it was part of a seminar or course related to student teaching. This timing will allow your master teacher to share books, articles, and other material to help you develop the specific and local knowledge base you need in order to achieve maximum success with her students. As you review the questions enumerated below and our occasional commentary (in parentheses), note the following:

1. In some cases the questions relate directly to one or more of the goals of multicultural education.
2. Some questions will serve other purposes.
3. Student teachers should not feel compelled to ask all of these questions.
4. In explaining the purpose of the interview, you should tell the master teacher that your main goal is to get a head start in learning about the students and selected practices and procedures in the class.
5. It would be ideal if this first interview was followed up by a second, and/or led to an ongoing two-way, question-and-answer dialogue within the pages of an interactive journal.
6. Student teachers who have interviewed teachers and principals have reported that, in response to questions about multicultural education, the educators occasionally asked the student teachers what they meant by multicultural education. Thus, be prepared to share the definition that is most meaningful to you. Of course, we recommend the seven-goal definition because it is clear and relatively easy to grasp. If you choose to use it, you can also make use of the visual image in the text to support your explanation.

The Questions

1. Part of my assignment is to learn a bit more about your teaching background. For example, how many years have you been a teacher, in what grade levels and in which school districts?
2. In terms of general ideas about teaching, which beliefs influence most the way you organize and manage the learning in your classroom?

3. Do you use specific rules or standards to help establish and maintain an effective learning environment? If yes, which rules or standards do you work with, and how were they selected or developed?

4. Is the development of self-esteem or self-direction in learning an explicit part of the curriculum in your class and, if so, what strategies do you use to help students develop self-esteem or self-direction?

5. What roles do parents play in helping you achieve your educational objectives? In what different ways do you communicate with parents?

6. Does your school district have a set of curriculum objectives (or standards) which you are expected to teach toward?

7. Do you place your students in groups to facilitate instruction and, if so, what kinds of groups do you use and what criteria do you employ to structure these groups?

8. Is multicultural education or educational equity an important curriculum emphasis in your school district? If so, what kinds of staff development or programs support educational equity and/or multicultural education? (Your major goal with questions 8 and 9 is to learn how a school district and master teacher respond to and conceptualize multicultural education. You should be open-minded and nonjudgmental as your master teacher responds. As you continue your questioning, you may discover that she employs teaching strategies associated with multicultural education but does not use the same terminology that your teacher education program does. In this area, the master teacher's response to question 13 should be revealing.)

9. Do you provide multicultural education in your classroom? If yes, what specific strategies help you to do so?

10. What types of evaluation and grading procedures do you use in your classroom? In this district, what are teachers required to do in the area of evaluation and grading, and what is left up to the teacher's discretion?

11. Do students in this class take standardized tests during the school year? If yes, on what are they tested, and how do you and your colleagues make use of the data generated by these exams?

12. How is homework handled in your classroom, and does the school district have a specific policy that requires teachers to give a certain amount of homework on a regular basis?

13. Are there individual students or groups of students in your class who receive special attention, special services, or modified instruction because of one or more of the factors listed below? If yes, I'd like to gather some specific information about each of these students today and then perhaps continue to discuss them in later sessions. So, are there students who receive special instruction because of:

    a. learning disabilities or capabilities?

    b. language background or capabilities (i.e., limited English, non-English proficiency, or potential English proficiency—LEP, NEP, PEP—or bilingual proficiency or bidialecticism)?

    c. recent immigration to, or migration within, the United States (and neighboring countries)?

    d. cultural, ethnic, or religious background?

    e. socioeconomic status or gender?

    f. Other factors related to recent family events such as separation from a parent, divorce, or death in the family?

    (If you choose to work with this strategy during student teaching, or are required to, it might be wise to save question 13 for a separate session, in which you and the master teacher can work together to complete a classroom demographic profile. The profile will be discussed in greater detail shortly. Secondary candidates are encouraged to complete a demographic profile for just one of their classes, perhaps the one that appears to be the most challenging.)

14. When did you first have access to the record cards or portfolios of your students? What information is kept in these files, and how do you use this database? At some point during the school term, may I review these files?

15. What strategies do you use to help students relate to each other in positive ways?

16. What do you consider to be your most important legal responsibilities? In this district, how do teachers become aware of their legal responsibilities?

17. In the context of your day-to-day curriculum, do you explicitly set out to promote/develop citizenship skills? If yes, please identify some of the practices you employ in this endeavor.

18. In our teacher education program, I will be expected to teach at least one unit of instruction during this assignment, and I will also be expected to spend approximately five weeks planning the unit and to employ a multicultural perspective as I design and implement the unit. With this in mind, are there any specific units you would like me to plan or special areas of the curriculum you would like me to direct my unit assignment toward?

Initial Interview with Principal

If there are other student teachers at the school site, try to arrange a joint meeting with the principal and also with the school psychologist. The principal will likely want to greet you when you arrive at the campus but may be surprised when you request an interview. With the principal, we recommend that you keep your interview short. You should ask the principal if she would like to see your questions in advance. Possible topics and questions for the principal include the following:

1. School and Community Characteristics and Special Programs
   a. Compared with other schools in the district, does your school have special demographic, social, and/or economic characteristics?
   b. Does your school have special programs to meet the educational needs of special groups of learners? If so, can you provide a few examples?
   c. How would you describe the overall mission of this school and your school district?
   d. In terms of mobility and cultural patterns, resources for children, health facilities, and other data, how would you describe the surrounding community?
   e. How would you describe the relationship between your school and the community? Please describe some programs and activities that help to create this relationship.

2. At-risk Children

   If at-risk students were not mentioned above, the following questions may prove illuminating:
   a. I have seen the term *at risk* used in recent educational articles. Are there children in your school who are considered to be at risk?
   b. If yes, how are such students identified, and do they receive special attention from teachers and other specialists on your staff?
   c. If yes, can you give some specific examples of such special support?
   d. Do you think this label is functional and productive for educators to employ? Why or why not?[o]

3. Educational Equity, Multicultural Education, and Democracy
   a. Do teachers and administrators in this district and school talk about *educational equity* and *multicultural education?* If yes, what do you think these terms mean to most of them?
   b. In this school district are there any districtwide policies pertaining to educational equity and multicultural education?
   c. In terms of ethnic and cultural background, has the student population in your school or school district been changing during the last five or ten years?
   d. If yes, have these demographic shifts led to changes in curriculum and instruction, specific patterns of communication, social events, or clubs at your school?
   e. Are teachers in your school expected to play a role in cultivating in students what might be called democratic character, or a propensity for living and participating in a democratic society? If so, how and when is this responsibility called to the teachers' attention?

   f. Are there schoolwide activities or clubs in your school which have been set up to prepare students to play a constructive role in their local community and/or the larger democratic society?

   g. Do you think it is important for future teachers to think, plan, and teach with a multicultural perspective, and can you provide some reasons for your response?

   h. Can you identify conferences or professional organizations in this region that might provide more sources of information about educational equity and multicultural education?

With your principal, as with your master teacher, you may find an educator carrying out practices associated with multicultural education but not using the same terms employed by the teacher educators at your university. With the school psychologist you can use the questions delineated earlier in the chapter (see The First Four Weeks and Beyond section), and you can also ask her or the principal to name some of the specific community agencies and organizations that serve the children in your school (libraries, parks and recreation, Boy Scouts and Girl Scouts, weekend cultural programs for specific immigrant groups, and others). If you have not already done so, now might be a good time to walk around and drive through the community your school serves. The more aware you are of community conditions and community resources, human and physical, the better able you will be to provide sensitive, equity-oriented instruction and advice to your students.

The Classroom Demographic Profile

After you have had initial interviews with your master teacher, principal, and school psychologist and have spent time observing in your local community, and perhaps observing in special classrooms at your school site, you are ready to sit down with your master teacher for a more detailed discussion about the individual students in the classroom. If possible, this conversation should occur before your assignment begins, so that you can observe with a multicultural perspective from the very first day of your assignment.

In Chapter 1 we said that the educators who teach with a multicultural perspective will see their students as unique individuals as well as members of family, ethnic, and cultural groups that influence their behavior to a greater or lesser degree. During student teaching, or in earlier field assignments, you can collect data to inform this dual vision by filling out a classroom demographic profile with your master teacher.

The Classroom Demographic Profile is a form (see Figure 2.5) that allows your master teacher to accomplish the following:

   1. introduce you to the ethnic, cultural, and instructional diversity that exists in the classroom;

Student
Teacher
Name:

Cooperating
Teacher
Name

Date:

Grade: School: District:

Types of students
(Students are or have a[n])

Instructionally relevant
information about specific students*

A. Linguistically different (LEP/NEP)
   (first name only)
   1. _____
   2. _____
   3. _____

B. Individual education plan (IEP/ILP)
   1. _____
   2. _____

C. Suspected learning disability but no IEP
   1. _____
   2. _____

D. Of ethnic minority background**
   (first name and ethnic identification)
   1. _____
   2. _____
   3. _____
   4. _____
   5. _____
   6. _____
   7. _____
   8. _____
   9. _____
   10. _____

E. Migrant students
   1. _____
   2. _____
   3. _____
   4. _____

F. Receiving special medication
   1. _____
   2. _____

G. Gifted and talented
   1. _____
   2. _____
   3. _____

Figure 2.5   The Classroom Demographic Profile

H. Other categories used by classroom teachers and/or school

_____

_____

_____

_____

I. Extra spaces

_____

_____

_____

_____

*This could include information about resource room instruction, modification of regular class instruction, special arrangements stemming from religious background, health and medication, individual education plans (IEPs), individual language plans (ILPs), learning styles, and so on.

**Include here students of Hispanic-American, Native American, Asian-American, Iranian-American, Punjabi-American, etc., background *only* if this classroom teacher believes the student's cultural background or ethnicity has, or might have, instructional implications.

Figure 2.5 continued The Classroom Demographic Profile

2. provide you with instructionally relevant information about specific special learners who are included in the database;

3. share with you new categories for students that the district finds useful for instructional or funding reasons. For example, some teachers can readily identify their at-risk learners and the extra resources that can help these learners expand their potential for success; and

4. share with you his or her views about the various labels that are used to classify students.

Note that the demographic profile provides you with instructionally relevant information about a range of special learners in the classroom. This information should enhance your ability to provide equity-oriented instruction to help your students achieve their full academic potential. As valuable as this database can be at the beginning of the student teaching experience, it is only a point of departure for further observation for all the students in class, those mentioned in the profile and those not mentioned. For this purpose we encourage you to keep a loose-leaf binder at home in which you set aside two or three pages for selected students or each student in your class depending on whether your assignment is elementary or secondary. Alternatively, if you are a secondary candidate, you can fill out a demographic profile for the class that appears to be most challenging. The names in the binder should be alphabetically arranged. Your profile data should be transferred to this notebook, which can also serve as a reflections journal and a catalyst for planning and teaching. If you are like many other teachers, the act of writing about your students will stimulate new ideas for helping them maximize their learning.

The structure of the profile will encourage you to think about your students in terms of socially relevant groups (ethnic and cultural, for example), and the alphabetical arrangement in the loose-leaf notebook will encourage you to think about each student as an individual. Both documents provide you with a knowledge base that will help you think and plan from a multicultural perspective. The synthesis of your *general* knowledge about the goals of multicultural education and related teaching strategies, your *general* knowledge about characteristics of, and diversity within, selected ethnic and cultural groups, and your *specific* knowledge about each of your students and their families will allow you to teach insightfully from a multicultural perspective. Another instrument that helps prospective teachers comprehend the wide range of strategies associated with multicultural education is a tool we call the Typology of Multicultural Teaching. In the next section, we will briefly discuss the typology and its relationship to the demographic profile and planning lessons, lesson sequences, and units of instruction.

The Typology of Multicultural Teaching

The Typology of Multicultural Teaching is a listing of strategies that help teachers achieve each of the various goals of multicultural education. Each goal has its own list, but the strategies, such as cooperative learning, that helps to achieve more than one goal will appear on more than one list. When prospective and veteran teachers ask us what strategies we employ when we teach with a multicultural perspective, we invariably mention a few and then refer them to the typology. Most teachers find some strategies they use and a few that they could easily adopt or adapt. When you examine the full typology in Appendix 1, you should have a similar realization—namely, that multicultural teaching is well within your reach.

Because educational equity is a main theme in this chapter, we will enumerate the teaching strategies listed under educational equity in the typology. The lists in the typology are meant to be suggestive rather than definitive.

The Typology
I. Examples of Type I Multicultural (MC) Planning and Teaching (Planning and teaching that is directly aimed at educational equity)
The teacher:
   A. makes sophisticated use of the elements of instruction (selecting an objective at the appropriate level of difficulty, teaching to an objective, monitoring and adjusting, using the principles of learning, etc.).
   B. selects and utilizes a classroom management system that maximizes the amount of time he or she has available for individual tutoring.
   C. modifies his or her oral pace and syntax to facilitate the learning of language and content material for English learners as well as other special learners.
   D. allows one student to serve as a buddy tutor, interpreter, or assistant teacher to facilitate the learning of another student.

E. makes appropriate use of cooperative learning strategies and tactics associated with specially designed academic instruction in English (SDAIE).

F. uses a variety of techniques and content to demonstrate powerfully that in contemporary America, men and women of all colors and ethnic groups are succeeding in a wide range of occupations, such as

1. Friday afternoon "career awareness" interviews in which a wide range of successful Americans are interviewed by students;
2. classroom bulletin boards;
3. magazines such as *Ebony* and *Hispanic* (which regularly contain stories about successful African Americans and Hispanic Americans);
4. book and video reports;
5. "Upward Bound" visitors (junior high school and high school students who attend special activities to prepare them for college);
6. trips to local businesses and universities to meet successful role models.

G. uses teaching techniques and curriculum materials from specially designed projects such as the Complex Instruction Project (Rachel Lotan, Stanford University, 415-723-5661); Success for All/Roots and Wings (Robert E. Slavin, Center for Social Organization of Schools, 800-548-4998); Accelerated Schools (Claudette Spriggs, Stanford University, 415-725-7158); Multicultural Reading and Thinking (Janita Hoskyn, National Consultant, McRat Program, 501-225-5809); and Advancement Via Individual Determination (Mary Catherine Swanson, AVID Center, San Diego, 619-682-5050).

H. pays serious and consistent attention to the idea that specific teacher behaviors and knowledge can make classroom learning more efficient and equitable for both girls and boys.

I. employs rules consistently across ethnic, racial, cultural, and gender groups—for example, does not allow boys to call out and expect girls to patiently raise their hands.

J. employs and models nonsexist language, such as saying "police officers" rather than "policemen" and "firefighters" rather than "firemen."

K. utilizes texts, videos, websites, speakers and so on to accurately portray the contributions of women and other cultural, ethnic, and racial groups, and the struggles these groups have had to wage to achieve full-status citizenship in the United States.

L. creates and maintains a classroom environment free of ethnic, racial, sexual, or other forms of harassment.

M. promotes junior high school and high school graduation and college attendance by engaging in "follow-through" and "future prediction" oral behavior, such as the following:

1. "I want you (all) to let me know when you graduate from high school (or junior high school)."
2. "When you children are in high school (or college), you are going to remember this lesson."

3. "I know that some of the children in this class will want to become classroom teachers, and if this is your goal I'll do what I can to help you achieve it." An example of follow-through behavior is the work of one local first-grade teacher who sends out congratulation cards to her students when they graduate from high school, 10 or 11 years later.

N. engages in student, peer, and self-evaluation to monitor, assess, and perhaps modify the distribution of attention, higher level questions and wait-time, and leadership opportunities to various individuals and groups in the class, women and men, African Americans and Whites, and so on.

O. employs a flexible mastery-learning model of instruction (pretest/posttest, carefully constructed teaching units, carefully prepared backup teaching strategies).

P. includes self-confidence and self-esteem building as part of the affective/cognitive curriculum.

Q. seeks out and makes professional use of parent volunteers and bilingual/trilingual aides if needed.

R. makes use of informal "interest" and "learning style" inventories to more insightfully address the student's interests, learning preferences, and learning style or strengths.

S. develops a multiability curriculum that allows a variety of academic skills to receive classroom and teacher recognition as important.

T. makes certain that students receive their fair share of instructional resources and technology.

U. creates a collaborative/supportive learning environment—We're all in this together; we're here to learn and grow as individuals and partners; in this class we will be facilitators for each other's success."

V. examines attendance records to get an early start on implementing plans designed to lower the absence rate of specific learners.

W. collects and analyzes data from a survey of television watching to increase his ability to modify patterns of excessive viewing where appropriate, and follows up with a second survey later in the semester.

X. strives to keep academic expectations high and within reach of the learners.

Y. teaches students that error, failure, struggle, and success are natural parts of the learning process, particularly when one is studying a wide range of required subjects (which is the basic K–12 reality).

Z. works with other teachers to create interdisciplinary units that connect school learning to real-world issues.

AA. seeks to create learning experiences that capitalize on and expand students' strengths and weaknesses.

AB. uses a variety of instructional materials (videos, computer programs, guest speakers, various print materials, etc.) to present the official curriculum and allows students to provide input to help shape that curriculum.

AC. works with other teachers and professional organizations to make certain that students are getting a "fair shake" when it comes to the allocation of resources within the school, school district, and state.

AD. develops a plan to learn *all* student names and other background information as quickly as possible in the school semester, constantly uses the names, and encourages students to learn and use each other's names—this reinforces the community-of-learners concept.

AE. reveals to students in specific numerical terms the payoff that may follow from hard work in general and a college education specifically (Jaime Escalante, for example, brings back former students who are college graduates to tell his current students how much money they are making). You should help students see the useful things they can do for themselves, their family, and their community after they graduate from high school (and perhaps college).

AF. reflects on and analyzes her own pedagogy. For example, if you teach in tracked or quasi-tracked settings, monitor and question your own practices.
   For instance:
   1. Are the teaching strategies employed in one of my classes different from those in another, and, if so, is this warranted?
   2. Am I providing a more challenging curriculum in one section than another, and, if so, is this warranted? Could the degree of challenge in the "lesser" class be increased?

AG. analyzes seating patterns in various sections to see whether racial, ethnic, and/or gender (self-) segregation is occurring; if so, attempts to determine whether this pattern is antithetical to course objectives.

AH. accepts, supports, and dignifies the first language (L_1) or dialect that students bring to school, and encourages students to use L_1 as they develop second-language capability, and also encourages the development of bilinguality but respects the decision of students and parents who opt for monolinguality.

AI. supports plans to modify or eliminate tracking systems that channel students away from appropriate educational opportunities (i.e., honors and AP classes in high school).

AJ. employs portfolio and other forms of authentic assessment that allow the teacher to share the responsibility of assessment with the learner.

AK. provides support for, or helps to create, a Future Teachers' Club, and uses this club as a vehicle to help recruit a broader group of individuals into the teaching profession.

With regard to learning names, a strategy we use in our college courses may be adaptable in some K–12 settings. During the first or second session of our courses, we have students provide the following information on the back of a 3-by-5 card:

   a. name, phone number, and E-mail address
   b. four adjectives that accurately describe the student's personality

    c. hobbies

    d. future career aspirations

    e. favorite relaxation strategies

    f. key cultural group affiliations (this is filled in after a presentation and exercise on culture and identity)

    g. favorite movies (or books, etc.)

    h. specific program information (secondary mathematics, counseling and guidance, elementary education, etc.)

During the session we also photocopy each student's I.D. card (which has a photograph) and then tape the photocopy to the front of the index card. Thus, prior to our second meeting, we have a picture to help us memorize names, and a conveniently accessible database that can be used in a variety of ways to personalize instruction and build rapport. In particular, this has proven to be a valuable strategy for getting to know the quiet, back-of-the-room type of students who are often the last to make a footprint in our short-term memory banks.

SUMMARY

When you understand the goals of multicultural education, are aware of strategies associated with these goals, have completed a first round of interviews with educators at your school site, and have extended the demographic profile into a more expansive notebook, you are ready to apply your synthesis of this database to the lessons and units you will implement in your student teaching assignment. In the next chapter, "before" and "after" examples of individual lesson and lesson sequences from various content areas and grade levels will be presented and discussed to show how lessons that reflect a monocultural, Eurocentric orientation can be modified to become multicultural. We call this process *multiculturalizing* the curriculum; we accomplish this expansion in many different ways as we draw on strategies associated with the various goals of multicultural education. However, we urge you, before venturing on to Chapter 3, to spend time with the discussion questions and recommended activities that follow. They were formulated to help you flesh out your own multicultural perspective and will encourage you to observe teachers who are effective practitioners of cooperative learning and specially designed academic instruction in English, which is still referred to as *sheltered English instruction* in various parts of the United States.

DISCUSSION QUESTIONS

1. Consider once again the words of Chief Justice Earl Warren and then select one or more of the following questions to respond to:

   "In these days, it is doubtful that any child may reasonably be expected to succeed in life if he is denied the opportunity of an education. Such an opportunity, where the state has undertaken to provide it, is a right which must be made available to all on equal terms."

a. Analyze the ideas of *equal terms* or *equal opportunity* from the perspective of a district superintendent, school principal, and classroom teacher. What are some important responsibilities each should assume or activities each can carry out to promote equality of educational opportunity for all their students?

b. What are some practices in your university or former high school that you consider to be strategies designed to promote equality of educational opportunity? From your perspective, how well did these strategies work? What are your personal feelings about equality of educational opportunity and associated strategies?

c. Have you or any of your friends benefited directly or indirectly from equity-oriented or affirmative action strategies? If so, describe them. If there have been negative repercussions associated with these benefits, identify and discuss these as well.

d. In 1954 when Justice Warren wrote his famous opinion, the issue at hand was segregated schools versus integrated schools. Currently, in schools in which 90 to 100 percent of the students are White American, Black American, or Latino American, can there be equality of educational opportunity? If so, what conditions and programs in the ethnically homogeneous school would be associated with such equality? If you respond to this question, consider both qualitative and quantitative conditions.

2. Given a high-SES elementary school (no students eligible for free or subsidized free lunch, etc.) and a low-SES elementary school (85 percent of students eligible for free or subsidized free lunch, etc.) in the same school district, if you were the district superintendent:

a. What data would you examine to ensure that at each school a strong effort was being made to provide "equality of educational opportunity" to each student?

b. What special programs would you initiate at the low-SES school if you discovered that students there started out one to two grades behind the high-SES students, and fell further behind each year they attended school?

3. In the section on "Class-building" Activities we say that you can promote a democratic and collaborative [classroom] ethos by (a) holding classroom meetings to help establish a set of classroom rules and consequences and (b) explaining to your class that your use of classroom meetings is part of a larger objective, namely the establishment of a democratic listening, thinking, questioning, learning environment. With such an environment in mind, answer one or more of the following questions:

a. Given the top/down nonconsultative nature of much classroom and school-site decision making, is it meaningful and/or realistic to talk about the establishment of a democratic classroom learning environment? Why? Why not?

b. Based on your idea of what makes a classroom learning environment democratic as opposed to authoritarian or autocratic, identify three to five things you would do at the beginning of the school year to set a democratic learning environment in motion in a specific instructional setting (e.g., an eighth- or eleventh-grade math class or a third- or sixth-grade elementary class).

c. What critical characteristics, in your opinion, make a democratic learning environment different than an autocratic learning environment?

4. Earlier in this chapter we wrote: "Increasingly since the 1970s, educational equity and educational excellence have become intertwined concepts. Because of this integration of meaning, when we evaluate the quality of K–12 educational organization, we no longer look only at overall graduation rates, overall admittance to community colleges, overall anything; excellence is now closely related to the

organization's success with the varied ethnic and cultural groups that make up its student body."

    a. Do you think this new group-oriented conception of organizational excellence is sensible? Why or why not? In what sense might your opinion be only part of the truth?

    b. If the integrated, multigroup conception of excellence is accurate and you aspire to be an excellent teacher, what specific implications does the integrated concept have for you in terms of classroom teaching, evaluation of students, teacher self-evaluation, and your own professional development?

5. In the section on student records, we wrote: "We consider the examination of [student] files [and portfolios] to be the professional responsibility of a multicultural educator and encourage you to pay attention to the information shared by your colleagues as well as your own professional instincts." After examining a duplicate set of real records (with all names removed and surrogates inserted) provided by your professor, discuss the strengths and weaknesses of our opinion about early, prior-to-school-opening, examination of your students' files (and portfolios, if available). In your response, specify (a) the type of information you discovered that would contribute to your ability to be effective as a multicultural educator and (b) the information you did not find but would like to see made a part of the official cumulative file.

6. In chapter 2 we suggest that teachers should learn as much as possible about the traditional communication patterns, educational values, and culture of new American immigrant and refugee groups they are interacting with, as well as the communication patterns of indigenous American minorities—African Americans and Native Americans.

    a. Does this seem reasonable to you? If so, explain why.

    b. Does this recommendation seem unreasonable to you? Do you feel that too much emphasis is being placed on Americans learning about immigrant cultures (from all over the world), when, in fact, these immigrants and refugees have come here to become Americans? If you lean toward this feeling, indicate what you think teachers should learn about the various immigrant, refugee, and indigenous American groups they will be teaching.

    c. Do you think it is wise for schools to send home letters in the language that is spoken at home, as well as in English? Why or why not? Where possible, share personal experiences as well as research pertinent to your opinion.

7. In a school or classroom in which cooperative learning groups (with consistent heterogeneous grouping) are employed for approximately 40 percent of instruction, and in which cooperative learning and other strategies have produced, for three consecutive years, modest gains on standardized test scores, should the teacher or school faculty accept a proposal that would dramatically reduce the cooperative learning in the school or classroom? In developing your response, indicate

    a. whether you are considering this issue from the classroom or from school-site perspective (in either case, you take the role of teacher);

    b. what other kinds of data should be examined and why they should be included; and

    c. other recommendations that might be appropriate for a multicultural curriculum-oriented educator to make.

    d. Would your position on cooperative learning (40 percent of the time, with emphasis on heterogeneous grouping) and your specific recommendations change if the test scores had shown a slight decline for the past two years?

Where possible, share personal experiences as well as research that supports your response.

8. In chapter 2 we suggest that classroom teachers should give serious attention to recruiting students of color (as well as White-American students) into the teaching profession. However, well-intentioned educators, like us, are constantly placing new demands on classroom teachers without significantly adding to their resources (fewer students, more school days or hours, more funds for instructional programs, etc.). Focus on the specific grades you teach or expect to teach (K-3, 4-8, 9-12) and then answer one or both of the following questions.

   a. Should teachers (new and veteran) be concerned—month after month across the school year—with the short- and long-term recruitment of teachers into the profession? Explain your response.

   b. If you consider the recruitment recommendation to have merit, what specific tactics could a teacher employ in developing an ongoing, subtle, and sometimes explicit recruitment campaign? In answering this question, consider the possible use of the content of your curriculum.

9. Describe the school, in terms of socioeconomic levels, ethnic composition, and locale (urban, suburban, rural), that you would like to teach in for the first year or next three years of your career, and then answer the following questions:

   a. On what basis did you decide this would be your ideal school? Be as candid as possible in delineating your reasons.

   b. Were you surprised by the characteristics of the school you described? Speculate about the reasons for your response.

   c. Does the school setting in which you would like to teach require any special preparation? If yes, what would you do to gain such experience and knowledge?

10. On occasion, the values embedded in the various goals of multicultural education (e.g., intergroup and interethnic harmony, freedom, cultural pluralism, educational equity) may conflict with one another if the teacher tries simultaneously to achieve all the goals with each student in the class. For example, it would be difficult to promote gender, ethnic, and cultural equity and, at the same time, provide respect and support for a family, ethnic, or cultural group that explicitly promotes racism or sexism. How would you, as a fifth- or tenth-grade teacher, handle the following situation?

A husband and wife asked you to stop reading and discussing a specific book in your class because they feel it promotes radical feminism. (You can modify this question by substituting another term, such as interracial dating, atheism, racism, satanism, or secular humanism.) The couple met with you to discuss the problem. You listened patiently and respectfully (you thought) and suggested that they were overinterpreting both the theme of the story and your intent in selecting the story. Although you appreciated their concern, you intended to continue reading and discussing the story in question. Now they and another parent, whom you have not met, have complained to your principal, and they have enlarged their complaint to include what they call your "persistent use of cooperative learning groups to promote feminism and secular humanism." Your principal would like you to meet with all three parents to hear their concerns.

Assuming that you agree to the meeting, how could you use the school district's support of multicultural education to address the concerns of these parents? Should you meet the parents alone or invite the principal to attend?

11. We recommend that elementary and secondary school teachers (in their effort to achieve educational equity) consider speaking with parents whose children have

a poor attendance record. In this discussion the teacher would suggest that, by collaborating, the teacher and the parents could improve the student's attendance rate and academic achievement. We make this recommendation because of studies like the Aspira Five Cities High School Dropout Study, which suggests that absences, grades, and age are critical factors in predicting whether Latino students will finish high school or drop out.[97]

- a. Do you consider the monitoring of attendance to be a significant aspect of multicultural education? Why or why not?
- b. A Mexican-American student in fourth grade has been absent for 23 days in the first grade, 31 days in the second grade, and 28 days in the third grade, and is one to two years below grade level in all tested academic areas. Would you share this information with the parents at an early meeting? If so, how would you go about it? Would you do the same for any student in your class?
- c. If you would not share the information at the beginning of the year, what is your rationale for not doing so?

12. We believe that what the teacher selects to teach (concepts, books, films, etc.) and how the teacher chooses to present required content is strongly linked to educational equity. In other words, the selection and treatment of content greatly influences the motivation and achievement levels in your class and also influences students' perception of reality.

- a. Drawing on your own experience as a learner and your more general experience as a student who has interacted with other learners, discuss your reactions to this assertion.
- b. Assuming that the aforementioned assertion is true, do you think that, for a unit on the Civil War in a fifth- or eleventh-grade class, the specific instructional decisions regarding content and treatment would differ according to whether the students were
  - (1) 90 percent African American, with the remainder Latino American;
  - (2) 80 percent White American, with some Asian-, African-, and Latino-American students;
  - (3) 80 percent Latino American, with some African-American and Asian-American students?
    - a. If yes, please specify how your selection and treatment of content might vary and explain the rationale for the variation.
    - b. If no, explain why the set of instructional resources and treatment of content would remain the same.
    - c. Would anything change in (1) or (2) if the unit was taught in a former Confederate state—for example, Georgia or South Carolina? What new factors and opportunities might come into play when you add geography to the context of this question?

13. Earlier we wrote: "The synthesis of your *general* knowledge about the goals of multicultural education and related teaching strategies, your *general* knowledge about characteristics of, and diversity within, selected ethnic and cultural groups, and your *specific* knowledge about each of your students and their families will allow you to teach insightfully from a multicultural perspective." In your own words explain what this statement is trying to communicate. In identifying three categories of knowledge that will allow you to teach with a multicultural perspective, have we left out a fourth and perhaps a fifth category of pertinent knowledge? If so, identify and discuss its relationship to insightful multicultural teaching.

14. Programs that aim at equal educational opportunity and equal educational results can lead to some confusing situations. Some teachers think that to pursue these goals, they must treat all their students equally—or the same—although the law and common sense suggest otherwise. For example, we believe it is practical and wise to distribute praise and classroom responsibilities in a fair and roughly equivalent manner but dysfunctional to try to give each child a quantitatively equal amount of attention or individual tutoring on a daily basis. Indeed, the at-risk concept would suggest that some students should receive more individual tutoring than others on a regular basis.

   a. In what areas of schooling, if any, should teachers and administrators strive to achieve quantitative equivalency in the education of their students?
   b. In what areas of classroom and school activity should teachers ignore quantitative equivalency as they seek to establish a fair learning environment for all students? Be as specific as possible in your responses and explain your choices.

15. Recently, a fifth-grade teacher, Mr. Roberti, in a graduate course that focuses on the interaction of culture, education, and learning, made the following statement:

   "Now that I know that in Mexico many parents do not have a tradition of actively participating in their child's school life—they turn education over to the teacher—I will not criticize my Mexican-American parents or take it personally when they do not show up for events like Back-to-School Night."

   a. What is your reaction to this statement?
   b. If this were a staff development meeting in which teachers were discussing how their new knowledge of Mexican culture and Mexican-American culture had influenced their teaching, and you were the staff development specialist and moderator of the meeting, how would you respond if a teacher asked you, in the group setting, what you thought about Mr. Roberti's "application of new knowledge"?
   c. What else do you want to know about Mr. Roberti's new attitude toward Mexican-American parents? What main message do you want him to take back to his classroom?

16. Create and answer your own questions about the educational equity or empowerment component of multicultural education, or any of the empowerment elements discussed in this chapter.

17. In the overview to this chapter, we wrote that "dramatic inequality of educational opportunity still prevails in many schools, school districts, and states," and that "this inequality is accepted as the natural order of things by a major segment of the American population."

   a. Indicate whether you agree or disagree with the statements; and support your response by alluding to specific legislation, educational conditions or programs, and/or statistical data.
   b. Do you believe that politicians in your state, province, or nation value equality of educational opportunity as much as or more than they value inequality of educational opportunity? Explain your response by alluding to specific legislation, educational conditions or programs, and/or statistical data.

18. What do you think were the three or four most important points made in this chapter? Why were these your choices?

19. What question(s) would you like to ask the authors? Try to answer one of these yourself. If time permits, consider sharing your answer and/or question with us

via E-mail. We will do our best to respond in a prompt fashion. See the preface for our E-mail address, and note that we may list your question and all or part of your answer (but not your name) on our World Wide Web homepage.

RECOMMENDED ACTIVITIES

1. On your own or with the help of your professor, arrange to observe in one or more classrooms in which the instructor has a reputation for the creative and effective use of cooperative learning groups. If possible, observe on more than one occasion and pay close attention to the interaction within two different groups in the classroom. In addition, try to structure the observation so that you will be able to (a) interview a few students immediately after the lesson, (b) interview the teacher after you have completed your observation in the class, and (c) go with one or more of your fellow students or colleagues so you can observe different groups and share your perceptions. The Cooperative Learning Group Observation Form in Appendix 4 may help you focus your observation and provide a database from which to generate questions for your follow-up interviews. Feel free to add, delete, and rephrase questions.

2. On your own or with the help of your instructor, arrange to observe in one or more classrooms in which the teacher has a reputation for the effective use of "specially designed academic instruction in English" (SDAIE) strategies. These are techniques that nonbilingual teachers use to increase the comprehensibility of instruction, particularly in content areas like history, science, and math. The instruction by the teacher is typically in English, but students are sometimes encouraged to use their primary language to help themselves and other learners develop proficiency in the new language. Bilingual teachers also make use of SDAIE, but the technique is associated with teachers who are not fluent in their students' primary languages. To increase the value of your observation, follow instructions (a), (b), and (c) in activity 1 as you use the SDAIE observation form in Appendix 3.

3. Working individually, or as part of a cooperative learning group,
   a. expand the list of strategies delineated in part A of the Typology of Multicultural Teaching (see Appendix 1);
   b. examine the entire typology (in Appendix 1) and add one or two strategies to each category;
   c. in each category put an asterisk by the strategies you consider most appropriate for your classroom, or one of your classes, or your student teaching assignment;
   d. share your new items and selected strategies with a classmate or members of your cooperative learning group.

4. Arrange to have several local principals or superintendents address your class as a panel to discuss selected discussion questions from Chapter 2. Structure the presentation so that it resembles Meet the Press, the Sunday morning news show. If possible, arrange to have the panel discussion videotaped.

5. View the Association for Supervision and Curriculum Development (ASCD) videotape Multicultural Education Goals: Teaching Strategies and Evaluation. Compare and contrast the goals presented in this videotape with the goals and strategies presented in Chapters 1 and 2. Or carry out the same task with the videotape entitled Multicultural Education produced by ASCD in 1994.

6. Use the 1994 ASCD *Multicultural Education* videotape and its accompanying Facilitator's Guide to plan a three-hour workshop for your school faculty or another deserving group.

7. Select one of the questions (1)–(7) in the "Planning a Curriculum of Empowerment" section of this chapter. With your current class in mind, spell out a detailed response to one or two of the questions.
8. Interview the appropriate professor on your campus and/or educational administrator in your region regarding the state and federal court decisions that have been most influential in fostering educational equity in your state. Prepare a summary for your colleagues.
9. Equal opportunity under the law has been interpreted to mean the right to be employed or considered for employment without prejudice or discrimination on the grounds of race, gender, or physical challenge. Conduct interviews with human resources and/or affirmative action directors to help answer these questions.
    a. How have affirmative action policies in your school district or university served to create and maintain equal employment opportunity?
    b. In which situations, if any, have affirmative action policies clashed with the concept of equal employment opportunity?
    c. In the situations in which affirmative action and equal employment opportunity (or equal protection under the law) have clashed, was there a sound legal and/or moral principle to provide guidance to the decision makers?

Journal Entry

Since this chapter has put you in touch with ideas related to the creation of equity conditions in your own classroom, or the classroom to which you will be assigned during student teaching, your journal entry should concentrate on the most significant things you have learned about this important area of teaching. More specifically, you could comment on the following:

1. what educational equity and/or democratic practice now means to you—when trying to create equity and/or democratic conditions in your classroom, what will you be doing? (for the in-service teacher)
2. equity-oriented strategies that you think you will use during student teaching and then those you think you will use in your first year of teaching (for the prospective teacher)
3. unresolved questions and feelings that you may have regarding educational equity, democratic practice, and multicultural education
4. the relationship between your earlier understanding and more recent understanding of educational equity and/or democratic practice in the classroom.

NOTES

1. See *Simple Justice: The History of Brown v. Board of Education and Black America's Struggle for Equality* by Richard Kluger (New York: Random House, 1975) for details about the courageous legal campaign led by Charles H. Houston. For more information about Houston, see *Groundwork: Charles Hamilton Houston and the Struggle for Civil Rights* by Genna Rae McNeil (Philadelphia, University of Pennsylvania Press, 1983).
2. An excellent initial source is Lawrence H. Fuchs's *The American Kaleidoscope: Race, Ethnicity, and the Civic Culture* (Hanover, N.H.: University Press of New England, 1990). In addition, several chapters from *The Handbook of Research on*

Multicultural Education, ed. James A. Banks and Cherry A. McGee Banks (New York: Macmillan, 1995) will prove helpful. These include Eugene E. Garcia, "Educating Mexican American Students: Past Treatment and Recent Developments in Theory, Research, Policy, and Practice," 372–387, and Carol D. Lee and Diana T. Slaughter-Defoe, "Historical and Sociocultural Influences on African American Education," 348–371.

3. R. Freeman Butts, *Public Education in the United States: From Revolution to Reform* (New York: Holt, Rinehart, and Winston, 1978), 262–267.

4. Influential court cases or pieces of legislation include *Brown v. Board of Education of Topeka*, 347 U.S. 483 (1954); the Bilingual Education Act (PL 90–247); *Lau v. Nichols*, 414 U.S. 563 (1974), Titles VI and VII of the Civil Rights Act of 1964 (PL 88–352); and the Education for All Handicapped Children Act of 1975 (PL 94–142).

5. *Cooper v. Aaron*, 358 U.S. 1 (1958).

6. *Alexander v. Holmes County (Mississippi) Board of Education* 396 U.S. 19 (1969).

7. *Cisneros v. Corpus Christi Independent School District,* Civ. No. 68–C–95 (D.C.S.D. Tex. Corpus Christi Div. 1970).

8. *John Serrano, Jr. et al. v. Ivy Baker Priest,* 96 Cal. Rptr., 601 (August 30, 1971).

9. Charles Wollenberg, *All Deliberate Speed: Segregation and Exclusion in California Public Schools, 1855–1975* (Berkeley: University of California Press, 1976), 127.

10. Albert Camarillo, *Chicanos in California: A History of Mexican Americans in California* (San Francisco: Boyd and Fraser, 1984), 82.

11. Wollenberg, *All Deliberate Speed: Segregation and Exclusion in California Public Schools,* 1855–1975, 128.

12. *Abbott v. Burke,* 149 N.J. 145.

13. *Brown v. Board of Education of Topeka*, p. 493 (cited in Butts, *Public Education in the United States,* 328).

14. *John Serrano, Jr., et al. v. Ivy Baker Priest.*

15. *Abbott v. Burke,* 149 N.J. 145 at p. 201.

16. *Lau v. Nichols.*

17. Elementary and Secondary Education Act of 1965; the Indian Education Act of 1972, PL 92–318; Title IX, Education Amendment Acts, (1972); the Women's Educational Equity Act of 1974.

18. Isabel Bruder, "Restructuring through Technology," *Business Week,* December 10, 1990, 33–34, special education section.

19. Supreme Court of Kentucky, 88–SC–804–TG, *Rose v. Council for Better Education,* Opinion of the Court by Chief Justice Stephens, p. 2.

20. Deborah A. Verstegen, "The New Wave of School Finance Litigation," *Phi Delta Kappan* 76, no. 3 (November 1994): 243–250.

21. Ibid., 244.

22. Kerry A. White, "Finance Battles Show Solutions Remain Elusive," *Education Week* 16, no. 37 (June 11, 1997) 1 and 31. This article is available at www.edweek.org. Go to 'In Context' and click on 'Issues' and then 'School Finance.'

23. Verstegen, "The New Wave of School Finance Litigation," 244.

24. Ibid.

25. Caroline Hendrie, "New Jersey Schools Put Reform to the Test," *Education Week* 18, no. 32 (April 21, 1999): 1, 13–14.

26. Maria Newman, "State's School Commissioner Proposes $5.4 Billion Budget," *New York Times* (April 14, 1999): 6 (Section B).

27. After reaching the New Jersey homepage click on Education, then N.J. State Department of Education, and then Whole School Reform Models. Parenthetically, to reach the homepage of any other state substitute its letter abbreviation, that is, tx for Texas, for nj.

28. Robert E. Slavin and Olatokumbo S. Fashola, *Show Me the Evidence! Proven and Promising Programs for America's Schools* (Thousand Oaks, Calif.: Corwin Press, 1998), 12–35.

29. Caroline Hendrie, "New Jersey Schools Put Reform to the Test," 13.

30. Juan Williams, "Integration Turns 40: The New Segregation," *Modern Maturity* 37, no. 2 (April/May 1994): 24–32. The statistics cited in this article are from a 1993 report, *The Growth of Segregation in American Schools: Changing Patterns of Separation and Poverty Since 1968.* It is available from the National School Boards Association, P. O. Box 630422, Baltimore, MD 21263-0422. The phone number is 703-838-6753.

31. Gary Orfield and John T. Yun, *Resegregation in American Schools* (Cambridge, Mass.: Harvard University Civil Rights Project, 1999). The report is based on data compiled by the National Center for Education Statistics through 1996–1997. As of June 14, 1999, the report can be downloaded at www.law.harvard.edu/civilrights/.

32. Orfield and Yun, *Resegregation in American Schools.* The quoted material is from the media advisory summary which accompanies the report.

33. Orfield and Yun, *Resegregation in American Schools*, media advisory summary.

34. See Peter Schmidt's article "New Jersey Supreme Court Affirms Study of Merging 3 Districts," *Education Week,* June 23, 1993, p. 1, which discusses the court's decision to uphold a lower court ruling that required the state to consider merging three school districts to effect greater racial integration. See also Kerry A. White's article "Lengthy Trial in Charlotte Desegregation Lawsuit Winds Down," *Education Week,* June 23, 1999, p. 5 (vol. 18, no. 4) which discusses efforts by several white families to end Charlotte-Mecklenburg School District's 30-year integration plan and efforts by black families and school district officials to keep it in place.

35. For example, Jonathan Kozol, in a brief essay entitled "The New Untouchables" (*Newsweek,* Special Edition, *The 21st Century Family,* Winter/Spring 1990), points out that the schools serving the relatively wealthy communities of Great Neck and White Plains, New York, spend twice as much per pupil as the schools serving the children of the Bronx, New York. In a related article entitled "Children at Risk" (*Newsweek,* March 12, 1990), Kozol reports that "in 1980 the wealthiest school districts in New Jersey spent $800 more per child than the poorest districts. Today they spend $3,000 more." Similarly, the same gap in Texas was $600 in 1978, and today it is $5,000. Kozol summarizes and extends his remarks on inequality in American public schools in *Savage Inequalities* (Southbridge, Mass.: Crown, 1991). An interesting critique of one of Kozol's themes, equalization, appears in Peter Shrag's essay "Savage Inequalities," *New Republic,* December 16, 1991, 18–20.

36. Robert C. Johnston, "Study Reveals Funding Gap Across the States," *Education Week* 16, no. 25 (March 19, 1997): 1 and 30.

37. Aaron M. Pallas et al., "The Changing Nature of the Disadvantaged Population: Current Dimensions and Future Trends," *Educational Researcher* 18, no. 5, (1989): 16–22.

38. In a decision in 1974 (*Millikan v. Bradley*), the U.S. Supreme Court made clear that it would not support "metropolitanization" plans that would achieve integration of Whites and Blacks by requiring the merger of city school districts with surrounding, largely White suburban districts. See Percy Bates, "Desegregation: Can We Get

There from Here?" *Phi Delta Kappan* 72, no. 2 (September 1990): 13, for a discussion of *Millikan v. Bradley.*

39. Kerry A. White, "Wisconsin Plan to End Milwaukee Busing Advances," *Education Week* 18, no. 40 (June 16, 1999): 3.
40. Philip Kaufman, Steve Klein, and Mary Frase, "Dropout Rates in the United States: 1997 (NCES-082), (Washington, D.C.: National Center for Education Statistics, 1999) 16.
41. Thomas Nagel, "Desegregation, Education or Both" (1988), unpublished manuscript. Nagel can be contacted through the School of Education at California State University, San Diego, 619-594-1425.
42. See the Issues page at the *Education Week* website www.edweek.org to see a brief essay and links to relevant articles about reconstituted schools, privatization, vouchers, charter schools, school reform networks, gender equity, etc.
43. Kerry A. White, "New Jersey Plans to End Takeover in Jersey City," *Education Week* 18, no. 39 (June 9, 1999): 1 and 11.
44. See Nancy Gibb's article "Schools for Profit" (*Time,* October 17, 1994, 48-49), which describes a decision by the Hartford, Connecticut, School Board to hire Education Alternatives, Inc., a Minnesota-based private firm, to manage its $200 million budget and 32 public schools, and George Judson's article "Private Business, Public Schools: Why Hartford Experiment Failed" (*New York Times,* March 11, 1996, A-1) which explains why Education Alternatives, Inc. was dismissed without ever taking control of the district's finances.
45. Kenneth A. Sirotnick, "Equal Access to Quality in Public Schooling: Issues in the Assessment of Equity and Excellence," chap. 9 in *Access to Knowledge: An Agenda for Our Nation's Schools,* ed. John I. Goodlad and Pamela Keating (New York: The College Board, 1990), 159.
46. Ibid., 159.
47. Ibid., 169-173.
48. Elliot W. Eisner, "What Really Counts in Schools," *Educational Leadership* 48, no. 5 (February 1991): 17.
49. Ibid.
50. Christine I. Bennett, *Comprehensive Multicultural Education:Theory and PracticeI, 4th ed.* (Needham Heights, Mass.: Allyn and Bacon, 1999), 15.
51. Ibid., 12.
52. Ibid., 16.
53. Patrice LeBlanc Kohl and Elaine P. Witty, "Equity Challenges," chap. 39 in the *Handbook of Research on Teacher Education,* 2nd ed., ed. John Sikula (New York: Simon & Schuster Macmillan, 1996), 838.
54. Ibid., 837.
55. Ibid.
56. Ibid.
57. Christine I. Bennett, *Comprehensive Multicultural Education:Theory and Practice,* 15.
58. Carl Grant, "Challenging the Myths about Multicultural Education," *Multicultural Education* 2, no. 2 (Winter 1994): 4.
59. Robert Slavin, "Where Should the Money Go," in *Funding for Justice: Money, Equity, and the Future of Public Education,* ed. Stan Karp, Robert Lowe, Barbara Miner, and Bob Peterson (Milwaukee, Wis.: Rethinking Schools, 1997), 32-33.
60. J. Naughton, "Women in Division One Sports Programs: The Glass Is Half Empty and Half Full," *The Chronicle of Higher Education* 43, no. 31 (April 11, 1997): A39-A40.

61. Ibid.
62. Geneva Gay, "Ethnic Minorities and Educational Equality," chap. 9 in *Multicultural Education: Issues and Perspectives,* 2nd ed., ed. James A. Banks and Cherry A. McGee Banks (Boston: Allyn and Bacon, 1993), 183.
63. Ibid., 186.
64. Ibid., 172.
65. Ibid., 188–190.
66. Ultimately, when considering educational equity, the investigator must compare school districts with other school districts and states with states.
67. Robert B. Reich, "Metamorphosis of the American Worker," *Business Week,* November 1990, 58.
68. Iram Valentin, "Title IX: A Brief History," *WEEA Digest,* (August 1997): 1. The Digest is published by the Women's Educational Equity Act Resource Center, 55 Chapel Street, Newton, MA 0245 (800-225-3088). As of Sept. 1999, copies of this and other digests were available at www.edc.org/WomensEquity/pubs/digests.
69. Ibid., 4–5.
70. National Coalition for Women and Girls in Education, "Executive Summary—Title IX at 25: Report Card on Gender Equity," 1997, http://www.org/1000/summary.html (August 26, 1999).
71. Valentin, "Title IX: A Brief History," 1.
72. Judith Kleinfeld, "Why Smart People Believe that Schools Shortchange Girls: What You See When You Live in a Tail," *Gender Issues* 16, no. 1-2 (Winter/Spring 1998): 47–63. See also the debate between Janice Weinman and Judith Kleinfeld in "Do Public Schools Shortchange Girls on Educational Opportunities?" *Insight on the News* 14, no. 46 (December 14, 1998): 24–28, and Kleinfeld's article "Student Performance: Males versus Females," *The Public Interest,* no. 134 (Winter 1999): 3–20.
73. Jack Frymier, with Larry Barber, Ruben Carriedo, et al., *Growing Up Is Risky Business, and Schools Are Not to Blame,* Final Report, Phi Delta Kappa Study of Students at Risk, Vol. 1. (Bloomington, Ind.: Phi Delta Kappa, 1992), 161–164.
74. Ibid., 161.
75. John I. Goodlad, "The Occupation of Teaching in Schools," in *The Moral Dimensions of Teaching,* ed. John I. Goodlad, Roger Soder, and Kenneth A. Sirotnick (San Francisco: Jossey-Bass, 1991), 17.
76. Donald C. Lueder, "Tennessee Parents Were Invited to Participate and They Did," *Educational Leadership* 47, no. 2 (October 1989): 15–17; see also Jim Cummins, "Empowering Minority Students: A Framework for Intervention," *Harvard Educational Review* 56, no. 1 (February 1986): 18–36, in which he links student empowerment to improved communication between teachers and parents, student goal setting, and the use of minority students' language and culture in the school curriculum.
77. Madeline Hunter, "Join the 'Par-aide' in Education," *Educational Leadership* 47, no. 2 (October 1989): 36–41.
78. Robert E. Slavin, *Cooperative Learning: Theory, Research, and Practice,* 2nd ed. (Boston: Allyn and Bacon, 1995).
79. Ibid., 21.
80. Ibid.
81. Slavin and Fashola, *Show Me the Evidence! Proven and Promising Programs for America's Schools,* 37–38.
82. Slavin, *Cooperative Learning: Theory, Research, and Practice,* 52.
83. Walter Donway, "The Demographic Imperative, Undergraduate Mathematics, the Ph.D. Crisis, American High Schools, and the Cost of Change—A Wide Ranging

Interview with Uri Treisman, Ph.D.," Charles A. Dana Foundation Report 5, no. 1 (Spring 1990).

84. John O'Neil, "On Tracking and Individual Differences: A Conversation with Jeannie Oakes," *Educational Leadership* 50, no. 2 (October 1992): 18–21; see also Jeannie Oakes, *Keeping Track: How Schools Structure Inequality* (New Haven: Yale University Press, 1985) and *Multiplying Inequalities: The Effects of Race, Social Class, and Tracking on Opportunities to Learn Mathematics and Science* (Santa Monica, Calif.: Rand, 1991); Jeannie Oakes and Martin Lipton, "Tracking and Ability Grouping: A Structural Barrier to Access and Achievement," chap. 10 in *Access to Knowledge,* ed. Goodlad and Keating (New York: The College Board, 1990).

85. Thomas D. Snyder, Charlene M. Hoffman, and Claire M. Geddes, *Digest of Education Statistics, 1997* (Washington, D.C.: National Center for Education Statistics, U.S. Department of Education, 1997), 79. This publication is available at www.nces.ed.gov. See table 069 (selected characteristics of public school teachers: Spring 1961 to Spring 1996) in chapter two.

86. Ibid.

87. Ibid., 60. See table 045 (Enrollment in public elementary and secondary schools by race or ethnicity and state: Fall 1986 and Fall 1995) in chapter 2.

88. Ibid.

89. Women's Educational Equity Act Resource Center, "Equity Online," 1998, http://www.edc.org/WomensEquity/edequity/index. html (September 2, 1999).

90. See Imogene C. Brower, "Counseling Vietnamese," chap. 9 in *Counseling American Minorities: A Cross-Cultural Perspective,* 3rd ed., ed. Donald R. Atkinson, George Morten, and Derald Wing Sue (Dubuque, Iowa: William C. Brown, 1989). Margaret A. Gibson makes a similar point about Punjabi-Sikh immigrants in her chapter, "Punjabi Immigrants in an American High School," in *Interpretive Ethnography of Education at Home and Abroad,* ed. George and Louise Spindler (Hillsdale, N.J.: Lawrence Erlbaum, 1987). Bruce Thowpaou Bliatout et al. make a similar comment about Hmong Americans in chapter 2 of *Handbook for Teaching Hmong-Speaking Students,* Folsom Folsom-Cordova Unified School District, California, 1988. This book can be ordered by calling 916-635-6815.

91. See Brower, "Counseling Vietnamese" and Gibson, "Punjabi Immigrants in an American High School."

92. Spencer Kagan, *Cooperative Learning: Resources for Teachers* (San Juan Capistrano, Calif.: Resources for Teachers, 1989), chap. 2, 2.

93. Ibid., chap. 8, 4.

94. Ibid., chap. 7, 1.

95. Ibid., chap. 7, 3.

96. *Communicating with Parents,* by Marcia Boruta, Janet Chrispeels, and Mary Daughtery, is available from the San Diego County Office of Education, Graphic Communications, Room 212, 6401 Linda Vista Road, San Diego, CA 92111-7399 (619-569-5391). In 1999 the cost including shipping was $28 for one copy.

97. Ana Maria Schuhmann, "Learning to Teach Hispanic Students," in *Diversity in Teacher Education: New Expectations,* ed. Mary E. Dilworth (San Francisco: Jossey-Bass, 1992), 94.

CHAPTER 3

Teaching with a Multicultural Perspective in Activities, Lessons, and Lesson Sequences

CHAPTER OVERVIEW

We believe that in the first decade of the new century and beyond, classroom teachers at all levels of instruction will be strongly encouraged, and in some cases pressured, to modify the way they conceptualize and deliver instruction. Although teacher-directed instruction, in which teachers parcel out information to 25 to 35 students in the traditional competitive mode, will continue to be an influential model, we expect K–12 learners to experience more interactive and collaborative instruction, helping each other learn in various cooperative formats. The collaborative teacher will spend more time working with students in an indirect facilitative way, and students will have greater opportunity to engage in self-directed learning, determining the direction and magnitude of their own learning. In addition, students' interaction with technological facilitators will increase dramatically, albeit unevenly, because of extreme economic disparities between school districts and states. Despite these expected changes, for the purpose of elucidating what teaching with a multicultural perspective means, we believe that the curriculum K–12 students will receive can be categorized into four types of planned instructional events. These events are part of the traditional way of describing teacher-directed instruction but are easily adapted to interactive and self-directed modes of instruction. They are classroom activities, lessons, lesson sequences, and units of instruction.

The content of these instructional events will be based on preestablished schoolwide routines as well as curriculum objectives determined by districtwide committees. For various reasons related to the European-influenced history of the United States and other Western nations, these routines and curriculum objectives sometimes reflect a monocultural perspective (a Eurocentric or Western orientation) as opposed to a multicultural perspective (a European, African, Asian, and American orientation encompassing Western and Eastern points of view). As a teacher, you will be responsible for modifying monocultural routines, objectives, and curricula so that they incorporate and reflect a meaningful multicultural perspective. To illustrate more clearly what such modification might look like, we offer in this chapter a series of curriculum case studies, before-and-after treatments of activities, lessons, and lesson sequences. In addition, we delineate a set of evaluative questions based on the goals of multicultural education, and we examine the role of these questions in "multiculturalizing" selected instructional events.

INTRODUCTION

Chapters 1 and 2 suggest that there are numerous strategies that classroom teachers can employ to create multicultural curricula. For example, we have seen that teachers help to create such curricula when they:

1. create more time for instruction by utilizing time-efficient classroom management strategies;

2. plan and implement successful parent communication and parent education strategies;

3. develop and participate in class- and schoolwide student recognition programs;

4. provide ongoing inspirational talks to students about completing junior high school, high school, and college;

5. introduce their students to former students and community role models who have successfully entered the world of work after earning a high school diploma, associate in arts degree (two-year degree), bachelor of arts or science degree, master of arts degree, or other degree;

6. utilize instructional strategies such as cooperative learning, which give more students the opportunity to achieve cross-gender and cross-ethnic friendships and academic success; and

7. develop and implement strategies that increase the academic confidence and self-esteem of their students.

With these examples and others, and our description of the work of James Comer, Uri Treisman, Jaime Escalante, Bruce Davis, Susan Sherwood, Mary Catherine Swanson, Charles Vidal, and John Goodlad we have shown that teaching that aims to create a multicultural curriculum extends far beyond the traditional academic curriculum. However, by illuminating the diverse nature and wide-ranging parameters of a transformational multicultural curriculum, we did not mean to diminish the central importance of the content and delivery system of the formal academic curriculum—namely, the facts, concepts, generalizations, skills, and attitudes learned in mathematics, social science, art, music, science, and language arts.

In chapters 3, 4, and 5 we will underscore the importance of this curriculum as we focus on content that is delivered in the following instructional formats: activities, lessons, lesson sequences, and units of instruction. We will show how teachers can shape these instructional events so that they become vehicles for achieving one or more of the goals of multicultural education. In this chapter we will focus on before-and-after treatments of activities, lessons, and lesson sequences, and then move to units of instruction in chapter 4.

A major objective of this chapter is to provide you with a clear and diverse set of examples that show how to enhance the multicultural nature of an instructional activity, lesson, or lesson sequence; in the sections that follow, we will enumerate some fundamental multiculturalization questions, define key terms, and present several curriculum case studies. First to be discussed are the multiculturalization questions.

MULTICULTURAL PLANNING QUESTIONS

The basic strategy in our multiculturalization process is to evaluate activities, lessons, and lesson sequences in terms of questions that directly relate to the goals of multicultural education. In this exercise, each "before" activity, lesson, and lesson sequence will be examined with one or more of the following questions in mind:

1. Do the lesson content and strategies promote educational equity? For example, does the lesson content help to create an inclusive curriculum, one that attempts to maximize student participation in the overall class curriculum? Are boys and girls given equal opportunity to participate in the lesson or activity?

2. Do the lesson content and strategies make use of, or help to develop, collaborative, empowering relationships among parents, students, and teacher?

3. Do the lesson content and strategies promote cultural pluralism in society or intergroup harmony in the classroom?

4. Does the lesson content help to increase the students' knowledge of various cultural and ethnic groups, including their own?

5. Do the lesson content and strategies increase students' proclivity and ability to see and think with a multicultural perspective?

6. Does the lesson content (a) help to correct distortions in the historical, literary, or scientific record that may stem from historical racism or other forces linked to the oppression and exploitation of specific ethnic and cultural groups, and (b) present material in a manner that suggests that racism-related distortions are or may be part of the historical and scientific record that the class is studying?

7. Does the lesson content provide knowledge or skills, or promote attitudinal development, that will leave the students better equipped and more inclined to participate in, and help improve, the democratic institutions of their society?

8. Does the lesson content contribute to the students' willingness to cross ethnic and cultural boundaries to participate in and/or learn about different cultural and ethnic groups?

We hope that your examination of the modified lesson content and structures that result from this evaluative process will persuade you to apply these questions selectively to your own curriculum planning and evaluation efforts.

DEFINITION OF KEY TERMS

At this point a caveat about the treatments is in order, as well as some remarks about what the terms *lesson, lesson sequence, activity,* and *unit of instruction* denote in this text. The suggested modifications that appear in the "after" treatment and analysis sections obviously do not exhaust all possibilities, and the activities, lessons, and lesson sequences given as examples represent only a portion of the curriculum areas taught by teachers. Our choices here are dictated by educational logic as well as space considerations. Logic suggests that we do not need to select lessons from every content area to illustrate how instructional strategies in all content areas can be modified to create lessons and lesson sequences that are congruent with one or more goals of multicultural education. In addition, as we developed our examples, our choices were influenced by three assumptions. First, in terms of the breadth and depth of our lesson examples, we assumed that less could be constructive. Second, we assumed that in moving from activity to lesson to lesson sequence and unit of instruction, we would parallel the manner in which many teacher education programs introduce candidates to curriculum planning. Finally, experience suggested that the activity, lesson, lesson sequence, and unit of instruction categorization would also be meaningful to in-service teachers.

Regarding the meaning of *lesson plan, lesson sequence, instructional activity,* and *unit of instruction,* the following definitions have proven to be practical for prospective teachers at our university. Although we think it is appropriate for teacher education programs to define such terms as building blocks for clear communication, we would remind you that all of these terms, like most words in our language, have several valuable meanings.

Lesson Plan

A *lesson plan* is a plan of instruction for a single lesson, and the block of time can be anywhere from 15 minutes to 2 hours, depending on the way instructional time is allotted in a given school situation. The plan covers a predetermined block of time. There are different kinds of lesson plans for different purposes. Typically, a lesson plan will consist of most of the following components:

1. the instructional objective;
2. the instructional materials to be used in the lesson;
3. the procedures to be used in "teaching to the objective";
4. the method(s) to be used in evaluating the students' learning;
5. self-evaluation (the specific methods student teachers will employ during or after the lesson to evaluate their own teaching);
6. time estimate (an estimate of the length of time the lesson will take to complete, from beginning to end); and
7. lesson origins (Is this a lesson the student teacher adapted from one found in a library resource? Is it totally or largely original? Is it one that the master teacher gave the student teacher?).

As they supervise student teachers, some master teachers and supervisors will want different amounts of detail in the procedure part of the lesson, and some supervisors will ask for more detail—a script almost—at the beginning of student teaching and less (or more) as the assignment unfolds. Later, during your probationary years of teaching, your principal, who will also visit you to conduct a form of clinical supervision, will likely ask for a lesson plan. This lesson plan will probably consist of four or five of the aforementioned elements, but the principal may ask for a new component. The point is, during your teacher education program, you should perceive your lesson plan, first, as an agenda that gives purpose and direction to your teaching, and second, as an act of communication between you and experienced educators. These educators are trying to help you develop to your fullest potential and simultaneously are trying to assure that their students are receiving thoughtful, high-quality instruction.

Lesson Sequence

The *lesson sequence* derives from the lesson plan and is defined as a series of individual lessons, each containing a single, specific instructional objective. The individual lessons are a sequence because one objective and lesson typically builds on the lesson that preceded it. In a lesson sequence each individual plan and objective leads the learner in small increments toward a predetermined major goal or objective at the end of the sequence. A typical sequence will have between three and eight lessons but could have more.

Instructional Activity

A third type of planned event, the *instructional activity,* is an important element in the classroom curriculum and, as used in the educational literature, has several meanings. In our work we distinguish between two types of instructional activities. First, there is the activity that is an integral part of a lesson, designed to achieve one or more specific instructional objectives. In a mathematics lesson students might manipulate Cuisenaire rods or pentaminoes for a period of time as part of a sequence of events leading to the instructional objective. In another type of instructional event, the activity is not part of a specific lesson plan. Rather, the activity is the entire instructional event; and although a great deal of valuable divergent learning occurs during this type of instructional event, teachers typically do not plan or think about these events in terms of specific instructional objectives, lesson plan formats, and assessments (tests). Examples of this type of activity include:

1. field trips to museums, work settings, and so on;
2. chapter-by-chapter oral reading by the teacher of a specific piece of literature on a regular basis (elementary teachers often read on a regular basis to their students immediately after recess);
3. oral presentations by, and interviews of, guest speakers;
4. self-directed learning periods during which students can engage in any type of learning activity they wish;
5. classroom meetings to discuss current events, classroom rules, schoolwide controversies, or the proposed content for an upcoming unit;
6. the development of a class play;
7. class and schoolwide recognition programs like the "Word of the Week" program (this particular program, as well as current events sharing, will be discussed later in this chapter when we explore ways to increase the multicultural content of instructional activities); and
8. weekly visits to the library and the computer room (teachers should ask themselves how, and if, the curriculum in these important centers of learning contribute to the goals of multicultural education).

The reader will note that instructional activities come in all sizes and shapes, often have an emergent quality, are structured so that different students will learn different things, and sometimes occur on a weekly basis. Instructional activities (1) call for thoughtful planning and execution, as anyone who has planned and led a field trip can attest; (2) can reflect a monocultural or multicultural perspective; and (3) often receive thin coverage in teacher education and staff development programs because of their informal nature.

Unit of Instruction

The *unit of instruction* is our final example of a planned instructional event. We define it as a comprehensive, multidimensional plan of instruction for learning inside and outside the classroom. A unit of instruction may contain several lesson sequences and typically requires a greater amount of time for planning and implementation than a lesson sequence. In comparison to a lesson sequence, a unit contains a wider range of lessons and activities, incorporates a more precise evaluation, and extends over a greater period of time, ranging from 4 to 16 weeks. In our program, units typically contain many of the following elements:

1. a guiding set of questions or generalizations linked to a set of unit objectives;
2. a list of major ideas around which the unit will revolve;
3. a list of the concepts that will be taught or reviewed in the unit;
4. collaborative planning with students on the content of the unit;
5. an exciting introductory activity to set the stage for the unit;
6. a pre- and postassessment, or some other form of preteaching diagnostic activity;
7. development of one or more bulletin boards and/or learning centers related to the unit;
8. utilization of carefully selected and prepared guest speakers;
9. a field trip;
10. use of filmstrips, films, software, and videotapes that have been previewed and carefully integrated into specific lessons;
11. a schedule of lessons and special activities and a bibliography of reading and visual material related to the unit;
12. independent research and cooperative group activities for students;
13. a special type of culminating event (a play, a musical presentation, or luau) that summarizes the group's learning, put on for themselves and invited guests (parents, other classes, the principal, etc.); and
14. a decorated construction paper folder in which the student will keep documents related to the unit.

With these definitions set, we can now examine our before-and-after curriculum case studies; we will focus first on instructional activities (section one), then move to lesson plans (section two), and culminate with lesson sequences (section three).

SECTION ONE

Instructional Activities

I. THE WORD OF THE WEEK PROGRAM

Before Multicultural Restructuring

* **Major Objective:** Citizenship Education
* **Content Area:** Interdisciplinary
* **Grade Levels:** K–6 and 6–8 (Elementary and Middle School)
* **Time Period:** Entire School Year on a Weekly Basis

Background and Implementation Information

The Word of the Week program became popular in the late 1970s as schools across the nation attempted to design more powerful ways to influence positively students' behavior and social development. As typically implemented, it is a schoolwide program, but in nonadopting schools, individual teachers have implemented a modified program in their own classroom.

In its simplest form, the principal or a committee of teachers picks one word for each week of the school year; this word is prominently displayed in each classroom and the school auditorium, and is announced in the school assembly and the weekly newsletter. For example, a word such as *helpful* may be selected. On Monday of each week, as part of their ongoing language arts program, teachers discuss the meaning of *helpful* to make certain that each child understands. Each child also understands that every week all teachers in the school will select one or two children from their class to receive special recognition as the student(s) whose behavior best exemplified the word of the week. The recognition is usually given at a schoolwide event, such as an assembly, on Friday mornings. Although schools implement this program in various ways, most schools:

1. have the teachers send in the names, or filled-in recognition certificates, on Thursday afternoon;
2. have school aides or volunteers make calls to parents or caretakers on Thursday afternoons or Friday mornings to give parents the opportunity to be at the awards ceremony;
3. take group pictures of recognized students and display them prominently near the principal's office;
4. list recognized students in a weekly or bimonthly newsletter; and
5. use words that are widely accepted as positive attributes (in American culture) in the set of 25 to 30 words. Examples include *helpful, friendly, cheerful, responsible, reliable, polite, courteous, considerate, positive, generous, independent, scholarly, hardworking, disciplined, punctual, tenacious, competitive,* and *imaginative.*

Analysis

The structure of the typical Word of the Week program has many commendable features, but it lacks parental involvement, rewards only one or two students from each class per week, and does little to promote cultural pluralism, intergroup harmony, or the ability to see and think with a multicultural perspective. These and other limitations will be addressed in the "after" treatment delineated next.

I. THE WORD OF THE WEEK PROGRAM

After Multicultural Restructuring

- **Curriculum Area:** Citizenship Education
- **Content Area:** Interdisciplinary
- **Grade Levels:** K–6 and 6–8 (Elementary and Middle School)
- **Time Period:** Entire School Year on a Weekly Basis

Suggested Modifications

1. Representatives of the parent committee can work together with teacher and student government representatives to help identify the 25 to 30 words that will provide the focus for the year's Word of the Week program. This strategy ties in with multicultural education goal 2 (see chapter 1): creating empowering relationships among teachers, parents, and students on a class and schoolwide basis.
2. The teacher can explain that the two students who receive recognition at the award assembly will likely be *representatives* of a larger group of students in the class whose behavior in and out of class merits recognition in terms of the Word of the Week program. For these students, the teacher can provide oral recognition in class and provide written recognition (on a weekly or bimonthly basis) by class certificates, letters sent home to parents, or identification in a bimonthly newsletter. These strategies tend to reduce competitiveness and thus increase the potential for intergroup harmony (multicultural goal 4).
3. To promote greater equity in this program—that is, to allow a larger number of deserving students to be recognized on a weekly or bimonthly basis (multicultural goal 1)—the manner in which the program is carried out can be modified. During the first week of the month, the first two words can be announced, and during weeks one and two, each teacher can nominate up to three students for each word. Thus, from this recognition program alone up to six children per week can receive certificates if their behavior was exemplary. In week three, the next two words could be announced; during these weeks the teacher can award certificates for all four words and distribute from 6 to 12 awards per week. In the school assembly, the teacher can read the names of students receiving certificates, and the students stand up as their names are called to receive recognition from fellow students and the principal.

4. To promote cultural pluralism (multicultural goal 3), intergroup harmony (multicultural goal 4), greater knowledge of selected ethnic and cultural groups (multicultural goal 5), and the ability to think with a multicultural perspective (multicultural goal 6), the traditional list of "good" words used in the program should be expanded to include some that more explicitly promote the values and goals of multicultural education. We have in mind words such as *open-minded, tolerant, bilingual, assertive, curious, pluralistic, bicultural, humorous, athletic, musical, creative, cooperative, collaborative, well-rounded,* and *problem solving.* When teachers explain what *curious* means, they can highlight the many useful things students can be curious about: knowledge about history, values, and contributions of specific American (and international) ethnic and cultural groups would be appropriate. In addition, because the teacher in weeks three and four can give recognition for all of the month's words, having a word like *bilingual* in the collection allows teachers to recognize publicly students who are striving to become bilingual, without penalizing those children who are aiming to move through life as creative monolinguals. Finally, some words, like *pluralistic* and *tolerant,* should be presented as optional in week three of the month because some K–3 teachers might find them difficult to explain to their students. Thus the school can have its set of schoolwide words for all classes as well as a few optional words that individual classes can adopt.

5. To help teachers explain and use each word to its fullest, the school district can provide a packet of curriculum materials to accompany each Word of the Week. These packets can include brief biographical descriptions of Americans from a variety of cultural and ethnic backgrounds. The lives of these outstanding Americans should exemplify several different words of the week and tend, therefore, to reinforce efforts to promote educational equity and cultural pluralism. In addition, materials that illuminate where prejudice, bigotry, and racism have stained American culture would help teachers explain what it means to be tolerant.

6. To promote positive collaborative relationships among parents, teachers, and students (multicultural goal 2), a description of the goals and procedures of the Word of the Week program should be sent home by school newsletter in as many languages as necessary, and the program should be reviewed on Back-to-School night. This activity will help parents understand the goals of the program and help to avoid situations like the following, which occurred in Mesa Elementary School, one of the "newcomer" schools in Lucia Mar Unified School District, in Arroyo Grande, California. In 1991, two brothers who were immigrants from Cambodia were attending the same newcomer class, along with immigrants from Mexico and the Philippines, to establish a certain level of English proficiency and social skill before being reassigned to a neighborhood school. One of the brothers received a special award at the monthly awards assembly, and when he showed the award to his parents, he received another reward from them. Unfortunately, the parents, who were unfamiliar with the awards ceremony and objectives, also punished the son who did not get an award. However, teachers should not assume that sending notes home in the native tongue will automatically solve the communication problem. Some immigrant parents may not be print literate in their native tongue. Tactful questioning of older elementary students or bilingual or migrant aides (when available) should help to identify the population for whom bilingual written communications will not suffice. Schoolwide efforts to explain key school programs orally—perhaps by cassette tapes—will then be needed.

7. To link this activity to the cooperative learning program in the class,
    a. encourage already formed cooperative groups to exhibit the qualities of the word;
    b. choose words, early in the year, that overlap with the skills and attitudes needed for effective small-group participation;
    c. during some weeks, select individuals and groups for recognition (or do this every week).

II. CURRENT EVENTS

Before Multicultural Restructuring

- Major Objective: Citizenship Education
- Content Area: Social Studies and Language Arts
- Grade Levels: 3–8
- **Time Period:** Entire School Year on a Weekly Basis (15 minutes per day)
- **Objectives:**
    1. Students will demonstrate the ability to locate and summarize orally the contents of newspaper articles on current events.
    2. Students will develop the propensity to stay abreast of current events.

Background Information

In most elementary schools, sharing is a part of the daily and weekly routine of the classroom. During this time, primary grade students come to the front of the class to present something they have brought to show or discuss with classmates. Some teachers make this a required activity and others leave it optional, but practically all teachers encourage parents and students to participate in this informal public speaking event. Typically, the activity is arranged on a schedule so that students and parents will know the day of the week each student is expected to be a presenter.

In the upper grades (4th–6th and in some middle school classrooms) the sharing of personal experiences, toys, and other objects from home gradually gives way to activities more closely related to the academic curriculum. In one common extension of primary grade sharing, upper-grade students present one current events article on a weekly or biweekly basis in front of the class.

General Procedures

1. Teachers establish a rationale and routine for current events sharing and present it to their students. They might explain that staying aware of current events is a natural part of citizenship responsibilities and survival strategies for most adults in our society, and that most adults get their current events update from a variety of sources, including radio and TV news, newspapers, various newsmagazines, and the Internet.
2. The teacher might then say, "To help develop the desire to stay in touch with important news events, all students in the class throughout the entire year will have the weekly or biweekly responsibility to give an oral report on a news article of their choice."
3. Beyond this, the teacher will set up ground rules such as the following:

    a. Each student will be given a specific day of the week on which to give the oral report.

    b. On occasion, the students can pass up the opportunity to be a presenter but must let the teacher know before sharing time.

    c. Students will neatly cut out the articles they are summarizing, so these can be posted on the current events bulletin board.

    d. On their presenting day, all students will be responsible for providing a written and oral summary of their news articles. The summary will, minimally, answer these questions:

       (1) Who or what was the news story about?

       (2) What happened in the story?

       (3) Where did the story take place?

       (4) Why did you find this story interesting?

       (5) What questions, if any, do you have about this news story?

    e. After the oral summary, students can ask questions to be answered by the presenter or other students in the class. The teacher moderates this part of the presentation.

    f. After the oral presentation, the student's written remarks will be submitted to the teacher, and the student's newspaper article will be posted on the bulletin board with his or her name neatly written in. Articles will be posted and removed on a weekly or biweekly basis. When the articles are taken down, students can keep or discard them.

Analysis

This format has several positive features but also notable flaws. It follows the traditional individualistic pattern of teaching and learning—students work alone—for an entire year with no modification of structure. The sheer repetition of the activity would probably dull student motivation long before June. Thus, as structured, the activity does little to promote educational equity or intergroup harmony. Regarding educational equity, it is noteworthy that the teacher assumes that all children in the class will have access to newspapers. With one out of four young children growing up in poverty in America, this is an inappropriate assumption. Also, for limited English proficient speakers and others, a format that allowed the presenter to address a smaller group, say 8 students rather than 32, would likely be more constructive for this type of public speaking event. In addition, teachers utilizing this traditional format do not exploit the potential for involving students in collaborative deliberation in this year-long project, and typically do little to promote parental support for the activity. Finally, the routine nature of the instructional activity—where week after week the students have the same responsibilities—severely limits its instructional value. For example, as structured, the activity does little to promote awareness of:

1. the manner in which the news media select and "create" news;
2. the distinction between local, regional, state, national, and international news;
3. the distinction between profit-making, and nonprofit-making news organizations;
4. the fact that selected cultural and ethnic groups in the United States create their own sources of daily, weekly, and monthly news; and

5. the various ways in which telecommunications can expand students' and teachers' perceptions of current events by creating two-way electronic mail communication between classrooms in different school districts, states, and nations.[1]

Some of the deficiencies are addressed in the revised activity structure that follows.

II. CURRENT EVENTS

After Multicultural Restructuring

- Major Objective: Citizenship Education
- Content Area: Social Studies and Language Arts
- Grade Levels: 3–8
- Time Period: Entire School Year for Varying Amounts of Time (The activity may be dropped in certain weeks and months.)
- **Objectives:**
  1. The learner will demonstrate increased knowledge of news production and dissemination in the United States.
  2. The learner will demonstrate the ability to locate, summarize, and evaluate the contents of various forms of current events reportage (print, radio, and television news).
  3. The learner will develop an interest in staying abreast of the news.

Suggested Modifications

1. By newsletter, the teacher informs parents that a yearlong study of news gathering and reporting will soon commence, and that, within two weeks, students will be asking parents to donate newspapers, magazines, and other print sources for projects. Parents with experience in news gathering or reporting are encouraged to share their experiences with the class. Teachers can also solicit newspapers from professionals and various business organizations.
2. The teacher introduces the activity in an open-ended way by asking students what they think *current news* is, and what they think *current events* means; then the teacher has all students describe, in writing, what they do to stay aware of current events.
3. The teacher asks students to brainstorm the following question: "In what different ways could the students in this class, *working together*, become more knowledgeable about news gathering and reporting in our community, state, and nation?" The teacher then analyzes and uses some of the student ideas to establish the initial structure for current events sharing.
4. The teacher arranges to have a class library, in which a range of recently published newspapers and magazines will be made available for students to read and cut articles from; there will also be a weekly classroom newspaper from a source such as *Scholastic, Inc.* or *Weekly Reader,* if the school budget permits.
5. The teacher tells the class that for the first few months, the class will employ several strategies to increase their knowledge base. "After the new year we'll evaluate our progress, and perhaps adopt some new strategies. The strategies we will use now include cooperative group sharing of newspaper and magazine

articles, presentations by and interviews of local journalists and publishers, individual and buddy research papers on news-related topics, and weekly or biweekly discussion of articles from the class newspaper, *My Weekly Reader.*"

6. Every student in the class has one partner and is also a member of a four- or five-student team. The teams are established in late September and stay together for about 6 or 12 weeks; if 12 weeks, the students can switch partners. For reporting on newspaper or magazine current events articles as delineated in the "before" activity, two teams of four students each can be combined. Half the group of eight students can report on Tuesday while the other half reports on the following Tuesday, or the groups can rotate on a weekly basis. By utilizing small cooperative groups for the reporting activity, rather than having each child speak in front of 32 students, the teacher (a) creates a more supportive climate, (b) allows more time for other types of sharing, because the four-student group takes less reporting time than the whole-group model, and (c) provides a setting that permits more active language involvement for a wider range of students.

7. With this extra time, during certain weeks the teacher can report on a current events article he or she found interesting. In addition, in a modified *Meet the Press* format, the students can, on a biannual or more frequent basis, arrange to interview a local print or television journalist or publisher from the English and non-English media. If the more frequent basis is chosen, interviewing other community personalities like the junior high school principal, town sheriff, or school custodian may also prove illuminating. Student research projects about famous journalists, specialized ethnic and cultural publications, and current issues about problems facing the journalists and the newspaper industry can also be reported on occasionally.

8. The questions students ask journalists and publishers during the *Meet the Press* interviews should be as probing as possible. For this reason, the students will be encouraged to ask their parents and older siblings for ideas, and parents will be invited to the Thursday or Friday afternoon interview. These sessions can also be videotaped. The teacher can suggest questions that reveal the economic basis and political dimension of local newspapers. For example, why do some papers cost money while others are given away? How are "given-away" papers similar to television stations? In terms of expressing political preferences and opinions, what are some differences between newspapers and television? What is the difference between public radio and television and commercial radio and television?

9. During the course of the year, teachers will bring variety to the weekly activity by
   a. using articles from the class newspaper as the basis for thought-provoking discussions;
   b. encouraging students to vary the type of current events they report on, in terms of the source of the news (local, regional, state, national, and international levels of news), and type of news: sports, politics, entertainment, scientific, education;
   c. encouraging students to seek out current events from a wide range of newspapers and magazines, including those disseminated via the World Wide Web;
   d. having students carry out comparisons of local newspapers, local newspapers versus local television in their treatment of a specific story, and analyses of what is included and excluded from local newspapers as well as the class newspaper;

e. linking current events to historical anniversaries like the Columbus Quin-centennial (1992); the fiftieth anniversary of *Brown v. Board of Education* (2004), the passage of the McCarran-Walter Immigration Act by the U.S. Congress (2002); and the ending of the Korean War (2003);

f. having each group of eight students keep a scrapbook of the articles they have reported, and by occasionally inviting several students from each group to present one of their articles in front of the whole class;

g. having student volunteers go out to interview and videotape fellow students, teachers, parents, and administrators about a specific controversial current event. The class can view, discuss, and critique the videotaped interview.

Final Comments

The "after" treatment of the current events activity took a routine activity, almost a time filler, and transformed it into a more ambitious collaborative undertaking. Because the current events activity lacks a unifying theme and has the potential, with ongoing mod-ifications, to last an entire year, it does not fall within the lesson sequence or unit para-meters. But as the horizons of the activity are expanded, it takes on some unitlike characteristics. In addition, in any given month the teacher can make current events part of a more elaborate unit of instruction. For example, the teacher can lead the class into a unit related to the development and production of a class newsletter or paper.

III. ORAL READING BY THE TEACHER

Before Multicultural Restructuring

* Major Objective: Motivation Toward Reading
* Content Area: Language Arts and Interdisciplinary Studies
* Grade Levels: K–8
* Time Period: Entire School Year on a Weekly Basis
* **Objectives:**
  1. Students will develop an enlarged appreciation of various types of literature.
  2. Students will develop a heightened enjoyment of reading.

Background Information

In grades K–6 and some 7–8 classes, oral reading of literature by the teacher is a regular part of the school curriculum. In the primary grades it is almost a daily occurrence, and primary teachers, because of the brevity of storybooks at this level, sometimes read more than one book per day. On the other hand, in the upper grades, where books are lengthier, a teacher might take a week or two to finish the dramatic reading of a spe-cific book, sometimes reading daily but more often reading on a flexible schedule sev-eral times per week. Because the traditional academic goals of this activity are largely motivational, teachers typically select books they enjoy reading and that experience suggests their students will enjoy. Occasionally, teachers choose books related to a theme or unit they are teaching; sometimes they read selected chapters from a book the entire class is reading. Typically, the teachers' focus in reading these stories is on presenting the literature in an enjoyable way rather than on using the content for skill-related objectives, such as stimulating higher-level thinking. Increasingly, teachers are employing these stories as a prompt for journal writing and class discussion.

General Procedures

The procedures here are pretty straightforward:

1. Teachers semirandomly select the book(s) they will read from the collection of books in their class or their own collection. Typically, the class collection has been chosen from the school library to augment the language arts program, and the teacher's dramatic reading of these books will motivate the students to read them and others during a variety of regularly scheduled reading activities.
2. The teacher reads the book in a dramatic fashion, utilizing different voices for various characters to make the oral interpretation more interesting.
3. When the story is complete, the teacher may simply invite the students to read the book on their own or may ask questions such as "Who can tell me something they liked or didn't like about this story?" Sometimes the teacher might invite students to ask questions about the story or discuss the story with a partner.

Analysis

Many students and teachers look forward to story time as a desirable break in a school day that is often excessively oriented to skill-based lessons. It is a time to enjoy literature in a holistic manner rather than break it into little pieces for the purpose of learning discrete skills related to the test-oriented language arts curriculum. Here is material the student and teacher can relate to in an unhurried, relatively unfocused manner, material that is not tied to a specific instructional objective or test item, material that both student and teacher can approach in a spontaneous and creative manner. This does not sound like a picture one wishes to tamper with, and yet when examined from a multicultural perspective, this routine activity, like other desirable components of the K–8 curriculum, can be strengthened without totally changing its character.

There are several general ways to improve this routine instructional activity:

1. broadening the major objective to link it more clearly to the goals of multicultural education;
2. making the selection of stories less random and more purposeful;
3. placing less emphasis on "enjoyable" reading so that challenging and informative literature can be included;
4. encouraging the teacher to become more knowledgeable about the main characters in selected biographies and autobiographies.

Developing links to multicultural education is critical; literature can play too important a role in helping to achieve the goals of multicultural education to be selected on a random or semirandom basis. It is not enough for the teacher to select library books on the basis of variety and interest. Literature does more than entertain; it teaches important lessons. Literature has the power to develop self-respect, pride, and curiosity, as well as a deeper understanding of self, others, and history. Therefore, at least some of the books selected for oral reading should provide content that helps to accomplish these and other purposes.

Although these objectives can and should be achieved with various forms of literature—poetry, short story, novel, journalism—we encourage you to develop a repertoire of biographies to share with students throughout the year, and not just during African-American History month (February) or Women's History month (March). We believe that children of all ethnic and cultural backgrounds can draw inspiration from the story of individuals, such as Rosa Parks and César Chávez, whose courage and faith helped them transcend obstacles that racism, sexism, or religious bigotry placed in front of them. In addition, specific children will gain emotional nourishment and perhaps ethnic pride from these stories.

Such literature—which is, after all, a part of an American and world history replete with cultural and ethnic antagonism—will sometimes describe conflicts between White Americans, African Americans, American Indians, Mexican Americans, and Asian Americans. The presentation of such stories in multiethnic and monoethnic classrooms calls for thoughtful preparation rather than spontaneous interpretation, and the preparation, where possible, should extend beyond the single biography the teacher reads to students. To illustrate the type of focused selection and special preparation we mean, in the restructured example in the next section we draw on Eloise Greenfield's 1973 biography of Rosa Parks, a captivating story that is suitable for second to fourth graders and could be adapted for use with older students. This book was originally published by Thomas Y. Crowell and is now distributed by HarperCollins.

III. ORAL READING BY THE TEACHER

After Multicultural Restructuring

- Major Objective: Motivation Toward Reading, Self-Esteem Development, Cultural Pluralism, and Citizenship Education
- Content Area: Interdisciplinary
- Grade Levels: K–8
- Time Period: Entire School Year on a Weekly Basis
- **Objectives:**
  1. Students will develop a heightened enjoyment of reading and of various types of literature.
  2. Students will gain greater understanding of the contributions specific individuals and groups have made to American and world history.
  3. Students may gain increased pride in themselves as members of specific ethnic and cultural groups (as African Americans, Hispanic Americans, or simply as Americans).

Suggested Modifications

1. The major and specific objectives of this weekly, yearlong activity have been expanded so that they can more easily promote the goals of multicultural education.
2. As noted, instead of selecting books exclusively on the basis of variety and student interest, the teacher should choose books that will inform students about different ethnic and cultural groups, both in the United States and abroad.
3. Some should be biographical and inspire students by providing role models who have helped Americans overcome complex political and socioeconomic problems.

4. Some of these biographies should portray scenes of cultural conflict; these valuable stories should be carefully studied by the teacher and thoughtfully presented to students. Instead of interpreting these stories spontaneously as they are read, teachers should read them several days in advance. The early reading gives teachers time to think about (a) an appropriate introduction, (b) questions students might ask about key characters and events, (c) questions teachers might want to ask students, and (d) points they might wish to make that extend beyond the specific content of the biography or story in question.

The biography of Rosa Parks written by Eloise Greenfield, part of an excellent series of elementary-level biographies developed by Crowell, provides a case in point. This is a story about America's past and present. Although it does not mention racism, it is about racism; it contains important lessons that illuminate our common heritage and provides examples of strategies future citizens might use as they grapple with the social problems of their day. The story of Rosa Parks is one link in the chain of individual and collective struggles that are part of the centuries-long battle African Americans have waged to achieve full equality in the United States. Because of its heroic dimensions and lessons in character and citizenship, Mrs. Parks's story should be widely told. However, for some White, Hispanic, and African-American teachers, the challenge will be, first, to tell the story, and then to tell it well. Because the story describes several White people in a negative light and because it is a part of our contemporary history, White teachers, in particular, may be hesitant to read this story to ethnically integrated or nonintegrated classes. The following suggestions should help all teachers share this story, and similar material, with elementary school students.

a. The teacher should *not* lead into a reading of the Greenfield biography with a simple remark like, "This morning I'm going to read another story about a famous American." Students should be emotionally prepared to hear this story. They should be told that this story is about a heroic African American who overcame serious obstacles to make her community and all of America a freer place to live. An introduction for any third- or fourth-grade class could begin as follows:

"Future historians, this morning I'm going to read and tell you a story about a courageous American, a very brave African American who nearly _____ years ago helped African Americans confront and triumph over the unfair, humiliating, and oppressive conditions they faced in different parts of America. Her work specifically helped African Americans, but it also made America a freer and fairer place for all Americans. Does anyone have an idea who I'm talking about? Yes, that's right, and there are lessons we can all learn from a review of some of the key events in Mrs. Rosa Parks's life. To help us discover these lessons, right after I finish reading you Eloise Greenfield's biography entitled Rosa Parks, I'd like each of you to be prepared to share your thoughts and questions about the struggles Mrs. Parks faced as she grew up as an African American. We'll all do our best to answer your questions, and the ones we can't answer, we'll research."

This introduction sets an appropriate foundation for the children because they now know they will be hearing a story that deals with racial conflict and struggle. Thus they will not be shocked at the explicit racial encounter with which the story opens:

Rosa was not afraid although the white boy was near his mother. When he pushed her, Rosa pushed back. "Why did you put your hands on my child?" the mother asked. "Because he pushed me," Rosa said.

This type of introduction should also raise the teacher's comfort level with the story. Any concerns about the story's being divisive will be diminished by the teacher's own remarks, which emphasize that Mrs. Parks's freedom struggle was for *all* Americans. Although many White Americans opposed Mrs. Parks and the African Americans who joined her in collective struggle, her victory was for Americans of all colors, including Whites.

b. As he has done in the last sentence of his opening remarks, the teacher should emphasize that he has come to this biography as a student himself, and that the class as a group will seek out the lessons in the story. This opportunity to think cooperatively is valuable for students, and it should alleviate any concern teachers have about needing to be an expert on every biography they read to their class. On the other hand, as a result of the group inquiry process and the strategy of developing a repertoire of biographies, teachers, as they share this biography with different classes, will become increasingly knowledgeable about Rosa Parks, Thurgood Marshall, Charles Hamilton Houston, and others and may find themselves seeking out more detailed biographies of Rosa Parks. For such extended reading, teachers can consult the nine-volume series *The History of the Civil Rights Movement,* published by Silver Burdett in 1990. This series of well-written biographies for young people includes *Rosa Parks: The Movement Organizes* by Kai Friese, as well as books about Fannie Lou Hamer, Jesse Jackson, Ella Baker, Thurgood Marshall, and A. Philip Randolph. Teachers will also want to read Rosa Parks's autobiography (written with the help of Jim Haskins) entitled *Rosa Parks: Mother to a Movement* (Dial Books, 1992). After teachers finish the reading and discussion stimulated by Greenfield's 32-page biography, they can read a page or two from Friese's lengthier work, or Parks's autobiography. Such exposure will increase the possibility that some students will delve more deeply into Parks and her contribution to the civil rights movement.

c. Prior to reading the Greenfield biography to the class, teachers should list three to five questions they think their students might ask, and consider how they would answer them. The teachers' responses should be accurate and at the appropriate level of complexity and should deal with issues like collective struggle and racism. For example, if asked why the White people were so mean to the Black people, a teacher might, after listening to student responses to the question, say the following. (Our response is one we feel is accurate and comprehensible for third and fourth graders. However, teachers should not perceive it as the only one and should experiment with their own versions of an accurate, comprehensible response.)

Racism was at the root of many problems in the United States at the time of this story. Many White people believed that they were superior to Blacks and that Blacks had to be kept in their place, and this meant below and away from Whites—in separate schools, pools, hospital rooms, and in separate parts of buses and theaters. As the story tells us, to keep African Americans in their place and dominate them, some Whites, in organizations like the Ku Klux Klan, terrorized African Americans. Things have gotten a lot better, but today we still find unfortunate examples of racism in our nation and world.

> Teachers should realize that when they explain the motivation of Whites and explain why racism made sense to them but had to be fought by African Americans, they will be teaching with a multicultural perspective. Such teaching may help young students make sense of the racial conflicts they see portrayed on television or played out in their own neighborhoods; the teacher's reading of Rosa Parks and related stories may also lead to questions and discussions about current ethnic and racial relations in America, Ireland, the former Yugoslavia, Canada, Iraq, Japan, Israel, Nigeria, India, and other nations.

d. Teachers should perceive the story of Rosa Parks and similar stories as more than occasions for sharing historical knowledge. As they teach the facts of the story, they should be prepared to probe, dignify, and respond sensitively to the feelings such stories evoke. Students should have the opportunity to share these feelings privately in their journals (to be read just by the teacher) and publicly during the class discussion. During these discussions, teachers should be prepared for a wide range of reactions. For example, in their preliminary work, teachers may prepare themselves to answer questions about the Ku Klux Klan, the National Association for the Advancement of Colored People (NAACP), and boycotts as a strategy for collective struggle against economic and political oppression. They may find that many student responses are personal and local, having more to do with playground and community conflicts than with the plight of, for example, Blacks in South Africa. Teachers, when dealing with the complex issue of race relations, should meet students conceptually where they are and then transport the class to higher levels of understanding. For instance, after discussing with students the important issue of bullying or name-calling on the playground, the teacher can remind children that young Rosa's confrontation of a bully was part of her preparation for the battle she and other African Americans would ultimately wage against the system of legalized segregation in the state of Alabama.

e. Teachers should consider having more than one level of the Rosa Parks biography in the classroom: the Greenfield biography (3rd–4th grade), the Friese biography (5th–8th grade), and a brief, two-page treatment of Parks by Kathie White in "Women as Members of Groups" (2nd–6th grade) from the National Women's History Project (www.nwhp.org). This variety will allow upper-grade students to read material about Parks to younger students and will provide more challenging material for advanced readers. The strategy may raise productive questions about the difficulty of writing biographies, of getting all the facts "just right," and may stimulate in students a desire for further reading and research. For example, a comparison of Greenfield's biography with Friese's suggests a difference of opinion about how old Rosa Parks was when she was pushed by a "white boy who was standing near his mother." In Greenfield's book, Rosa is depicted as a child when this happens, but Friese reports that Rosa was married and over 20 years old when the shoving incident occurs. Whose depiction is more accurate, or could there have been two similar pushing incidents? Some future historians might well enjoy the opportunity to search out the answer to this discrepancy.

In terms of stimulating a desire for additional knowledge, students reading the Friese biography will be intrigued, and perhaps surprised, to learn that Sojourner Truth, another courageous African-American woman, successfully struggled to integrate the streetcars of Washington, D.C., during the Civil War, and that Mary Ellen Pleasant waged a similar struggle in San Francisco in 1866, and Ida B. Wells sued a railroad corporation in 1883 in Memphis, Tennessee, in an effort to keep the railway cars integrated. With some properly worded invitations for inquiry, several students will likely want to track down more information about these nineteenth-century civil rights workers. It is even possible that some highly motivated upper graders can do original historical work by letter writing and other methods, perhaps making use of the Internet and the listservs discussed in chapter 2. For example, Friese reports that in 1900—55 years prior to the boycott stimulated by Parks's refusal—another boycott was conducted by the Black citizens of Birmingham, Alabama. At that time the goal was to increase the number of segregated seats in the streetcars. Who were the African Americans who led this successful boycott, what pressures did they face, and how can fourth through eighth graders, making use of local as well as distant resources, pursue these questions? Other students might be interested in a research project on Irene Morgan, who in 1944 was convicted of refusing to move to the "colored" section of a Greyhound bus. The outcome of her struggle for freedom is described in "Forty-five Years in Law and Civil Rights" by A. Leon Higginbotham Jr., in *Ebony*'s forty-fifth anniversary edition (November 1990, pp. 80–86). Finally, some students might be interested in reporting on the life and legal triumphs of Vilma Martinez, a contemporary leader of the Mexican American Legal Defense and Education Fund (see the National Women's History Project catalog for curriculum resources pertaining to Martinez; for information regarding this catalog, call 707-838-6000).

f. Finally, to prepare themselves to make a positive contribution to the development of their students' ethnic, cultural, gender, and racial identity, teachers should consider reading books and articles that discuss the various stages through which students travel as they develop a healthy, integrated personality. A good place to begin such reading would be with Beverly Tatum's article "Talking About Race, Learning About Racism: The Application of Racial Identity Development Theory in the Classroom" (*Harvard Educational Review* 62, no. 1 [Spring 1992]: 1–24). A later article by Tatum will also prove helpful. The article, "Teaching White Students About Racism: The Search for White Allies and the Restoration of Hope," appeared in *Teacher's College Record* 95, no. 4 (Summer 1994): 462–476.

SECTION TWO

Lesson Plans

I. TO TELL THE TRUTH

Before Multicultural Restructuring

- Major Objective:Scientific Literacy
- Content Area: Science and Language Arts (Interdisciplinary)
- Grade Levels: 3–8
- Time Period: 90–120 Minutes (two to three sessions)
- Objectives:
  1. Students will be able to identify orally the major achievement of outstanding scientists.
  2. Students will demonstrate the ability to use various language arts skills (reading, writing, speaking, listening, selecting key facts) to play the game "To Tell the Truth."

Background and Implementation Information

In contemporary language arts, science, mathematics, and social studies education, a great deal of emphasis is placed on involving students in meaningful and enjoyable activities in these content areas. The development of meaningful activities that allow students to use writing, reading, speaking, and analytical skills has assumed a new importance in K-12 settings and teacher education. In this context, enjoyable, multi-skill activities like "To Tell the Truth," based on a past popular television game show, have gained legitimacy and popularity. They enable students to use various language arts and thinking skills and are not guided by one specific instructional objective.

The version of "To Tell the Truth" described next has been circulated in California by several county offices of education as one way to use writing to teach science. The instructions that accompany the suggested activity are these.

Instructions

1. Divide the class into groups—three students per group.
2. Each group is assigned a letter of the alphabet.
3. Each group looks in the index of the science textbook and selects a person whose last name begins with that letter.
4. Each student in the group reads the pages that deal with the group's scientist.
5. The group decides who will be the "real" person and who will be the impostors.
6. The students use 5-x-8-inch cards to write down the autobiographical information they want to provide the class.
7. The groups quietly rehearse how they will present their information.
8. The groups make their presentations in the order designated by the teacher.
9. The moderator ask contestants one, two, and three, "What is your name, please?" Each of the contestants then presents the autobiographical information.

10. The moderator asks for questions from the audience. Members of the audience can question any one of the contestants; the class may want to put a limit on the number of questions.
11. The class votes on who they think is the real scientist.
12. The moderator says, "Will the real _____ please step forward?"

Analysis

In providing an interesting activity in which students can use reading, writing, oral, and interpretive skills while learning facts about the accomplishments of outstanding scientists, this interactive, multidimensional language game is a good instructional choice for most students. However, with some modification of objectives and procedures, the lesson would have much greater potential for achieving multicultural objectives.

In terms of promoting educational equity, the process of selecting scientists is severely limited. The students can choose only the scientists that are mentioned in their text and must select from these a scientist whose name begins with the letter they have been assigned. Give these constraints, it is quite possible that the students would end up with a group consisting largely of White male scientists. This potential result, which for some students would reinforce the notion that outstanding scientists are White men, is exactly the type of knowledge that works against the academic interests of White female and male students and students of color, and the long-term interests of all citizens. In the twenty-first century, America and the world will encounter increasing shortages of scientists, engineers, and mathematicians. For this reason, we need to replace language games that may send negative messages to students of color and false impressions to White students with games designed to carry positive messages. The following revised game should be evaluated with this positive objective in mind. Note especially the change in objectives.

I. TO TELL THE TRUTH

After Multicultural Restructuring

- Major Objective: Recruitment for Scientific Careers and Scientific Literacy
- Content Area: Science and Language Arts (Interdisciplinary)
- Grade Levels: 3–8
- Time Period: Two Hours (two to three sessions)
- **Objectives:**
  1. Students will be able to identify various contemporary and past scientists and inventors who have made contributions to scientific knowledge. These scientists will represent various ethnic and cultural groups.
  2. Teacher will get students interested in a career in science and will demonstrate to students that scientists come from both genders and various ethnic groups.

Suggested Modifications

1. The teacher should show a videotaped segment of the game, if available, and provide a script that can be enacted so that all students will see exactly how the game is played. This demonstration will make the rules of the game more comprehensible to limited English proficient students who might be in the class.

2. For purposes of educational equity and intergroup harmony, teachers should use four-member cooperative learning terms. Three members of the team can be the contestants while one serves as moderator for that group. Team members, as usual, can help each other with the reading and writing tasks.
3. The teacher should pass out a sheet with information about a specific scientist or inventor and then illustrate how the four team members will proceed to develop three sets of autobiographical remarks on 5-x-8-inch cards. The teacher and students can write one or more sets of remarks on the overhead projector.
4. Instead of limiting the selection of scientists and inventors to those in the index of whatever science text the class is using, the teacher should assign specific resources to the teams. For example, assuming that the school library or teacher has copies of these texts, the teacher could give each team the following resources:
   a. Robert Hayden and Richard Loehle, *Seven African-American Scientists*, rev. and expanded ed. (Frederick, MD: Twenty-First Century Books, 1992) or Hattie Carwell, *Blacks in Science:Astrophysicist to Zoologist* (Norris, Tenn.: Exposition Press, 1977).
   b. Robert Hayden, *Nine African-American Inventors* (Frederick, MD: Twenty-First Books, 1992); "Superstars of Science," *Ebony*, June 1991, 42–50; "Fifty Years of Blacks in Medicine," *Ebony*, July 1995, 120–127; *African-American Medical Pioneers,* by Charles H. Epps, Davis G. Johnson, and Audrey L. Vaughan (Rockville, Md.: Betz, 1994); and *Eleven African-American Doctors*, by Robert Hayden (Frederick, MD: Twenty-First Century Books, 1992).
   c. Louis Haber, *Black Pioneers of Science and Invention* (New York: Harcourt, Brace and World, 1979); and *Black Contributors to Science and Energy Technology*, available from the U.S. Department of Energy, Office of Public Affairs, Washington, DC 20585, Publication No. DOE/OPA–0035 (79).
   d. Clark Newlon's *Famous Mexican-Americans* (New York: Dodd Mead, 1972).
   e. Ivan Van Sertima, ed. *Blacks in Science:Ancient and Modern* (New Brunswick, N.J.: Transaction Books, 1983); and "African American Inventors," *Cobblestone: The History Magazine for Young People* 13, no. 2 (February 1992): 2–23.
   f. Ethlie Ann Vare and Greg Ptacek, *Mothers of Invention: From the Bra to the Bomb, Forgotten Women and Their Unforgettable Ideas* (National Women's History Project—see appendix 6, section III of this text, for ordering information).
   g. Louis Grinstein and Paul Campbell, *Women of Mathematics:A Bibliographic Sourcebook* (Westport, Conn.: Greenwood Press, 1987).
   h. The index of the science text, which several groups could use to make their choices.

These resources may not be in all elementary and middle-school libraries, but they can be ordered. In the interim, teachers can utilize *Ebony* magazine, and other resources that highlight the contributions of inventors and scientists from various ethnic and cultural groups. Enterprising teachers may be interested in developing computer software that can be used in conjunction with this game. An effort should be made to identify scientists and inventors from various Asian-American and Hispanic groups. One helpful resource is entitled *Mexican-American Biographies: A Historical Dictionary* (1836-1987), by Matt S. Meier (New York: Greenwood Press, 1988). In it we learn, for example, of the accomplishments of Francisco Sanchez Alvarez (1928-1980), a research chemist and former principal scientist of Syntex Corporation, who is listed as the inventor in over 80 patents. Other helpful resources, all from Gale Research Corporation in Detroit, include: *Notable Hispanic American Women* (1993), which includes biographical information about astronaut Ellen Ochoa, planetary geologist Adriana C. Ocampo, and anthropologist Lydia Cabrera: *Notable Native Americans* (1995), which includes biographical information about physicist Fred Begay (Navajo) and anthropologists Arthur C. Parker (Seneca), Beatrice A. Medicine (Lakota), and George H. J. Abrams (Seneca); and *Notable Asian Americans,* which includes biographical information about nuclear physicist Samuel C. Ting, physicist Chen Ning Yang, biochemist Har Gobind Khorana, and astronauts Leroy Chiao, Ellison Onizuka, and Taylor G. Wang.

5. To reinforce what the teams and the class have learned about the various scientists and inventors, each team will have the responsibility of writing a short article about their scientist/inventor for the class's monthly newsletter. The teacher can also invite students to create a crossword puzzle using facts from the set of 5-x-8-inch cards. In these and other ways, the accomplishments and inspirational messages of these creative individuals should become a part of the class's ongoing conversation.

6. The other versions of this game can include doctors, lawyers, and artists, as well as scientists and inventors.

7. The teacher should consider following up this activity with guest speakers and videotapes. One videotape series, entitled *Women in Science,* is suitable for use in grades 5 through 12. Each tape is 30 minutes long, and titles include "Biomedical Fields," "Chemistry," "Computer Science," "Dentistry," "Engineering," "Geosciences, Physics and Astronomy," and "Scientific Careers for Women: Doors to the Future." The video series and the guide are available from the Agency for Instructional Technology, Box A, Bloomington, IN 47402; 800-457-4509. Previews are available free of charge except for return shipping.

II. THANKSGIVING

Before Multicultural Restructuring*

• Major Objective: To Learn About the Origins of an Important American Holiday
• Content Area: American History (Social Studies)
• Grade Levels: K–2
• Time Period: 30–40 Minutes
• Objectives:
  1. The learner will be able to identify several key facts about the first American Thanksgiving.
  2. Working in small groups, the learners will create a flannel-board story about the first Thanksgiving in the United States and will share that story with another group.

---

*This "before" and "after" treatment is based on Activity 156, "The First Thanksgiving in This Country," which is part of a collection of lessons entitled *US:A Cultural Mosaic:A Multicultural Program for Primary Grades.* The handbook was prepared by San Diego Unified School District curriculum consultants and teachers between 1975 and 1977 and is currently disseminated by the Anti-Defamation League of B'nai B'rith (823 United Nations Plaza, New York, NY 10017). The material is used with the permission of the Anti-Defamation League of B'nai B'rith.

Suggested Procedures

1. Create an anticipatory set for the lesson. "Who can tell me what this picture (a turkey) has to do with a holiday we will celebrate this month?"
2. "Do you know who brought the turkeys to the first American Thanksgiving?"
3. "These are good guesses. Let's listen to a story about the first Thanksgiving to see whose guess came closest to the truth. Be prepared to tell me something you learned about the first Thanksgiving that you didn't know."
4. Read the following story to your class.

The Story of the First American Thanksgiving

In 1620 a small ship named the *Mayflower* came to the United States, which was then an English colony. The people on this ship were Englishmen known as Pilgrims and were among the first Europeans to settle the eastern part of our country. They were Puritans who did not wish to break away from the Church of England.

Arriving on the bleak, rocky Massachusetts coast in December 1620 in a place called Plymouth, the sick and weak settlers had to spend the winter in extreme hunger. They had very little food left after a dangerous ocean voyage, and so about half of them died of hunger, disease, and bad weather. Luckily for them, the Englishmen found the natives of this land, Indians of the Wampanoag tribe, to be friendly. They provided advice, food, and other important help. The Indians, one of whom was Squanto, taught their new neighbors how to build houses, hunt for food, and survive in the wilderness. The Pilgrims learned much from their friends of the Wampanoag tribe, whose chief, Massasoit, was one of the most powerful native rulers of New England. The treaty Chief Massasoit signed with them at Plymouth in 1621 was faithfully observed until his death many years later.

In the spring the Englishmen planted the seeds they had brought with them, along with corn and other crops the Indians taught them to grow. When autumn arrived, the Pilgrims gathered their bountiful harvest of foods and stored away some for the next winter.

Everyone was grateful for the harvest, and the Pilgrims said, "We must give thanks for all the good food, our homes, our clothes, our Indian friends and all our blessings. We shall have a big feast and invite our Indian friends. We will call it a feast of Thanksgiving." Well might they offer thanks; the Indians had helped the Pilgrims survive the terrible conditions in their new land.

Therefore, Governor Bradford invited Chief Massasoit and his braves to the celebration. On that memorable day of the first Thanksgiving feast in December 1621, the Pilgrims covered their tables with food from their gardens. Massasoit's braves brought turkeys, deer, and other game they had shot with their bows and arrows. The corn, pumpkins, squash, beans, clams, oysters, and fish provided by the Indians were added to the Pilgrims' food so that this famous Thanksgiving feast lasted for three days.

Typical of most of the Indians of the United States, Wampanoags were good hunters; growing crops was not as important to them as killing game. Unlike the Plains Indians, but like most tribes of the Eastern Woodlands, Wampanoags did not move their homes; they stayed in one place.

Chief Massasoit and 90 of his braves came in their best dress to celebrate the feast day. Some of the Indians had wide bands of black paint on their faces. Some had feathers stuck in their long straight black hair, and some wore furry coats of wildcats hanging from their shoulders; others wore deerskins.

Before anyone ate, they bowed their heads, offering a prayer of thanksgiving. That was the first Thanksgiving—a day that is now a legal holiday and one of the most popular holidays in the United States, especially since we do not have to come to school on that day.

The Indians danced, acted out stories, and played games with the children. The colonists sang their songs. In addition, a target was set up, and the soldiers fired at it. Then the Indians, standing in closer, shot at it with their bows and arrows to see which side would win the contest. Most important, hearty fellowship and goodwill was felt between the colonists and the Indians. Peace and friendship had been established on a firm foundation. Without such a peace, the Pilgrims would never have won a footing on that bleak, rugged coast. Without it, Plymouth could never have survived.

Thanksgiving was not a new observance for the American Indians. We know that several Indian tribes were accustomed to observing several days of thanksgiving throughout the year. The Iroquois and Choctaw, for example, had an autumn festival known as the Green Corn Dance, which lasted three days. We are also familiar with the story of how the Wampanoags came to the first Thanksgiving feast at the invitation of Governor Bradford and the Pilgrims. It seems likely that the three-day period of Thanksgiving to which Massasoit and his Indians went was already customary for them.

The first Thanksgiving observance was held in December 1621, but it was not an annual affair as it is today. On July 30, 1623, Governor Bradford proclaimed a second Thanksgiving when a ship was sighted, heading for port carrying much-awaited, much-needed supplies from England. This second Thanksgiving Day was in no way connected with the harvest, but, later on, a day was set in the month of November that became associated with the gathering of the crops. Today Thanksgiving is a legal holiday in all the United States.

1. After reading the story, ask your students:
   a. "Which of our guesses came the closest?"
   b. "What did you learn from the story that was new information for you?"
   c. "Did any of the material in the story surprise you?"
2. Next, structure small groups so that each group will create a flannel-board story of the first Thanksgiving in this country. Be sure that the stories include the *Mayflower,* several Pilgrims, several Indians, some crude homes for the Pilgrims, corn and other crops, and the Thanksgiving table laden with food.
3. As possible follow-up or extension activities, consider having your class learn the songs "Thanksgiving Story" and "Indian Hunting Song" and listen to "Dances of Indian America."

Analysis

The lesson plan outlined previously is to be presented as part of a sequence of activities in *US: A Cultural Mosaic*; the entire set of 238 activities is designed to

1. help children see that the similarities among people are those traits that make them members of the human family, and that differences among people are those characteristics that make people special and unique; and

2. help children develop an understanding and appreciation of themselves and other persons in the communities.

The Thanksgiving lesson has a number of positive attributes: it illustrates the importance of friendliness and support from Native Americans—in this case, members of the Wampanoag tribe—to the survival of the Pilgrims. In addition, it shows some of the diversity that existed and still exists among Native Americans; it also presents some basic information about the Pilgrims and their first American Thanksgiving.

On the other hand, the lesson could be improved:

1. It could incorporate some invitations for inquiry: Who can find out when Thanksgiving became a national holiday? Has anyone written a biography about Chief Massasoit? In the years after they celebrated Thanksgiving together, did the Pilgrims and members of the Wampanoag tribe come in conflict with each other?
2. The lesson could make use of student partners to increase active student participation during the lesson; students could share the information they learned from the story with their partners before the teacher asks a few to share in front of the entire class.
3. The story might have been entitled "The Second American Thanksgiving" to emphasize that Native American groups had had celebration feasts prior to 1621, at which they likely thanked the "Great Spirit" for their good fortune. This would not diminish the historical significance of the first Thanksgiving the Pilgrims had in America but would help to dispel the idea that "American" history begins with the European experience in what would be called the Americas. These observations and others will be incorporated into the revised lesson sequence following.
4. The lesson should develop the understanding that even though Thanksgiving has been a national holiday since 1863, there are religious communities in the United States that do not celebrate it.

II. THANKSGIVING

After Multicultural Restructuring

- Major Objective: The Development of a Culturally Pluralistic Attitude
- Content Area: Interdisciplinary
- Grade Levels: K–2
- Time Period: 60–120 Minutes
- Objective:
    The learners will identify and develop an appreciation of the way several different groups celebrate their own version of Thanksgiving.

Suggested Modifications

1. Implement the "before" lesson with the modifications just mentioned— namely, to (a) call the story "The Second Thanksgiving in America," (b) make use of partners to increase active participation and of cooperative learning

groups to facilitate the flannel-board activity, and (c) incorporate invitations for inquiry to encourage critical thinking and self-directed learning.

2. Follow-up the presentation of "The Second American Thanksgiving" with lessons in which students learn about the following:
   a. the Jewish festival of Succot. Explain why many people believe that the Pilgrims patterned their Thanksgiving festival after Succot, which is described in the Bible as a festival of thanksgiving and rejoicing, related to the harvest.
   b. the Moon Festival, which is celebrated by some Chinese people in the autumn.
   c. the Octoberfest, which is celebrated in Germany at the end of the harvest in late September and early October.
   d. Specific suggestions regarding lesson content and materials for the Succot, Moon Festival, and Octoberfest are included in *US: A Cultural Mosaic* (pages 178–186), and in additional appendixes in the document.

Final Comments

Note that in the "after" treatment in this comparison, we not only changed the major objective but also transformed a single lesson into a more elaborate lesson sequence. However, we also changed the Thanksgiving lesson itself in ways that make it more congruent with the goals of multicultural education.

US: A Cultural Mosaic is filled with thoughtful sequences that promote cultural pluralism (multicultural goal 3), intergroup harmony (multicultural goal 4), an expanded multicultural/multiethnic knowledge base (multicultural goal 5), and the propensity and ability to think with a multicultural perspective (multicultural goal 6). Because it works consistently to enhance the students' sense of group and individual self-esteem, the entire collection contributes to educational equity. Other sequences in the volume that are related to the Thanksgiving story include

- A Crosscultural Look at Some New Year's Celebrations
- A Crosscultural Look at Some Independence Days
- A Crosscultural Look at Some Special Religious Days
- A Crosscultural Look at Some Days of Appreciation

US: A Cultural Mosaic is clearly a resource worthy of your attention.

III. INTERVIEWING ANCESTORS

Before Multicultural Restructuring

- Major Objective: To provide students with the opportunity to learn specific facts about their ancestors and to develop an interest in learning more about their ancestors.
- Content Area: Language Arts
- Grade Level: 2
- Time Period: 60–90 Minutes
- Objectives: Given instruction on how to conduct an interview, the learner will
  1. demonstrate the ability to interview an ancestor; and
  2. share the results of the interview in class.

Background Information

This lesson was taught by a student teacher as part of several integrated language arts activities carried out over a 10-week period to help students become more familiar and friendly with each other. The setting was a second-grade class with 30 students, in a school in which most of the students and families were monolingual and middle class. In this class, three of the students were labeled limited English proficient (LEP), with Spanish as their primary language and the language spoken at home. One of the students was more proficient in both English and Spanish than the other two; all three second-language learners were Mexican American; the remainder of the class was composed of White Americans of varying ethnic backgrounds. The student teacher in this class made use of a modified seven-step lesson plan to communicate his plan of action and also submitted a letter of context along with the lesson plan. The "letter of context" is a device used in the California Polytechnic student teaching program and other programs that have adapted it. It allows the student teacher to provide special information about (1) the lesson plan itself in relation to prior and future lessons, (2) changes in the demographic profile of the classroom, and (3) targeted learners in the classroom. The student teacher's lesson plan and letter of context follow, along with a letter that was sent home to selected parents.

THE LESSON PLAN

ANTICIPATORY SET

"Class, who remembers what we were going to do with our ancestor information? Very good. Now show me with a thumbs up when you remember one of the things you are supposed to tell the class when you share your interview data."

At this point I will elicit, and then orally reinforce, that students are to

1. tell which ancestor they interviewed;
2. recite the question they asked and what the answer was;
3. state what they learned from the interview.

STATEMENT OF PURPOSE

"Who thinks he or she can tell me one reason we are sharing our interviews today? Yes, we do want to develop good speaking and listening skills, and there is one more reason. We want to learn more about each other, the way we are alike and the way we are different. The more we know, the easier it will be to form a helping community in our classroom."

PROCEDURE

1. Review the characteristics of good speaking in this class.
2. Review the characteristics of good listening.
3. Role-play an interview presentation—I will share an interview that was conducted.
4. Proceed with the presentation.

CLOSURE

"What are some interesting things you have learned from your classmates' presentations? Tell your partner first and then be prepared to share with the whole class."

THE LETTER SENT TO PARENTS

Dear Parents:

Next week the students in Mrs. Boxer's class will be sharing the results of an interview with one of their ancestors. Mrs. Boxer and I would appreciate it if you would help your son or daughter complete the interview. Here are some of the basic facts about this assignment.

1. The interview
   a. can be done with a parent, aunt, uncle, or grandparent;
   b. can have more than four questions;
   c. is due by November 20.
2. The student is to write out the answer to the questions that are asked.
3. The questions to be asked are these:
   a. Where did you go to school?
   b. What was school like when you were my age?
   c. What were your hobbies?
   d. What important event in history happened during your childhood?

Your support of this project is appreciated.
Sincerely,

Michael Deukmajian
Denise Boxer

THE LETTER OF CONTEXT

Dear Dr. Davidman,

Today you will see a neat presentation by some of the students. Their assignment was to interview an ancestor. This assignment was given to them last week and was due yesterday. Today will be a presentation of those interviews. I am predicting that some students will not be prepared because of absences and lack of effort. I did not ask the three ESL students to participate in this. But they will be required to listen, and I think they will learn from this listening. The students will be asked to tell who they interviewed, read the question asked and the answer given, and tell something they learned from doing this interview.

Analysis

On the positive side, this teacher candidate designed an integrated language arts activity that would allow most of the students to share an interesting language arts experience with a relative; he structured the activity so that students would have the opportunity to learn more about each other. In addition, the candidate reviewed speaking and listening standards at the appropriate time—when the assignment was first given and then again just prior to the recitations. The candidate also employed selected lesson design components (anticipatory set, purpose statement, modeling, and closure) in a manner that promoted active and appropriate participation by a wide range of students. The candidate encouraged parent involvement by sending home a fairly clear letter. On the other hand, from a multicultural point of view, there is much room for improvement in this lesson. Several of these improvements will be mentioned next and then incorporated into the restructured lesson plan that follows the analysis.

1. From the perspective of the multicultural model, a major flaw in this lesson is the total exclusion of the limited English proficient (LEP), potentially bilingual students and their Spanish-speaking parents, from active participation. It is not clear why the student teacher, and the cooperating teacher who approved the lesson, opted for exclusion. It may be because they could not easily translate their letter into Spanish or because they thought the overall activity was too complex for the three second-language learners. But even if this was the case, the lesson should have been modified so that the second-language learners could still conduct an interview with a relative or significant other. The student teacher apparently thought that any student who was going to participate in the lesson would have to participate at the same level as everyone else. Nothing could be further from the spirit of multiculturalizing/individualizing assignments according to individual students' special strengths, learning disabilities, linguistic capabilities, and home environments. This lesson could have been adjusted in any number of ways to accommodate and include all the students in this second-grade class.

   a. If the teacher has parents who do not speak English, he should immediately seek out human resources to help open up oral and written communication with the parents. The excluded parents should have received a letter about this interview assignment written in Spanish and English. The teacher should have sought help from the English as a second language (ESL) teacher at the school site, and could also have received help from a parent or upper-grade bilingual student. In addition, the teacher should lobby the principal to bring a bilingual resource person to the school site.

   b. The three English/Spanish-speaking students should have been allowed to interview their parents in Spanish and share their findings in written or oral form with each other. The student who was more bilingually proficient could have helped the other two prepare an oral presentation and might have volunteered to serve as a translator for the other two, with the added benefit of showing this second-language learner and the entire class why bilingualism is so practical and valuable. However, as we learned from our dialogue with the two students, they did not need a translator. They would have been able to report in English to their classmates what they had heard in Spanish from their parents. And the teacher or student teacher could have facilitated this recital by giving the second-language learners an opportunity for rehearsal prior to the presentation in front of the entire class. The teacher could also have invited one or more English-speaking second graders to help the second-language learners prepare their oral remarks. There are usually students, often budding teachers, who would be delighted to help; indeed, by association, some of these monolingual learners might be attracted to bilingualism at a propitious age.

c. The teacher could have structured the lesson so as to combine small- and large-group sharing; the students in this class were seated in groups of five, which served as cooperative learning groups. Students could have had the opportunity to report their interview data in the small group or the large group. As it turned out, the oral reporting in this class took much longer than was anticipated, and half the class did not have a chance to present their information with the whole class. Also, some of the students who did speak could not be heard because their voices were too soft.

d. From a precise vocabulary point of view, the lesson should not have been titled "Interviewing Ancestors." Ancestors are relatives from whom descent is derived, but an ancestor is often considered to be a person further back in line than a grandparent. Typically, your ancestors are not alive when you are and thus cannot be interviewed. A better title, allowing more flexibility and thus increasing the success potential of the lesson, would have been "Interviewing Relatives and Close Friends."

e. The list of possible questions should be expanded so as to (1) increase students' knowledge of selected cultural and ethnic groups; (2) provide flexibility for students and interviewee, allowing them to decide which three or four questions they wish to ask or answer; and (3) avoid placing students in a position of sharing information they might find embarrassing. For example, it is conceivable that some parents might not have attended school when they were young.

Additional questions related to (1) above include (a) When you were my age, what was your favorite holiday or celebration? (b) When you were my age, what was most different from today's world? and (c) When you were my age, where did you live and how was that community different from San Luis Obispo? Note that the last question opens up a potential connection with geography, and the teacher can now provide a map with push pins and string indicating the towns, cities, and countries in which the interviewees lived when they were young.

f. The letter to parents might have to be modified unless the teacher knows that all of the students are indeed living with one or more parents. If this is not the case, the letter should be addressed to parents and caretakers, and should refer to son, daughter, foster child, and so on. In addition, the last line should read, "Your consideration of this request is appreciated," instead of "Your support of this project is appreciated." We believe there is a subtle difference here and that the former ending treats the parent more like a respected client; the latter ending is slightly pushy. We realize that the difference here is small and that some educators might be comfortable with the ending just as it is. What do you think?

g. On a slightly different note, we suggest that the teacher consider using a microphone to increase the ability of students to project their voices more easily without shouting. If all can be heard, the whole-group sharing will be more enjoyable for a wider range of second graders, thus increasing the equity potential of this lesson. Once a microphone has been set up, the teacher might also choose to tape-record the presentations and then place the tape at the class listening post for future listening. Such embellishments require some extra preparation but pay off handsomely in added motivation and additional potential for sharing. For example, some students who were absent can still hear their classmates' presentations.

III. INTERVIEWING ANCESTORS (NOW CALLED INTERVIEWING RELATIVES OR CLOSE FRIENDS)

After Multicultural Restructuring

- Major Objective: To provide students with the opportunity to learn specific facts about their relatives or close friends as well as the families and friends of their classmates.
- Content Area: Language Arts, History, and Geography
- Grade Level: 2
- Time Period: 120 Minutes (3 sessions)
- Objectives: Given instruction in how to conduct an interview, the learner will
  1. demonstrate the ability to interview a relative or close friend of the family;
  2. share the results of the interview in class.

Suggested Modifications

1. As noted, change the name of the lesson, the major objectives, and the length of the lesson (one session to explain the project, two for the sharing and possible playback of selected presentations).
2. Include the three second-language learners and their parents in this integrated language arts activity, as delineated in the analysis section. Set up a support team of second graders to help the second-language learners prepare their presentations; allow these students to engage in a bit of behavior rehearsal prior to their oral presentations.
3. Expand the list of questions and involve the students in making up the final list of six to eight questions. Let the students know that on the day of the sharing, each child will decide whether to make the presentation to the small group or to the entire class. Model for them on that first day how the microphone and tape recorder will be used to facilitate the oral presentations.
4. Let the interviewers and the interviewees know that they can choose the three to five questions the interviewers will ultimately share.
5. Add a geography component to this activity by using a map, push pins, and yarn to mark where the interviewees lived when they were young children.
6. Modify the letter to parents as noted in the analysis section. In addition, encourage interviewees to share material about holidays and celebrations that students might not know about because the holiday is associated with a culture the students are unfamiliar with.
7. Allow students to give their presentation with a partner. The partner can read the question that was asked, and the interviewer can share what the interviewee said.
8. As an invitation to inquiry, invite a second grader whose grandmother or grandfather is alive to interview the grandparent about the grandparent's mother or father, the child's most immediate ancestors. Invite the student to share these findings in an oral or written report. From this invitation to inquiry, the teacher might discover that some of the children have grandparents living in different states and nations, and the invitation could lead to some joint parent–child letter writing to carry out the inquiry. In addition, the invitation might allow the teacher to learn about the extended or dispersed family of several of the students and could result in rapport-building with parents who value school projects that reinforce the young student's connection with and respect for the extended family.

SECTION THREE

Lesson Sequences

I. SMOKING PREVENTION

Before Multicultural Restructuring

- Major Objective: To make students more knowledgeable about the dangers of smoking, so they will be more likely to avoid smoking if they have not begun, and more inclined to stop if they have already started.
- Content Area: Health, Language Arts, and Science
- Grade Levels: 5–8
- Time Period: 100–120 Minutes (two lessons)
- Instructional Objectives The learner will be able to
  1. recall verbally or in writing the harmful ingredients in cigarettes: nicotine, tar, and carbon monoxide (lesson 1);
  2. explain verbally or in writing why or how nicotine, tar, and carbon monoxide are harmful to the human body (lesson 1);
  3. explain verbally and in writing why people smoke (lesson 2);
  4. understand and explain verbally and in writing the psychology of cigarette advertisements and their inherent fallacies (lesson 2);
  5. explain and/or model techniques on how to say *no* (lesson 2).

Background Information

These lessons were prepared by a preservice candidate as part of a senior project. The lessons were implemented in several upper-elementary classrooms (fifth and sixth grades), and the candidate made use of elements associated with a specific seven-step lesson plan to design and implement these lessons. The lesson plans and selected materials follow.

LESSON PLAN ONE

ANTICIPATORY SET

"How many of you have been near a person who is smoking?
"How did the person's smoke affect you?
"There are poisonous ingredients in cigarettes that cause unpleasant reactions in our bodies."

STUDENTS' OBJECTIVE

"Today we're going to learn about the dangerous ingredients in cigarettes and what harm they cause to people who smoke."

PURPOSE STATEMENT

"By learning about the harm caused by smoking cigarettes, each of us will be able to make a more knowledgeable decision about whether or not to smoke."

INPUT

"Cigarettes are made with leaves that come from the tobacco plant.

"Cigarettes and cigarette smoke contain three main harmful ingredients—nicotine, tar, and carbon monoxide—three items that I will now begin to tell you more about.

"*Nicotine* is a poison found in tobacco. It causes our blood vessels to constrict, reducing the flow of blood and oxygen through the body. This reduction causes an increase in blood pressure and heart rate that is not healthy. Nicotine also paralyzes the cilia in the bronchial tubes. *Cilia* are tiny hairlike structures that clean the lungs. When the cilia are paralyzed, dirt and germs are not removed from the lungs and sickness can result. There are billions of tiny particles of *tar* in cigarette smoke. When tar cools inside the lungs, it forms a brown sticky mass that contains chemicals that are believed to cause cancer.

"*Carbon monoxide* is found in cigarette smoke. It reduces the amount of oxygen carried in the blood. This means that the cells are demanding more oxygen than the blood is able to supply. Now we are going to learn about harm caused to the *lungs* and *heart* from smoking. First, let's think about what the lungs do. What is their function? Yes, the lungs allow us to breathe. When we breathe, oxygen comes into our lungs and goes to the *alveoli,* where it enters our blood and can then travel through our bodies and feed our cells. On our outline next to function of the lungs, let's write, 'The organ that allows us to breathe.'

"Next, let's think about what the *heart* does. The heart is the organ that pumps blood through our body so that our cells can get oxygen from the blood. The heart is a muscle. On our outline next to function of the heart, let's write, 'The organ that pumps blood through our body.'

"Smoking is very harmful to our lungs. Cigarette smoking is a major cause of emphysema, chronic bronchitis, and lung cancer.

"*Bronchitis* is an inflammation of the bronchial tubes. Smoking can cause bronchitis by irritating the cells in these tubes. Chronic bronchitis means that the bronchial tubes are always inflamed; this makes breathing very difficult, since the passageway for air is smaller.

"*Emphysema* is a stretching of the structures in the lungs. This makes it more difficult for oxygen to enter the blood at the alveoli.

"*Lung cancer* is a disease caused by the uncontrolled growth of abnormal cells. These abnormal cells destroy the healthy lung cells. Cigarette smoke contains chemicals that can cause the healthy lung cells to become cancerous cells.

"Smoking is also very harmful to our hearts. Cigarette smoking is a major cause of heart disease, heart attacks, and atherosclerosis. *Atherosclerosis* is caused when nicotine and carbon monoxide damage the inner walls of the arteries. This damage allows fat cells and other abnormal cells to build up on the walls of the arteries. The arteries carry blood away from the heart. This thickening of the artery walls by fat and abnormal cells that have built up causes narrowing and hardening of the arteries. When the arteries are hard and have a narrow opening, it is difficult for blood to pass through. This means the heart has to work harder to pump the blood.

"*Heart disease* is caused when the heart does not have the proper conditions to function. It means the heart is not healthy. Heart disease can lead to *heart attacks.* Heart attacks are caused when the heart does not get enough blood. The blood brings oxygen to the heart, so when the heart does not get enough blood, it lacks oxygen as well. The lack of blood and oxygen to the heart during a heart attack causes damage to the heart, since the heart cells can be killed when they do not get oxygen."

CHECK FOR UNDERSTANDING

1. "I want all of you to look at your outline (see Figure 3.1) and go over all the major points I just had you write down. Then discuss with your neighbor the harmful ingredients in cigarettes and how your lungs and heart are harmed by smoking.
2. "Now listen to me carefully and show me with thumbs up or down whether the material I mention is one of the three main harmful ingredients of cigarettes.
3. "Now let's do the same as I mention possible harmful effects that smoking produces in the lungs."

GUIDED PRACTICE

"Check your outline with your neighbor and then color in the illustrations of the heart and lungs."

FIGURE 3.1   Example Lesson Outline 1

Day 1 Outline

Key

nicotine   tar   carbon monoxide   cilia   emphysema   bronchitis
lung cancer   heart disease   heart attacks   atherosclerosis

Function of the lungs:
The organ that allows us to breathe.

Function of the heart:
The organ that pumps blood through our body.

I. Harmful ingredients in cigarettes
   1. nicotine
   2. tar
   3. carbon monoxide

II. Harm caused to the LUNGS
   1. bronchitis
   2. cilia
   3. emphysema (alveoli)
   4. lung cancer

III. Harm caused to the HEART
   1. heart disease
   2. heart attack
   3. atherosclerosis

CLOSURE

"I'd like each of you now to think about what we learned today, and then turn to your neighbor and tell him or her, first, what our lesson was about today and, second, what some harmful effects of smoking are."

INDEPENDENT PRACTICE (HOMEWORK)

"Complete this worksheet (see Figure 3.2) by filling in the correct term in each sentence."

LESSON PLAN TWO

ANTICIPATORY SET

"I'd like everyone to think back to our previous lesson on smoking and tell yourself one thing you learned about cigarette smoking.
    "Who can tell us three harmful ingredients of cigarettes and cigarette smoke?
    "Who can tell us some ways in which cigarette smoke harms the heart and lungs?"

STUDENTS' OBJECTIVE

"We know that cigarette smoking is harmful in many ways, so today we'll discuss and try to figure out why people might choose to smoke. We'll learn the major reasons people smoke, and we'll study the tactics advertisers use to promote an image that makes smoking acceptable and desirable to many consumers."

PURPOSE STATEMENT

"The information we study today should help us avoid the pressure to smoke and help us to say *no* to anyone who asks us to smoke."

FIGURE 3.2 Example Lesson Worksheet

Key

carbon monoxide   bronchitis   tar   emphysema

cilia   nicotine   atherosclerosis

Using the words listed above, write in the correct word to complete each sentence.

1. A poison in tobacco that constricts blood vessels and paralyzes cilia is <u>nicotine</u>.
2. A substance in cigarette smoke that forms a brown sticky mass in the lungs when it cools is <u>tar</u>.
3. An ingredient of cigarette smoke that decreases the oxygen in our blood is <u>carbon monoxide</u>.
4. A disease that makes gas exchange at the alveoli more difficult is <u>emphysema</u>.
5. The disease causing inflamed bronchial tubes is called <u>bronchitis</u>.
6. The disease that would cause narrowing of the passageway in an artery of the heart is called <u>atherosclerosis</u>.
7. The hairlike structures that keep the bronchial tubes clean are the <u>cilia</u>.

INPUT

1. "First, let's discuss *why people smoke*. On our outline (Figure 3.3), we can fill in the three reasons that people are most likely to smoke, and why they continue. (1) Parents, friends, or idols smoke; (2) cigarettes, matches, and ashtrays are easy to obtain; (3) nicotine is a very addictive drug.

2. "Advertisers spend over a billion dollars a year to get people to spend their money on cigarettes. These advertisements try to make smoking seem desirable. They do this by making the consumer want to be like the people in their ads. Different companies create different images of the people who smoke their cigarettes. They try to make you believe that by buying their brand of cigarettes you will be like the people in their ads. There are two things we should know about cigarette ads. They contain hidden messages, and the hidden messages contain fallacies, or incorrect statements.

3. "As you get older and go on to junior high and high school, your friends or acquaintances may offer you a cigarette and pressure you to smoke. We know the health reasons for why we should say *no* to smoking cigarettes. I am going to tell you of three ways to *say no* to someone who asks you to smoke. These same examples can be used to say *no* to drugs. First, you could simply ignore the question and walk away or change the subject; second, you could say, 'No, I'd rather not'; or third, you could say, 'No, I'm not going to smoke because it is bad for the heart and lungs, and I want to stay as healthy as I can.' This is an example of giving reasons why you don't want to smoke. By using the third example, you may even persuade the other person not to smoke. You should use the method of saying *no* that you feel most comfortable with.

4. "Now, I'd like you to look at your outline (Figure 3.3) and discuss with your neighbors why people smoke, how advertisers create a false image of smoking, and ways to say *no* if someone asks or pressures you to smoke."

FIGURE 3.3 Example Lesson Outline 2

Day 2 Outline

Key

parents, friends, or idols   easy to obtain   nicotine addiction   hidden message

false message   ignore   say <u>no</u>   say <u>no</u>, give reasons

---

I. Why People Smoke
  1. Parents, friends, or idols smoke
  2. Cigarettes, ashtrays, and matches are easy to obtain
  3. Nicotine addiction

II. Advertisements
  1. Hidden message
  2. False message

III. How to say <u>no</u>
  1. Ignore
  2. Say <u>no</u>
  3. Say <u>no</u>, give reasons

CHECK FOR UNDERSTANDING

"I'm going to ask some questions. Listen carefully and show me with your thumbs if the answer is correct or not. Why do people smoke? How do advertisers try to get people to buy their brand of cigarettes? What are some ways we can say *no* to someone who asks us to smoke?"

CLOSURE

"With your neighbor, do a role-play in which a parent or relative is asking you what you learned in school today that was interesting. In your response, among other things, identify the ingredient in cigarettes that is addictive and the ways you can say *no* to a person offering you a cigarette."

INDEPENDENT PRACTICE (HOMEWORK)

1. "For homework, complete the sheet with true/false and fill-in sentences." (See Figure 3.4.)
2. "Examine the activities listed on the Follow-up Activities worksheet and identify one you'd like to participate in, or add your own project to the list." (See Figure 3.5.)

Lesson Analysis

These lessons can be critiqued and improved from a variety of perspectives. On the plus side, the teacher candidate has selected a very appropriate content area for her fifth and sixth graders. Despite the warnings from the U.S. Surgeon General's office, the labeling on cigarette packages regarding the harmful effects of smoking, and the increasing sophistication of television antismoking commercials, in the United States

FIGURE 3.4 Example Lesson Outline 2

True or False

T   F   1. Smoking is harmful to the lungs.
T   F   2. Cancer and heart attacks can be caused by smoking.
T   F   3. There is poison in cigarette smoke.
T   F   4. Smoking is an easy habit to break for people who have smoked for a long time.
T   F   5. Bronchitis and emphysema are diseases caused by smoking.
T   F   6. Smoking does not affect the heart.
T   F   7. Smoking makes kids look and seem grown up.
T   F   8. If a friend asks us to smoke, it is okay to say <u>no.</u>

Fill in the blank with one of the following words:

Key

oxygen   cilia   lungs   heart   advertisements

1. When we breathe in, <u>oxygen</u> goes into our blood and feeds the cells.
2. <u>Cilia</u> are hairlike structures that sweep out our air passages to keep them clean.
3. We breathe with our <u>lungs</u>.
4. The <u>heart</u> is the body organ that pumps blood through the body.
5. <u>Advertisements</u> try to show an image that people will want to copy.

Possible Follow-Up Activities

1. Public Service Announcements
    Have a contest among the students to write and recite public service announcements about the hazards of smoking. Do the announcements in class or contact radio or television stations beforehand to find out about airing the announcements.

2. Awareness in the School
    Have the students design antismoking posters. The students could start a campaign to inform the entire school about the hazards of smoking.

3. Math
    Have students investigate how much a pack of cigarettes costs and determine how much a one-, two-, or three-pack-a-day smoker would spend on cigarettes in a year.

4. Interview
    Have students interview smokers and nonsmokers as to why they do or do not smoke and their attitudes toward smoking.

5. Current Events
    Have students look for information about cigarette smoking in newspapers.

FIGURE 3.5   Example Follow-Up Activities Worksheet

we still have large numbers of teenagers who begin smoking each year. Thomas Glynn found that each day more than 2,000 American adolescents smoke their first cigarette,[2] and the University of Michigan Institute for Social Research reported that 18.1 percent of American high school seniors smoked every day in 1988.[3] Given the linkages between cigarettes and lung cancer and emphysema, and the status of cigarettes as a gateway drug with the potential to lead to other serious forms of drug abuse, prevention education related to cigarettes is clearly warranted.

In addition to selecting an appropriate content area, the teacher candidate, utilizing resources from the American Lung Association, has selected meaningful facts to call to the attention of the fifth and sixth graders who received these lessons. In particular, the candidate attempted to incorporate a no-use message into her lessons. Beyond these positives there is ample room for improvement, and we will use several of the evaluation questions for multiculturalization to structure our improvement remarks.

Does the lesson content and structure promote or impede educational equity? These lessons were initially prepared for fifth and sixth graders in general and not a specific classroom, so as we respond to this question and the ones that follow, we will keep in mind the wide range of learners teachers often encounter, even in classrooms that are relatively homogeneous in terms of ethnicity.

For this wide range of learners and their various learning style preferences, points of view, prior knowledge of, and perhaps experience with, cigarettes, the candidate's decision to view her learners as empty vessels who would be filled up with important knowledge is a weakness. Before you can consider more subtle questions related to teaching effectively with a multicultural perspective, you must consider some very basic questions about making the most effective use of the model of instruction you are employing. For these lessons the candidate employed a teacher-directed approach that leaned heavily on a seven-step lesson design format familiar to many prospective and veteran teachers. It is a format many teachers use well as they employ it flexibly and integrate it with other approaches to teaching and learning. In this sequence, however, there is no creative or flexible use of this lesson format. The format is disconnected from the mastery-learning model of which it is a part. Thus, the candidate is cut off from the diagnostic and task analysis process that would put her in touch with what students already know about the topic, and what they would like to know, to help her sequence the material she would ultimately teach.

In addition to diagnostic work, teachers who draw on the seven-step format as they make instructional design decisions often use selected ideas about learning to promote efficient learning for all students; these ideas lead teachers to employ teaching tactics related to anticipatory set, active participation, reinforcement, retention, motivation, and closure. In these lessons the candidate's attempts at active participation—keeping the students' minds consistently engaged in the lesson—were limited to having them fill out a worksheet after listening to her present information orally. Occasionally, the students would be directed to share and discuss their worksheet with a neighbor. The candidate, perhaps because she was working in classrooms that were not her own, fell back on the oldest and least effective way of transmitting information—the lecture. These lecture remarks were not illuminated by slides or other visuals, or punctuated by thought-provoking questions. The candidate does not know what her students know because she has not done any diagnostic work prior to sharing information about nicotine, carbon monoxide, and cilia. In lesson one, she should ask students what they know about these terms and then connect her remarks to their comments. In addition to an increase in questioning, the candidate could create more active participation by incorporating more variety in modes of information delivery. Directed reading, thinking, and discussion activities would serve this purpose, as would the selective use of videotape or slide/cassette tape presentations, role-playing, or brainstorming.

Another area worthy of revision concerns the relationship between the major objective of the lesson and the purpose statement in lesson one. The major objective incorporates a strong and appropriate no-use message. The goal of this lesson is prevention, to keep young people away from cigarettes, or to persuade them to stop smoking if they have already begun smoking or experimenting. In the statement of purpose, however, the candidate's words suggest that the objective of the lesson is to provide information that will help the students make a more informed decision about whether to become a smoker. Ultimately, of course, that is what each student will do, but current research suggests that the teacher should be a partial, rather than an impartial, disseminator of information. The teacher should be willing to say something like this:

> The purpose of today's lesson and this entire sequence is to persuade and prepare each of you to avoid smoking and cigarette smoke, and to stop experimenting with cigarettes if you've already begun. If you wish, you can consider today's lesson one big antismoking commercial. I care about you and your health, and that's why I don't want you to smoke.

It is noteworthy that the purpose statement and the entire approach employed by the candidate appear to be closely aligned to the "information-only" program of alcohol and drug prevention that was the dominant mode of drug prevention in the 1970s and 1980s. Writing in 1987, John Van de Kamp, attorney general of California, described this method in the following way:

This approach relies heavily on scare tactics and provides some information on the effects of drug and alcohol in the human body. It assumes that the individual uses drugs because of the lack of information, and that by providing that the individual will choose not to use drugs. This method is outdated and some researchers even claim that it may contribute to increased drug and alcohol abuse.[4]

Furthermore, in discussing constructive alternatives to the information-only approach, Van de Kamp said that "the essential ingredient seems to be the comprehensive approach of a K–12 curriculum. Such a curriculum must emphasize development of a strong level of self-esteem . . . must emphasize effective decision-making skills, and must be age-appropriate. It must give special weight to teaching social skills and refusal skills in difficult situations. And it must be supported by parental and youth involvement at every level with peer support being especially important."[5]

One of the main ideas in the model of instruction employed by the candidate is that after selecting an appropriate instructional objective, the teacher should teach directly to that objective with relevant behaviors (which is another way of saying appropriate strategies). In addition, in our Typology of Multicultural Teaching (see appendix 1), we say that teachers should use the direct instruction model in a sophisticated manner. This means knowing when to use and not use it, when to integrate it with other models, and how to use it well when using it. In this instance, Van de Kamp's statements strongly suggest that the candidate was not using appropriate strategies. The candidate included the idea of refusal in her lesson but thought that all she had to do was provide information about refusal. However, research suggests that to increase the age at which individuals begin to experiment with tobacco, alcohol, or marijuana, or to prevent it altogether, students need the opportunity to role-play refusal and to discuss the difficult choices many will encounter. The addition of role-playing and discussion related to the role-playing scenarios suggests that this two-lesson sequence will need to be lengthened. A review of curricula designed to prevent drug and alcohol abuse reveals that several popular research-based prevention curricula for grades five through eight contain 10 to 12 lessons in their sequence. Although some prevention curricula and programs focus on tobacco exclusively, more recently designed curricula integrate prevention education for tobacco with prevention education for alcohol and marijuana and also link this content to larger health considerations. Such curricula are described in *Schools and Drugs: A Guide to Drug and Alcohol Abuse Prevention Curricula and Programs*,[6] and K–8 educators interested in designing sophisticated and multiculturalized lesson sequences in this area should review the 19 curricula described in this document. Particularly noteworthy are Project SMART—grades six through nine (developed by the Institute for Health Promotion and Disease Prevention Research at the University of Southern California); Ombudsman: A Classroom Community—grades five and six (developed by the Drug Education Center, Charlotte, North Carolina); and Parent and Substance Use Prevention/PASS-UP—grades six and seven (developed by the American Lung Association of Los Angeles County and the Institute for Health Promotion and Disease Prevention Research, University of Southern California). In the latter curriculum, both classroom and homework activities involve parents; follow-up research conducted 18 months after the 10-session curriculum was implemented revealed that a high level of parent involvement was a critical factor in maintaining a low usage rate of alcohol and marijuana.[7] This research result relates to the second question in our multiculturalization process.

Does the lesson content or structure make use of, or help to develop, collaborative, empowering relationships among parents, students, and teachers? In our model, the goal of collaboration among parents, teachers, and students is eminently sensible for a variety of reasons. Logic suggests that classroom teachers and parents, functioning as guides and educators in different settings and sometimes differing cultural contexts, will be more effective in motivating and supporting students when they share information about students' proclivities and progress, and work together as a team.

What we learn from drug prevention research is that, in this area of the curriculum, parent involvement is not only desirable but critical. The introduction to a recent drug prevention guide put it this way:

> There is little evidence to challenge the basic premise that prevention is the most human and cost-effective response to drug and alcohol abuse and related problems among youth. But preventing drug use takes more than classroom instruction. Research shows that no curriculum has much impact on students' behavior concerning drugs, unless it is delivered in the context of a comprehensive prevention program encompassing school instruction, parent involvement, and community support.[8]

Like many lessons designed and implemented by student teachers who are in classrooms for relatively short periods of time, the lesson sequence outlined above did not have a parent-involvement component. However, whether the instructor is a student or a veteran teacher, there are several good reasons for involving parents in drug prevention instruction. In terms of long-term prevention or overall effectiveness, parent involvement is an influential factor in the prevention equation. Even if parent involvement did not make the curriculum more powerful, the teacher working with a multicultural perspective would want to communicate with parents prior to implementing this sequence because this teacher, more than others, wants to maintain rapport and open lines of communication between parents and teacher and parents and students.

The maintenance of such smooth, two-way communication is a major goal of the multicultural model. Thus, because the multicultural perspective encourages the teacher to habitually think about the learner in the broader context of family and community, it will be second nature for the teacher oriented to multicultural instruction to consider the effects of the lesson content on the students' extended families. This consideration will likely lead the teacher to see that this content is not neutral, innocent information devoid of social or family implications. Because parents or relatives of the students may be smokers, we believe the teacher, in planning this sequence, is ethically bound to consider the social implications of the content. Minimally, parents should receive an overview of the objectives and content in this set of lessons in the monthly newsletter that precedes the sequence, and parents should be invited to attend any of the sessions. Parents who have quit smoking can make brief presentations as part of a panel; homework assignments can be designed with a component that involves parents and child, so that parents are also learning or being reminded about the prevention content. In addition, students should have the opportunity to discuss the way this content, and antismoking advertising in general, might make smokers in their extended families feel, and how and if they should use their new knowledge in the family context. In leading this discussion, the teacher should make clear that although politeness is an obvious consideration, there are no easy answers to this question. Various responses should be expected because of the different values and relationships that exist in different families. This content might produce sadness or fear in some students because of their relatives' smoking. Therefore, teachers should encourage students to write about these and other feelings in their classroom journal so the teacher can address their individual concerns.

Another observation is that the structure of the candidate's sequence did little to use or develop collaborative relationships between students. The student teacher's plan had neighbors checking and discussing each other's worksheets, but *neighbor* is a vague term; students can change neighbors from one part of the lesson to the next, and some students may not find a neighbor easily. This sequence, in a variety of ways, would improve if it were implemented in a "classroom community" in which partners and cooperative learning groups were integral elements. Smoking is not just an individual problem. It is also a social problem, and the solutions for the individual and the society are intertwined. Therefore, cooperative problem solving and support groups provide the logical context in which to receive prevention knowledge. Commitments made to peers, who in a cooperative learning environment have a responsibility to help each other, should strengthen everyone's individual resolve to resist pro-use media messages and local peer pressure.

Collective and critical analysis of pro-use and antismoking advertising can help to strengthen students' resolve not to smoke. It can also show students how certain corporations in America and elsewhere attempt to use knowledge of cultural groups, such as women, and ethnic groups, such as African Americans and Hispanic Americans, to sell products like cigarettes and alcohol. We will discuss this further under our next evaluative question, the last one to be considered in this analysis.

Does the lesson content help to increase students' knowledge regarding various cultural and ethnic groups? The candidate's sequence, which dealt with advertising in a very general way, did not add to her students' knowledge of cultural and ethnic groups. Significant improvement could be made here in the lesson plan, because cigarette product development has been described as "the epitome of what advertisers call *niche* marketing, with more than 300 brands, targeted by gender, race, and socio-economic group."[9] With concrete examples, students should be made aware that specific groups such as the poor, women, Blacks, Hispanics, and the young in general are routinely targeted by cigarette corporations, and that the objective of the corporations is to lure members of these groups into smoking. Consider the story of Uptown. In 1988, R. J. Reynolds developed Uptown, a new cigarette aimed at the African-American market. The new cigarette "had less menthol flavoring, was packaged in black and gold . . . and was packed with the filters facing down after market research indicated that Black-American smokers tend to open cigarette packs from the bottom. Six months of test marketing were scheduled to begin in January 1990 in Philadelphia, which has a Black population of some forty percent, through heavy advertising in Black newspapers, on billboards and buses, and through point-of-purchase displays."[10] The Uptown story shows students how individuals and groups can fight back to protect their own communities and children. In late January 1990, Reynolds canceled its plans to pilot and market its new product, losing an estimated five to seven million dollars. The cancelation resulted from the combined protest efforts of antismoking groups, African-American community leaders, and Louis Sullivan, then U.S. Secretary of Health and Human Services.[11] The story also reveals the tenacity of the cigarette industry. In 1990, R. J. Reynolds tested two additions to its Salem line, Salem Gold and Salem Box. Each has the lower level of menthol that Black smokers prefer, according to R. J. Reynolds's market research.[12]

Other case studies can be used to show products and advertising that have been developed to target different groups: Rio and Dorado cigarettes for Hispanics,[13] Virginia Slims for women, and Dakota, a cigarette aimed at young uneducated White women, aged 18 to 24, who are considered to be virile females.[14] This may not be the type of ethnic and cultural knowledge practitioners have in mind when they think about multiculturalizing the curriculum, but in learning how to grow in a positive and healthy way in our society, students need to learn that some corporations and advertising agencies will exploit cultural and ethnic patterns to attract individuals to various addictive and dangerous products such as cigarettes.

I. SMOKING PREVENTION

After Multicultural Restructuring

- Major Objective: To provide students with a variety of reasons and skills to help them (1) avoid the smoking habit and (2) stop smoking if they have already begun.
- Content Area: Health, Language Arts, Science, and Social Science
- Grade Levels: 5–10
- Time Period: 4 to 8 Weeks
- Instructional Objectives The learner will be able to
  1. assertively and constructively turn down offers of cigarettes in role-playing situations;
  2. give specific examples of the way cigarette advertising, packaging (shape and design of box and cigarette), and promotion of sports events is designed to attract young people to cigarette smoking;
  3. identify and describe specific examples of cigarette companies developing cigarette products and advertising campaigns targeted at specific cultural and ethnic groups;
  4. identify several reasons for saying *no* to cigarettes;
  5. identify specific locations where smoking is prohibited (e.g., airplanes, Carl's Jr. restaurants);
  6. identify the harmful ingredients in cigarettes (nicotine, tar, and carbon monoxide) and explain how these elements harm an individual's health;
  7. explain why young people begin smoking and why some veteran smokers find it difficult to stop.

Suggested Modifications

1. To enhance effectiveness, during the planning stage, analyze curriculum packages that incorporate the latest knowledge regarding tobacco prevention; review periodical articles and texts to make certain your content and strategies reflect current research.
2. Consider expanding the sequence to include lessons on alcohol and marijuana prevention.
3. Design the sequence and class newsletter so that parents and other caretakers have the maximum opportunity to participate in the sequence as learners, volunteer instructional assistants, guest lecturers, and homework assistants for their child when possible. Help with homework should be requested in a polite and sensitive manner.
4. In the class newsletter, several weeks prior to the unit, provide an overview of the sequence content and objectives and invite parents and caretakers to discuss the content with you at a special meeting prior to sequence imple-

mentation. Provide other means of communication for the adults who cannot attend the special meeting.

5. During the planning stage, conduct diagnostic work to learn what your students already know about this topic and what they would like to learn. To the greatest possible extent, incorporate collaborative and self-directed approaches to learning in this sequence.

6. Consider, during the planning stage, having students design inquiries to learn
   a. how many, or if any, fifth or sixth graders have experimented with cigarette smoking;
   b. what kinds of cigarette advertising they see in their communities and homes.

7. Organize the students into learning teams and give each team the responsibility for designing and implementing a special citizenship project related to the sequence. Brainstorm possibilities within groups and then the whole class.

8. Diversify the methods used to disseminate sequence content and significantly reduce the amount of time lecturing; devote at least one period to role-playing, giving each student the opportunity to practice refusal communication.

9. Disseminate brief descriptions of tobacco products and advertising campaigns that have targeted specific ethnic and cultural groups in the United States. Consider showing a film such as *Seeing Through Commercials,* which is described in *Schools and Drugs* as a 15-minute film appropriate for fourth through sixth graders.[15] The film shows how commercials are made and certain techniques are used to induce people to buy products.

10. Design invitations for inquiry that will
    a. allow your students to play a role in shaping the ongoing sequence. You might encourage some students to preview films and videos available in your district's instructional media center and select one or two the class would benefit from seeing;
    b. give them the opportunity to analyze new cigarette advertising to learn whether they can discern who is being targeted for "disease recruitment";
    c. give them the opportunity to learn whether other nations like Mexico, Canada, France, Japan, or Nigeria put warnings on cigarette products, and if not, why not. Can American companies sell cigarettes in other countries without the warning labels? If yes, is this fair?
    d. give them the opportunity to correspond with or interview citizens like Louis Sullivan, U.S. Secretary of Health and Human Services during the Bush administration, who have publicly taken strong antismoking positions;
    e. give them the opportunity to learn whether the U.S. Congress and Department of Agriculture still provide subsidies to American farmers who grow tobacco.
    f. encourage your students to analyze the latest findings regarding nicotine addiction. The article "Nicotine Plays Deadly Role in Infant Death" by L. Seachrist, in *Science News,* July 15, 1995, 39, will prove helpful in this inquiry, as will T. Adler, "Infants' Deaths Become Less Mysterious," in *Science News,* March 11, 1995, 151.

Final Comments

The restructuring of this sequence was similar to prior restructuring in that a variety of techniques was used to "multiculturalize" the content. However, the restructuring in the "Smoking Prevention" sequence provided an opportunity to introduce a different type of multicultural/multiethnic knowledge. Students became aware that some American corporations actually target specific ethnic and cultural groups for what might objectively be called "disease recruitment." The impulse to think, wonder, and see with a multicultural perspective is shaped, over time, by "social facts" such as these. Such facts clearly indicate that some very powerful organizations think deeply about culture and ethnicity when they make influential marketing decisions. Informed citizens need to be aware that corporations use gender, culture, and ethnicity to sell their products; such knowledge helps consumers evaluate the real intent of the marketing message. Teachers can help their students in becoming informed consumers by a thorough examination of marketing strategies such as those discussed here. In addition, they can foster empowerment by inviting their students to participate in social action projects designed to countervail media campaigns aimed at the recruitment of new smokers.

II. Discovering New Pilgrims in America

Before Multicultural Restructuring

- Major Objective: To enhance teacher awareness of a wide range of traditional Thanksgiving literature and ways to utilize it.
- Content Area: Language Arts and Social Studies
- Grade Levels: 3–8
- Time Period: One Week

Background and Implementation Information

The "before" and "after" sequence of lessons that follow was designed by us and used in our graduate and undergraduate methods courses to illustrate how the selection of curriculum materials can promote or impede the development of a multicultural curriculum. The direction of the sequence is from more traditional Thanksgiving stories and activities toward those with the potential to promote intergroup harmony; increase students' knowledge of selected cultural and ethnic groups; and increase students' willingness and ability to examine an issue, word, or political situation from a new and perhaps multicultural perspective. Note that, at the end of the sequence, we tell our teachers and future K–8 teachers that the implementation procedures for the sequence of stories they will use can roughly parallel our procedures, but should also diverge creatively.

Because (1) our initial objective is to make our students more aware of a wide range of traditional Thanksgiving materials and (2) our classes are divided into cooperative learning groups, we structure this sequence in the following way:

1. Working in their cooperative learning groups, students tell whether their families have a tradition of celebrating Thanksgiving; if so, how they celebrate it; and what their own personal feelings are about Thanksgiving. (Is this a holiday they look forward to? Why? Why not?)
2. After this, we distribute to each group a different set of traditional Thanksgiving materials (stories, songs, poems, craft activities, etc.) from the university library. Each group collectively examines the materials and develops a con-

sensus about the three or four they would most likely use in their own classrooms. The materials distributed include the following:

a. "Thanksgiving," in *Twenty-five Plays for Holidays* (Boston: Plays Inc.,
   1952), 124–177.
b. "November: A Play for Thanksgiving—The Case of the Gone Gobbler," in
   Teacher's Activity Calendar (New York: Instructor Publications, 1981),
   56–57.
c. "Thanksgiving," in *Holiday Plays for Little Players* (Boston: Plays Inc.,
   1957), 92–111.
d. *The First Thanksgiving* (New York: Knopf, 1942).
e. *Let's Find Out About Thanksgiving* (New York: Watts, 1964).
f. *The Plymouth Thanksgiving* (New York: Doubleday, 1967).
g. *A Charlie Brown Thanksgiving* (New York: Random House, 1974).
h. *The Harvest Feast: Stories of Thanksgiving Yesterday and Today* (New
   York: Dutton, 1938).
i. "Thanksgiving," in *Holiday Storybook* (New York: Crowell, 1952),
   290–314.

3. Each group indicates its consensus choices with one or two other groups,
   using the following routine: the spokesperson, using notes created by the
   scribe, shows and identifies all the materials examined and then introduces
   the team members who will present one of the consensus choices, one or
   more reasons for the choice, and the grade levels they consider most appropriate for their selected materials.

4. The next step is to ask each group to identify what its materials have in common with those presented by the other groups. The answers for each group
   are put on the board, and the groups will generally discover that their material included traditional elements and symbols of the historical American
   Thanksgiving story: Pilgrims, Indians, a turkey, family togetherness, giving
   thanks.

5. When this analysis is completed, the teachers and student teachers are asked
   whether they have found any stories, songs, poems, or craft activities that
   introduce new elements into the traditional Thanksgiving story or that treat
   the old elements in a new and thoughtful way. The discussion that follows
   leads into the next step in the sequence where the authors present two stories and one film; these together help to achieve objectives related to multiculturalization questions 3, 4, and 5 enumerated at the beginning of this
   chapter.

6. In our sequence, the main story we offer is *Molly's Pilgrim* by Barbara Cohen
   (Bantam Skylark by arrangement with New York: William Morrow, 1990). The
   book was originally published in 1983. We use it because it is a touching,
   well-written book but also because the story was made into a film that is easily available to teachers in our region; the film, produced by Jeff Brown, won
   an Academy Award for Best Short Film in 1986. We discuss the book by using
   a set of into, through, and beyond activities to illustrate how this approach to
   language development can relate to effective teaching and multicultural education. *Molly's Pilgrim* introduces elementary readers to an immigrant Russian Jewish family who has moved to America to find religious freedom. In the
   story we find Molly, the protagonist, in conflict with Elizabeth and several
   other classmates who ridicule her, do not generously accept her differences in
   speech and dress, and are particularly insensitive to the wrenching change

Molly's family has recently experienced. The story line moves from rejection and bigotry to acceptance and tolerance as Molly's mother encourages her to share in class the insight that she, Molly, and Molly's dad are modern-day pilgrims. Molly, in response to her teacher's homework assignment, nervously shows a pilgrim doll that closely resembles her mother dressed in Russian garb instead of a Puritan or Indian doll as requested. The stage is then set for Miss Stickley, who in several ways resembles an old-fashioned teacher, to tell Molly's classmates that "I'm going to put this beautiful doll on my desk where everyone can see it all the time. It will remind us that pilgrims are still coming to America." Then she says that the Pilgrims got the idea for Thanksgiving from reading in the Bible "about the Jewish harvest festival of Tabernacles." This festival is called Sukkot by contemporary Jews.

7. In our university classroom, to set the stage for appreciating and understanding our initial reading of *Molly's Pilgrim,* we review a number of words from the story and read the story in a slow, dramatic way. This illustrates how we would attempt to make our oral rendition more comprehensible for limited English proficient (LEP) listeners. We review these words with contextual clues—the word in a sentence—with pictures and maps, and also with concrete experiences where appropriate, such as a peppermint stick. Some of the words we preview from *Molly's Pilgrim* are *Cossacks, Russians, pilgrim, peppermint, tenement, synagogue, Goraduk, embroidered, tabernacles, religious freedom, Oi Malkelah, shaynkeit, paskudnyaks, Nu Malkelah,* and *Yiddish.* With our largely English-speaking, monolingual teachers and prospective teachers we spent a bit of extra time explaining the meaning of these Yiddish phrases to emphasize the value that this type of "sheltered English" preparatory activity will have for all learners, especially the limited English proficient learners who will be encountering strange-sounding, strange-looking English and Yiddish words for the first time. For those who want to use Molly's Pilgrim in class, the following translations are based on information in Leo Rosten's *The Joys of Yiddish* (New York: Simon and Schuster, Pocket Book edition, 1970).

   a. "*Nu Malkelah,*" as used in this book (p. 22), means "So, little Malke." However, the reader should know that *nu* (pronounced nōō, to rhyme with *moon*) is a versatile expression that can have many meanings, depending on how it is said and where it is placed in a sentence. Rosten shows us that it can mean "How are things with you?" "What's new?" "Well," "So," as well as at least 15 other things. In addition, Malke is a Yiddish name, and was Molly's name when she lived in Russia.

   b. *Oi, Malkelah,* as used in this story (p. 10), is meant to communicate dismay and regret, as if to say, "I'm sorry, little Malke." Leo Rosten says *Oy* is not a word but rather a vocabulary. Like *nu,* it is an expression that can take on many meanings.

   c. *Shaynkeit* (pronounced shānkīte) means "beautiful child" or "my beautiful child." *Schön* (pronounced shān) in German means pretty, and *shayner* in Yiddish means "beautiful" or "pretty." In Yiddish, *shayner* denotes goodness more than physical beauty.

   d. *Paskudnyaks* is a Yiddish word that derives from *paskudne,* a Polish/Ukrainian word for "nasty," "dirty," or "sloppy." A *paskudnyak* is a person who is nasty, mean, insensitive, petty, or simply contemptible.

    e. Yiddish, according to Leo Rosten, is a language that is about 1,000 years old. Rosten writes that "Yiddish is descended from a form of German heard by Jewish settlers from Northern France about a thousand years ago,"[16] but the letters used to write Yiddish words were from the Hebrew alphabet rather than the German. The use of Yiddish in modern times was severely diminished by the destruction of East European Jewry during World War II.

8. After the vocabulary study, we deliver the first oral reading by ourselves without the help of students, but students are asked to listen carefully and to jot down any questions they may have about the story. After the story is read, we ask a general question such as, "Well, what did you think about this story?" Then we listen to the students' reactions before answering their questions.

9. After the question-and-answer period, we discuss and list the different ways elementary students might read this story after the teacher's oral presentation. Some of these ideas include assigning parts to various readers for a whole-class rendition, allowing cooperative learning groups to read the story within groups in a round-robin fashion, and allowing partners to read the story to each other page by page. As a part of this exercise, we distribute questions to our prospective teachers, instruct them to discuss one or more questions of their choice, and create and answer a question of their own after the reading is completed. With this component we remind future teachers about the importance of self-directed learning and self-initiated questioning, and the fact that structure (a set of questions) and self-directed learning can go hand in hand. By providing meaningful choices and appropriate amounts of time, the teacher in a clear and deliberate way begins to share classroom power with the learners. In this component the opportunity to choose is also diagnostic because several of the questions deal with the nastiness and prejudice displayed by Elizabeth, Molly's antagonist in this story. Questions such as "Why do you think Elizabeth was so mean and intolerant?" and "Where do you think her ideas about Russian immigrants came from?" provide teachers and their students the opportunity to discuss their feelings about intolerance. Parenthetically, whether or not students have chosen to respond to the questions that relate to intolerance, we encourage our teachers to spend time discussing these important multicultural questions with their students.

10. When these discussions are completed, our students are asked to go back to the story one more time to identify the characters who spoke (Molly, Elizabeth, Mama, Miss Stickley, and Emma), the characters who were mentioned (Papa, Mr. Brodsky, Hilda, Kitty, Faye, Emma, Arthur, Michael), and important icons, artifacts, or symbols from the story (Molly's Pilgrim Doll). This analysis sets the stage for viewing the 23-minute film version of *Molly's Pilgrim* from Phoenix films. As an advance organizer, students are told that, in addition to discussing their general likes and dislikes about the film version, the class will focus on the following questions:

    a. In the film what was new in terms of characters, dialogue, and setting?

    b. What appeared in the novel that did not appear in the film?

    c. What was left in but modified?

    d. Why do you think there was a difference between the book and the film?

    e. Which of the changes did you like? Why? Which changes did you not like? Why?

After the students assimilate the idea that storytelling in different media requires some changes, we ask them through a series of invitations for inquiry to engage in some creative writing, drawing, acting, and general research. What follows is a sampling of these inquiries:

    a. Develop a readers' theater script for *Molly's Pilgrim* or modify one that exists and then select a cast, perform, and possibly videotape it.

    b. Develop a movie script for one or more scenes from *Molly's Pilgrim,* select your actors and actresses, practice parts, perform, and possibly videotape it.

    c. Write an entirely new play based on the character of Molly—possible titles include *Molly's Christmas Story, Molly's Return to Russia,* or *Molly Visits Relatives in Mexico.*

    d. Make drawings of several of the characters and possibly a doll representing your favorite character in the book.

    e. Write a report that discusses the history of Yiddish.

11. In our college course, after we have completed a series of into, through, and beyond activities based on *Molly's Pilgrim,* we read another story that introduces or reminds our student teachers about another type of modern-day pilgrim, in this case boat people leaving their country to seek political freedom in the United States. The story we read is a picture book for primary graders and older students entitled *How Many Days to America: A Thanksgiving Story,* written by Eve Bunting (New York: Ticknor and Fields, 1988).

12. After we have engaged our students in the aforementioned activities, we have them review multiculturalization questions 1 through 8. Then, with a partner, students design a sequence of activities based on *Molly's Pilgrim,* and other Thanksgiving resources to meet the objectives of several of these questions.

Analysis

The sequence described contains a number of positive elements. For one, it shows how to build a multicultural curriculum by combining older curriculum elements with new resources. This is positive because it provides a response to critics of multicultural education. Often they claim that such instruction is anti-White, anti-European, and antimale; they maintain that it consistently devalues European contributions to American culture at the same time that it uncritically celebrates the accomplishments of indigenous Americans and Americans of all colors save White. From this sequence, and other commentary in this text, it should be clear that we, along with many other advocates of multicultural education, favor an approach that is well-rounded, balanced, and accurate in terms of its distribution of praise and criticism.

Second, the sequence demonstrates that awareness of relatively new literary resources, published in the 1970s, 1980s, and 1990s, greatly facilitates the multiculturalization of a holiday that is a deeply entrenched part of the American K–8 curriculum. By extension, future and veteran teachers should perceive that the curriculum experiences for other widely celebrated holidays in February (the month of presidents, Valentine's Day, and African-American History month) and March/April (Easter, Passover, and Women's History month) can be multiculturalized by combining older and newer curriculum resources. The sequence also makes use of cooperative learning groups and integrated whole-language teaching strategies that lead to higher-level thinking activities (the invitations for inquiry); it brings to the readers' attention a print and film resource that is useful for multicultural education, teacher education, and general literary enjoyment.

On the other hand, there is clearly room for improvement in this sequence at the university level or in an adapted format at the elementary or middle-school level. For example, as presented in our course, not much is done with *How Many Days to America: A Thanksgiving Story*, beyond reading it in class and asking students how they might use it in an elementary setting. Because this brief picture book does not name the island or nation the newcomers are fleeing, the story should be reinforced by books and other media that make it clear that we are talking about real people here. The following print resources could be used in a university or elementary/middle-school classroom:

1. Carol Olsen Day and Edmund Day, *The New Immigrants* (New York: Franklin Watts, 1985).
2. Joan McCarthy First, *New Voices: Immigrant Students in U.S. Public Schools* (Boston: National Coalition of Advocates for Students, 1988).
3. James Haskins, *The New Americans: Vietnamese Boat People* (Hillside, N.J.: Enslow, 1980).
4. James Haskins, *The New Americans: Cuban Boat People* (Hillside, N.J.: Enslow, 1982).
5. Brent Ashabranner, *Children of the Maya: A Guatemalan Indian Odyssey* (New York: Dodd, Mead, 1986).

There is nothing in this sequence to remind students that some parents and students may not celebrate Thanksgiving at all, although some students may share such information in their cooperative learning groups. Even though the thrust of this sequence is on discovering new pilgrims to America, future and veteran teachers should be reminded that Thanksgiving has been, but should no longer remain, a holiday during which false information about Native Americans has been disseminated. As an example, Michael Dorris wrote in an essay entitled "Why I'm Not Thankful for Thanksgiving":

> A year ago my older son brought home a program printed by his school; on the second page was an illustration of the "First Thanksgiving," with a caption which read in part: "they served pumpkins and turkeys and corn and squash. The Indians had never seen such a feast!" On the contrary. The Pilgrims had literally never seen "such a feast" since all foods mentioned are exclusively indigenous to the Americas and had been provided, or so legend has it, by the local tribe.[17]

The moral here, and the message to be included in the sequence, is that as we make use of new themes such as those embodied in *Molly's Pilgrim,* we should also do a much better job of conveying accurate information about Native Americans and Pilgrims and new immigrants to America, during Thanksgiving and throughout the school year.

II. Discovering New Pilgrims in America

After Multicultural Restructuring

- Major Objective: To enhance teacher awareness of a wide range of traditional Thanksgiving literature as well as more contemporary literature that develops the theme of new pilgrims to America.
- Content Area: Language Arts and Social Studies
- Grade Levels: 3–8
- Time Period: One to Two Weeks

Instructional Objectives

The learners will be able to

1. specify how *Molly's Pilgrim* and *How Many Days to America: A Thanksgiving Story* can be used to incorporate new themes into the traditional Thanksgiving curriculum;
2. explain how they would use *Molly's Pilgrim* as the basis for a class discussion related to tolerance and intolerance;
3. identify and describe traditional and contemporary material they would use to create a meaningful Thanksgiving instructional sequence for a specific grade level.

Suggested Modifications

1. Utilize the new major objective to introduce the topic to future or veteran teachers so that everyone is working toward the same objective from the very beginning and to avoid the suggestion at any point in the lesson that the instructors are trying to reveal to the teachers what they, the teachers, do not know and should be aware of.
2. When teams are evaluating and selecting traditional Thanksgiving material, encourage the team members to (a) identify and set aside materials that treat Native Americans stereotypically or inaccurately, and (b) identify and select materials that describe accurately the interaction between the Pilgrims and the local Indians.
3. Allow teams to discuss the materials that have been set aside because of stereotyping and inaccuracies.
4. Develop a packet of information about Barbara Cohen, the author of *Molly's Pilgrim,* and some of her other novels.
5. When presenting *How Many Days to America: A Thanksgiving Story,* discuss other nonfiction materials that accurately describe the varied experiences and feelings of new immigrants to America; develop new invitations for inquiry based on these materials.

DISCUSSION QUESTIONS

1. We identify four types of planned instructional events: instructional activities, lessons, lesson sequences, and units of instruction. Does this seem like a practical division to you? How do these categories compare to (a) the language used in your teacher education program, (b) the language used by teachers in your region, and (c) the realities of your own day-to-day teaching?

2. We suggest that the multicultural nature and potential of a given lesson or instructional activity can be evaluated by asking eight basic questions that encompass the seven goals in our model:

   a. Do the lesson content and strategies promote educational equity?

   b. Do the lesson content and strategies make use of, or help to develop, collaborative, empowering relationships among parents, students, and teachers?

   c. Do the lesson content and strategies promote cultural pluralism in society or intergroup harmony in the classroom?

   d. Does the lesson content help to increase the students' knowledge of various cultural and ethnic groups, including their own?

   e. Do the lesson content and strategies increase students' proclivity and ability to see and think with a multicultural perspective?

   f. Does the lesson content (a) help to ameliorate distortions in the historical, literary, or scientific record that may be linked to historical racism or other forces related to the oppression and exploitation of specific ethnic and cultural groups, and/or (b) present material in a manner that suggests that racism-related distortions are or may be part of the historical and scientific record?

   g. Does the lesson provide knowledge or skills, or promote attitudinal development, that will leave the students better equipped and more inclined to participate in, and help improve, the democratic institutions of their society?

   h. Does the lesson content contribute to the students' proclivity to cross ethnic and cultural boundaries to participate in and/or learn about different cultural and ethnic groups?

   - To help evaluate the multicultural nature and potential of a lesson or lesson sequence, does this set of questions seem adequate? What would you add or delete and why?

   - Should the fourth question be modified so as to focus on specific ethnic and cultural groups such as African Americans, Hispanic Americans, and Native Americans, or is the question phrased appropriately in your opinion?

3. Another popular example of a weekly, ongoing instructional activity is Celebrity (or VIP or Star) of the Week. This activity is oriented toward building self-esteem. It is used most often in K–3 classrooms but is occasionally found in fourth- through sixth-grade classrooms as well. In this activity each child in the class, for an entire week, becomes the focus of attention; in some classes two children may share the spotlight. In various ways during the week, the entire class learns about the life and family of the student VIP through photographs, favorite toys and art work, an autobiographical statement and/or class interview, a "my favorites" web, and possibly an experience chart written by the class. These materials and others are displayed on a bulletin board or in a learning center. Thus, during a given week the "facts" of each child's life become a central part of the class curriculum.

   In a specific grade, how could a teacher sensitively structure this activity so that the VIP of the Week activity, in addition to contributing to individual self-esteem, helps to accomplish selected goals of multicultural education, such as the development of a pluralistic attitude and increased knowledge of the various cultures and ethnic groups represented in the class?

RECOMMENDED ACTIVITIES

1. In a K–12 setting, identify an ongoing activity such as homework and review, uninterrupted silent reading or writing, or a 15-minute daily recess period; (a) describe the current structure (content/process) of the activity, and (b) make a list of proposed changes to increase the multicultural nature and potential of the activity.
2. Develop a plan for increasing student involvement in the Word of the Week program at the classroom or school level of operation. Your plan, on a weekly or monthly basis, should give as many students as possible the opportunity to shape the school world they inhabit.
3. Pick a biography, like *Rosa Parks*, in which the biographer's subject experiences some explicit form of political or economic discrimination that he or she overcomes. Prepare responses for questions you think students might ask as well as questions you would like to ask students. Read the story to your own or another class, and then answer one or more of the following questions:
   a. Was this the first time you had discussed discrimination (racism) with elementary school students? If so, how do you think it went?
   b. Which questions from students surprised you? Which questions, if any, were difficult for you to answer?
   c. Did your advance preparation lead to a fruitful discussion? Were you able to use any of your prepared responses in the postreading discussion? If yes, specify the response.
   d. Do you think that discussing such stories helps to create a more intimate bond between you and your students? If yes, explain your response.
   e. Do you think that the consistent reading of such stories may help to reduce prejudice in the student body?[18]
4. Locate some printed material in which an author has written about Rosa Parks or some other historical figure inaccurately. Develop and describe a plan for using such material in a critical thinking lesson. For example, in *It Was on Fire When I Lay Down on It,* Robert Fulghum describes Rosa Parks as "a quiet, conservative, church going woman with a nice family and a decent job as a seamstress" and points out that "she was not an activist or a radical."[19] However, Friese's biography, cited in section one of this chapter, makes clear that from 1943 to 1955, Parks was much more than a quiet, conservative, churchgoing woman. During this period she served as secretary of the local NAACP, helped register voters, and challenged the "bus laws" to the point of being ordered off a bus.
5. Using the eight planning questions, write an evaluation of a key text or course in your teacher education program or major. If appropriate, write a set of recommendations for enhancing the multicultural nature and potential of the curriculum material or course. Do the questions appear to be helpful for evaluating materials and courses in higher education?
6. Locate several individual lessons, a lesson sequence, or a unit of instruction in your university library or with your instructor's help. Evaluate the multicultural nature and potential of this lesson. Discuss (a) the major instructional steps or procedures in the lesson, (b) your list of suggested modifications, and (c) the rationale for your modifications.
7. Pick one of the curriculum case studies in this chapter; (a) critique the "after" treatment, and (b) extend or improve the "after" treatment.
8. If you are designing a lesson, lesson sequence, or unit for another course in your teacher education program, your student teaching assignment, or your own class-

room, use the eight-question planning format to enhance the multicultural nature and potential of your lesson. If the questions lead to specific content or structural inclusions or modifications, make a list of these.

9. Evaluate the following lesson sequence; then, working with a partner, decide whether multiculturalization of the sequence is desirable. If it is, specify how you would multiculturalize this sequence. As you evaluate it, first imagine yourself in a class that is predominantly African American or Native American (90 percent), one that is predominantly White American (90 percent), and one that is ethnically diverse (Black, White, Hispanic, and Asian American) with no dominant majority. If you choose to multiculturalize the sequence, indicate whether the different groups in the class would lead you to modify the sequence in different ways.

- Sequence Title: A Rainbow of Poems by Great Poets
- Major Objective: Poetic Literacy and Enjoyment of Poetry
- Content Area: Language Arts
- Grade Levels: 4–
- Time Period: 90–120 Minutes (three to four 35-minute sessions)
- Objectives: Students will
  1. give specific examples of pairs of poems that illustrate the various ways poems can differ from each other (rhyming and nonrhyming, funny and serious, compressed and expansive);
  2. provide some biographical information regarding the following well-known poets: John Masefield, John Ciardi, Carl Sandburg, Robert Frost, and Shel Silverstein.
  3. be more likely to enjoy listening to poetry produced by others and to writing their own poetry.

General Procedures

1. In session one, the teacher read poems such as "Sea Fever" by the British poet John Masefield and "Lost" by the American poet Carl Sandburg to contrast rhyming versus nonrhyming poetic structures, discussed the meaning of each poem, compared and contrasted the two poems, and shared background information about the two poets. Students were then invited to write their own rhyming or non-rhyming poems or listen to the teacher and other pupils recite favorite poetry.

2. In session two, selected poems by the American poets John Ciardi, Robert Frost, and Shel Silverstein were used to contrast humorous and serious poetry. The activities in session two were identical to those of session one except that students who had completed poems during or after session one were invited to read their poetry.

3. In session three, poems from all five poets were used to contrast brief compressed poems with lengthier, more expansive poetry. Again, the structure of the lesson was identical to the format of session two.

4. Session four was devoted to silent reading or poetry writing. Poetry that was produced, in first-draft form, was shared orally, and when revised, was sent home in the next class newsletter.

Journal Entry

This chapter focused on strategies for modifying the academic curriculum to bring it more in line with the goals of multicultural education. It would, therefore, be appropriate in your journal entry to comment on the following questions as well as your own questions or feelings about this chapter.

1. Did you learn anything of value from the chapter's "before" and "after" treatments, discussion questions, and activities? If yes, summarize what you have learned.

2. Has the experience of reading chapters 1, 2, and 3 influenced the development or refinement of your own multicultural perspective? If yes, describe and discuss the changes that have occurred.
3. Which aspects of the multicultural review and restructuring process recommended in this chapter seem questionable or ambiguous to you?

NOTES

1. For more information regarding the way telecommunications can positively influence classroom learning, see "Telecommunications and Language Learning" by Patricia Mulligan and Kay Gore, *Language Arts* 69, no. 5 (September 1992): 379–384.
2. Thomas J. Glynn, "The Essential Elements of School-Based Smoking Prevention Programs: Research Results," *Journal of School Health* 59, no. 5 (May 1989): 181–188.
3. Sara Glazer, "Who Smokes and Starts, and Why," *Editorial Research Reports* 1, no. 11 (March 24, 1989): 151.
4. John Van de Kamp, "A New Solution to an Old Problem," in *Schools and Drugs: A Guide to Drug and Alcohol Abuse Prevention Curricula and Programs* (Sacramento: Office of the California State Attorney General, 1987), I–iii.
5. Ibid., ii–iii.
6. Ibid., 33–66.
7. Ibid., 47.
8. *Drug Prevention Curricula: A Guide to Selection and Implementation* (Washington, D.C.: Office of Educational Research and Improvement, U.S. Department of Education, 1988), iii.
9. Carol Matlack, "Smoke-Free Advertising," *National Journal,* February 24, 1990, 452–455.
10. *Standard and Poor's Industry Surveys,* May 17, 1990, F-36.
11. Ibid.
12. Walecia Konrad with Mark Landler, "Reynolds Draws a Bead on the Marlboro Man," *Business Week,* December 24, 1990, 47–48.
13. Jeff Bingaman, "Tobacco Has Dead Aim on Latinos," *Los Angeles Times,* February 11, 1990, M5.
14. Shari Roan, "Under Fire: Women and Smoking," *Los Angeles Times,* April 17, 1990, E5.
15. *Schools and Drugs: A Guide to Drug and Alcohol Abuse Prevention Curricula and Programs* (Sacramento: Office of the California State Attorney General, 1987), 111.
16. Leo Rosten, *The Joys of Yiddish* (New York: Simon and Schuster, Pocket Books, 1970), 439.
17. Michael Dorris, "Why I'm Not Thankful for Thanksgiving," *Spectrum: The Newsletter of Multiracial Americans of Southern California* 5, no. 5 (November/December, 1991): 3.
18. See James A. Banks, "Multicultural Education: Its Effects on Students' Racial and Gender Role Attitudes," in *Handbook of Research on Social Studies Teaching and Learning*, ed. J. P. Shaver (New York: Macmillan, 1991), 459–469, for evidence that sharing stories about ethnic heroes is a helpful strategy for reducing prejudice.
19. Robert Fulghum, *It Was on Fire When I Lay Down on It* (New York: Villard/Random House, 1988), 112.

Creating a Multicultural Curriculum with Integrated Social Studies, Language Arts, and Science-based Units of Instruction

CHAPTER OVERVIEW

In chapter 4 various types of units are described—the basic unit of instruction, the content-specific unit, the literature-based unit, the resource unit, the integrated unit, and the multiethnic unit. In addition, several integrated units are discussed to illustrate how teachers' awareness of the goals of multicultural education can help them multiculturalize the content and process of selected units.

The thought processes and evaluative questions employed in this multiculturization process are almost identical to those used with activities, lessons, and lesson sequences. However, the multiculturalization process with social studies and science-based units of instruction is, typically, more challenging, because we deal with more complex categories of knowledge, such as generalizations, main ideas, and interdisciplinary concepts. Also, because of space considerations, in chapter 4 we use selected unit components rather than entire units to make our points and have integrated our "before" and "after" analysis into one set of remarks rather than the separate treatments employed in chapter 3.

INTRODUCTION

To gain a greater appreciation of how units of instruction in general, and integrated, social studies–based units in particular, can help you achieve the goals of multicultural education, we will make several important points. First, you should understand that there are different types of units; some have greater potential for multicultural education than others, but all have some possibilities. Second, to be well prepared to apply a multicultural perspective in curriculum development you should be knowledgeable about a specific set of interdisciplinary concepts that James Banks calls "key concepts for a multicultural curriculum."[1] Third, you need to remember that a multicultural perspective is both an orientation and a skill; it is simultaneously a way of viewing and thinking about the world, and a capability that is shaped by your belief system and multicultural/multiethnic knowledge base. You must be convinced that cultivating a multicultural perspective and knowledge base is critical, and, further, that the perspective and knowledge base are worthy of development in students. You should be concerned about, but not overwhelmed with, this responsibility, and be encouraged by knowing that your efforts in working with a multicultural perspective will lead to an enhanced multicultural/multiethnic knowledge base for you and your students. Last, recall the eight evaluative questions that can help you make judgments about the multicultural quality of units or other materials under consideration.

Before examining the different types of units, we need to explore the interdisciplinary concepts that are the fundamental building blocks for *anyone's* multicultural perspective. These include culture, ethnic group, ethnic minority group, cultural assimilation, acculturation, cultural conflict, prejudice, discrimination, race, racism, ethnocentrism, values, self-concept, socialization, intercultural communication, historical bias, power, social protest, collective struggle, colonialism, migration, and immigration. Some teachers will be quite familiar with these ideas; others will benefit from a review. An excellent text for this purpose is James Banks's *Teaching Strategies for Ethnic Studies,* particularly chapters 1 through 4. This text, better than any other, introduces the reader to multicultural/multiethnic units of instruction that involve key multicultural concepts as well as the comparative study of two or more ethnic groups.[2]

Veteran teachers realize that units of instruction come in all sizes and shapes and that "the way units are planned and taught varies greatly from one teacher to another."[3] Because of this diversity and the key role units can play in developing a multicultural curriculum, teachers should be familiar with several types of units and the distinctions between them. Below, we discuss selected characteristics of a general unit of instruction, a content-specific unit of instruction, a literature-based unit of instruction, an integrated unit of instruction (sometimes referred to as a comprehensive unit), a multiethnic unit, and a resource unit.

TYPES OF UNITS

A *unit of instruction* is a comprehensive, multidimensional plan of instruction for learning inside or outside the classroom. A unit may consist of several lesson sequences, and typically requires more time to plan and implement than a lesson sequence. Also, the unit will usually have greater diversity in lessons and activities than a sequence and will incorporate a more precise type of evaluation.

In chapter 3 we presented 14 elements that are commonly found in the units produced by student teachers in our program. It would be helpful to review these elements before reading further. Also, note that the unit described here is often referred to as a *teaching unit* to distinguish it from a *resource unit.* The teaching unit contains only those objectives, activities, materials, bibliographies, and so on that the teacher and students will use during the unit. In contrast, the resource unit is an extensive collection of objectives, activities, and materials the teacher can use as a resource to help develop the teaching unit. Typically, the resource unit contains many more suggestions for study than any single teacher can pursue.

A *content-specific unit* has a good deal in common with a teaching unit and could conceivably contain all 14 elements listed in chapter 3; typically, however, it would not be guided by generalizations unless it was a social studies or science unit. The chief distinguishing characteristic of the content-specific unit is that its contents are linked to one area of the elementary curriculum and there is little or no intent to stretch the unit's content beyond that one area. For example, we could have a content-specific unit in language arts entitled "Japanese Forms of Poetry." The focus of this unit would be the structure of various forms of Japanese poetry. Student activities would consist mainly of (1) reading and reciting Japanese poems and creating images stimulated by the Japanese poetry, and (2) using Japanese forms, such as haiku, to write original poetry. Students would be invited to illustrate selected poems, but this would be the only non-language arts–related activity. Japanese poetry would not be related to Japanese history, other aspects of Japanese culture, or the literary traditions of other Asian nations, such as China. It is noteworthy that this particular unit, "Japanese Forms of Poetry," in addition to being a content-specific unit, has the potential to be a literature-based unit.

The development of *literature-based units* is a relatively recent phenomenon and is related to the evolution of "whole-language" approaches to the teaching of language arts, including reading. These methods represent an increasingly popular approach to language arts education and include an emphasis on (1) helping students read, write, and speak in a natural, less formal, way; and (2) allowing more time in class for students to use language in activities that receive less quantitative teacher evaluation. In addition, students are not divided into ability groups (high, middle, and low) in which reading and related language arts instruction are delivered separately to each group by different level basal readers. All the children simultaneously read the same whole piece of well-written, enjoyable literature, and the teacher uses the document as the primary resource from which a series of language arts–related activities are developed. Units that revolve around a single piece of literature are typically not guided by a set of generalizations and related main ideas. However, the literature-based unit need not be restricted to language arts activities. For example, a book about the life of George Washington Carver could easily serve as a catalyst for lessons related to science, history, geography, music, and art. If it involves language arts activities exclusively or primarily, the literature-based unit is a special type of content-specific teaching unit. But, like many content-specific units, the literature-based unit can incorporate lessons that extend into several different content areas. When this occurs, we have created a different type of unit—the integrated unit.

An *integrated teaching unit* cuts across the boundaries of subject areas and integrates the curriculum. Students learn how the content areas relate to one another and how specific skills apply to real-life situations. They experience the application of reading and other language arts, mathematics, science, art, music, and physical education (PE) through meaningful and relevant life-related activities. Further, because it encompasses activities from a diverse array of content areas, the integrated unit is sometimes referred to as a thematic or comprehensive unit. Comprehensive units are often associated with social studies education, perhaps because social studies, as a content area, is itself informed by content from a variety of disciplines such as geography, anthropology, history, sociology, economics, and political science.

The final type of unit, the *multicultural/multiethnic unit,* has qualities that allow it to fit into the content-specific and integrated categories. The multiethnic/multicultural unit involves the comparative study of two or more ethnic groups, typically from the same culture. Because ethnic studies in the university setting is increasingly considered a discipline or content area, a multiethnic unit can be perceived as content specific. On the other hand, as described by James Banks, a multiethnic unit is guided by interdisciplinary concepts that stem from a variety of social science disciplines. Therefore, almost by definition, it is an integrated unit. In Banks's conception, multicultural/multiethnic units are part of an ongoing curriculum in which concepts such as racism, discrimination, prejudice, social protest, and culture will play a central role. Because these units allow for the consistent study of American ethnic groups, they contribute directly to the student's multicultural/multiethnic knowledge and indirectly to the capacity to think from a multicultural perspective. These direct and indirect contributions allow such units to provide a significant form of multicultural education.

CURRICULUM CASE STUDIES

With these units defined, we are ready to examine more closely the thought processes that educators employ as they create material for a multicultural curriculum. Toward this end, we will analyze two groups of units. The first group, one through four, consists of units developed at California Polytechnic State University (Cal Poly) at San Luis Obispo by adjunct professors (elementary school teachers) and student teachers who have recently worked in Cal Poly's elementary teacher education program. The first two, "Winning of the West" and "Ancient Egypt," are first-draft units developed to help us model how to design, implement, and evaluate units that reflect and incorporate a multicultural perspective. As a part of the modeling process, the adjunct professor produces the first draft of a planned unit; then the draft is used to stimulate dialogue about the different ways the unit could be *multiculturalized.* The versions of units one and two examined here are the first-draft units; the units that were actually taught emerged from these plans after considerable revision. In contrast, units three and four, "Support and Movement of the Human Body" and "Famous Fairy Tales," were designed by student teachers, and classroom implementation closely followed the plans delineated below.

The second group of units to be analyzed, "Thinking Logically: A Study of Common Fallacies" (unit five) and "Prejudice in Group Relations" (unit six), were designed by Brant Abrahamson and Fred C. Smith as key components of a required course in sociology taught at Riverside–Brookfield High School in Brookfield, Illinois. The units have been taught to several thousand students during the past few decades and have been systematically evaluated and refined. Because these units are now commercially produced and distributed, our "before" and "after" treatments will be compressed.[4]

Finally, as you contemplate these units and our recommendations, remember that while there are many ways to multiculturalize a unit, there is only so much a teacher can do at a given time. It would be incorrect to assume that the adjunct professors, for example, in creating their revised versions, should incorporate all the suggestions we make. The recommendations we offer are for teaching purposes. Our main objective is to show how selective use of eight multicultural planning questions can help teachers design units incorporating a multicultural perspective.

UNITS OF INSTRUCTION

Unit One: Winning of the West: 1775–1850

The first unit to be reviewed, entitled "Winning of the West: 1775–1850," was developed by an adjunct professor, Mrs. Anderson (the names employed in this section are pseudonyms), for a bilingual fifth- and sixth-grade class in which 95 percent of the students were Mexican American. Before discussing this unit, we will enumerate several components from Mrs. Anderson's first-draft unit, so that you can form your own preliminary opinions about the content:

1. Categorization of unit content and strategies by content area
2. Unit objectives
3. Generalizations, main ideas, and supporting information
4. Introductory, selected developmental, and culminating activities
5. Statement of multicultural perspective
6. Bibliography
7. A week-by-week schedule of unit activities

Categorization of Unit Content and Strategies

SOCIAL STUDIES

Mountain Men/Trappers
First Women to Travel
Trails/Routes/Roads
Land Ordinance
Northwest Ordinance
Territories
Modes of Transportation
Frontier Life
Treatment of the Indians
Gold Rush
History of State Annexations and
 Statehoods

Indian Leaders:
Sacagawea
Tecumseh, Sitting Bull, Black Hawk,
 Stand Waite

Contemporary Indian Personalities:
Will Rogers
Orville Moody
Buffy St. Marie
Jim Thorpe

Carlos Montezuma

American Leaders:
Sam Houston
Daniel Boone
Jim Bridger
Lewis and Clark
George Rogers Clark
Andrew Jackson
Zebulon Pike
Davy Crockett
Stephen Austin

LANGUAGE ARTS

Simulations
Writing Newspaper Articles
Poetry
Outlining, Charting
Research Writing
Cooperative Grouping
Reading for Information
Role-Playing
Diary Entries
Oral Discussions

Tableaux
Oral Presentations
Biography Writing
Persuasive Writings
Readers' Theater
Interviews, Similes
Students will read *Sign of the Beaver*
 by Elizabeth Speare

ART

Make Covered Wagons/Conestoga
 Wagons Dioramas/Murals
Portraits of Famous Leaders and/or
 Pioneers
Tableaux
Make Flatboats/Keelboats/Forts
Build Wilderness Shelters

INDIAN CULTURE

Weaving, Food
Clothing, Cooking
Dancing, Customs

VALUES

Appreciation of the courage and
 determination of the pioneers
Understand the point of view of Indians and Mexican settlers in regard to
 their treatment during this period

MATH/CRITICAL THINKING

Mapping

Graphing
Similarities and Differences
Decision Making
Time Lines
Charting
Comparisons
Kilometers
Word Problems
Computer Programs

SCIENCE

Survival Skills in the Wilderness
Endangered Animals
Preservation of the Environment/
 Ecology
Animal Tracks
Natural Resources

MUSIC

"Clementine"
"Oh! Susanna"
"Battle of New Orleans"
"Old Dan Tucker"
"John Henry"
"Wait for the Wagon"
"Sweet Betsy from Pike"
Indian Songs

PHYSICAL EDUCATION

Invent a game from natural materials
Play games as described in *Sign of
 the Beaver*

Unit Objectives

COGNITIVE

1. Students will know why different groups of pioneers traveled west.
2. Students will know when the various states and sections of the country became a part of the United States and the history of these events.
3. Students will know the early pioneers and leaders of the westward movement and their contribution to the history of this period.
4. Students will realize the hardships endured by the pioneers as they traveled and then settled in new lands.
5. Students will know the reasons the American Indians were treated unfairly.
6. Students will know the hardships the American Indians experienced.
7. Students will know the history of the Mexican Americans in California and in the Southwest and the impact of their culture in the United States.
8. Students will know of various contemporary Indian and Mexican personalities.

SKILLS

1. Students will be able to map the removal of the Eastern Indians.
2. Students will be able to map the westward growth of the United States.
3. Students will be able to map the United States at different times in its history.
4. Students will work cooperatively and harmoniously in their groups.
5. Students will use reference materials independently as they seek information.

AFFECTIVE

1. Students will appreciate the perseverance of the American pioneers and their determination to settle new lands.
2. Students will appreciate the hardships and perspective of the American Indians regarding their plight during the westward expansion.
3. Students will appreciate the attitude of the Mexican-American people when they became outnumbered in their own land.

Generalizations, Main Ideas, and Supporting Information

Generalization   People with pioneer spirit will always meet challenges and endure hardships to improve their lives.

Main Idea 1   Early pioneers traveled west in search of better farmlands and greater opportunities.

Information
1. Some of the first Americans to move to the Old Northwest were land speculators.
2. Most pioneers were poor people who wanted land on which to build a home and start a farm.
3. By 1820, two and a half million people lived between the Appalachian Mountains and the Mississippi River.
4. Deserts, mountains, and rivers were explored by hardy fur trappers and mountaineers.
5. In 1849, more than 80,000 hopeful newcomers arrived in California in search of gold.
6. By 1835, there were 30,000 settlers in Texas.
7. Pioneers endured many hardships and dangers in their travels and in settling the frontier.

Main Idea 2   Mexican Americans migrated to the United States in search of jobs and opportunities.

Information
1. In 1910, because of political problems in their homeland, many Mexicans migrated to the United States.
2. Today the Mexican people make up the largest Hispanic group in the United States.

Generalization   Adversity breeds leadership.

Main Idea 1   A number of aggressive leaders were prominent during the westward expansion.

Information
1. Daniel Boone was the first White person to lead a group of settlers through the Appalachian Mountains.
2. Thomas Jefferson was responsible for the Louisiana Purchase.
3. Lewis and Clark and Pike were the pioneer pathfinders into the West.
4. Sacagawea guided Lewis and Clark much of their way through the unexplored areas.
5. President Jackson ordered the removal of Indians in order to make their fertile grounds available to the White man.
6. Jim Beckwourth was a famous mountaineer and trapper who later became a chief of the Crow tribe.
7. Davy Crockett was a famous hunter, scout, soldier, and congressman.
8. Kit Carson was a scout who guided some of the most important U.S. Army expeditions across great areas through which he alone knew the way.
9. Jim Bridger led expeditions through the mountains.
10. Stephen Austin brought 300 American families to settle in Texas.
11. Sam Houston led the army that won Texas its independence.

Generalization   When an advanced civilization meets a less-advanced civilization, the less-advanced civilization will be assimilated or lose its national identity.

Main Idea 1   American Indians were dominated and eventually conquered by the White man.

Information
1. Treaties were made and then broken between the American Indians and the American government in regard to land.
2. In 1830, Congress passed a law ordering all American Indians to move west of the Mississippi.
3. The Cherokees were forced to leave in the middle of winter. Their march west is known as the Trail of Tears.
4. American Indians were defeated in various battles and consequently lost their lands.
5. President Jackson did not support the Cherokees in their dilemma even after they had fought with him to defeat the Creeks in 1814.
6. By 1827, most of the tribes in the Old Northwest had moved west of the Mississippi.

Main Idea 2   In the mid-1800s, it became harder for Mexican Americans in California and in the Southwest to protect their rights and property.

Information
1. Mexican Americans were soon outnumbered in their own land.
2. Mexican Americans were not treated as well as English-speaking settlers in many ways.

Generalization   It is human nature to want to rebel when personal interests are not being represented in government.

Main Idea   Americans who settled in Texas wanted their independence from Mexico.

Information
1. Many of the Texans from the United States did not get along with the Mexican government and would not assimilate into the Roman Catholic culture of Mexico.
2. Mexico sent troops to Texas. Two hundred fighters held off about 5,000 Mexican soldiers for 12 days at the Alamo, a mission in San Antonio.
3. In 1836 the Texans declared their independence from Mexico.
4. The victory of Sam Houston's army over Santa Ana of Mexico led to the creation of the Republic of Texas, with Sam Houston as president.

Introductory, Selected Developmental, and Culminating Activities

Introductory Activity   A time line will be charted. After it is presented and various study prints and pictures have been previewed, students will be encouraged to ask questions for study in the unit. Their questions will be charted.

TIME LINE

1775	Daniel Boone opened the Wilderness Road and made possible the first settlement of Kentucky.
1778–1779	George Rogers Clark's campaign won the Northwest Territory for the United States.
1785	The Land Ordinance provided an orderly system for surveying and selling government lands.
1794	Victory over the Indians and a treaty with Great Britain brought peace to the Northwest Territory.
1795	Pinckney's Treaty with Spain opened the mouth of the Mississippi River to American navigation.
1803	The Louisiana Purchase opened a vast area beyond the Mississippi River to American settlers.
1804–1806	Lewis and Clark explored the Louisiana Territory.
1825	The Erie Canal opened, providing improved transportation westward.
1838–1839	The Cherokee Indians were forced to migrate to Oklahoma from Georgia.
1845	The United States annexed Texas.
1846	A treaty with Great Britain added the Oregon country to the United States.
1846–1848	War with Mexico resulted in the acquisition of California and the Southwest.
1848	The discovery of gold in California inspired the gold rush.
1862	The Homestead Act promised free land to settlers in the West.

Developmental Activities (Lessons)   Some of the activities are self-explanatory; following is a description of the others (the complete list is included in the week-by-week schedule; see Figure 4.1).

January

Monday	Tuesday	Wednesday	Thursday	Friday
15	16	17	18 Introductory activity (see description under Introductory activity). Lesson plan will be provided.	19 What types of people traveled across the frontier? Activity #1: Mapping the Old Northwest on individual maps.
22 Activity writing. Activity #2: (see description under Activities).	23 Westward movement. Activity #3: Chart advantages and disadvantages of settling west. Chart similarities and differences.	24 Daniel Boone. Activity #4: Write poem on Daniel Boone.	25 Frontier life. Activity #5: Chart similarities and differences between frontier life and life today. Lesson plan will be provided.	26 Outline Daniel Boone's life.
29 Across the Mississippi. Louisiana Purchase. Lewis and Clark. Activity #6: Map the Louisiana Purchase.	30 More on Lewis and Clark. Activity #7: Newspaper writing (see description under Activities).	31 War of 1812. Review meaning of words of "Star Spangled Banner." Activity #8: Teach song—"Battle of New Orleans."		

Figure 4.1 Week-By-Week Schedule

Activity No. 2   As a result of hearing about and discussing the various personalities who traveled west, children will pretend they are one of these individuals and will write creatively about their reasons for coming west.

Activity No. 7   Students will write a newspaper article on the adventures of Lewis and Clark. The article will include a headline. The first sentence will contain information answering questions of who, what, when, where, and why. Remaining paragraphs will elaborate on the incident.

February

Monday	Tuesday	Wednesday	Thursday	Friday
			1 Trail of Tears. Cooperative groups. Lesson plan will be provided. For homework have students inquire of any prejudiced behavior toward family in history.	**2** Jackson and the Indians. Activity #9: Map the removal of the Cherokee and other Indian groups.
5	**6**	**7** Indian personalities. Activity #10 (see description under Activities).	**8** Manifest Destiny/trappers missionaries, pioneers, Conestogas. Lesson plan wil be provided.	**9** Activity #11: Make Conestoga wagons.
12	**13** War in Mexico.	**14** Writing activity #13: Newspaper writing (see description under Activity #7).	**15** Learning centers.	**16** Resource person in for presentation to answer interview questions. Students interview parents about ancestors moving west.
19	**20** California Gold Rush.	**21** Simulation. Lesson plan will be provided.	**22** Values. Lesson plan will be provided.	**23** Paint murals and portraits.

Figure 4.1   (Continued)

March

Monday	Tuesday	Wednesday	Thursday	Friday
26	27 Mexican Americans in the West.	28 Hispanic Americans today.	1 Graphics. Lesson plan will be provided.	2
5	6 Practice for culminating activity.	7 Practice for culminating activity.	8 Culminating activity. Lesson plan will be provided.	9

Figure 4.1 (Continued)

Activity No. 10   Using instructor curriculum materials on North American Indian personalities, children will work in their cooperative groups to prepare presentations on assigned Indian personalities. Each cooperative group will be responsible for two to three personalities.

Activity No. 12   After a study of the Alamo, students will present a brief tableau.

Activity No. 14   Students will imagine that they are in New York City in 1848. They have heard of the discovery of gold at Sutter's Mill and have decided to join the rush to California. Students will be divided into three groups—each taking a different route.

Each group will be prepared to (1) draw the route on a map provided, (2) describe the weather conditions the group members expect to face, (3) explain how they will deal with those weather conditions, and (4) tell what other dangers they expect and how they plan to deal with them.

Also used at another time during the day will be an Interact simulation curriculum resource entitled *Pioneers*. This resource consists of various simulation activities involving decision making on a wagon train.

As settlers heading west during the 1840s, the students face problems such as floods, droughts, blocked trails, snakes, Indians, and a lack of food. The would-be homesteaders must make numerous individual and small-group decisions. While learning about wagon trains and pioneer life, students participate in individual and small-group decision making. In addition, they learn how to take notes, how to outline material, and how to write a brief research paper.

Culminating Activity   Throughout the unit, a time line will be maintained showing important events in the westward expansion. Charts will also be displayed illustrating the addition of land to the United States and other information learned in the unit. Various groups will be assigned to portray these important events in a creative manner; tableaux, creative drama, choral verse, story writing, poetry, and readers' theater will be employed.

Statement of Multicultural Perspective

How do I plan to create educational equity?   To assure achievement and success for all, I will organize student groups of two or three and will encourage them to use cooperative learning. These techniques help to ensure peer support that stimulates learning. SDAIE techniques, such as the use of pictures to help make history come alive, will be employed.

Material is also provided in Spanish. Because our social studies Spanish material is not as comprehensive as that provided in the English texts, I translate much of the material to ensure educational equity. I also make use of tableaux, creative drama, and films to stimulate understanding and comprehension.

How do I plan to create intergroup harmony?   In forming the cooperative groups, careful attention will be paid to ensure that there are both boys and girls in each group and a mixture of Hispanic children and the rest of our classroom population. Rewards are provided for harmonious, cooperative behavior. All groups work together toward a total classroom reward.

How do I plan to help children recognize, value, and respect the diversity among their classmates?   Encouraging students to respect the opinion of their peers and of others has been the main method used to teach and promote respect for others. I act as a model by listening attentively to my students.

Compiling a chart of our similarities and differences as human beings has been an effective strategy in realizing how we are the same and different. Through a discussion of how boring the world would be if we ate the same foods, played the same physical education games, dressed the same, looked the same, and spoke the same, students will learn the value of diversity. Again, using the chart, students can appreciate the commonalities we all share.

In this unit in particular, students will have the opportunity to appreciate their differences and commonalities as they share the results of family interviews in which they will attempt to discover

1. the reasons their family has settled on the central coast of California; and
2. hardships that their families have incurred and may still be experiencing in the settlement process.

How do I plan to help the children feel what the Indians felt or the Mexican Americans felt when absorbed into mainstream U.S. culture or banished from their land and culture?   I will ask the children to express their feelings when I move them away from a friend or when groups of children move them and their friends away from a play area in the playground. Also, the students should provide insights if asked how they would feel if their family was forced to move by a group of individuals who wanted to live where the family does.

Another strategy would be to ask how they would feel if they had to stand in line for quite a while and before reaching their goal, they were sent to the end of the line to start waiting again.

I plan to read accounts written by Cherokee Indians and Mexican Americans of their feelings during this period when the "Americans" won the West.

Bibliography

Buggey, Joanne L., Gerald A. Danzer, Charles L. Mitsakos, and C. Frederick Risinger. America, America! Glenview, Ill.: Scott, Foresman, 1982.

Eibling, Harold. Great Names in Our Country's Story. Sacramento: California State Department of Education, 1962.

Hoover, Sharon. North American Indian Personalities. Troy, Mo.: Instructor Publications, 1980.

Life History of the United States. New York: Time, 1963.

McCracken, Harold. Winning the West. Garden City, N.Y.: Doubleday, 1955.

Peck, Ira, and Steven Jantzen. A Nation Conceived and Dedicated. Albany, N.Y.: Scholastic Book Services, 1983.

Vuicich, George. United States. New York: McGraw-Hill, 1983.

World Book Encyclopedia. Chicago: Field Enterprises, 1970.

Analysis of the Unit

Do the lesson content and strategies promote or impede educational equity? Overall, in planning for this unit, Mrs. Anderson has done a very good job of providing for educational equity. She plans to use sheltered English strategies, cooperative learning, the bilingual capability of several of her students, and her own fluency in Spanish and English to facilitate comprehension and learning for all her students. In addition, to increase motivation, she has selected interesting and diverse activities that should appeal to a wide range of learners (music, arts and crafts, writing, creative dramatics, and interviewing). She has modified the unit to include content that will be personally meaningful to many students in the class. For example, in an attempt to relate the historical material more directly to her students' lives, interests, and ethnocultural background, Mrs. Anderson broke out of the time boundaries of her unit. In doing so, she included twentieth-century content about the Mexican migration to the United States as well as the contributions of contemporary Mexican-American and Native American leaders. This addition will allow her students to compare the nineteenth-century east-to-west migration/emigration of mainly White Americans with the primarily south-to-north migration/emigration of Mexican Americans. As described next, Mrs. Anderson also found a way to make each parent or caretaker a resource for this unit through her homework assignments.

Do the lesson content and strategies make use of, or help to develop, collaborative, empowering relationships among parents, students, and teacher?
Mrs. Anderson's plans call for extensive use of cooperative learning with groups as heterogeneously structured as possible. In addition, in two specific homework assignments Mrs. Anderson placed parents or caretakers in a position to serve as important information resources for this unit. Students would interview family members to learn whether (1) the family had experienced any prejudicial behavior and (2) any of their ancestors had been a part of the westward movement. The latter assignment would be more multicultural or "multiperspective" if the homework assignment included the northern movement (of Mexican Americans and others) and the west-to-east movement of various Asian Americans and Pacific Islanders to America. In addition, sharing the geographic perspective of the American Indians in question—namely, that they saw themselves as the center of all things—would be illuminating.

Analysis of the first draft of the unit suggests that it could be improved by some simple steps designed to elicit greater parent participation. For example, a class newsletter to parents could inform them about the upcoming interviews, as well as the unit content; parents could be invited to (1) offer any special knowledge they possess and (2) visit the class for the unit's culminating activity, in which the students will present a variety of creative unit-related projects. Parent involvement in the unit, if only as an audience for student presentations, should heighten motivation and learning for some students. A different point of view could be introduced to the unit content if at least one parent volunteers to be a guest lecturer, poet, artist, or dramatic actor, presenting material related to the unit.

Do the lesson content and strategies promote cultural pluralism in society or intergroup harmony in the classroom?
In terms of promoting cultural pluralism—the ability and propensity to understand and value different cultures—a unit entitled "Winning of the West: 1775–1850" holds great potential. But many teachers who grew up in schools that denigrated Native American cultures may find it difficult to present a balanced portrayal of the interaction and clashes among the European, Mexican, and Native Americans. Even teachers like Mrs. Anderson, who clearly intends to present accurate information regarding the way successive American administrations unfairly treated Native Americans, may fall into the trap of comparing "White-American" culture and "Native American" culture in ways that

1. work against attempts to understand and appreciate various American Indian cultures on their own terms;
2. imply that American civilization, in all dimensions, was more advanced than the culture(s) of the American Indian; and
3. obscure the diversity that was characteristic of the various American Indian tribes.

For example, in several places in the unit plan, the language suggests that in telling about the winning of the American West, Mrs. Anderson will favor the U.S. settlers and soldiers. Since most American teachers and textbook writers consciously or unconsciously identify with the White settlers and the soldiers—the victors—one might wonder whether this favoritism was both natural and inevitable. In fact, it is neither, and it is the teacher's responsibility to provide an accurate, balanced portrayal of both cultures, key events, and key actors—heroes and scoundrels—on both sides of the struggle. To help achieve accuracy and balance when teaching this and related units, we recommend the following ideas as worthy of consideration:

1. The title or theme of the unit should be examined to see whether it orients the unit toward one or another perspective. To increase the orientation to multiperspectivism of this unit, we would change the title to "The Expansion of the American Nation: 1775–1850."

2. The categorization of unit content should be reviewed for evidence of possible bias. For example, under "Values" in the web, why will students have the opportunity to appreciate the courage and determination of the pioneers but not the courage and determination of American Indians who, against all odds, steadfastly attempted to hold onto their land and way of life?

3. In stating unit objectives, the teacher should be more specific in describing the plight of the American Indian. Through the media, particularly motion pictures made prior to 1980 and shared folklore, American students become aware of Indian massacres and atrocities; rarely, however, do they hear about atrocities carried out by U.S. soldiers, such as the Sand Creek Massacre. Thus, unit objective 6 might read:

   Students will learn about the forced marches, massacres, broken treaties, burned villages, destroyed crops, and inadequate reservations the American Indians experienced during their struggles with the "Americans."[5]

   And, where possible, when students learn of this tragic history, they should hear about it from Native American authors as well as authors who bring a traditional Eurocentric viewpoint to the creation of their historical tale.

4. Some of the generalizations in this unit and the main ideas and facts they lead to are also worthy of revision. The third unit generalization, states: "When an advanced civilization meets a less-advanced civilization, the less-advanced civilization will be assimilated or lose its national identity." As structured, this generalization and its related main ideas suggest that one civilization or culture (that of the White European) was more advanced than, or superior to, the civilization of the American Indian and Mexican American. A related generalization, designed to avoid the less advanced/more advanced comparison, would read:

   When cultures with different values come into conflict over land (and over other economic and political rights), the group with the technological advantage in weaponry will usually prevail.

Note that the word "usually" is included to indicate that this behavioral science generalization, like most others, is tentative and nonconclusive. As Banks notes, such generalizations "will have some exceptions," and "they often contain qualifying words."[6]

The second generalization, "Adversity breeds leadership," has this main idea: "A number of aggressive leaders were prominent during the westward expansion." It, too, is worthy of rethinking. On the one hand, it is a bit narrow, almost a cliché like "Necessity is the mother of invention"; on the other hand, it doesn't seem to be supported by the main idea or the accompanying information. For example, Sacagawea and Lewis and Clark were not "aggressive leaders" and their exploits were not directly related to adversity or hard times. In fact, Sacagawea was not an Indian leader. In addition, all the men who are presented as "aggressive leaders" were White except for Jim Beckwourth, whose racial heritage was a blend of Black and White. In planning integrated units, the generalizations, concepts, main ideas, and facts need to be logically related and mutually supportive and the generalizations should be testable and verifiable.

A broader generalization that simultaneously meets these criteria and leads to the content Mrs. Anderson wants to present is this: As cultures struggle to survive and thrive, various types of leaders will typically emerge.

Main ideas supporting the validity of this generalization could incorporate information about Mexican-American, American Indian, and White-American leaders. This would help to increase the students' knowledge of pertinent cultural/ethnic groups and reinforce their growing ability to analyze events with a multicultural perspective. The following main ideas would serve these purposes:

1. The groups that came into conflict during the country's westward expansion were served by various kinds of leaders.
2. Various types of leaders played key roles in creating opportunities for White Americans to settle in the ever-expanding "American West."
3. Various types of leaders played key roles in the American Indians' attempt to maintain their way of life.

These main ideas would allow Mrs. Anderson to include all the White-American leaders she originally listed and to discuss their lives and contributions in a well-rounded manner. It would also allow students to learn about a more diverse set of "American" leaders—namely, those who made contributions as representatives of the Mexicans and American Indians who struggled to maintain their way of life.

Does the lesson content help to increase the students' knowledge of various cultural and ethnic groups? The unit's objectives, generalizations, and main ideas indicate that in addition to the historical figures mentioned, who are mainly White, information about contemporary Native American and Mexican-American personalities would be included. Several of the aforementioned suggestions show how the generalizations could be modified to increase the amount of knowledge students gain about specific nineteenth-century ethnic groups—namely, Mexican Americans and Native Americans. But the refinement and multiculturalization of this unit could extend beyond the generalizations and content proposed by Mrs. Anderson, and in a manner that would expand students' knowledge of ethnic groups outside the United States.

The story of the country's westward growth is filled with significant and traumatic conflict between the cultures that confronted each other on this part of the continent. Because of this, the concept of cultural conflict should receive special emphasis in this unit. Generalizations, main ideas, and facts related to this concept would provide the students with a richer understanding of why the Whites and American Indians found it impossible to coexist peacefully. A study of cultural conflict might also help students understand the complexity of contemporary U.S. relationships with nations such as Iran, Iraq, and Cuba, as well as conflicts in Peru, Venezuela, Brazil, and Malaysia, where the land and economic and political freedom of indigenous rain forest tribes are rapidly being destroyed by a combination of private and governmental forces.

Units that link the past to the present and provide students with conceptual tools to help them understand ethnic and nation-to-nation interaction throughout history are both motivating and educationally appropriate, particularly from the perspective of citizenship education. What follows now is a broad generalization, a related main idea, and several facts that, together, illustrate the type of understanding that generalizations about cultural conflict can produce.

The Generalization

When cultures with very different beliefs about religion, land ownership and usage, and government confront each other on the same land, clear communication and peaceful coexistence will often be difficult to achieve.

A Related Main Idea

Major differences between European-American cultures and American Indian cultures made clear communication and peaceful coexistence between the two cultures difficult to achieve.

Some Related Facts (or Supporting Information)

1. In European culture, it was assumed that land was a commodity that could be broken into parts and owned by individuals; these individuals could prevent others from using the land.
2. The Indians believed that all people could use the land as long as they treated it with respect; they thought the land was sacred and could not be sold any more than the air or the sea.
3. When, in exchange for gifts, American Indians gave Europeans permission to use their lands, many did not realize that from a European viewpoint they were also giving up their own rights to use the land forever.
4. Because of their feudalistic background, the Europeans looked for monarchs among the Indians and assumed that Indian chiefs had absolute authority over their tribes. However, the authority of most chiefs was limited by the tribal council. In a sense, the Indian tribes and councils had a ratification process that the Europeans did not take into account.[7]

Final Comments

In teaching this unit, Mrs. Anderson used an integrated approach to language arts, one that allowed her to select whole pieces of literature (books, poems, newspaper articles, etc.) that *all* her students would read simultaneously to advance their literacy skills. To add depth to this unit and to help bring the historical period to life, Mrs. Anderson chose to have her entire class read (in English and Spanish versions) the *Sign of the Beaver* by Elizabeth Speare; this was an excellent choice for her generalizations as well as the ones we have added, and the choice is worthy of emphasis as we study how to increase the multicultural dimension of units of instruction.

The selection of written and visual materials for units is a pivotal aspect of multicultural teaching, and the content of a novel can work for or against the goals of multicultural education. In this instance the teacher's selection supports several goals of multicultural education as well as her own specific unit objectives. *Sign of the Beaver* highlights a pre–Revolutionary War (1768) relationship between two teenage boys, Matthew Hallowell, the son of a White settler in Maine, and Attean, the grandson of Saknis, a Penobscot Indian chief. The development of their relationship allowed Mrs. Anderson's students to see two boys transcend the barriers created by their own cultural stereotypes to establish a relationship based on respect and mutual support. In addition, the interaction between Attean and Matthew provided an opportunity for students to gain appreciation for the substantial cultural differences that led to conflict between the Indians and Whites, such as different beliefs about owning and using land, and the complexity and rewards of cross-cultural relationships. Such opportunities contribute greatly to achieving the general goals of multicultural education as well as the specific objectives of this unit.

Finally, beyond the fine *Sign of the Beaver* activities included in this unit, it would be appropriate to encourage the students to conduct inquiries regarding the present-day status of the Penobscots. Did they disappear from history, or are they a part of contemporary American history? And if the latter, how are they faring? Among other things, the students will learn from sources like *Academic American Encyclopedia* that in the 1950s approximately 400 Penobscots joined the Passamaquoddy Indians in a successful lawsuit against Maine to recover lands originally lost through illegal state treaties in the 1790s. And in 1980, according to Lawrence Fuchs in his wonderful *The American Kaleidoscope: Race, Ethnicity, and the Civic Culture* (Hanover, N.H.: University Press of New England, p. 215), "both the Passamaquoddy and Penobscots gained status as 'federal' tribes in 1978, and both were accorded the status of state municipalities with exclusive jurisdiction over internal tribal matters, small claims, civil matters, minor criminal offenses involving Indians, and issues of domestic relations."

Unit Two: Ancient Egypt

The second unit to be discussed in this chapter, "Ancient Egypt," will integrate elements drawn from several units. A number of teachers participated in its development, but Mrs. Jackson was the major contributor, so we refer to her as the designer of the unit. Mrs. Jackson prepared this integrated unit for her sixth-grade class, which was diverse in ethnicity and socioeconomic status; half the class was White American and the remaining half was Hispanic, Asian, and African American. As we did with "Winning of the West," prior to discussing the multiculturalization of Mrs. Jackson's unit, we will enumerate its various components.

Overview Statement

The purpose of this unit is to help students understand how and why ancient Egyptian culture developed, and to be familiar with selected characteristics of the culture and its influence on other cultures.

Categorization of Unit Content and Strategies Selected Unit Objectives

HISTORICAL/SOCIAL STUDIES

Geography of Ancient Egypt:
Trade Routes
Resources
Regions
Climate
Location—Size

Life of the People:
Family Life
City Life
Language
The People

Work of the People:
Agriculture
Manufacturing
Trade–Transportation

Activities of the People:
Education
Religion
The Arts
The Sciences

Invasions

Contributions to Civilization

SCIENCE
Mummification/Embalming

ART
Murals
Draw/Create Hieroglyphics

Illustrate Family Life, Homes, Fashion
Make Mummies
Make Temple
Make Pyramid
Make Masks
Duplicating *ka* (invisible twin)

MATH
Egyptian Numerals and Fractions
Dimensions in Pyramids: Height—feet; Weight—tons; Area—acres

LANGUAGE ARTS
Dramatic Play
Role-Playing
Writing Projects
Poetry
Report Writing
Spelling
Simulations
Cooperative Learning
Oral Reports
Tableaux
Interviews
Outlining
Monologues
The novel *His Majesty, Queen Hatshepsut* by Dorothy Carter will be read to the class

GUEST SPEAKER
Mortician

Selected Unit Objectives

COGNITIVE

1. Students will demonstrate their knowledge of the geography of ancient Egypt—its location, size, natural resources, and climate.
2. Students will demonstrate their knowledge of ancient Egyptian family life, city life, and language.
3. Students will demonstrate their knowledge of the various types of work ancient Egyptians engaged in, including agriculture, manufacturing, and mining.
4. Students will describe various facets of ancient Egyptian culture, including its education, religion, arts, and science.

5. Students will identify different invaders and conquerors of ancient Egypt and reasons the invaders were successful.

SELECTED SKILLS

1. Students will be able to locate Egypt, the Red Sea, the Mediterranean Sea, and the Nile River on maps and globes.
2. Students will be able to trace on maps and globes the trading routes used by the ancient Egyptians to and from other countries.
3. Students will be able to trace on maps and globes the coastal, desert, and fertile regions, plus Upper and Lower Egypt.
4. Students will be able to research, prepare, and present written reports about ancient Egypt.
5. Students will work cooperatively in their groups to complete various assignments.
6. Students will use higher-level thinking skills in class discussions.

AFFECTIVE (ATTITUDES)

1. Students will appreciate the beauty of the pyramids and the great amount of labor required to build them.
2. Students will appreciate the way of life of the ancient Egyptians and how it is both similar to and different from contemporary life.
3. Students will appreciate the dependence of the ancient Egyptians on the Nile River.
4. Students will appreciate the beauty and antiquity of the treasures of ancient Egypt that today can be seen in museums.

Generalizations, Main Ideas, and Supporting Information

Generalization   In both ancient and contemporary cultures, human beings develop various ideas about life after death.

Main Idea   Ancient Egyptians took great care in preparing for life after death.

Information
1. They denied that death ended the existence of a person who led a good life.
2. They believed that the next world would be like Egypt in its richest and most enjoyable form.
3. They built stone tombs and filled them with clothing, food, furnishings, and jewelry for use in the next world.
4. They embalmed their dead and wrapped their bodies in layers of cloth.

Generalization   People tend to congregate and form societies in areas that have natural resources.

Main Idea   The ancient Egyptians built most of their villages and towns along the banks of the Nile River.

Information
   1. Floodwaters of the Nile deposited rich black soil on the land year after year.
   2. Egyptian farmers planted their crops on this fertile soil.
   3. Near the First Cataract, Egyptians mined granite and sandstone.
   4. In the desert and hills to the east lay deposits of copper, manganese, and turquoise.
   5. Without the Nile River, no one could live in Egypt.

Generalization   In many ancient and contemporary societies the people are divided into separate groups along social, religious, and economic lines.

Main Idea   The ancient Egyptians were divided into four social classes.

Information
   1. The four social classes were royalty and nobles; artisans, craftsmen, and merchants; workers; and slaves.
   2. The professional army gradually became almost a separate class.
   3. Egypt had no fixed caste system.
   4. A person of the poorest class could rise to the highest offices in the land.

Generalization   In ancient cultures, as in contemporary societies, people developed religious beliefs to help them deal with aspects of life they did not fully understand.

Main Idea   The ancient Egyptians believed that gods and goddesses took part in human activity from birth to death.

Information
   1. The Egyptians believed in many different gods.
   2. At one time each city had a god of its own.
   3. Later, all Egyptians worshiped Amon—one of the great gods.
   4. However, the people still felt loyalty to the god who lived in the temple of their hometown.
   5. Following are three gods who were known throughout the land.
      a. Amon of Thebes was worshiped as king of the gods.
      b. Ptah, the god of Memphis, was the patron god of craftsmen.
      c. Bes, a comic dwarf god, brought good luck and happiness in the home.

Generalization   In both the ancient and contemporary world, certain societies stand out as leaders in political, economic, and technological development.

Main Idea   In its time, ancient Egypt was an enlightened, advanced society.

Information
   1. Pyramid design and construction showed architectural expertise.
   2. The embalming/mummification process is still studied and admired by scientists today.
   3. Egyptians made significant contributions to recorded history and language development.

Introductory, Selected Developmental, and Culminating Activities

Introductory Activity   A series of overheads will be shown to introduce the students to ancient Egypt, accompanied by a brief overview of the country and its culture. Students will be encouraged to create questions for study in the forthcoming unit. Students will work in their cooperative groups.

Possible Introductory Questions
1. Why and how did the ancient Egyptians build the temples?
2. How did they embalm their dead?
3. Why did they bury their dead with valuable jewels and treasures?
4. Where are the treasures today?
5. What do the different hieroglyphics mean?
6. Why did the ancient Egyptians gather papyrus?
7. What are the names of some of their gods?
8. Who was Tutankhamen and what were some of the treasures found in his tomb?
9. Where is Egypt on the map?
10. How did the ancient Egyptians live? What was their work like, and their family life? What kind of games did they play, and what were their homes like? How did they dress?

Developmental Activities (Lessons)

Activity No. 1   On individual maps students will locate ancient Egypt, the Nile River, regions of Upper and Lower Egypt, trading routes, surrounding countries, and important cities. The lesson on geography will stress five themes: location, physical and cultural features that give an area an identity, interaction between humans and the environment, communication and transportation systems, and regional considerations.

Activity No. 2   Children will work in their cooperative groups supporting and helping each other as they learn new information. A leader will keep the group on task. Questions are written on the board for the groups to work on. Groups receive points according to good cooperative behavior exhibited. When students return to their regular seats, all write the answers, and two papers are chosen from each group as representative answers for further points for their groups. A reward is given when all groups accumulate 10 points.

Activity No. 3   After a study of hieroglyphics and their meaning, students will create hieroglyphics for each letter of the alphabet. Each cooperative group will be responsible for five to six letters. Students then will write notes to each other using their hieroglyphics. Also, groups will be responsible for re-creating original hieroglyphics for display.

Activity No. 4   As a result of studying the mummification process, students will work in their cooperative groups and pretend they are creating a mummy. In each group there will be the priest, the embalmer, the cutter, the remover, and the organ wrapper. Each group will receive one dough body shape made out of salt and flour, two plastic knives, one shoe box, five cotton balls, and a small container of spices. The dough shape that the group will receive will have the internal organs inside represented by rubber bands and candies. Students work according to what their role dictates.

Activity No. 5 Alone or with the help of a partner, students will trace on craft paper their shadow picture. Each student will cut out a *ka,* or invisible twin. Students in turn guess who each *ka* belongs to. This activity reinforces the Egyptian belief that each person had a *ba,* or soul, and a *ka.* When the individual died, the *ba* and *ka* were released from the body and lived on in the tomb. The *ba* would maintain contact with the person's family and friends while the *ka* traveled back and forth at night from the body to the new world. In order for the person to live forever, the *ba* and the *ka* had to be able to recognize the body or they could not return to it.

Activity No. 6 This activity will focus on temple building. The book *Make This Egyptian Temple,* by Ashman (Tulsa, Okla.: EDC Publishing, 1990), lends itself well to this activity; it is a cut-out model of a temple. Different portions of the temple will be distributed to the groups to assemble. Finished group products will then be joined so the class can see its re-creation of a complete Egyptian temple.

Activity No. 7 This activity will focus on mask making. Papier-mâché is applied to a paper plate that has had eyeholes cut out. The dried papier-mâché is painted white. The face is brilliantly colored with tempera paints. Some students will continue to work on the re-creation of the Egyptian temple.

Activity No. 8 This activity centers on poetry writing and reading. Drawing on material learned in this unit, students will be encouraged to write one or more poems that use patterns introduced in class, such as the cinquain, limerick, question poem, or biopoem. Students will be invited to enhance their writing with a drawing.

Activity No. 9 Working in their cooperative learning groups, students will exchange the most interesting facts they learned in the process of completing their research report and will ask questions of each other. Selected students will present their reports to the entire class.

Culminating Activity During the unit's culminating activity each child, or a small group of students, will present one or more of the following:

1. a special poem, story, song, drawing or painting, craft project, original readers' theater presentation, or other expressive project related to the unit;
2. the results of their special report on ancient Egypt;
3. the information in the unit that they found most interesting; or
4. the questions they are still pondering.

For this activity the class will be transformed into an ancient Egyptian temple and special guests (parents and other relatives, the principal, His Majesty Queen Hatshepsut, the Pharaoh Djoser, and his great architect and adviser Imhotep). The latter three will be special "spiritual" guests to whom all the students would direct their remarks.

Statement of Multicultural Perspective

How do I plan to promote educational equity? I will use various strategies that have been shown to stimulate widespread academic achievement. Most notably, I will make use of several forms of cooperative group learning during the unit. All the students in my class are members of a dyad or triad as well as a larger cooperative group, and students are quite used to helping each other learn. In addition, part of the direction of the unit will be influenced by questions the students themselves generate. My students like to engage in collaborative planning and enjoy seeing their names next to the questions they have created, even when they themselves do not follow up on research to answer the question. In my class, creating questions is an activity worthy of recognition. During the unit I will include activities that I know my students find interesting. This class is an expressive group; they like to write, paint, construct, perform, and listen, particularly when I read to them. Therefore, this unit will have a variety of imaginative and expressive activities. To bring history alive during the course of the unit, I will read and tell them the story of *His Majesty, Queen Hatshepsut,* and will have Hatshepsut and others make an appearance at our culminating event. Finally, with regard to equity, my students like to contribute to the specific content of the culminating unit quiz; they find this motivating and it favorably influences the achievement of many of the students. In other areas of the curriculum, I make use of mastery learning strategies, but I find this approach less applicable for my integrated units of instruction.

How do I promote positive intergroup harmony? My main strategy here is cooperative learning. I am quite open with my students; we all know, from current events reports and class discussions during January and February about Black history, that in terms of getting along with each other, most Americans have ample room for growth. I share the research about cooperative group learning with them, and then throughout the year place them in heterogeneous cooperative learning groups. In addition, during my current events time I will occasionally tell stories that illustrate integrated groups of people successfully working together to solve problems. Parenthetically, this unit will provide an example of an ancient multiracial civilization in which people of various colors apparently worked together with the relative absence of prejudice and racism that has been a major part of modern history. Finally, I try to build in all my students a positive, success-oriented identity; when they feel good about themselves, I think they will be in a better position to have positive relationships with others.

How will I promote collaboration among myself, parents, and students? My parents know that I welcome their support and presence. About every six weeks parents receive a class newsletter that updates them on the general curriculum objectives for the next two-month period and invites them to participate in various ways. For this unit, for example, parents with special interest in or expertise about ancient Egypt will be invited to contact me, and all parents will be invited to witness or participate in our culminating event. Parents have also accepted the responsibility of monitoring their child's homework packet for neatness and completeness.

How will I promote cultural pluralism? I believe that exposure to the contributions that different cultures have made, as well as to the complexity of these cultures, will produce in my students a more positive attitude toward cultures and civilizations different from their own. The content of this unit on ancient Egypt will serve this objective well.

How will I use this unit to promote in my students a multicultural perspective vis-à-vis current events and history?
I will address this mainly by introducing my students to the socioeconomic diversity that existed in ancient Egypt. They will contrast the lives and attitudes of slaves and the royalty and artisans of ancient Egypt. This will remind them that history can be viewed from more than one perspective. As they study about different civilizations, they should wonder about the story that would be told by people in different segments of a society.

Bibliography

Aliki. Mummies Made in Egypt. New York: Harper & Row, 1979.

Allan, Tony. The Time Traveler Book of Pharaohs and Pyramids. Tulsa, Okla.: EDC Publishing, 1977.

Carter, Dorothy Sharp. His Majesty, Queen Hatshepsut. New York: HarperCollins, 1987.

Casson, Lionel, and the editors of Time-Life Books. Ancient Egypt. New York: Time, 1965.

Champollion, Jacques. The World of the Egyptians. Bergamo, Italy: Minerva, 1989.

Glubok, Shirley. The Art of Ancient Egypt. New York: Atheneum, 1962.

Hart, George. Exploring the Past: Ancient Egypt. New York: Harcourt Brace, 1989.

Ions, Veronica. Egyptian Mythology. New York: Bedrick, 1983.

Macaulay, David. Pyramid. New York: Houghton Mifflin, 1975.

Nesbit, E. The Story of the Amulet. New York: Dell, 1987.

Sethus, Michel. The Days of the Pharaohs. Morristown, N.J.: Silver Burdett, 1986.

Stuart, Gene S. Secrets from the Past. Washington, D.C.: National Geographic Society, 1979.

Unstead, R. J. An Egyptian Town. Lanham, Md.: Barnes & Noble, 1986.

World Book Encyclopedia. Chicago: Field Enterprises, 1970.

Unit Analysis and Multiculturalization Remarks

Once again we will use several of the evaluative questions for multiculturalization to guide our analysis.

Do the lesson content and structure promote or impede educational equity? There are various ways to think about educational equity in this unit. Earlier in this text we focused on maximizing the achievement of each student in the classroom and encouraged teachers to give special consideration to students who were members of groups who have experienced oppression and unequal access to political and economic resources. The objective is to make certain that such inequalities are not reproduced in contemporary classrooms. It is clear from Mrs. Jackson's remarks that she is taking steps to ensure that *all* the students in her class have a successful learning experience. To motivate her students toward the unit content, Mrs. Jackson will employ a number of commendable strategies. These include collaborative planning of unit content; heterogeneous cooperative learning groups; imaginative arts activities that include Mrs. Jackson's own telling of the story of Queen Hatshepsut; and presentations by intriguing visitors, in this case a mortician. In this class one senses, first, that the needs and interests of special learners have received professional consideration and, second, that the unit activities have been designed to stimulate intellectual growth in all the students, and not just among a top level of rapid learners. In short, in this class there appears to be equal access to learning for all 32 students.

This judgment notwithstanding, in the lives and lessons of teachers there is usually room for improvement, or at least for considering ideas. This unit is no exception. For her 32 students Mrs. Jackson did much to promote equity of access to learning and actual participation and achievement. But it is also appropriate to ask: Is the content of this unit equitable compared with what good sixth-grade students are learning about ancient Egypt in other parts of the country? In other words, are my students being challenged at the same level as yours? Is the content of my unit as rigorous as that in units designed elsewhere?

With this comparative sense of equity in mind, we believe there is room for conceptual improvement in Mrs. Jackson's unit. To illustrate this point, we will draw on selected components of a sixth-grade ancient Egypt unit designed by Jon Wiles and Joseph Bondi.[8]

In their interdisciplinary resource unit Wiles and Bondi identify the following conceptual goals among others. They want their unit to

1. acquaint students with the sources of our knowledge of the past: material remains, artifacts, oral traditions, pictorial data, and written records;
2. train students in the use of source materials so they can draw valid conclusions or frame reasonable hypotheses on the basis of the evidence, and thus learn elements of the historical method;
3. help students understand the values and limitations of various source materials in reconstructing our account of the past;
4. lead students to see that all racial and ethnic groups have similar innate capacities and intelligence and that historical circumstances and environment, as well as heredity, determine a people's cultural achievement.[9]

From these goals we can infer that Wiles and Bondi are not interested in merely exposing students to textbook chapters written for sixth graders by reputable scholars and pictures gathered by archaeologists. They want students to have the opportunity to *think* and *hypothesize* like archaeologists, anthropologists, and historians. The attempt to create situations in which students will engage in higher and more complex levels of thinking is illustrated in one of the unit's behavioral objectives. They state that the learner will be able to "write a description of Egyptian religion and hypothesize reasons for the form it took."[10] By including such goals and behavioral objectives in their unit, Wiles and Bondi place teachers in a good position to remind their students of the difficulties in creating an accurate or definitive history of ancient Egypt. This, in turn, will help students understand why the history of ancient Egypt—indeed, history in general—is open to ongoing review and reinterpretation. It is healthy for future scholars to see that the experts of their day still have important disagreements about ancient Egyptian civilization and, further, that such debate is part of the continuing scholarly conversation, a dialogue to which they someday may contribute. In addition, because the reinterpretation is influenced by relatively new scientific tools, such as radiocarbon dating to determine the age of fossils and the use of the magnetometer to locate ancient cities, students should be invited to make special reports on these and other new procedures.

Although Mrs. Jackson's objectives and activities would engage her students in creative activities, Wiles and Bondi's goals more clearly view the students as future scholars and scientists. The overriding goal of their unit is not just to uncover information about ancient Egypt but to begin the training and recruitment process that provokes sixth graders to see themselves and their fellow students as the scientists, historians, and artists of the future. Educational equity and teachers' expectations are interrelated, and both influence future careers as well as current academic achievement.

The fourth goal of Wiles and Bondi, which pertains to the similar capacities and intelligence of various racial and ethnic groups, indirectly relates to the recruitment process as well as to the continuing debate among scholars about important aspects of ancient Egyptian civilization. With regard to recruitment, what is it that stimulates 12-year-old children to dream that someday they may be creative scientists, authors, teachers, entertainers, architects, or doctors? Surely, part of the stimulus comes from the world around them. In the world they live in, do they see people who resemble themselves serving in such positions? The study of the past can be a part of this stimulus if such study reveals (1) that men and women of various colors made important contributions to the civilizations that have paved the way to our own, and (2) that, in different times and places, racism and sexism prevented men and women from making the contributions they were capable of. In the case of ancient Egyptian civilization, students should learn that over a 3,500-year period, the leaders and creators of this civilization were people of various colors—tan, brown, and black. Although this multicolored depiction of ancient Egyptians may seem obvious or perhaps trivial to some contemporary teachers, it is noteworthy that for African-American scholars of the stature of W. E. B. DuBois[11] and St. Claire Drake,[12] the color and racial types of the ancient Egyptians was an issue of great importance. As Drake explained:

> Crucial in the Afro-American coping process has been their identification, over a time span of more than two centuries, with ancient Egypt and Ethiopia as symbols of black initiative and success long before their enslavement on the plantations of the New World. Great myths are always part of the group-coping strategies.[13]

At the same time that African Americans were identifying with the creators of ancient Egyptian civilization, however, influential twentieth-century European historians like Arnold Toynbee were writing a history that strongly contradicted the African contribution to Egyptian civilization. In *A Study of History,* a work that was later serialized in the widely read *Reader's Digest,* Toynbee asserted that "the only one of the primary races . . . which has not made a creative contribution to any one of our twenty-one civilizations is the Black race.[14]

Although Toynbee's remarks were made several decades later, it was to counter such flagrant distortions that Du Bois and others created the American Negro Academy in 1897. Today, when teachers introduce sixth, seventh, and eighth graders to what may be their first systematic exposure to Egyptian history, they can choose to ignore the debate about Egyptian racial and ethnic characteristics, or, because of the work of DuBois and Drake, among others, teachers can focus on it as a main element in the unit or introduce it through a series of invitations for inquiry. We recommend choosing one of the latter two options and will discuss our rationale under the next evaluative question.

Do the lesson content and structure increase students' proclivity and ability to see and think with a multicultural perspective, or is the content monocultural and/or inaccurate? First, we consider the content of Mrs. Jackson's unit slightly monocultural and inaccurate because it does nothing to suggest that, for significant periods in ancient Egyptian history, Egyptian pharaohs, soldiers, priests, artisans, and slaves were Black Africans. If this basic fact is ignored, the unit silently endorses the contention that ancient Egypt was in no way influenced by Black-African men and women from Egypt and other African nations such as Kush, which in fact conquered ancient Egypt somewhere around 750 B.C.[15] This is an extreme Eurocentric perspective, and it is within this perspective that ancient Egypt is described as a "near Eastern" civilization rather than an "advanced African civilization" as DuBois and other vindicationist African-American scholars stressed.[16]

In addition to essentially ignoring Black-African participation and contributions to Egyptian civilization, Mrs. Jackson, by reading passages of Carter's *His Majesty, Queen Hatshepsut* to her class, subtly reinforces the contention that Egyptian pharaohs were non-Negroid. Where it is not subtly reinforcing, it is sending a mixed message. Consider the following data from the novel:

1. In the picture on the book cover, Hatshepsut has copper or light brown skin, large lips, a broad strong nose, and eyes that appear more or less Asian. The women attendants have their hair in thick black braids similar to the "cornrows" contemporary African-American women wear occasionally.
2. In the black-and-white pencil drawings in the book, the skin coloring of the Egyptians suggests some degree of darkness, but the noses and lips of the Egyptians—royalty and servants—have shapes commonly considered "White" rather than "Black."
3. Descriptions of Egyptian, Libyan, and Syrian characters subtly reinforce the non-Black image. On page 40 it is suggested that Libyans have crinkly hair, but this adjective is never used to describe Egyptian hair (and the pictures uniformly suggest straight hair for the Egyptians):

> His majesty's pet monkey . . . Ini . . . yanked the wig off the Vizier's wife . . . then dropped it neatly on the Libyan ambassador's head. The very ambassador who is so vain of his thatch of crinkly hair.

And, in describing the Syrian ambassador and her future lover and adviser, Senmut, Hatshepsut, who is the narrator throughout the novel, gives us a contrast in noses and a slight sense of the Egyptian concept of beauty filtered through Dorothy Carter's imagination:

> The Syrian envoy is as always obnoxious. With his greasy face and dirty beard and little piggy snout.[17]

> His face (Senmut's) is strong rather than handsome, the nose a prominent beak, lines about the mouth deep as though slit by a knife, a brow cut off by the kind of short curly wig that went out of fashion years ago.[18]

Finally, in describing her 15-year-old stepson, Thutmose III, on his return from a 3-year sojourn in the Egyptian desert, we hear more about royal Egyptian noses:

> He appears bursting with health, taller, tanner, more robust. And his nose—that too, has grown. A true Thutmosid beak, wide and hooked, it dominates his face.[19]

So, in this novel published in 1987, we see two wide, prominent beaked noses on two leading eighteenth-dynasty leaders, and tan skin on Thutmose III, but no metaphor or language to suggest that either of these individuals was Negroid in appearance. Provocatively, Drake, whose book *Black Folk Here and There: An Essay in History and Anthropology* was also published in 1987, notes that the pharaohs of the eighteenth dynasty, during the time Hatshepsut reigned, were Negroid in appearance. In describing the Pharaoh Tutankhamen and his family, Drake wrote,

"This family was negroid, as was the entire Eighteenth Dynasty. The most highly respected Egyptologists admit that."[20] And in various other places in his text, Drake makes clear his conviction that Negro pharaohs were a factor in all the Egyptian dynasties. For example, he states:

> Sculpture in the round, bas-relief friezes, and colored paintings on walls and papyrus provide enough data for stating conclusively that some distinctly Negro pharaohs appeared in all the dynasties and were numerous in a few. Portraits of others give the impression of a Negro ancestral strain. In addition to the Kings, their wives, and members of the courts, religious functionaries and officials of the state show similar tendencies, as do other individuals in a wide variety of occupations.[21]

What should elementary teachers do with the claims of respected scholars like Drake, when other apparently informed authors, such as Carter and the writers of the ancient Egypt chapter in the 1991 Houghton Mifflin series, choose not to mention the Negroid presence that Drake and other scholars see so vividly in ancient Egyptian history?[22]

We believe that teachers should not ignore the strong assertions made by Drake and others, such as Martin Bernal[23] and DuBois; but they should not accept them uncritically either. What they should do is keep an open mind to the idea that in ancient Egyptian history we might have another example of "Black" history lost, stolen, or strayed. Indeed, racist attitudes that have been so prevalent in the West in the eighteenth, nineteenth, and twentieth centuries may well have prevented European scholars from seeing the physical pattern so clearly perceived by Drake and others. On the other hand, it is not clear that identifying ancient Egyptians as "Black" or "negroid" based on nostril size and high cheekbones represents good scholarship.[24] But, as noted, it is not the fact of Negro-looking pharaohs that we want young Black, White, Hispanic, and other students to read about. It is the theory, or possibility of such a fact, that we would call to their attention, and then by pictures, essays, interviews, and other evidence we would encourage them to draw their own tentative conclusions. In this case, discussing the Eurocentric "Near Eastern" White version of ancient Egypt alongside the Afrocentric version of a Black/Negro-dominated ancient Egypt would provide students an important opportunity. They could consider history writing and making from different perspectives, and see that the history they read is sometimes shaped by the political purposes and social needs of the author.

Finally, although we believe that the precise ethnic and racial background of many Egyptian pharaohs is open to question, we consider it fair to assume that a good number of Egyptian pharaohs and queens did not look like Yul Brynner and Anne Baxter in Hollywood's *Ten Commandments*. At the minimum, a unit on ancient Egypt should convey that many of its pharaohs and citizens were people of color (non-White), people who were apparently much less color- and race-oriented than contemporary Americans, Canadians, Australians, Japanese, and others. Perhaps ancient Egypt has more to offer us than pyramids and mummies.

Unit Three: Support and Movement of the Human Body

The third unit to be reviewed, entitled "Support and Movement of the Human Body," was developed by a student teacher, Stacy Williams (pseudonym), for a combination fourth-fifth-grade class in a small, semirural, coastal school district. Her class of 23 students was 98 percent White American, coming for the most part from middle-class or lower-middle-class families (22 out of 23 students). It was relatively free of special learners. One child had an individual education plan (IEP) and was also designated limited English proficient (LEP); one other student participated in the school's free breakfast and lunch program. The IEP/LEP learner received one-to-one instructional support from a learning disability (LD) teacher who pulled her out for 30- to 45-minute sessions three days per week. The content of these lessons was heavily influenced by classroom teacher input. Before we discuss the unit taught in this class, we display several components from Ms. Williams's unit plan so that you can form your own preliminary opinions about the content:

1. Introductory statement
2. Generalizations and main ideas
3. General objectives
4. Key questions
5. Introductory, culminating, and selected developmental activities
6. Statement of multicultural perspective
7. Evaluation procedures
8. Unit evaluation
9. Bibliography

Introductory Statement

This science unit is designed for both the fourth and fifth graders in this combination class. The unit focuses mainly on the skeletal and muscular systems of the human body, which provide for support and movement. The human body is a highly complex organism, and through studying these systems, the students will begin to understand that many components must work together to create a properly functioning body.

The unit will last approximately three weeks, and although it is primarily a science unit, literature, physical education, art, and math will be integrated into it. The fourth graders will read Lynne Reid Banks's *The Indian in the Cupboard,* which tells of a plastic miniature Indian who comes to life; the fifth graders, who have already read this book, will read Scott O'Dell's *Island of the Blue Dolphins.* During the unit we will draw on *The Indian in the Cupboard* by discussing "what makes something real" and will connect this discussion to the systems of the body that sustain life.

Generalizations and Main Ideas

Smaller components work together to create larger systems.
  I. The healthy human body is a complex organism of interdependent systems successfully working together.
    A. Individual bones work together to create the skeletal system.
    B. Individual muscles work together to create the muscular system.
    C. The skeletal system, muscular system, and other systems work together to move and support the human body.
  II. When a system is not working properly, complications occur that can often be compensated for or corrected.
    A. Injured bones and muscles often heal and become healthy bones and muscles again.
    B. Some disabilities are permanent but can be compensated for with special equipment or training.

General Objectives

1. Students will describe the functions of the skeletal system.
2. Students will identify several major bones of the human body.
3. Students will identify the four types of joints and give examples of each type.
4. Students will compare the functions of ligaments, tendons, and cartilage.
5. Students will describe the functions of the muscular system.
6. Students will compare voluntary and involuntary muscles.
7. Students will describe the effects of exercise on muscles.
8. Students will identify injuries to bones and muscles.
9. Students will become familiar with adaptations made by persons with disabilities.
10. Students will learn the proper care of muscles and bones.

Key Questions

1. What are the functions of the skeletal system?
2. What are the functions of the muscular system?
3. (From picture) Identify four bones that are labeled (common names).
4. What are the four types of joints? What is an example of each?
5. How do muscles move the body?
6. (From picture) Which muscle is contracting? Which is relaxing?
7. What do voluntary muscles do? What do involuntary muscles do? Why do we need both?
8. How does exercise affect muscles?
9. What are some injuries to muscles and bones?
10. What are some ways people compensate for physical disabilities?

Introductory, Culminating, and Selected Developmental Activities

Introductory Activity   Tell the students that they will learn about the human body and systems that have specific functions. Discuss the definition of *system*. Assign students to different systems, give them their physical positions, and as a group have them simulate the human body. Have them walk from place to place in a group to see that all components must work together for the larger system to function correctly. The students will simulate the human body by taking the roles of different systems in the body. The students will understand that systems in the body must work together to perform properly.

Culminating Activity   Have a "healthy body" party with healthy snacks, healthy games, and so on to promote the proper care of bones and muscles.

Selected Developmental Activities
1. Read textbook pages 314–318: "Your Body's Framework." Discuss functions of bones; begin notes. Activity: In small groups, make life-size skeletons and label bones. (The students will identify the functions of the skeletal system. The students will locate individual bones in the context of the entire skeleton.)

2. Discuss cartilage, ligaments, and the four types of bones. Add to notes. Continue to work on skeletons. (The students will identify the four types of bones. The students will locate individual bones in the context of the entire skeleton.)

3. Using a cow bone, discuss the parts of a bone. Add to notes. Activity: Compare strength of round bones to other possible bone shapes. (The students will identify the parts of a bone. They will experiment with different bone structures to determine the strongest shape.)

4. Using other objects, discuss the four types of joints and examples in the body. Read textbook pages 319–320. Add to notes. (The students will identify the four types of joints and will give examples of each type.)

5. Read textbook pages 321–323: "Muscles Move Bones." Discuss the functions of muscles and how they work, using your own muscles as examples. Add to notes. Activity: In pairs, students perform simple exercises to see how muscles fatigue over time when we exercise. (The students will identify the functions of muscles. The students will affirm that muscles fatigue as they are used.)

6. Activity: In pairs, students investigate blinking, discover that it is both voluntary and involuntary. Read textbook pages 325–326. Discuss voluntary, involuntary muscles, three types. Add to notes. (The students will compare voluntary and involuntary muscles. The students will identify the three types of muscles.)

7. Students do exercises and flexibility tests and answer questions about which muscles are used and how flexible they are. (The students will identify which muscles are used for certain exercises and will identify the extent of their flexibility.)

8. Read textbook pages 327–328: Bone and muscle injuries. Discuss injuries. Students complete "Determine the Fracture" worksheet, draw X rays with broken bones. (The students will identify injuries to bones and muscles.)

9. In pairs, students take a blind walk around campus. Students try out wheelchair and discuss possible problems, feelings, compensations, and so on. (The students will identify problems facd by people with disabilities and become familiar with adaptations made by them.)

10. Read textbook pages 329–331. Discuss what is necessary for healthy bones and muscles. Brainstorm healthy choices. Plan "healthy body" party. (The students will identify what is necessary for the proper care of bones and muscles.)

11. During free time, students can play a matching game at the "Bone Zone" interactive bulletin board. The bulletin board will consist of a large drawing of a human skeleton along with two envelopes, one labeled "scientific names" and the other "common names." The students will be able to label bones on the skeleton with either the common names or the scientific names of the bones; they will tack the names in the envelope to the bones of the skeleton on the board. There will be a labeled skeleton available to help the students with the scientific names; the object is to give the students practice with the names.

Statement of Multicultural Perspective

Intergroup Harmony in the Larger Culture   This unit will encourage students to see life from other people's perspective—specifically, the perspective of a disabled person. Through activities such as a blind walk and spending time in a wheelchair, students will be encouraged to think about the special challenges and obstacles that face persons with physical disabilities. These activities should help them see that not all people are the same, and that understanding and accepting people who are different is important.

Educational Equity Each lesson is planned with specific objectives to be reached, and appropriate strategies are used to reach these objectives. A variety of lessons and activities are planned so that students with different learning styles will succeed. Reading, writing, oral discussion, drawing, experimenting, and physical activities will all be used. Cooperative learning will be used, with students assigned specific roles within groups to complete tasks as a team. The cooperative groups are diverse in terms of ability level and sex, so students can draw from each other's strengths and learn to work together successfully. Regarding the five R's (routine, relevance, rigor, ritual, and mutual responsibility) that we discussed in class as one approach to creating educational equity, I make use of the routines of taking notes and reading in class, and my assignments have students thinking about their *own* bodies (relevance). In addition, in this class the students answer in unison when a question is asked and the answer is clear (ritual). I maintain high standards throughout the unit (rigor). For example, students must retake a quiz if they misspell the names of bones. Finally, through the practice of cooperative learning we establish mutual responsibility.

Cultural Pluralism The literature book *The Indian in the Cupboard* is being taught with this unit, and connections will be made to the book concerning what makes the miniature Indian in the book *real*. This book will provide opportunities to discuss different cultures—specifically, the Iroquois Indians and cowboys in American history. The class will study these cultures from the point of view that not all peoples do things the way we now do in America. Through these discussions, students will realize that different cultures and ways of doing things have value.

Evaluation Procedures

The students will be evaluated throughout the unit on their participation in discussions and their cooperation with other members during group activities. On some days the students will receive marks of a check, check plus, or check minus, depending on their participation and teamwork. I will stress to the students the importance of working with classmates and of participating in group discussions, and they will know they are receiving grades for these activities.

The students will also be evaluated on their mastery of the content areas taught in the unit. There will be a test at the end of the unit on the major concepts covered, and smaller quizzes and activities that will be graded during the unit. Students will understand what they are expected to know for each quiz and for the end-of-unit test.

Unit Evaluation

Overall, I think this has been a very successful unit. The students have enjoyed learning about the systems of the body, and they have been meeting the planned objectives. I have learned that activities generally take longer than I think they will, so I did not accomplish everything I had planned, but I am pleased with what we did.

In my initiating activity, the students acted out the different systems of the human body to see that they have to work together to function properly, and this activity was quite successful. It was fairly simple, but it was different and interesting for the students, and I think the point of it was clear. It was rewarding to start the unit in a simple but unusual way.

We did experiments and activities throughout the unit that were good learning experiences, even though they did not always turn out as I had planned. In an especially good experiment, the students stacked books on paper structures to determine why bones have a circular shape. The results led all students to the correct conclusions. In an especially difficult and confusing experiment, the students did exercises and extended periods of writing to see how muscles behave when they are tired. Many of the students got results that I did not anticipate and came to conclusions different from those I had hoped for. It was still a good learning experience, however, because we discussed the results, what should have happened, and how I might change the experiment in the future to make it better. I would use this experiment again, but I would definitely have fewer variables. I really liked having the students discover things on their own. I have seen that children need to be encouraged to think for themselves and draw their own conclusions, so I will continue to incorporate these types of activities into my teaching.

If I could change something about my unit, it would be to integrate it more into other parts of the curriculum. There was a tie into the literature book *The Indian in the Cupboard,* but it was a very limited connection and little time was spent on it. I am still not exactly sure how I would integrate the unit into other subject areas, but this is something I would like to work on. Writing could be done, such as traveling through the human body, and art projects could also be tied in. If I had control of the material being taught in all subject areas, I would work on ways to integrate more. I enjoyed planning this unit and presenting it, and I am happy with how it turned out. I am especially pleased that the students enjoyed learning the content.

Bibliography

Allison, Linda. Blood and Guts, pp. 21–58. Boston: Little, Brown, 1976.

Conway, Lorraine. Superific Science Series: Body Systems. Carthage, Ill.: Good Apple, 1984.

Mallison, George G. Silver Burdett Science 5, pp. 314–331. Morristown, N.J.: Silver Burdett, 1985.

Analysis of the Unit

Do the lesson content and strategies promote or impede educational equity? Overall, Ms. Williams, in her second student teaching assignment (11 weeks/full time) with approximately five weeks available for planning prior to unit implementation, has done a fairly adequate job. On the positive side, she used a diversity of activities (oral discussion, reading, drawing, experimenting) to achieve her instructional objectives, and also used cooperative learning in a manner designed to enhance learning for the various individuals in her class. Ms. Williams reports that she maintained high standards, helped her students see the relevance of unit content by relating material to their own bodies, and made good use of routines, rituals, and feelings of mutual responsibility. Ms. Williams also promoted maximum learning for individuals and groups in the class (boys and girls, for example) by including in the unit some very interesting experiments and activities (e.g., the blind walk around the campus, the time spent in a wheelchair, the interactive bulletin board) and attempted to add an interesting dimension by linking the unit content to a popular fictional story her fifth graders had already read and her fourth graders were reading as the unit unfolded. These virtues notwithstanding, there is significant room for improvement in the design of this unit in order to provide maximum opportunity and motivation for learning unit content.

Use of the following strategies and content would likely have improved the motivation and learning of more students in this class:

1. The content in this unit appears to be dominated by the textbook chapter, and this may be inevitable: where textbooks exist, teachers will likely use them, particulariy for content areas like science and math. Nevertheless, some individual and collaborative brainstorming at the beginning of the unit might have created a need to go beyond the textbook in the search for information. In her introduction to the unit, Ms. Williams could have said something like, "Children, a lot of what you and I learn in this unit will be determined by what these textbook authors (names on board) thought we should learn, but they might not have anticipated all our needs or our collective curiosity. Based on my own reading of this chapter, I believe it would be quite valuable for us to spend some time generating questions based on what we want to know about muscles and bones. After the brainstorming I could let you know which of your questions are answered by the text and which will require external research. I can tell you already that the text does not answer three questions I am interested in: (a) Do men and women in the United States, and all over the world, have the same skeletal bones and muscles? (b) Are there new ways and materials used to help broken bones heal? (c) What are steroids, how do they affect muscles, and why are they illegal in sports but used by doctors to treat certain diseases?" With these questions and the opportunity for self-initiated questioning, the teacher moves the class toward inquiry-oriented learning in the self-directed learning mode. Question a might, in a limited way, contribute to a sense of community and intergroup harmony within and outside the class. Students, by themselves and on the street and through the media, will learn about the physical differences between men and women, and the alleged differences between members of different ethnic groups and races. This unit provides an excellent opportunity to teach about what men and women all over the world have in common. In addition, question c would allow the teacher to connect this unit to the topic of drug abuse (past, present, and future) in the world of sports.

2. Following up on the list of "student and teacher" questions, the class could have generated a list of individuals whose occupations or special interests might connect to the content in the unit. For example, an interview with a local chiropractor, medical doctor or surgeon, athletic coach, or gym owner could enhance the material presented in the unit. It would also be appropriate, particularly in the context of a three-week unit, for the teacher to recruit guest speakers well before the unit was introduced and to locate nontraditional practitioners, such as a woman chiropractor, physical therapist, or medical doctor. The recruitment of minority practitioners as guest speakers could, as part of a cumulative program, contribute to increased equity in terms of opportunity and outcomes as well as a reduction in stereotypes.

3. This unit also appears to be devoid of invitations for inquiry. Requiring students to spell correctly all the names of the skeletal bones is one approach to

high standards and expectations, but another powerful strategy is to communicate to your learners that you expect them to define and carry out their own inquiries. Perceiving your students as active creators of knowledge, as well as energetic analysts of knowledge already created, is another significant way to contribute to equity in your classroom. For example, any child who recently suffered a broken bone would be a natural to do research on new techniques for healing bones. Anyone who doubts the efficacy or feasibility of this activist, learning-by-doing approach to knowledge creation should study the Foxfire experience, created and sustained by Eliot Wigginton and his students across 25 years of community interviews.[25]

4. Ms. Williams's multicultural perspective statement says nothing about special steps taken to enhance the potential learning of Carmen, the LEP student whose learning disability made reading and learning new words more difficult for her than for the average learner; indeed, no such preparation was made for Carmen. In this class, where a learning disabilities specialist was available and quite willing to link her tutorial session to whatever content the teacher desired, it was the student teacher's responsibility to provide the specialist with ideas and materials to facilitate Carmen's academic learning and positive participation in the unit. Although the debate about the relative virtue of pull-out programs continues, it is clear that the full advantages of this equity resource will not be realized unless there is a rich dialogue between the classroom teacher and the resource specialist. This holds true as well for Ms. Williams, who accepted the responsibility for educating Carmen when she stepped into this assignment.

5. Finally, although a diverse set of activities was incorporated into this unit, there was no mention of films, videos, filmstrips, or computer software. This unit appears to have relied too heavily on the textbook as a source of information.

Do the lesson content and strategies promote cultural pluralism in society or intergroup harmony in the classroom?   The use of cooperative learning may contribute to intergroup harmony as well as to the acceptance of different groups in society. The content of *The Indian in the Cupboard* might also contribute positively in this regard, but this novel has the potential to reinforce negative stereotypes about American Indians (p. 174) at the same time that it presents some stereotype-reducing information regarding Iroquois Indians (p. 21) and calls into question the portrayal of Indians on American television (p. 29). For promoting cultural pluralism, this novel is not a good choice. In addition, as Ms. Williams notes in her evaluation, the connection between the plot of this story and her unit was quite thin.

A biography much better suited to the content of this unit, and coincidentally available from the National Women's History Project, is *Wilma Rudolph: Champion Athlete,* by Tom Biracree (New York: Chelsea House, 1989). Parts of the story could have been read orally to the students during the three-week unit. This 112-page book is about a child stricken with polio who was unable to walk until age 11; with the help of her family, however, she won several Olympic gold medals in track. The book's content—an inspiring story of a child the same age as the students who overcame a severe physical disability—relates directly to the objectives of this unit. Also, in this class and community, in which there are very few African Americans, the story of Wilma Rudolph will give students the opportunity to identify with a courageous role model from an ethnic group, and perhaps gender group, different from their own. Such exposure and sense of identification throughout the K–8 curriculum should contribute to greater acceptance of and more positive relationships with individuals who are different.

Do the lesson content and strategies make use of, or help to develop, collaborative, empowering relationships among parents, students, and teachers? Efforts to involve parents in this unit were minimal. For example, no letter was sent home notifying parents about the upcoming unit or inviting them to attend the culminating activity (the "healthy body" party). Until she asks, a teacher will not know whether a parent or friend of a parent possesses special knowledge that might tie into the unit. A parent who is a soccer coach, former ballet student or dancer, jazzercise instructor, or other athletic type might have knowledge that could enrich the unit.

Does the content of the unit help to lessen distortions in the historical, literary, or scientific record that may be linked to historical racism or other forces that have led to the oppression of specific ethnic and cultural groups? As designed and implemented, this unit made no contribution toward discovering racial or cultural distortions in history, and the content does not lead itself to this objective in a clear way. Nevertheless, the question we raised earlier regarding whether men and women from different parts of world have the same skeletal structure and muscle groups can show that the differences between the so-called races are skin deep at best.

Unit Four: Famous Fairy Tales

The fourth unit to be reviewed, "Famous Fairy Tales," was developed by a student teacher, Carol Sanchez (pseudonym), for a second-grade class in a small, rural, central coast school district in California. Ms. Sanchez's class had 28 students, was 93 percent White American; most of the students came from families who were middle- and lower-middle class ($N = 25$ out of 28 students), and there were few special learners. One child was designated limited English proficient (LEP), and another student was non-English proficient (NEP); both were Mexican Americans. Three students in the class participated in the school's free or partially subsidized lunch program. The LEP and NEP learners were pulled out of class five days a week (30 minutes per session) to participate in a second-grade ESL (English as a Second Language) class, in which they were taught English by a Spanish/English teacher. The classroom teachers in the second grade had little input into the content of the ESL class, and there was little effort to create continuity between the curricula in the school's three second-grade classrooms and the curriculum of the ESL classroom. Although there was little dialogue and continuity, relationships among all teachers in the setting were quite good, and the potential for more curriculum dialogue and exchange was favorable.

Following is a list of several key components of Ms. Sanchez's unit from which you can form your own preliminary opinions about the content:

1. Introductory statement
2. Categorization of activities by content area
3. Main ideas
4. General objectives
5. Key questions

6. Introductory, closing, and selected developmental activities
7. Statement of multicultural perspective
8. Evaluation procedures
9. Unit evaluation
10. Bibliography

Introductory Statement

This is a literature-based unit featuring well-known fairy tales and folktales. Such stories as "Jack and the Beanstalk," "Strega Nona," "The Frog Prince," "Little Red Riding Hood," "The Three Little Pigs," "Goldilocks and the Three Bears," "Cinderella," and "The Gingerbread Man" will be read, compared, acted out, and written about. This unit is to be incorporated into a four-week period for a second-grade class. The students will be engaged in exciting and interesting activities that will make these well-loved stories even more important to them.

Categorization of Activities by Content Area

LANGUAGE ARTS
Beginning, Middle, End
Sequencing Events
Changing Endings
Oral Language
Charades
Drama
Similarities/Differences
Point of View
Characters
Setting
Create Own Fairy Tale
Magic Bean Writing

SCIENCE
Senses
Taste
Smell
Touch
Growth of Plants
Wolf Information
Bear Information
Life Cycle of Frogs

COOKING
Gingerbread Men/Women
Porridge Making
Cookie Making

MATH
Counting
Graphing
Estimating
Map Reading
Sequencing
Measuring
Pumpkin Activities
Estimating/Graphing
Time Lines
Cinderella's Day
Jellybean Activities
Pasta Activities
Classification

SOCIAL STUDIES
Italy—Map Reading
Reading Maps
Native Americans
Appalachian Mountains Location
Folktale Homes
Creating Fairy-Tale Maps

ART
Fairy-Tale Quilt
Gingerbread Men/Women
Making Pigs
Basket Making

Main Ideas

1. Fairy tales and folktales differ from culture to culture.
2. There are similarities and differences between popular childhood fairy tales and folktales.
3. Fairy tales and folktales may be communicated in many different forms.

General Objectives

1. Students will gain awareness of fairy tales and folktales from other parts of the world.
2. Students will become aware of the similarities and differences between some fairy tales and folktales.
3. Students will gain knowledge in sequencing events of a story by using pictures and words.
4. Students will be able to compare and contrast two similar fairy tales or folktales.
5. Students will gain knowledge in estimating and graphing their results.
6. Students will understand the different components of a fairy tale and a folktale: plot, characters, and setting.
7. Students will be able to explore their sense of taste, smell, and touch.
8. Students will be able to determine the difference between fantasy and reality.

Key Questions

1. What differences lie between familiar fairy tales and those of different cultures?
2. What is point of view?
3. What does the term *main characters* mean?
4. What is setting?
5. What is the difference between fantasy and reality?
6. How does our sense of smell affect our sense of taste?
7. Where is Italy located?
8. How do we sequence a story?
9. Are there differences between the same fairy tale or folktale told by different authors?
10. Are wolves that we read about in fairy tales and folktales the same wolves that are in the forest?

Introductory, Closing, and Selected Developmental Activities

Introductory Activity   This unit focuses on many different stories, and the introductory activity I have selected has something to do with all of them. The students will be involved in a lesson that asks them to differentiate between statements of reality and fantasy. This activity, in turn, will lead into a discussion about fairy and folktales and whether they are reality or fantasy. I will then read one of my favorite fairy tales from my childhood, "The Princess and the Pea," and will ask the students to guess why this tale was one of my favorites.

Closing Activity   The students will present to their parents the work they have completed in this four-week unit. They will also present several of the stories we read in a play version for their parents to enjoy. Refreshments will be served to the parents and students.

Selected Developmental Activities

1. Opening lesson. Students differentiate between fantasy and reality. I will read "The Princess and the Pea." (The students will learn about the difference between fantasy and reality.)
2. Introduce vocabulary for "Jack and the Beanstalk." Show students vocabulary cards, which have words and pictures. I will read the story and students will use the vocabulary words in sentences. (The students will be able to use the new vocabulary words in sentences of their own.)
3. Students will sequence the story "Jack and the Beanstalk" by coloring pictures about the story and placing them in correct order. They then have their own story. (After reading "Jack and the Beanstalk," the students will color six pictures based on the story and be able to sequence them in the correct order.)
4. Students will plant beans in cups and measure their progress over the next few weeks. We will talk about the different parts of the plant. (The students will take part in planting their own "beanstalk" and then measure the progress of its growth. They will also be able to identify the different parts of a plant.)
5. I will read "Strega Nona." The students will complete a map activity of Italy. (After reading "Strega Nona," the students will be able to find Strega Nona's hometown on their map of Italy; then they will color Italy.)
6. I will read "The Magic Porridge Pot" and the students will compare and contrast the two stories. (After reading "Strega Nona" and "The Magic Porridge Pot," the students will be able to describe the differences and similarities between the two stories.)
7. I will read "The Frog Prince"—students will learn about the life cycle of the frog and sequence the different phases in illustrations.
8. I will read "Little Red Riding Hood" in several versions. (The students will develop their sense of hearing and comprehension.)
9. I will read "Lon Po Po," a Chinese version of "Little Red Riding Hood," and we will discuss the differences and similarities between the stories. (The students will learn how storytellers in China narrate the story we know in a different form.)
10. Students will create their favorite scene in an illustration and then cut the picture into three panels, similar to the panel art found in "Lon Po Po." (The students will learn about the Chinese art form of panel pictures.)
11. "Little Red Riding Hood" tells about eye color, so students will create a graph to discover which eye color is the most prevalent in our classroom. (The students will gain knowledge in predicting eye color, graphing their results, counting their results, interpreting data, and comparing their data.)
12. I will read "The Three Little Pigs" in several versions. (Students will listen attentively to the story and will be able to answer questions when it is completed.)
13. The students will act out the story "The Three Little Pigs" as I read it again. (The students will be able to show their comprehension of the story by acting it out. They will also understand what a "part," or character, is.)

14. I will read "The True Story of the Three Little Pigs!" which is told from the wolf's point of view. We will then discuss point of view. (The students will understand what *point of view* means after reading "The True Story of the Three Little Pigs!")

15. I will read "Goldilocks and the Three Bears"; the students will learn about their sense of taste and smell, senses that Goldilocks used in finding and tasting the bears' porridge. (The students will be able to label items given to them to taste as sweet, sour, bitter, or salty. They will complete the assigned activity in groups of four.)

16. I will read "Cinderella." (The students will be able to listen attentively.)

17. The students will become more familiar with telling time and will be able to sequence Cinderella's day based on time; they will also sequence their daily events. (The students will be able to match times written out with the corresponding times on clocks.)

18. I will read "The Indian Cinderella" and the students will compare and contrast the events in the story with the more familiar "Cinderella." (The students will be able to compare and contrast different and similar elements in the two Cinderella stories.)

19. I will read "Yeh Shen," a Chinese version of "Cinderella," and will compare this story to the version we know best. (The students will be able to compare and contrast the similar and different elements in the two stories.)

20. As wrap-up activities the students will survey ten classmates to learn which of the fairy tales we read during the unit was their favorite. We will collect the information and compose a class graph showing the results. (The students will be able to collect data, graph the findings, and make an inference.)

21. As a class, the students will create a "fairy-tale quilt." Each student will cut out of construction paper one item that relates to fairy tales (frog, glass slipper, etc.), and we will make a class quilt out of their construction paper items to hang on the wall. (The students will be able to create one object related to fairy tales or folktales, cut it out, and mount it on paper. They will be able to use their creativity for this lesson.)

22. Students will present to their parents what they have done in their fairy-tale unit and will perform several plays based on the fairy tales and folktales we have read in class. (The students will be able to use the knowledge they have acquired throughout the unit to perform works informed by that knowledge.)

Statement of Multicultural Perspective

Educational Equity   I hope that each student achieves success in my classroom. To help to ensure this, during the presentation and implementation of my unit I will incorporate appropriate teaching strategies that enable each student to acquire the necessary information. I have incorporated heterogeneous seating groups, set up to ensure that each student has an equal opportunity to learn in my classroom. These groups will also enhance peer involvement, support, and teamwork.

To present vocabulary for the fairy tales that I will read during this unit, I have made vocabulary cards that have the word and a picture to illustrate the word. The pictures will give all students, including my non-English-proficient student, a visual reference to associate with vocabulary words.

Intergroup Harmony   In forming the groups in which students will work cooperatively, I will group them by gender, ability, and capability to work effectively together. I will also talk with the students to make sure we know what it means to work as a team. My bilingual student will be placed next to my non-English-proficient student so as to increase both students' self-confidence and opportunity for success. As students are placed in groups, some may not get along. Students will understand that in life they do not always have to like someone but may have to work side by side with this person, and teamwork should help them learn cooperation.

Valuing Diversity   I value and encourage all the opinions of the children in my classroom. Through modeling, the students will learn that even when they disagree with someone, that person's opinion is also important. Diversity should be encouraged. I will point out diversity among classmates when we discuss the versions of fairy tales we each know best. Also, diversity will be addressed when we examine the same fairy tale as told in different cultures. All people are important, and that is what will be stressed.

Knowledge of Other Cultures   A large portion of this unit focuses on the students examining the similarities and differences between versions of fairy tales from our country and from other countries and cultures. We will then talk about those cultures and why their fairy tales are different from the versions we know. This exercise will help students see that our knowledge of other cultures helps us to understand why their fairy tales are different.

Evaluation Procedures

During this unit on fairy tales and folktales, I will evaluate students' progress in learning the material on an ongoing basis. The students will be evaluated on participation, both in the large group and in their teams of four. Also being evaluated will be their completed assignments. By the end of the unit, each child should have completed four sequenced picture books based on what we read in class. The students' final presentation for parents, classmates, and staff members will be evaluated and will also allow the students to share the work they complete during this unit. I hope that this unit will be a positive experience for the students and that they will be excited about participating and completing assignments.

Unit Evaluation

For my initiating activity I tried to incorporate something that would be useful for all the fairy tales and folktales we would be reading. The students participated very well in our discussion of what was reality and what was fantasy. They showed great imagination!

Overall, I feel that the entire unit went very well. With unexpected things that occur in school days, I found that I had planned too many activities for the amount of time allotted. Writing lessons, for example, tended to take a few days. We incorporated math concepts such as graphing, estimating, classifying, and counting. In language arts we spent a great deal of time sequencing and distinguishing characters, setting, and point of view in the story. The students grasped the concept of point of view much better than I had anticipated. Hearing "The True Story of the Three Little Pigs!" really made the concept clear to them. The students were also introduced to different versions of fairy tales and folktales, which we compared and contrasted. They seemed to enjoy hearing versions from different countries.

If I were to do this unit again with second and, perhaps, third graders, I would use some fairy tales and folktales that they did not know, especially those from other countries. I think I might also read fewer stories and go into greater depth with the stories we studied. With second graders I felt as if I needed to keep their interest high by using many stories, but I think that older students could do much more with the overall topic without as much stimulation.

Bibliography

Children's Stories Utilized In Unit

1. "Cinderella," ed. Marcia Brown (New York: Scribner, 1954).
2. "Goldilocks and the Three Bears," by Jan Brett (New York: Putnam, 1987).
3. "Jack and the Bean Tree," by Gail Haley (New York: Crown, 1986).
4. "Johnny Cake" in *English Fairy Tales,* by Joseph Jacobs (New York: Putnam, 1904).
5. "Little Red Riding Hood," by Jacob Grimm and Wilhelm Grimm (New York: Scholastic, 1986).
6. "Lon Po Po," ed. Ed Young (New York: Putnam, 1989).
7. "Red Riding Hood," ed. James Marshall (New York: Dial, 1987).
8. "Strega Nona," by Tomie de Paola (Englewood Cliffs, N.J.: Prentice-Hall, 1975).
9. "The Frog Prince," by the Brothers Grimm (Mahway, N.J.: Troll, 1979).
10. "The Frog Prince Continued," by Jon Scieszka (New York: Viking Child Books, 1991).
11. "The Magic Porridge Pot," by Paul Galdone (New York: Houghton Mifflin, 1976).
12. "The Soup Stone," by Iris VanRynbach (New York: Greenwillow, 1988).
13. "The Teeny Tiny Woman," by Paul Galdone (New York: Ticknor and Fields, 1986).
14. "The Three Billy Goats Gruff," by Janet Stevens (San Diego: Harcourt Brace Jovanovich, 1987).
15. "The Three Little Pigs," by Gavin Bishop (New York: Scholastic, 1990).
16. "The True Story of the Three Little Pigs!" by Alexander Wolf and Jon Scieszka (New York: Viking Kestrel, 1989).

Teacher Resources

1. *Fairy Tale Sequencing,* by Evan Moor
2. Project AIMS, Fall into Math and Science; Spring into Math and Science; Glide into Winter

Analysis of Unit

Do the lesson content and strategies promote or impede educational equity? Overall, Ms. Sanchez, who was in her second student teaching assignment

(11 weeks/full time) with approximately five weeks available for unit planning prior to unit implementation, has designed and delivered a strong unit. Among the positive attributes, several are important for promoting educational equity for the 28 second graders in this class. First, Ms. Sanchez employed a wide range of lessons, activities, and teaching strategies to achieve her instructional objectives; this diversity no doubt reinforced the learning styles and preferences of specific learners at the same time that the variety increased the overall level of motivation in the class. In addition to the variety of methods and lessons, the selection of content and activities was diverse. The specific stories selected and the wide range of intriguing hands-on activities (cooking, map making, basket making, quilt making, and picture making), along with the well-developed integration of the fairy tales with math and science activities (the eye color graph and life cycle of the frog) and the presence of parents at the culminating experience, all promoted a high degree of student interest and achievement in this unit.

Ms. Sanchez made good use of cooperative learning, created word/picture flash cards for the two Spanish-speaking learners, and arranged her seating so that the limited English proficient student could help the non-English-proficient student in her first steps toward the English language. For a student teacher this was certainly a well-rounded effort to promote equity. Nevertheless, as in most lessons and units, the advantage of hindsight and reflection leads to new ideas regarding teaching strategies and content. One idea, although intended to increase motivation for the two Spanish-speaking students, might also serve, in a limited way, to promote bilinguality for the second graders in this rural, heavily monolingual (English) community.

The strategy is to make available some Spanish-language translations of selected fairy tales (such as "Caperucita Roja/Little Red Riding Hood") for optional reading by Juan and Rosita, assuming that one or both can read in Spanish. Ms. Sanchez might read aloud one of the fairy tales in Spanish. Within the unit, the second graders will hear several versions of the Cinderella story from several nations. Why not also hear a version translated into Spanish, so the children can experience a dramatic reading in a language other than English? If the teacher cannot read in Spanish, perhaps an older elementary school student, parent, bilingual aide, or another teacher can help out.

An excellent resource for locating literature available in Spanish is *Recommended Readings in Spanish Literature: Kindergarten Through Grade Eight* (Sacramento: California Department of Education, 1991). The book can be ordered from the CDE Press, Sales Office, California Department of Education, P.O. Box 271, Sacramento, CA 95812–0271. In 2000 the book sold for $7.00 plus $5.95 for shipping. Call 1–800–995–4099 for the current prices. Also, Group Editorial Grijalbo, Barcelona, Spain, publishes a series of fairy tales that are available in the United States. Series One and Two in its collection titled Ediciones Junior S.A. includes "El Mago de Oz," "Peter Pan," "Los Viajes de Gulliver," "Las Aventuras de Pinocho," and "Hansel y Gretel."

Do the lesson content and strategies promote cultural pluralism in society or intergroup harmony in the classroom? With regard to intergroup harmony, the use of heterogeneously structured cooperative learning groups, as noted in chapter 2, is a very strong choice. In a more limited way, the selection of fairy tales from different nations suggests to the learners that their teacher values the countries and cultures from which these fairy and folktales have emerged. A teacher will rarely say this explicitly; instead, over time, from one grade to another, students form the impression based on their teachers' cumulative choices about which tales and nations to include. This unit contained two lovely tales from China—"Yeh Shen" (a Cinderella story) and "Lon Po Po" (a Red Riding Hood story)—as well as "Strega Nona" (Grandma Witch), a delightful story with an Italian cast of characters. Because this story was in the unit, the second graders learned where Italy is located and colored a map of Italy. All this represents *very* good planning.

To promote appreciation and acceptance of a wider range of cultures, it would have been appropriate for Ms. Sanchez to include one or more tales from Africa and/or Central and South America. Teachers have a Caldecott Honor Book available to serve this purpose: *Mufaro's Beautiful Daughters: An African Tale* by John Steptoe (New York: Lothrop, Lee and Shepard Books, 1987). This story incorporates several Cinderella-like elements. Beyond the beauty of its illustrations and its well-crafted prose, this story has other virtues, ones not usually associated with fairy tales. For example, on the introductory page to *Mufaro's Beautiful Daughters* we learn that (1) the illustrations in the book were inspired by the ruins of an ancient city in Zimbabwe as well as the flora and fauna in that region, (2) the names of the characters in the story are from the Shona language, and (3) the author dedicated this book to the children of South Africa. We now have two more nations, Zimbabwe and South Africa, for students to locate on the map; with the addition of this tale, the unit transports the second graders to Asia, Europe, and Africa. In addition, we have an interesting question to share with the students: Why do you think John Steptoe dedicated this book to the children of South Africa? After discussing the children's opinions, the teacher could use this question to stimulate interest in further research on South Africa.

Does the unit allow students to expand their knowledge of other cultures and ethnic groups? In this unit students did not really explore different cultures as much as they experienced literature from several different cultures. From these experiences they learned that cultures that existed long ago and in widely separated locations developed quite similar folktales and fairy tales. Thus these stories allow the second graders to catch a glimpse of a common humanity unfolding, through literature, in several different cultures. In addition, the reading of *Mufaro's Beautiful Daughters,* which introduces the second graders to the idea of a beautiful and ancient African kingdom, could be augmented by several nonfiction articles about ancient African kingdoms. Taken together, the tale and extra readings could serve to diminish contemporary distortions regarding African history. Including content that pertains to Africa, along with efforts to provide accurate information about Blacks in American history, could promote better relationships between Blacks and Whites and people of color in general. At the minimum, children of all colors and cultural backgrounds deserve the opportunity to see themselves and their ancestors sensitively portrayed in the school's literary selections; it is the responsibility of teachers to know where to locate such materials. An excellent resource is the videos produced for the Reading Rainbow series, seen on Public Broadcasting Stations (PBS) around the nation. The series, hosted by Levar Burton, has one video that celebrates the music, dance, and literature of Africa. On the 28-minute video, also entitled *Mufaro's Beautiful Daughters,* actress Felicia Rashad reads the story, which is accompanied by close-ups of the artwork from the book. The reading is followed by a brief, informative discussion about drums and other ancient African instruments made from indigenous materials, such as gourds, bamboo, and conch shells. In the final part of the video, several elementary school students talk about other books with African themes. This video helps teachers integrate literature with music, art, craft, dance, and history. Local education agencies around the country are likely to have copies of the Reading Rainbow series.

Finally, if we were teaching the unit, we would add at least one more variation on the Cinderella theme: a captivating little tale named "Atalanta," written by Betty Miles. This tale, which does not exactly fit into the traditional Cinderella mode, adds a modern twist that second graders would notice and enjoy. This tale introduces primary graders to a bright and clever princess who speaks her own mind and is determined to select her own husband. It will demonstrate to students that in the creation of their own folktales and fairy tales, it is appropriate to develop and incorporate new themes and relationships. The story of "Atalanta" appears in *Free to Be You and Me* (New York: McGraw-Hill, 1974), a project conceived by Marlo Thomas and developed and edited by her, Carole Hart, Letty Cottin Pogrebin, and Mary Rodgers.

Unit Five: Thinking Logically: A Study of Common Fallacies

Abrahamson and Smith's "Thinking Logically" unit is one of five that comprise a semester-long required course in sociology at their high school. Within the course, besides the unit on common fallacies in thinking, there are units on prejudice formation and reduction, on authority, on family, and on influences; a term paper project is another element in the course. The logical fallacies unit serves as the foundation for the course; it develops or refines analytical skills that enhance the potential for deeper insights into the units that follow, as well as content the students encounter in and out of school. The 13 fallacies the unit revolves around are based on the work of Stuart Chase in his 1956 book *Guides to Straight Thinking*.[26]

The major goal of the logical fallacies unit is to increase each student's ability to engage in critical thinking. For the authors, this skill "implies a questioning world outlook" and "means an ability to actively investigate aspects of the world in a structured way—as opposed to blind acceptance of tradition, authority or folk wisdom."[27]

Course Goals

In the "Thinking Logically: A Study of Common Fallacies" teacher's manual, the authors list 16 course goals and include a footnote explaining that the goals were inspired by and adapted from Raymond S. Nickerson's article "Why Teach Thinking?"[28] Although presented as goals, with a little bit of rephrasing, the goals could be presented as behavioral objectives. For example, goal 1 could read: At the completion of this course, students will be better able to *systematically use evidence, organize their thoughts, and avoid common fallacies.* Next, we list five of the course goals exactly as they appear in the teacher's manual.

1. Systematically uses evidence, organizes thoughts and avoids common fallacies.
2. Recognizes the difference between searching for a solution and rationalizing a predetermined one.
3. Understands that expressing deeply held beliefs is different from making factual claims.
4. Listens carefully to opponents' ideas. Can state these in a manner acceptable to the people involved.

5. Can suspend judgment when evidence is lacking. Is capable of saying, "I don't know."[29]

The Logical Fallacies

Fallacies, as defined by the authors, "are logical faults as these have been understood by scholars in the Western World beginning with the Greeks and Romans."[30] A fallacy can also be defined as a mistaken belief, especially one that is based on an unsound argument, or simply as faulty reasoning that leads to the presentation of a misleading or unsound argument.[31] This faulty reasoning could be described as mental errors, and Abrahamson and Smith do indeed write that "mental errors—or childish thought patterns—are often called logical fallacies."[32] The 13 logical fallacies in this unit are the wise men fallacy, overgeneralization fallacy, false cause-and-effect fallacy, crowd appeal fallacy, self-evident truth fallacy, thin-entering wedge fallacy, getting personal fallacy, you're another fallacy, guilt by association fallacy, black/white fallacy, false analogy fallacy, arguing in circles fallacy, and the facts and figures fallacy.[33]

Teaching Strategies

The teaching strategies employed, and the actual content of the logical fallacies and prejudice units, were strongly influenced by Abrahamson's experiences in teaching a required course on race relations at Riverside–Brookfield High School in the early 1960s. Referring to that period, Abrahamson has written:

> At that time I believed that non-violent direct action would end segregation in America, that students learned best through discussions where they were free to express themselves, and that people-to-people interaction would end out-group hostilities. Fairly rapidly I realized that my simplistic enthusiasms were not well grounded in the reality of my classroom. The Riverside–Brookfield community was in a white flight corridor from Chicago. Many of my students' families had gone through real estate block-busting. Their experiences or those of relatives and friends resulted in a high degree of bigotry that they freely expressed during class discussions. As students verbally battled, I stood on moral high ground inserting little ethical lectures. As a result, I found myself siding with some students and alienating others. My teaching was not having the effects intended.[34]

From this experience, Abrahamson and his colleagues developed what they called a "remedial thinking unit" using, as previously noted, Chase's *Guides to Straight Thinking*. Ideas were kept simple, and, in the current rendition of the unit, students, in heterogeneously grouped classes, proceed through four well-defined phases in the two- to three-week unit.

In phase one, each fallacy is studied for about 10 to 15 minutes and follow-up classroom and homework assignments help each student memorize and understand each fallacy. In phase two, in a mastery-learning format, four quizzes are completed; after the fourth is completed, students, avoiding the use of fallacies, writes a brief essay on a social injustice. When the essay is completed, students enter phase three. Here they either help students who are still working on assignments or work on the electives that are an optional part of the unit. Finally, in phase four, students exit the unit by passing the final exam with a score of about 60 percent or higher.

Analysis of Unit

This unit has numerous positive attributes; we will only mention a few here. To begin with, it is refreshing to read about a course that has been taught, refined, and evaluated over a 25-year period. Second, we like the idea of students developing, or refining, their understanding of common fallacies prior to engaging a unit on prejudice and that this critical-thinking, empowering unit is part of a required, untracked course. In addition, the variety of strategies employed promote equity while underlining the significance of the material taught. There is a nice balance between required material (the quizzes), invitations to inquiry and service (the electives and cooperative learning), and application and choice (the students' selection of the social injustice they will write about).

For those readers who choose to adapt material from the teacher's manual and the student text, we offer the following suggestions for multiculturalizing the unit:

1. The overview in the student text strongly associates the study of fallacies with Greek philosophers and Roman translators. We would point out, first, that the study of fallacies quite possibly predates the work of Greek philosophers and, second, that alongside and prior to the work of the Greeks, thoughtful men and women probably critiqued the positions advanced by others, on the basis of the faulty reasoning inherent in the arguments. In other words, while we recognize the significant contributions of Greek philosophers like Aristotle, we should avoid giving students the impression that all logical, nonflawed thinking began with the Greeks.

2. Change the name of the "wise men fallacy" to the "wise people fallacy."

3. In the student text (p. 1) the authors associate logical fallacies with "childish thought patterns." We would delete the reference to childish thought patterns, or at least before assigning the reading, we would emphasize that fallacy-influenced reasoning is something many adults fall prey to. In short, the use and misuse of fallacies characterize the thought processes of many children *and* adults, including teachers, professors, media pundits, politicians, religious leaders, and so on. As students become more knowledgeable about specific fallacies, some of them will recognize that individuals whom they admire—members of their family, faith group, and/or community—consistently make use of fallacies to advance their arguments. Out of respect for these individuals and the cultures they may represent, we do not describe their thinking as childish. It is enough that we characterize it as unsound and misleading. If this unit is taught in the context of the seven goals of multicultural education enumerated earlier, the teacher can show how a unit that supports the goal of empowerment can conflict with some of the values associated with cultural pluralism (tolerance, respect, and/or celebration of cultural diversity). Teachers may also be interested in seeking out points of view that advocate accepting one or more of the 13 fallacies as a valid form of social argument, or may want to read about nations like Canada and China, which are grappling with related issues as they define what is appropriate evidence for the medical practice that will be provided to various majority and minority groups.[35]

Unit Six: Prejudice in Group Relations

The three-week unit "Prejudice in Group Relations" was developed during the same time period (1960s–1990s) and for the same course as the logical fallacies unit; indeed, the prejudice unit immediately follows the fallacies unit. The focus of this unit is on prejudice comprehension and reduction; to facilitate this, the authors have developed a teacher's manual, student text, student workbook, and a packet of supplemental materials. Abrahamson and Smith discuss the origin of this unit in the introduction to the "Prejudice in Group Relations" teacher's manual. They explain what led to the development of the unit: "We often found that our attempts to teach about prejudice had effects opposite of those we desired. Some students used class discussions to defend their prejudiced beliefs . . . [and] classes tended to become polarized."[36] Introducing the unit enabled the authors to deal with these problems. In addition, the authors comment that "by treating prejudice objectively—almost clinically—emotional argumentation is reduced" and, further, that their materials help an instructor "make prejudice so indefensible intellectually as to render it inoperative even for youngsters surrounded by prejudiced peers."[37] Understood in context, the latter is more of a goal than a claim regarding the success of the unit.

The unit is divided into five sections. Each section attempts to answer one basic question:

1. How do social scientists group people?
2. What is prejudice, and how does it relate to love, hate, and society?
3. What are the causes of prejudice?
4. What effects does prejudice have on those who give it and those who receive it?
5. In what ways can an individual take a stand against creating, maintaining, or tolerating prejudice? (This part of the unit is optional.)

In responding to these questions, Abrahamson and Smith draw on the work of a variety of social scientists. However, they make clear that it was Gordon Allport's classic work *The Nature of Prejudice* that was most influential in the development of their unit.[38]

Course Goals

As noted, the major goal of this unit is to leave the student more knowledgeable about prejudice and its repercussions, and less likely to create, maintain, or tolerate prejudicial thinking or behavior.

Teaching Strategies

In general, the unit progresses through three stages. In stage one, basic concepts are didactically presented, and in stage two, students demonstrate their mastery of concepts via quizzes and writing exercises. In stage three, students apply the concepts to their own lives and participate in class discussions about prejudice in the media and in their own communities. It is noteworthy that the high school students do not participate in a wide-ranging, whole-class discussion about prejudice until they have demonstrated mastery of a series of social science concepts. Among others, these concepts include sociologist, groups, in-groups, out-groups, biological groups, ethnic groups, racial groups, ascribed groups, achieved groups, nationality groups, primary and secondary in-groups, positive and negative prejudice, rationalization, social approval of prejudice, projection, stereotype, scapegoat, selective perception, overgeneralization, guilt by association, false cause and effect, self-hatred, discrimination, reverse prejudice, and the self-fulfilling prophecy. A clear attempt is made, in this unit, to base the class discussions on conceptual knowledge, so that they will be more illuminating and less polarized and emotional.

Beyond the direct teaching of these concepts, across the three stages a variety of teaching strategies is employed. These include lectures and guided student note taking, directed reading-thinking-writing activities, role-playing, a series of quizzes implemented within a mastery-learning structure, well-structured discussions, and writing activities that allow students to apply prejudice-related concepts to their own lives. The writing exercises also occur within a mastery-learning structure; the students are told, "I'll reevaluate as long as you rewrite and resubmit." In addition, as in the fallacies unit, there are intriguing optional assignments for students who move through the quizzes and writing activities more rapidly than others. One activity, for example, invites students to identify and discuss song lyrics that focus on prejudice reduction.

Analysis of the Unit

As was true with the fallacies unit, there are many positive elements in this unit; only a few are mentioned here. We value the unit's conceptual approach to prejudice comprehension and reduction. Because there is a significant emotional, nonintellectual, irrational component to prejudice in the real world, it makes eminent sense for high school students to explore prejudice-related concepts before they (1) analyze how prejudice may have influenced their own lives and (2) engage in open-ended discussions about prejudice in the media and in their own communities. The mastery-learning structure of the quizzes and written assignments is another positive feature, as is the untracked nature of the class and the opportunity to participate in cooperative learning to gain mastery over the unit's key concepts. We also value the opportunities students have to explore ways in which they personally can take a stand against prejudice, and the fact that the authors made this an optional assignment. From our vantage point, the more developmentally appropriate choices we provide students, the more likely that they will leave our courses empowered. Finally, we are delighted that for over 25 years this unit has been required for every student at Riverside–Brookfield High School; we consider the requirement, and the ongoing 5-year reviews of the unit, to be excellent modeling for other high school faculties.

To help make this unit more consistent with our synthesis model of multicultural education, we offer the following suggestions:

1. At the beginning of the unit, incorporate a section on the social construction of knowledge. The goal is, first, to make students aware that many of the terms they will use in this unit have a set of competing definitions. And, second, to make students aware that the definitions were created by fallible human beings who were influenced by their era and their culture as they created concepts like prejudice, stereotype, and ethnicity, let the students know that the definitions (verbal inventions) are not fixed in concrete. This might undermine the motivation of some learners to memorize all the unit's definitions, but we believe it is more important to introduce the students early on to the real world of conceptual conflict. Indeed, as one of the electives within the unit we would introduce the students to competing definitions and perspectives on such topics as prejudice, race, racism, ethnic group, and reverse discrimination.

2. With this revision of concepts and definitions in mind, we would modify the section entitled "How Persons Are Grouped" (in the student text) as follows. In this section two broad categories, biological and societal groups, are introduced. Biological groups are subdivided into four categories: sex or gender groups, age groups, racial groups, and physical anomaly classifications. Because the word anomalous is linked in some dictionaries to the pejorative terms abnormal, deviancy, and abnormality, we would change "physical anomaly classifications" to "nonracial physical classifications." In addition, although we would continue to use the term racial groups, we would include statements making clear that many distinguished social scientists and laypeople consider race to be a false and misleading category. At the same time, to have a meaningful discussion about racism, one must carefully make use of the categories that have been historically associated with racial prejudice. Thus the instructor must simultaneously use the categories and undermine their legitimacy.

3. Along similar lines, but for different reasons, we would introduce the students to more than one definition of stereotype. In the student text a stereotype is initially presented as a perception (p. 20) and then as a preconceived idea about a person, place, or thing (p. 21). Abrahamson and Smith's perception of the stereotyping process allows them to say or imply that "one cannot say that stereotyping is wrong anymore than one can say that being fearful is wrong"[39] and that stereotypes can be positive or negative.[40] This assessment is consistent with the authors' remarks about positive and negative prejudice: "An adequate definition of prejudice must include positive prejudice as well as negative prejudice."[41] While we agree with the authors, we want to emphasize that a presentation about positive prejudice or positive stereotypes should be organized so that students are not left with the idea that prejudice or stereotypes can be a good thing. Toward this end, and consistent with our strategy of sharing several definitions with students, we would point out that stereotype can be usefully defined as "a rigidly held, erroneous belief or generalization about an entire group of people." It follows from this definition that individuals who hold stereotypes will interact with whole groups of people on the basis of incorrect ideas. Whether the stereotype is positive or negative, the interaction will be misguided and will likely create problems for all concerned. The message we want to get across to high school students is that stereotypes and stereotyping are wrong.

4. In addition, we would recommend lengthening the unit a bit to incorporate two specific videos, primarily because they support two of the unit topics (prejudice in the media and taking a stand) and also set the stage for student discussion about, and inquiry into, racism and sexism in American culture and beyond. This unit on prejudice stops short of introducing these critical concepts but provides a foundation for students and faculty who want to go beyond the unit's parameters. The two videos are *Ethnic Notions* and *The Shadow of Hate.*[42] *Ethnic Notions* traces the evolution of the deeply rooted stereotypes that have fueled anti-Black prejudice and White racism from the antebellum period to the civil rights era. Supplementing this, *The Shadow of Hate* chronicles the legacy of intolerance toward Native Americans, African Americans, religious minorities, European and Asian immigrants, and others.

5. While we like having the "take a stand" component of the unit optional, we believe that all students in the class should take part in a discussion in which the action-oriented prejudice-reduction ideas and commitments of individual students are presented. Instructors could invite students to share their ideas,

or they could structure the activity so that all authors would know that later in the unit or semester their ideas would be anonymously shared with the entire class, or they could integrate the two options.

6. Finally, in the elective component of the unit we would invite students to consider whether the definition of prejudice provided by Abrahamson and Smith, or the definition we shared above, would be improved by changing "whole groups" or "an entire group of people" to "most members of a group." (The Abrahamson and Smith definition is a simplified version of Gordon Allport's definition; they state that "prejudice involves deep-seated feelings toward whole groups or specific people just because they are members of some group. These feelings are excused—or rationalized—by faulty reasoning.")[43] This elective exercise would allow students to wonder if an individual can feel prejudice toward most members of a group at the same time that he or she recognizes the individual merit of some members of that group. In short, is prejudice an all-or-nothing attitude, or are there differing degrees of group prejudice?

DISCUSSION QUESTIONS

1. In discussing the unit "The Winning of the West," we suggested that the title "The Expansion of the American Nation: 1775–1850" might lend itself better to a unit oriented toward multiculturalism.
   a. How do you think we would defend this title change?
   b. Can you suggest a different and possibly better title? If so, explain.
   c. Is "The Westward Movement: 1775–1850" better than both of the above titles? Why or why not?

2. We believe that elementary and middle-school teachers, using divergent inquiry-oriented questions and activities, should call attention to the various skin colors of the ancient Egyptians as well as the African context of the ancient Egyptian civilization.
   a. What strikes you as logical about this belief? Explain your reasoning.
   b. If you see little merit in this suggestion, spell out your reasons.

3. A frustrated teacher in one of our graduate courses lamented that multicultural education constantly seemed to highlight the achievements of people of color (non-Whites) and diminish or comment negatively on the behavior of Whites.
   a. Does this complaint seem accurate to you?
   b. How would you respond to this teacher?

4. In an essay entitled "The Danger in Multiple Perspectives," the late Albert Shanker, then president of the American Federation of Teachers, presents a point of view regarding multiperspective teaching that we consider erroneous and misleading. In discussing the danger he perceives, Shanker writes:

   > Now "multiple perspectives" is an excellent phrase. It sounds open-minded, which is what the pursuit of knowledge should be. But when you put the concept into the classroom, what does it mean?
   >
   > For a teacher presenting a historical event to elementary school children, using multiple perspectives probably means that the teacher turns to each child and asks the child's point of view about the event. To an African-American child this would mean, "What is the African-American point of view?" To a Jewish child, "What is the Jewish point of view?" And to an Irish child, "What is the Irish point of view?"
   >
   > This is racist because it assumes that a child's point of view is determined by the group he comes from. But is there a single African-American or Jewish or Irish point of view? A child may have a point of view based on the fact that he is rich or poor or that he has read extensively or that he comes from a family of conservative Republicans or Marxists. In a society like ours, we are often, and delightfully, surprised that people do not carry with them the views that stereotypes call for. Is it a teacher's job to tell children that they are entitled to only one point of view because of the racial, religious, or ethnic group they come from? Should schools be in the business of promoting racial stereotypes and fostering differences where they may not exist?

   Answer any or all of the following questions:
   a. What do you consider to be insightful in Shanker's remarks? Explain your reasoning.
   b. What do you consider to be questionable in Shanker's remarks? Explain your reasoning.

    c. Why do you think we consider Shanker's remarks erroneous and misleading? Be as specific as possible in your comments and support your reasons with remarks made elsewhere in this text.

Note that Shanker's article is part of the series of brief position papers that appear as paid advertisements under the auspices of the American Federation of Teachers. The essay mentioned above appeared in the December 2, 1991, issue of *The New Republic* and is reprinted in appendix 5 with permission of Shanker and the American Federation of Teachers. It is noteworthy that Shanker's concerns about "multiple perspectives" were provoked by a curriculum proposal entitled "One Nation, Many Peoples: A Declaration of Cultural Interdependence," which was accepted by the New York State Board of Regents. There are some serious problems with the idea of "multicultural perspectives" as it is discussed in this curriculum proposal, and Shanker insightfully discusses one of these problems in another portion of his essay.

5. In a revealing essay entitled "Sacrificing Accuracy for Diversity," Albert Shanker continued to discuss problems with the type of multicultural curriculum apparently supported by the New York State Board of Regents as a result of its approval of a social studies curriculum document entitled "One Nation, Many Peoples: A Declaration of Cultural Interdependence." In this essay Shanker develops his argument by presenting a critique of selected components—the science essay in particular—of the African-American Baseline Essays, a key element in the evolving Afrocentric curriculum movement. In the portion of the essay leading up to the critique, Shanker says the following about ancient Egyptian civilization:

> The Portland essays present ancient Egypt as an African culture that strongly influenced the development of European civilization, and this is fair enough. It is a view most reputable scholars have agreed with for 40 years, and it corrects distortions of previous historians who were inclined to ignore Egypt's contributions or to disregard the fact that Egypt was an African civilization. But the baseline essays go far beyond discussing Egypt as an African society, and they assert a number of ideas that are inconsistent with the best scholarship. For instance, they maintain that the inhabitants of ancient Egypt were black Africans.
>
> Scholars of Egyptian history and archeology say that the evidence suggests an entirely different story. Far from being all black (or all white), ancient Egypt, they say, was a multiracial society with a variety of racial types much like that of modern Egypt. In any case, our concept of race—a relatively modern invention—would not have made much sense to the ancient Egyptians, who did not look at people in terms of skin color or hair texture. So the baseline essays not only misrepresent the evidence by insisting that Egypt was a black African society; they distort the example that Egypt has to offer our own multiracial society to make a political point.

Answer any of the following questions.

    a. Do Shanker's remarks support our critique of Dorothy S. Carter's novel *His Majesty, Queen Hatshepsut,* or does it perhaps reveal grounds for a new line of criticism? Explain your reasoning.

    b. Shanker and the historians and archaeologists he refers to suggest that ancient Egyptians did not look at people in terms of skin color or hair texture. But their artists did draw, paint, and sculpt Egyptians who looked different, suggesting that they were aware of physical differences. However, it seems likely that although they noticed and depicted these differences, the ancient Egyptians did not categorize their people by race nor assume that people with different physical characteristics had different moral and intellectual capacity.

(1) In teaching a unit on ancient Egypt to sixth, seventh, or eighth graders, would you discuss the likely absence of racial categories in ancient Egypt, and if so, how could you make use of contemporary Egyptian society to characterize the diverse, multicolored nature of ancient Egyptian society?

(2) Regarding the reduced emphasis on color consciousness in ancient Egypt, what questions might you ask your students, and toward what end?

c. In your junior high school, high school, college, and postgraduate education, were you taught that reputable scholars have believed since 1950 that (1) ancient Egypt was a multiracial African culture and (2) Egyptian culture strongly influenced the development of European civilization? If yes, in what circumstances did you learn this information? If not, why do you think this point of view was excluded from your education?

The article referred to above, another of Shanker's position papers, appeared in the December 9, 1991, issue of *The New Republic*. With the permission of Shanker and the American Federation of Teachers, the entire essay is reprinted in appendix 5.

6. In units five and six we discuss a high school program in which all the students at the school are required to study, discuss, and take exams related to a wide range of prejudice-related concepts.

a. Do you think it is appropriate, at this point in American history, to make a three-week unit on "prejudice in group relations" a high school requirement? Why or why not?

b. If yes, do you consider the three-week time period to be adequate?

RECOMMENDED ACTIVITIES

1. Identify specific resources from your school district, university, public library, museum, or other source that would allow you to create an inquiry-oriented activity on ancient Egypt—specifically, one that would allow students to speculate about the colors and racial background of ancient Egyptians. Develop a lesson to indicate how you would use such resources.

2. Examine chapter 7 ("Ancient Egypt") in Houghton Mifflin's (1991) sixth-grade text *A Message of Ancient Days*. See specifically pp. 204–205, the exercise "Interpreting Egyptian Art"; see also the activity on p. 100 of the teacher's and students' editions, which depicts Cro-Magnon people as very European looking.

a. With the goals of multicultural education in mind, which components of this chapter, if any, would you modify? Describe and explain the changes.

b. The Houghton Mifflin writers state: "Scientists say that in modern-day clothing Cro-Magnon people would look very much like Europeans." Why do you think these writers find it appropriate to comment on the physical and racial appearance of Cro-Magnons but choose not to comment on the physical/racial appearance of the ancient Egyptians?

c. Identify those things you like about the Houghton Mifflin chapter.

3. Examine the way ancient Egypt is treated in a textbook series other than the one by Houghton Mifflin; describe and discuss the strengths and shortcomings of these

chapters. Do the same for the chapters that deal with the westward expansion of the United States.

4. Working alone or with other teachers, select a unit you have taught or plan to teach. Using our eight evaluative questions as a point of departure, specify what you could do to increase the multicultural nature of this unit.

5. Plan a three-hour workshop for your fellow teachers or prospective teachers on multiculturalizing units of instruction. Specify what information you would share. Do not hesitate to go beyond the content and prescriptions discussed in this text.

6. Purchase the units developed by Abrahamson and Smith and critique the materials as well as our analysis of the units. In addition, if appropriate, adapt the materials for future teaching in one of your classes.

Journal Entry

This chapter has provided you with another opportunity for adapting content and strategies to increase the multicultural elements of the curriculum. The next chapter will link multicultural education to other curriculum areas such as citizenship education, global education, and environmental education. Before we move forward, it would be helpful for you to write a summary of your current thoughts about multicultural education; before doing so, you should review your prior journal entries.

NOTES

1. James A. Banks, *Teaching Strategies for Ethnic Studies,* 5th ed. (Boston: Allyn & Bacon, 1991), 57.
2. Ibid., 487–509.
3. John Jarolimek, *Social Studies in Elementary Education,* 8th ed. (New York: Macmillan, 1990), 275.
4. For information on ordering the student text or the teacher's manual for "Thinking Logically: A Study of Common Fallacies" or the student text and teacher's manual for "Prejudice in Group Relations," contact GSP, Inc., 9361 North Camino del Plata, Tucson, AZ 85742. The phone number is 520-498-2050. For information regarding permission to reproduce content from the above texts for noncommercial use, or for purchasing information, contact Brant Abrahamson, The Teacher's Press, 3731 Madison Ave., Brookfield, IL 60513. The phone number is 708-485-5983; their website address is (www.angelfire.com/biz/tchpr).
5. See Dee Brown, *Bury My Heart at Wounded Knee* (New York: Bantam Books, 1971), 85–91, for an example of American history written from a Native-American viewpoint.
6. Banks, *Teaching Strategies for Ethnic Studies,* 47.
7. The related facts are based on information in James Banks's chapter, "American Indians: Concepts, Strategies, and Materials," in *Teaching Strategies for Ethnic Studies,* 131-166.
8. John D. McNeil and Jon Wiles, *The Essentials of Teaching: Decisions, Plans, Methods* (New York: Macmillan, 1990), 382-392.
9. Ibid., 382-383.
10. Ibid., 383.

11. W. E. B. DuBois, *Black Folk Then and Now: An Essay in the History and Sociology of the Negro Race* (New York: Octagon Books, 1939).
12. St. Claire Drake, *Black Folk Here and There: An Essay in History and Anthropology* (Los Angeles: University of California, Center for Afro-American Studies, 1987).
13. Ibid., xv.
14. Ibid., 158
15. This date appears on p. 212 in chapter 7, "Egypt and Kush," in *A Message of Ancient Days,* the sixth-grade text in the Houghton Mifflin social studies series. The copyright date is 1991.
16. Drake, *Black Folk Here and There,* xviii.
17. Dorothy S. Carter, *His Majesty, Queen Hatshepsut* (New York: HarperCollins, 1987), 38.
18. Ibid., 59.
19. Ibid., 131.
20. Drake, *Black Folk Here and There,* 218.
21. Ibid., 173.
22. Beverly J. Armento, Gary B. Nash, Christopher L. Salter, and Karen K. Wixon, *The Message of Ancient Days* (Boston: Houghton Mifflin, 1991), 186-217.
23. Martin Bernal, *Black Athena: The Afroasiatic Roots of Classical Civilization* (New Brunswick, N.J.: Rutgers University Press, 1987).
24. Robin Sewell, a Black-American graduate student working in Egyptian archaeology; expressed this viewpoint in a letter to *The New Republic,* December 31, 1990, 6. See also Mary Lefkowitz's article "Not Out of Africa: The Origins of Greece and the Illusions of Afrocentrists," *The New Republic* 206, no. 6 (February 10, 1992): 29-36, for a thought-provoking article on this topic. Commentary regarding the article appeared on pages 4-5 of the March 9, 1992, issue of *The New Republic.* Additional material will be found in Mary Lefkowitz's book *Not Out of Africa: How Afrocentrism Became an Excuse to Teach Myth as History* (New York: Basic Books, 1996).
25. Ann Meek, "On 25 Years of Foxfire: A Conversation with Eliot Wigginton," *Educational Leadership* 47, no. 6 (March, 1990): 30-35; see also Eliot Wigginton, *Sometimes a Shining Moment: The Foxfire Experience* (New York: Doubleday, 1985).
26. Stuart Chase, *Guides to Straight Thinking* (New York: Harper, 1956).
27. Brant Abrahamson and Fred C. Smith, *Thinking Logically: A Study of Common Fallacies (Teacher's Manual),* 3rd ed. (Brookfield, Ill.: The Teacher's Press, 1994), 1.
28. Raymond S. Nickerson, "Why Teach Thinking?" in *Teaching Thinking Skills: Theory and Practice,* ed. Joan Boykoff Baron and Robert J. Sternberg (New York: W. H. Freeman, 1987), 29-30.
29. Abrahamson and Smith, *Thinking Logically (Teacher's Manual),* 3.
30. Ibid., 1.
31. These definitions are based on the definitions provided in *The Concise Oxford Dictionary* (Oxford: Clarendon Press, 1990), 442.
32. Brant Abrahamson and Fred C. Smith, *Thinking Logically: A Study of Common Fallacies (Student Text),* 3rd ed. (Brookfield, Ill.: The Teacher's Press, 1993), 1.
33. Ibid., 3.
34. Brant Abrahamson, "Understanding Prejudice: A Focus on Critical Thinking," *Multicultural Education* 3, no. 3 (Spring 1996): 44-45.
35. David Young, Grant Ingram, Ming Liu, and Constance MacIntosh, "The Dilemma Posed by Minority Medical Traditions in Pluralistic Societies: The Case of China and Canada," *Ethnic and Racial Studies* 18, no. 3 (July 1995): 495-514.

36. Brant Abrahamson and Fred C. Smith. *Prejudice in Group Relations (Teacher's Manual),* 2nd ed. (Brookfield, Ill.: The Teacher's Press, 1991), 1.
37. Ibid., 2.
38. Gordon W. Allport. *The Nature of Prejudice* (New York: Addison-Wesley, 1954).
39. Brant Abrahamson and Fred C. Smith. *Prejudice in Group Relations (Student's Text),* 2nd ed. (Brookfield, Ill.: The Teacher's Press, 1991), 20.
40. Ibid., 21.
41. Ibid., 7.
42. *Ethnic Notions* is a 56-minute, Emmy-award-winning video produced in 1987 by Marlon Riggs. Information about renting or purchasing the video is available from Resolution Inc./California Newsreel, 149 Ninth Street, San Francisco, CA 94103; the phone number is 415–621–6196. *The Shadow of Hate: A History of Intolerance in America*, a video and text kit for secondary students, includes a 40-minute video and a 128-page illustrated text *Us and Them* and a teacher's guide. One kit per school, university department, or community organization is available free upon written request on letterhead from principal, department chair, or director. Mail request to Teaching Tolerance, P.O. Box 548, Montgomery, AL 36101-0548. This information was taken from the Southern Poverty Law Center website, www.splcenter.org on 9/15/99.
43. Abrahamson, and Smith, *Prejudice in Group Relations (Student Text),* 8.

CHAPTER 5

Creating a Multicultural Curriculum with Content That Links Environmental, Global, Citizenship, and Multicultural Education

CHAPTER OVERIVEW

This chapter provides working definitions of global, environmental, and citizenship education and a rationale for creating units that link these curriculum areas to multicultural education. To illustrate the distinctive characteristics and special value of this unique type of multicultural unit, a profile of an integrated rain forest unit is given along with discussion questions and recommended activities.

INTRODUCTION

In chapter 4, two of the units we discussed had social studies themes: "Winning of the West" and "Ancient Egypt." These units were considered integrated because the teachers who planned them attempted to connect their social studies content to art, music, science, math, and language arts activities. Thus, the units integrated into one entity the traditional content areas of the K–12 curriculum. Now we present a different type of integrated unit, one in which the teacher starts with themes that are *global* and *environmental* in nature, like rain forest depletion, and then broadens these themes to include content related to *citizenship* and *multicultural education*. We refer to this special type of integrated unit as an environmental multicultural unit (EMC) and will show that the synthesis of these four interdisciplinary curriculum areas (global, environmental, citizenship, and multicultural education) can lead to units that are timely for students and society. As background we will discuss the synthesis approach to extending multicultural education, and then provide brief definitions for three of the four curriculum areas.

In chapter 1 we discussed conceptions of multicultural education that integrated it with other curriculum concepts such as multiethnic education (James Banks) and social reconstructionism (Carl Grant). In addition, various authors, particularly Christine Bennett,[1] have linked multicultural education to global education. In discussing our integrated multicultural model of curriculum and instruction, we noted that there were other important models of instruction worthy of teachers' attention. One such model would link effective instruction to a vigorous, open-minded form of citizenship education. Within this citizenship model "effective instruction" could be defined as instruction that successfully prepares students to be active, productive, citizens of their national and world societies. Carl Grant and Christine Sleeter, in their "Education That Is Multicultural and Social Reconstructionist" model, have included a focused version of citizenship education in their conception of multicultural education by linking it to the philosophy of social reconstructionism. As noted in chapter 1 of this text, Sleeter and Grant distinguish their model from multicultural education as follows:

> Education that is Multicultural and Social Reconstructionist deals more directly than the other approaches have with oppression and social structural inequality based on race, social class, gender, and disability . . . It prepares future citizens to reconstruct society so that it better serves the interests of all groups of people and especially those who are of color, poor, female, and/or disabled.[2]

Clearly, this is a heightened, focused, and politically directed form of citizenship education that would presumably go far beyond preparing students to create a more efficient and dynamic version of our current capitalist democracy. For our target population, K–12 students, and our sense of what is appropriate in citizenship education, the reconstructionist emphasis is too focused, even though the oppressed groups Sleeter and Grant highlight are quite worthy of attention by younger and older citizens.

In slight but important contrast, our conception of multicultural education includes goals such as cultural pluralism, maintenance and expansion of freedom and democracy, intergroup harmony, an expanded multicultural/multiethnic knowledge base, and empowerment of students and parents and, by implication, teachers; all of these goals develop skills and knowledge associated with citizenship education. Furthermore, in our model, citizenship education should be viewed as a major strategy for preparing students to maintain and expand freedom and democracy in our nation. But, while citizenship education contributes to the goal of "maintenance and expansion of freedom and democracy," it is not equivalent to this goal. Thus, we can simultaneously view citizenship, environmental, and global education as critical components of the overall K–12 curriculum, and multicultural education and citizenship education as tightly connected but distinct elements within that curriculum. This view allows citizenship education, like any other content area, to be analyzed in terms of being more or less multicultural. Also, our approach to citizenship education is not as sharply defined or politically directed as Sleeter and Grant's. The citizenship content we propose does not explicitly aim at preparing K–12 students to reconstruct society in the interests of all people or, more specifically, those who are of color, poor, female, and/or disabled. Rather, the citizenship curriculum we espouse would develop in students a positive attitude toward being an active citizen in their class and school as well as the local, state, national, and world society. It would show K–12 students that, by individual and collective political and economic action, they can make a difference at one or more of these political levels. Because we are focusing on students 5 to 17 years old, most of the citizenship projects should be at the local school, community, and county levels, with active involvement in state, national, and world issues as appropriate. This, of course, does not preclude specific discussions or real-world projects pertaining to oppression, social structural inequality, or racism and sexism in the United States and other nations.

In our view, the formation of a positive attitude toward citizenship is the quintessential function of schools, and the major strategy for developing this attitude goes far beyond preaching to students and having discussions about citizenship responsibilities. On a recurring basis, students should have the opportunity to read about, discuss, and *do* citizenship. However, for this to happen, teachers must vividly see their own classrooms, schools, and local communities as politically formed communities in which power and conflict of interests exist; in these settings, students can learn through citizenship projects that their own decision making and action can improve their classrooms, school, and local communities. In short, local politics is highly significant politics, particularly for developing a healthy attitude and inclination toward active, responsible citizenship.

A related nationwide research project was completed in 1989 among American youth aged 15 to 24 by People for the American Way. The researchers concluded that the youth interviewed:

1. considered personal success, family life, and personal happiness far more important than community involvement and public life;
2. equated being a good citizen with being a good person rather than as being politically engaged; and
3. displayed no compelling drive to participate in the political system because their focus tended to be directed inward.[3]

These findings were supported by another nationwide survey completed in 1998. In this study of over 250,000 American college freshmen, researchers at UCLA's Higher Education Research Institute reported that:

1. "a record low 25.9 percent of freshmen believe that keeping up to date with political affairs is a very important or essential life goal . . . compared with a high of 57.8 percent in 1966"[4];
2. "only 14 percent of freshmen frequently discuss politics" compared with 29.9 percent in 1968[5]; and

3. "76.9 percent of freshmen report that they are going to college to be able to make more money while only 62 percent say they are in college to gain a general education and appreciation of ideas."[6]

With these results in mind, and because the citizenship projects discussed are closely linked to global citizenship, three ideas are worthy of emphasis. First, it is critical that young students utilize democratic skills (voting, debating, writing letters, challenging authority figures, shaping class and school rules) *on a regular basi*s in their own classroom, school, and local community. Second, teachers and students can engage in an important and productive form of citizenship education without committing themselves and their students to the more radical form of "reconstructionist" citizenship education. There is much good work to be done in directing students toward social responsibility in their own communities and away from an exclusive concern with personal success; K–12 teachers from all over the political landscape (Republicans, Democrats, Independents, Christian Democrats, members of Labour or Green parties, etc.) should see in multicultural education an approach to citizenship education they can strongly identify with. Finally, as Jack M. Hamilton illustrates in his book *Main Street America and the Third World*,[7] students and teachers can discover in their local community many connections to the world community and therefore many opportunities for global education.[8]

DEFINITIONS OF CITIZENSHIP EDUCATION, GLOBAL EDUCATION, AND ENVIRONMENTAL EDUCATION

Set against these two approaches to citizenship education, the following definitions of citizenship education, global education, and environmental education should help teachers to make choices about creating or adapting the type of thematic unit described in this chapter. For the purposes of our discussion, *citizenship education* will consist of all the school lessons and experiences that help students develop the ability and desire to be an active responsible citizen at various levels in our emergent democracy. One major responsibility involves being a reflective and informed voter; this requires a growing knowledge about pertinent local, state, and national issues. Given the obvious importance of this knowledge, it is easy to view *global education* as a key component of citizenship education; a definition by Kenneth A. Tye and Williard M. Kniep affirms this viewpoint. They wrote, "Global education involves learning about those problems and issues that cut across national boundaries, and about the interconnectedness of systems—ecological, cultural, economic, political, and technological" and added that global education also "involves learning to understand and appreciate our neighbors with different cultural backgrounds from ours; to see the world through the eyes and minds of others; and to realize that all peoples of the world need and want much the same things."[9] Global education so conceived clearly enhances the citizenship curriculum because it places current and future citizens in a more informed position to attempt to influence the domestic and foreign policy of their nation and other nations by voting, writing letters, and creating special advocacy groups. Given the problems that cut across national boundaries, such as deforestation and nuclear proliferation, one could argue that global education should be a major component of a well-rounded citizenship curriculum rather than an add-on. For K–12 students, global education can complement an emphasis on learning to be politically effective in one's own local community. As teachers and students strive to accomplish this effectiveness, it is appropriate for them to discover that problems they experience locally, such as pollution, poverty, and homelessness, are global in nature, and that the political and economic behavior of Americans, Japanese, Mexicans, Canadians, and others can contribute in a positive or negative way to the local problems experienced in different areas of the globe.

Learning that human consumption affects local as well as distant communities brings us close to the central concerns of environmental educators. Although *environmental education* has been defined in various ways, most environmental educators would agree that an environmental curriculum attempts to teach people to live more harmoniously with the earth and each other. Some link it strongly to citizenship education. For example, Michael Weilbacher, in describing the central mission of environmental education, wrote, "It's to assist learners in developing awareness, knowledge, skills, and commitment that result in informed decisions, responsible behavior, and constructive action concerning wildlife and the environment upon which we all depend."[10]

These definitions suggest that environmental education, global education, and citizenship education are overlapping curriculum areas, and that each can mesh neatly with the major goals of multicultural education. Citizenship education will show K–12 students that by individual and collective political action, they can influence the course of local political events. Environmental education will help them learn how to take constructive action concerning wildlife and the environment, and global education will teach them about problems and issues that cut across national boundaries. If we as classroom teachers define curriculum units that accomplish these objectives, and simultaneously achieve selected goals of multicultural education, we will productively link four critically important curriculum areas that too often receive brief, unsystematic treatment in the busy and overcrowded K–12 curriculum.

DEVELOPING ENVIRONMENTAL MULTICULTURAL UNITS

Classroom teachers working in the first decade of the new century and beyond will not have to start from scratch as they develop these multiemphasis, environmental multicultural units. An excellent resource for developing such units is the 17-volume, K–8 NATURESCOPE series developed and distributed by the National Wildlife Federation.[11] Each volume provides background information for the teacher, activities to help students understand key concepts, a set of copycat pages (ready-to-copy games, puzzles, coloring pages, and worksheets), and lessons aimed at specific age groups: the primary grades (K–2), the intermediate grades (3–5), and the advanced grades (6–8). Titles in the series include *Incredible Insects, Astronomy Adventures, Diving into Oceans, and Discovering Deserts.* A 24-minute video, entitled *Special Report: You Can Make a Difference,* shows how students around the country are taking action to protect the environment. It was developed to accompany the NATURESCOPE series. This video is an excellent vehicle for showing how environmental awareness and knowledge can lead to productive, age-appropriate citizenship activities.

All the volumes in this series are excellent resources for environmental education, but several are particularly well suited for the development of environmental multicultural units. This subset includes the volumes entitled *Pollution: Problems and Solutions, Endangered Species: Wild and Rare, Trees Are Terrific*, and *Rain Forests: Tropical Treasures*. For illustration, we will work with the tropical rain forest volume to show how a unit based on a specific volume of the NATURESCOPE series will successfully integrate all four curriculum areas. We will begin by analyzing content from the volume and will then show how this content can be selectively multiculturalized.

THE TROPICAL RAIN FOREST
AS AN ENVIROMENTAL MULTICULTURAL UNIT

Analysis of the content in the tropical rain forest volume quickly reveals why this theme lends itself to a multiemphasis unit. The global and environmental education dimensions of tropical rain forests, both as an amazing physical reality and as a human problem that cuts across national boundaries, are illuminated through various rain forest topics. Students study the forests in terms of their location, unique qualities, flora and fauna, indigenous human groups, and the various problems associated with the quickening pace of rain forest depletion throughout the world. Instructional objectives related to the lessons and activities in this volume could be stated in the following way. Students will demonstrate the ability to

1. describe the four levels of tropical rain forest growth and the special characteristics of each;
2. describe the special nature of weather in the rain forest overall and at the four levels of the rain forest;
3. identify two prevalent myths about the rain forest;
4. describe specific characteristics of certain rain forest flora and fauna as well as supportive relationships that exist between selected animals and plants;
5. describe several ways that plants have adapted to life in tropical rain forests;
6. identify several continents and nations where tropical rain forests exist and locate the tropical rain forests within these nations;

7. explain how tropical rain forests differ from other types of forests, particularly the forest closest to the students' school;

8. identify common foods (banana, coffee, etc.) and products (quinine, rubber, and mahogany) that originate in tropical rain forests;

9. identify indigenous tribes who live in rain forests on different continents such as the Kayans or Penans in Borneo, the Efe in Zaire, the Lacandon Maya in Mexico, the Yanomamo and Kayapo in Brazil;

10. identify problems and consequences associated with the rapid depletion of the world's tropical rain forests;

11. provide 6 to 10 reasons that help to explain why it is important to protect tropical rain forests;

12. identify five ways K–12 students can try to improve the health of the world's tropical rain forests.

These objectives are relevant to environmental and global education and clearly set the stage for an active form of citizenship education, but they fall short of engaging students in a planning process related to citizenship education. This situation, however, is easily remedied. Both the *You Can Make a Difference* videotape and the "Problems and Solutions" section of *Rain Forests: Tropical Treasures* provide well-selected citizenship projects for upper-elementary and middle-school students. Suggestions include (1) raising money to support organizations that seek to protect the world's rain forests, wildlife, and indigenous tribes; (2) making a commitment to modify consumption of wood products and food in ways that might positively influence the health of the world's rain forests; and (3) writing letters to chief executive officers and government officials in the United States, Japan, and Brazil, urging these leaders to support legislation and industrial practices favorable to the tropical rain forests.

We need not elaborate further because most of the information an elementary or middle-school teacher would want is well covered in the NATURESCOPE volume and its bibliography. What is less well covered is content that would allow for selective multiculturalization of the unit; therefore, we will turn our attention to this curriculum area.

In previous chapters we used seven different goals of multicultural education as guides in adapting various lessons; in this chapter we will focus on two goals, the ones that pertain to (1) expanding students' knowledge of different cultures and ethnic groups and (2) developing in students a pluralistic, open-minded attitude toward individuals and groups whose culture differs from their own. These goals are obviously related, but they are not the same. It is possible to expand students' knowledge of different cultures and ethnic groups in a manner that increases rather than diminishes ethnocentrism, and this possibility is heightened when students from technologically advanced societies, with a history of racism, study the cultures created by tribal groups who are less technologically advanced. The "multicultural" challenge for educators presenting information about the hundreds of thousands of humans who inhabit the planet's tropical rain forests is to do so in a manner that reinforces cultural pluralism while avoiding the distortion or idealization of the rain forest cultures in question.

Any unit dealing with the tropical rain forests should provide specific facts about the great diversity that exists among the indigenous people of these areas,[12] and we recommend that the teacher provide information about different tropical rain forest cultures as often as possible. This activity will extend the teacher's knowledge base and should lead to units that are progressively richer in terms of cross-cultural comparisons. Simultaneously, students should be encouraged to do individual and cooperative group research into other rain forest cultures, perhaps those that have been taught in prior years by their teacher. Although the specific rain forest culture to be presented will vary according to personal preference, we recommend that teachers consider the following criteria as they make their decisions. Where possible, the indigenous group selected for study should be one that:

1. has been studied by one or more anthropologists or other social scientists so that there are ethnographies (written descriptions of the culture) as well as photographs and possibly films or videos that can be used in the development and implementation of the unit;

2. takes into account the location of the class or special interests of the students. It is conceivable that students would show a bit more interest in a group located on their own continent, or in a country like Mexico, which has a special relationship to the United States and which may be the ancestral home for a number of students in the class; and

3. links to material taught earlier in class or as part of the K-12 social studies curriculum.

Finally, the indigenous group selected should be one whose special accomplishments and characteristics will highlight the skills, knowledge, and wisdom needed for survival in the tropical rain forests. Such a choice will help students increase their appreciation of the sophisticated skills developed by various tribal cultures, groups who are sometimes described as "primitive," with much negative connotation loaded into the word.

With these criteria in mind, we have identified a small, indigenous, tribal culture, the Lacandon Maya, for study. This group lives in the Selva Lacandone in Chiapas, Mexico, the largest remaining tropical rain forest in North America, and is a good choice for an environmental multicultural unit. The group highlighted in the NATURESCOPE volume—the Efe Pygmies of the Ituri rain forest in Zaire, Africa—is interesting and suitable for a primary grade unit; however, the Lacandon Maya should interest older students in the United States, Canada, Brazil, and other nations for various reasons. First, it is likely that the students would have already spent some time studying the ancient Mayan civilization and its mysteries. Second, studying the past and present history of the Lacandon Maya would provide students with the opportunity to:

1. review the extreme cruelty visited upon the South and Central "Native Americans" by the conquering soldiers and missionaries of Spain;

2. study the changes that occur when a relatively isolated culture begins to make contact with outside influences;

3. learn about the highly successful form of swidden (slash and burn) agriculture the Lacandon Maya have practiced for centuries; and

4. increase their knowledge of the past and present of Mexico, a nation whose history and economic realities are of increasing importance to the United States and other nations.

The Lacandon Maya have been studied by several types of social scientists, and at least three books and two films, as well as assorted photographs of the tribe members, are available to teachers.[13]

To facilitate the development of a unit that contains information about the Lacandon Maya, in the next section we will provide brief information about them in a question-and-answer format. To close the chapter, we will discuss the rationale for developing environmental multicultural units in an era when the information available to students and teachers is exploding at unprecedented rates. One estimate suggests that the information accessible in 1990 was just 3 percent of the amount that will be available in the year 2010.

THE LACANDON MAYA: BRIEF QUESTIONS AND ANSWERS

1. Who are the Lacandon Maya, where do they currently live, and where did they originate?

   The Lacandon Maya are a small group of Yucatecan-speaking Maya descendants who have lived in and around the Selva Lacandon rain forest in eastern Chiapas, Mexico, for approximately 400 years. Most authorities believe they moved into the area around Najà, Mexico, to escape persecution from Spanish soldiers and missionaries in western Guatemala, but a few others believe they are the direct descendants of the Mayans who built the temples located at Palenque and Yaxchilan in Chiapas. Today, the Lacandon Maya are one of the few remaining non-Christian Indian groups in Mexico.

2. Are the Lacandon Maya a homogeneous group?

   There are two distinct groups of Lacandon Maya: the northern Lacandon—the non-Christianized Lacandon who live in Najà and Mensäbäck—and the southern Lacandon, who live in Lacanha. The groups differ in customs, speak slightly different dialects of Yucatecan Maya, and rarely intermarry. The northern Lacandon have traditionally avoided the southern Lacandon because they consider them extremely violent.[14]

3. What is the origin of the term *Lacandon*?

   In the sixteenth century, according to R. Jon McGee, "the Spanish used the term to refer to non-Christian Indians within a geographical area covering Chiapas and a part of the modern state of Tabasco. There are two competing theories regarding the word's origins. The first claims that *Lacandon* "is derived from lacum tun, or 'great rock,' the name of the Chol Maya fortress settlement on Lake Miramar."[15] The second theory, proposed by Robert Bruce, suggests that the word *Lacandon* was derived from the Mayan words *ah acantum*, which means "to set up stone, stone pillars, or stone idols." In essence, this would be a way that Christianized Maya could refer to the non-Christianized as pagans or idolators, those who worship stones.

4. There are other contemporary Mayan descendants living in Mexico, like the Chol Maya and Tzeltal Maya (Chol and Tzeltal are Mayan dialects). What makes the Lacandon Maya worthy of study by elementary and middle-school students as well as social scientists?

   The Lacandon Maya are unique in several ways. First, practically every other Mayan group in Mexico has been Christianized to some extent. The Lacandon Maya are the only contemporary group in Mexico whose daily life and rituals may approximate what peasant and religious life could have been like among the ancient Maya. They are also one of the few remaining groups who make use of "the practical environmental knowledge which accrued within the ancient Mayan civilization," and a number of contemporary social scientists believe that "aspects of Lacandon Maya subsistence and forest management systems have significance and viability for modern tropical forest production schemes."[16] Beyond this, the northern Lacandon Maya are interesting because of their continued efforts to keep their ancient religion alive even though their culture tolerates change that does not threaten the religion.

5. What are some of the key characteristics of the Lacandon Maya agricultural system?

   According to James D. Nations and Ronald B. Nigh, "The Lacandon subsistence strategy centers around a multipurpose land-use system which takes advantage of a number of food-producing resource areas: The primary forest, secondary forest growth, marshes and rivers, and lakes and streams." The authors further note that "the basis for Lacandon resource management is tropical swidden agriculture (variously called shifting cultivation, slash and burn agriculture, or in Central America, the Milpa)," and that the "Lacandon approach . . . centers on felling primary and secondary forest, burning the dried cuttings, and planting selected species in the clearing."[17]

The phrase *slash and burn,* which may suggest to some a careless approach to farming and natural resources, can be quite misleading. The Lacandon approach is a patient, sensible, and long-term method of using the forest's resources in a way that does not deplete the rain forest as a source of food or as a natural habitat:

> Lacandones plant and harvest a milpa for two to five consecutive years, then plant the area in tree crops and allow it to regrow with natural forest species. When regrowth reaches a height of four to seven meters (usually within five to seven years), they clear and burn the area for a second round of cultivation, or allow it to regenerate into mature secondary forest, a process which requires twenty years of fallowing. Lacandones prefer to cut milpas in regrowth areas (acahuales), and historical accounts demonstrate that this preference has long been a feature of their agricultural system.[18]

Much more can be said about the extent and sophistication of the agricultural knowledge base that has accrued within the Mayan culture, past and present. Nations and Nigh discuss:

1. the Lacandon knowledge of soils, which is based on the types of trees in the area—for instance, when the Lacandones see the Ceibra tree and the breadnut ramon in abundance, they know the soil is rich and well drained;

2. the wise precautions the Lacandones take before burning rain forest to create a milpa;

3. the strategy of dispersing crops throughout the milpa to prevent large clusters of a single species;

4. planting crops like corn with a portion purposely allotted to wild mammals such as deer, squirrels, and raccoons; these animals ultimately provide the farmer with necessary meat protein; and

5. maintaining the acuahal (or planted tree milpa) as a secondary source of crops, rubber, and wildlife. Nations and Nigh point out that the acuahal "is essentially a managed wildlife area."[19]

This description of the Lacandon Maya milpa agricultural system is only a thin slice of the whole picture. The intent was to show that a study of the Lacandon Maya can provide much useful information for fourth- through eighth-grade students. Learning about the Lacandon Maya will help students appreciate the depth and complexity of human cultures in general, and in this case those rain forest tribes who at first glance appear to be primitive, backward, and without wisdom that could inform the modern world. For teachers who choose to develop a rain forest unit that includes the Lacandon Maya as an example of a rain forest culture, there is much more information about Lacandon milpa agriculture in the Nations and Nigh article; R. Jon McGee has also provided a brief informative chapter on the topic as well as a thorough bibliography of resources on the Lacandon Maya.[20]

SUMMARY

This chapter has demonstrated ways to develop another type of integrated unit, one that links four pivotal but often sparsely treated curriculum areas: citizenship education, environmental education, global education, and multicultural education. The problem of omission or superficial treatment will grow rapidly as the amount of information increases geometrically in the coming decades. As a result, emphasis on teaching students to think critically and to discover and use knowledge on their own will become an overriding concern. As we grapple with these concerns, part of the solution will come from restructuring the curriculum and organizational categories that have traditionally made up the K–12 curriculum. The new combinations of knowledge and curriculum areas that should emerge will allow educators to be more creative in meeting the demands of a new era in knowledge production and consumption. As we move into this uncertain future, we believe that teachers should highlight the importance of knowledge and skills associated with the four curriculum areas stressed in this chapter. The content of a carefully designed environmental multicultural unit should influence attitudes in a way to make our future a bit more promising. For this reason we recommend that teachers give serious thought to implementing one or more environmental multicultural units per year, or find other ways to weave these curriculum areas into their ongoing curriculum.

DISCUSSION QUESTIONS

1. We conclude the chapter by saying that the content of a carefully structured environmental multicultural unit should influence student attitudes positively so as to make our future a bit more optimistic.
   a. Why do you think we have this opinion and how valid do you believe it is?
   b. Do you think it is the public schools' responsibility to develop in students a specific mind-set toward democracy, the environment, and personal health? Is it appropriate for public school teachers and the public school curriculum to present a point of view with the hope that students will adopt it? If yes, explain your reasoning and discuss specific pitfalls or problem areas of a curriculum designed to shape attitudes. If no, explain your reasoning.
2. We have four reasons to believe that it is appropriate and practical to distinguish multicultural education from three other significant curriculum emphases (citizenship education, environmental education, and global education): first, each emphasis has its own specific domain; second, by keeping them distinct, we can more easily step back to evaluate the multicultural nature of these three emphases; third, in our seven-goal model citizenship education can be viewed as a set of strategies to help achieve the goal of freedom; and finally, multicultural education is sufficiently complicated without incorporating a set of new goals related to these curriculum emphases. On the other hand, respected multicultural theorists such as Christine Bennett, James A. Banks, Carl Grant, and Christine Sleeter have developed conceptions of multicultural education that incorporate one or more of these curriculum areas.
   a. If you were planning a workshop for pre- and in-service classroom teachers and their administrators, how would you define *multicultural education*?
   b. Would it be wise in your workshop to offer competing definitions of *multicultural education*? Why? Why not?

    c. Is there a way to define multicultural education that clarifies both its unique-
ness and its connection to other curriculum emphases? What sort of visual
image would be helpful in supporting this explanation?

3. We suggest that it would be valuable for fourth- through twelfth-grade students,
in the context of a unit that linked environmental, global, and citizenship concerns, to study the Lacandon Maya, an indigenous, relatively obscure Mexican ethnocultural group of about 350 people, a group that may become extinct within
two to three generations.

    a. Reading into and beyond the material presented in this chapter, why do you
think we believe this group is worthy of inclusion in the fourth- through
twelfth-grade multicultural curriculum?

    b. Based on your reading and experiences inside and outside this course, what
do you think of our selection? Can you identify a better choice? Explain your
reasoning.

4. Within this chapter we assert that students' knowledge of different cultures and ethnic groups can be expanded so as to increase rather than diminish ethnocentrism.

    a. From your own personal experience as a learner, can you identify school- or
non-school-related learning experiences in which your exposure to a specific
ethnocultural group increased rather than decreased your own ethnocentrism? If so, please describe the learning experience and its repercussions.

    b. To increase your own positive orientation to cultural pluralism, how should
the material in this learning experience have been arranged?

RECOMMENDED ACTIVITIES

1. Drawing on your professor's knowledge base or your own network, identify one
or more teachers with a strong reputation for teaching units that link together all
or several of the curriculum areas discussed in this chapter. Observe and interview this teacher (or teachers) to discover resources and tactics that will prove
useful in your own teaching.

2. Develop and prepare to implement an environmental multicultural unit that
focuses on tropical rain forest issues; to the extent possible, work collaboratively
with one or more teachers or student teachers in an attempt to make the unit as
interesting as possible.

3. Examine the instructional media center in your local school district, county or
regional office of education, or university to identify specific curriculum materials that would be helpful in designing an environmental multicultural unit that
revolves around pollution, overpopulation, the spread of acquired immunodefi-
ciency syndrome (AIDS), or some other environmental/global problem area. One
work that could be helpful as an initial source of information is *The Global Ecology Handbook: What You Can Do About the Environmental Crisis.* The book
was edited by Walter H. Corson and published by Beacon Press (Boston) in 1990
with the help of the Global Tomorrow Coalition. The text, which is now out of
print, is a rich compendium of environmental information and can be a practical
supplement to the Public Broadcasting System's series entitled *Race to Save the
Planet.* In addition, for teachers there are several valuable sources of information
about global and multicultural education. Two of the most important are the Social
Science Education Consortium, www.ssecinc.org, Inc., 3300 Mitchell Lane, Suite
240, Boulder, CO 80301-2272, phone 303-492-8154, and the Center for Teaching

International Relations, www.ctironline.com, Graduate School of International Studies, University of Denver, Denver, CO 80208, phone 303-871-3106. Seven titles and brief descriptions are listed below to give you a clearer sense of the curriculum resources made available by these organizations.

a. *Global Issues in the Elementary Classroom.* Boulder, CO: Social Science Education Consortium, revised edition, 1993. Ideas, activities (lesson plans, student handouts), and strategies for teaching global awareness and studying human values, global systems, global issues, and global history. Includes an annotated bibliography of additional resources for teachers.

b. *Global Issues in the Middle School Classroom: Grades 5–8.* Boulder, CO: Social Science Education Consortium, third edition, 1994. Ideas, activities (lesson plans, student handouts), and strategies for teaching global awareness, global interdependence, and cross-cultural understanding. Practical, hands-on approach.

c. *Teaching About Cultural Awareness: Grades 5–12.* Denver, CO: Center for Teaching International Relations, revised edition, 1994. Lesson plans and reproducible handouts to stimulate positive attitudes about cultural differences.

d. *Teaching Writing Skills: A Global Approach* (grades 6–12). Denver, CO: Center for Teaching International Relations. This book uses global issues as bases for developing writing skills while enhancing understanding of the concepts of human rights.

e. *Teaching Reading: A Global Approach for Secondary Students.* Denver, CO: Center for Teaching International Relations. This book has nine sections: reading texbooks; reading propaganda; reading maps; reading newspapers; vocabulary; and concept development.

f. *Multicultural Activities for the American History Classroom.* The Center for Applied Research in Education, available from the Center for Teaching International Relations, 1996. This curriculum reviews four centuries of diversity, from the 1600s to the present. The document includes 130 ready-to-use activities to build students' understanding and appreciation of diverse people and points of view.

g. *English Teacher's Portfolio of Multicultural Activities* (grades 7–12). The Center for Applied Research in Education, available from the Center for Teaching International Relations, 1996. Over 75 reproducible literature sections with ready-to-use lessons based on a variety of multicultural fiction and nonfiction books written by authors of varying cultural and ethnic backgrounds. Each lesson offers students a chance to hone their critical thinking, literary analysis, writing, and reading comprehension.

Journal Entry

This chapter focused on the rationale and procedure for developing units linking citizenship, global education, environmental education, and multicultural education. It would be appropriate in your journal entry to comment on the following questions as well as on your own questions or feelings about this chapter.

1. Did you learn anything of value from this chapter's content, discussion questions, and recommended activities? If yes, summarize what you have learned.

2. Has the experience of reading chapter 5 or participating in discussions or activities related to the chapter given you some new insight into multicultural education? If yes, discuss your new insights.

3. Which, if any, of the comments made about environmental multicultural units seemed questionable or ambiguous to you?

NOTES

1. Christine L. Bennett, *Comprehensive Multicultural Education: Theory and Practice* (Boston: Allyn & Bacon, 1995).
2. Christine E. Sleeter and Carl A. Grant, *Making Choices for Multicultural Education: Five Approaches to Race, Class, and Gender* (Columbus, Ohio: Merrill, 1988), 176.
3. *Democracy's Next Generation* (Washington, D.C.: People for the American Way, 1989).
4. Linda J. Sax, Alexander W. Astin, Willima S. Korn, and Kathryn M. Mahoney, *The American Freshmen: National Norms for Fall 1998* (Los Angeles, Calif.: Higher Education Research Institute, UCLA), 4.
5. Ibid.
6. Ibid.
7. Jack M. Hamilton, *Main Street America and the Third World* (Washington, D.C.: Seven Locks Press, 1988).
8. In "Identifying Local Links to the World," *Educational Leadership* 48, no. 7 (April 1991), 50–52, Roselle Kline Chartok offers a very practical approach to helping students of all ages discover the links between their local communities and various nations of the world.
9. Kenneth A. Tye and Williard M. Kniep, "Global Education Around the World," *Educational Leadership* 48, no. 7 (April 1991), 47–49; a similar definition appears in *Global Education: From Thought to Action,* ed. Kenneth A. Tye (Alexandria, Va.: Association for Supervision and Curriculum Development, 1990), 5.
10. Michael Weilbacher, "Education That Cannot Wait," *E: The Environmental Magazine* 2, no. 2 (March/April 1991), 30. In describing the mission of environmental education, Weilbacher drew on a direct quote from the director of Project Wild, Dr. Cheryl Charles.
11. Individual copies of the entire 17-volume set can be ordered by writing to the National Wildlife Federation, P.O. Box 50281, Hampden Station, Baltimore, MD 21211, or by calling 410-516-6583. In 1999, an individual copy cost $12.95 plus shipping and handling. The entire set costs $185.00 plus shipping and handling. The homepage of the National Wildlife Federation is located at www.nwf.org/atracks.
12. Two useful resources for learning about this diversity are the following:
    a. *People of the Tropical Rain Forest*, ed. Julie Sloan Denslow and Christine Padoch (Berkeley: University of California Press in association with the Smithsonian Institution Traveling Exhibition Service, 1988).
    b. *Tropical Rain Forests: A Disappearing Treasure*, a booklet published by the Smithsonian Institution (1988) in conjunction with the exhibition Tropical Rain Forests: A Disappearing Treasure.

13. Each of the following three books is about the Lacandon Maya; each was written at the beginning of a recent decade: the 1970s, 1980s, and 1990s. The first book listed, by a professor of anthropology, will be most valuable for classroom teachers.

   a. R. Jon McGee. *Life, Ritual, and Religion Among the Lacandon Maya* (Belmont, Calif.: Wadsworth, 1990). This should be the first book read by a teacher planning a unit on the Lacandon Maya. It focuses primarily on the religious beliefs of the Lacandon Maya but also contains several chapters that provide an excellent introduction to this group. Chapter titles include "Introduction to the Lacandon Maya," "The Conquest of the Yucatan and Origins of the Lacandon Maya," "Social Organization in Najà" (one of the Lacandon Maya villages), "Lacandon Subsistence and Economics," and "Lacandon Culture and the Future." The book's 10 chapters, independent of the glossary, appendixes, and index, total 131 pages and can easily be read over a weekend. This book contains less photography than the two books listed next.

   b. Christine Price (author) and Gertrude Duby Blom (photographer), *Heirs of the Ancient Maya: A Portrait of the Lacandon Indians* (New York: Charles Scribner's Sons, 1972). Of the books listed here, this is the oldest and briefest (56 pages) and is now out of print. When you teach the unit, this would be a good resource to have available because of its photographs and because many upper-grade students can read it on their own. In addition, it could be read to the entire class. Sections of this book could be contrasted with information in the more up-to-date McGee book to show how the Lacandon Maya are both changing and remaining the same as the pace of contact with the outer world increases.

   c. Victor Perera and Robert D. Bruce, *The Lacandon Maya and the Mexican Rain Forest* (Boston: Little, Brown, 1982). This is the longest (303 pages) and the least conventional, perhaps because one of the authors, Robert Bruce, is an atypical linguist and anthropologist. To get as close as he could to the Lacandon worldview, Bruce attempted to live the life of a Lacandon Maya to the greatest extent possible. This book, which contains many interesting observations about the Lacandon Maya, is harder to read than the McGee book. We recommend that the Perera/Bruce work be consulted after the McGee book is read. The Perera/Bruce book also contains many interesting photographs.

      In addition to these books, two ethnographic films about the Lacandon Maya, both produced by R. Jon McGee, can be rented or purchased through the California Extension Media Center in Berkeley in either [[1/2]]-inch VHS or [[3/4]]-inch U-Matic format. Call 510-642-0460 for further information. The films are titled *Swidden Agriculture Among the Lacandon Maya* and *The Lacandon Maya Balché Ritual.*

14. McGee, *Life, Ritual, and Religion,* 1.
15. Ibid., 17, 18.
16. James D. Nations and Ronald B. Nigh, "The Evolutionary Potential of Lacandon Maya Sustained-yield Tropical Forest Agriculture," *Journal of Anthropological Research* 36, no. 1 (1980), 2.
17. Ibid., 8.
18. Ibid.
19. Ibid., 13.
20. McGee, *Life, Ritual, and Religion*, 15.

The Idea of Multicultural Education Revisited

A quick review of the preface and chapter 1 would reveal that the main focus of this text is on design and implementation of multicultural education at the classroom level. There is some mention of designing school projects to serve the local community (AVID and Hanshaw Middle School), the different levels at which multicultural education should be taught (the school site, district and university levels), the James Comer approach to schoolwide restructuring, and John Goodlad's approach to simultaneous renewal between K–12 public schools and institutions of higher education; much of this text, however, channels teachers' multicultural thinking into the confines of their own classrooms. This individual classroom focus, which in part derives from our belief that classroom teachers are the ultimate and critical agents of change in the multicultural restructuring process, is both a virtue and a weakness.

A CLASSROOM-FOCUSED CONCEPTION OF MULTICULTURAL EDUCATION: VIRTUE AND WEAKNESS

The classroom-focused conception is helpful because this is where the vast majority of teachers do their most significant work. This level of analysis allows us to clearly show the many ways you can restructure your classroom curriculum to achieve various goals of multicultural education. This clarity and emphasis is needed for implementation. Too often a single university-level course, in attempting to deal with the full range of multicultural concepts and issues, will provide incomplete treatment of the critical classroom applications of these elements.

To attain this clarity, however, we have neglected discussing the important ways that school counselors, nurses, nutritionists, staff development specialists, principals, superintendents, parents, and community representatives can help to create a total school environment conducive to multicultural education. This is an important limitation to be aware of. As James Banks has noted, "To implement multicultural education successfully, we must think of the school as a social system in which all of its major variables are closely interrelated. Thinking of a school as a social system suggests that we must formulate and initiate a change strategy that reforms the total school environment to implement multicultural education."[1]

If, after reading and discussing the content of this text and completing various recommended activities, you choose to become an agent of multicultural change in your classroom and school, you should realize that introducing the new concepts in your classroom alone is a bit like Don Quixote jousting with windmills. Throughout the text we have suggested that for teaching to be effective, it must occur within the context of a multicultural curriculum; to that we now add the idea that your multicultural change efforts, to be truly meaningful for your students—whom you will most likely teach for only one year—should be part of a wider systematic change effort. This means, simply, that the umbrella of multicultural change should cover all aspects of education in the entire school district. Teachers interested in creating an effective multicultural curriculum in their own classrooms will need to work together with other like-minded teachers, administrators, school counselors, parents, and curriculum specialists to initiate school and district change. There are many ways to move toward a comprehensive schoolwide approach to multicultural education, but perhaps the most logical first step is to discuss with your fellow teachers and principal the notion of making multicultural education, in all its rich variety, a short- and long-term priority in staff development.[2] Creating integrated units with other teachers is another logical step, and planning a schoolwide approach to increase parental participation in school governance is a third area worthy of exploration. Beyond this, delving into the resources listed in the appendixes should also prove helpful in preparing you to be a more effective change agent and advocate for students and citizens who are being shortchanged in our schools and society.

Finally, we hope we have encouraged you to continue your study of the emergent multicultural education literature. It is a literature of optimism; it fosters a movement that challenges teachers to enhance and extend our democracy by reaching out to all learners with enthusiasm, sensitivity, and democratic practice. It is a movement we feel obligated and privileged to serve. We are delighted, with the help of your instructor, to have brought it to your attention.

DISCUSSION QUESTIONS

1. We acknowledge that we have lightly treated a critical dimension of multicultural education—the necessity of thinking comprehensively about schoolwide change when creating an effective multicultural curriculum.
   a. Based on your own readings in and beyond this course, what are some other important multicultural topics that have not been adequately addressed in this text?
   b. Are you aware of specific resources that shed light on these topics? If yes, delineate them.
   c. What are some instructional strategies for addressing these concerns in your multicultural restructuring effort?
2. For practical reasons, we have suggested defining multicultural education in terms of its goals—what it is setting out to accomplish. Toward this end we have iden-

tified goals for our classroom-oriented conception of multicultural education. After reviewing these goals (in chapter 1) and the planning questions they suggest (in chapters 2 and 3), discuss the adequacy or inadequacy of our conception of multicultural education. Multicultural goals delineated by other authors may help. For example, in "Multicultural Education: Characteristics and Goals" (see endnote 1), James Banks describes "The Dimensions of Multicultural Education" which provide a set of goals on pages 20–23, and Christine Bennett lists an overlapping, but different set on pages 29–32 in her text Comprehensive Multicultural Education: Theory and Practice, 4th. ed. (Boston: Allyn & Bacon, 1999).

3. What is your own working definition of multicultural education? Has it changed as a result of your readings and discussions in this course? If so, how?

4. There will always be competing conceptions of multicultural education, just as there are competing theories about cooperative learning, classroom discipline, and democracy. As a result, an educator hearing about these various conceptions may comment, "Forget about this multicultural education. It's too confusing and complex, and people can't make up their minds what it is supposed to mean."

   a. How do you think we would respond to this educator?

   b. How would you respond to this educator if he or she made this comment to you after you had just presented the first hour of a three-hour workshop on multicultural education?

NOTES

1. James Banks, "Multicultural Education: Characteristics and Goals," chap. 1 in Multicultural Education: Issues and Perspectives, 3rd ed., ed. James Banks and Cherry A. McGee Banks (Boston: Allyn & Bacon, 1997), 23.

2. A helpful document for this purpose is the position statement of the National Council for the Social Studies entitled "Curriculum Guidelines for Multicultural Education," in Social Education 56, no. 5 (September 1992), 274–294. The primary author of this statement, which updates the 1976 position statement, is James Banks, director, Center for Multicultural Education, University of Washington, Seattle, Washington. (The phone number of the center is 206-543-3386.)

Appendix 1
The Typology of Multicultural Teaching

In the mid-1980s, to facilitate the dissemination of information about multi-cultural education and multicultural teaching to master teachers, university supervisors, principals, and student teachers, we developed the Typology of Multicultural Teaching. The typology was included as part of a memorandum sent to all student and teachers in the California Polytechnic (Cal Poly) teacher education program prior to the beginning of student teaching. It was also referred to at the student teaching orientation meetings held each quarter to reinforce the importance of multicultural education within the Cal Poly teacher education program. We reprint the memorandum and the typology with minor revisions.

To: Fall Quarter Twelve Unit   Date: September 15, 1999
      Multiple Subject Student Teachers,
      Cooperating Teachers, Principals, and   File No.: Version #9
      University Supervisors

From: Leonard and Patricia Davidman

Subject: A Typology of Multicultural Teaching Designed to Help Participants
          Understand What the Teacher Education Program Means When It
          Uses the Term *Multicultural Teaching*

GENERAL REMARKS TO STUDENT TEACHERS

Multicultural instruction provides us with a significant and sophisticated model of curriculum and instruction. The sophistication pertains to the wide range of instructional decisions that a teacher needs to make to create a comprehensive multicultural curriculum. In your first and second student teaching assignments you will be able to make some of these multicultural instruction decisions but not others. For those you can make, it is important that you have a clear understanding of what multicultural teaching is and are prepared to incorporate elements of the model into your own teaching repertoire as soon as possible. To help you achieve these objectives, a typology of multicultural teaching with examples is provided for your future study and discussion. As you become increasingly familiar with the seven major components of the current Cal Poly conception of multicultural education, you will begin to discover other, perhaps better, examples. When you do, we would appreciate your passing them along to your ED 435 instructor. Finally, as you analyze these examples, please remember that effective multicultural teaching occurs during specific lessons but also before, after, and between lessons in a variety of contexts both inside and outside the classroom. It includes communication with parents and students; it affects and takes place within the entire school curriculum. While we focus on the classroom level, students should recall that multicultural education is concerned with reforming school, districtwide, and societal practices when such practices are in need of change.

GENERAL REMARKS TO MASTER TEACHERS

As a part of the evolution of the Cal Poly teacher education program and because of the instructional challenges facing contemporary and future educators in the state of California, the Cal Poly multiple subject program has embraced and is now transmitting a conception of multicultural education that emphasizes the teacher's role in creating educational equity at the classroom level. We understand educational equity to be strongly related to (1) maximizing opportunities for the educational success of all students in a classroom and (2) analyzing the results of our educational programs to ensure that the opportunities lead to successful educational results for a wide range of students.

Following one of the principles of effective communication, we are trying to develop a common vocabulary in the area of multicultural education and teaching. This vocabulary will allow for clearer communication about multicultural teaching among professors, master teachers, university supervisors, and student teachers. The typology listed next presents an incomplete list of possible teacher behaviors and is basically a communication tool. It is not a list of requirements, and it will not play a formal role in the assessment of student teachers. It is a shorthand device we are using to create a clearer vision of what multicultural teaching could look like in behavioral terms at the classroom level, and a source of ideas for all those involved in teacher education. Finally, it is an invitation to further dialogue and growth in the area of multicultural education for all concerned.

The Typology

A. Examples of Type I Multicultural (MC) Planning and Teaching (Planning and teaching that is directly aimed at educational equity) The teacher:
   1. makes sophisticated use of the elements of instruction (selecting an objective at the appropriate level of difficulty, teaching to an objective, monitoring and adjusting, using the principles of learning, etc.).

2. selects and utilizes a classroom management system that maximizes the amount of time he or she has available for individual tutoring.
3. modifies his or her oral pace and syntax to facilitate the learning of language and content material for English learners as well as other special learners.
4. allows one student to serve as a buddy tutor, interpreter, or assistant teacher to facilitate the learning of another student.
5. makes appropriate use of cooperative learning strategies and tactics associated with specially designed academic instruction in English (SDAIE).
6. uses a variety of techniques and content to demonstrate powerfully that in contemporary America, men and women of all colors and ethnic groups are succeeding in a wide range of occupations, such as
   a. Friday afternoon "career awareness" interviews in which a wide range of successful Americans are interviewed by students;
   b. classroom bulletin boards;
   c. magazines such as *Ebony* and *Hispanic* (which regularly contain stories about successful African Americans and Hispanic Americans);
   d. book and video reports;
   e. "Upward Bound" visitors (junior high school and high school students who attend special activities to prepare them for college);
   f. trips to local businesses and universities to meet successful role models.
7. uses teaching techniques and curriculum materials from specially designed projects such as the Complex Instruction Project (Rachel Lotan, Stanford University, 415-723-5661); Success for All/Roots and Wings (Robert E. Slavin, Center for Social Organization of Schools, 800-548-4998); Accelerated Schools (Claudette Spriggs, Stanford University, 415-725-7158); Multicultural Reading and Thinking (Janita Hoskyn, National Consultant, McRat Program, 501-225-5809); and Advancement Via Individual Determination (Mary Catherine Swanson, AVID Center, San Diego, 619-682-5050).
8. pays serious and consistent attention to the idea that specific teacher behaviors and knowledge can make classroom learning more efficient and equitable for both girls and boys.
9. employs rules consistently across ethnic, racial, cultural, and gender groups—for example, does not allow boys to call out and expect girls to patiently raise their hands.
10. employs and models nonsexist language, such as saying "police officers" rather than "policemen" and "firefighters" rather than "firemen."
11. utilizes texts, videos, websites, speakers and so on to accurately portray the contributions of women and other cultural, ethnic, and racial groups, and the struggles these groups have had to wage to achieve full-status citizenship in the United States.
12. creates and maintains a classroom environment free of ethnic, racial, sexual, or other forms of harassment.

13. promotes junior high school and high school graduation and college attendance by engaging in "follow-through" and "future prediction" oral behavior, such as the following:
    a. "I want you (all) to let me know when you graduate from high school (or junior high school)."
    b. "When you children are in high school (or college), you are going to remember this lesson."
    c. "I know that some of the children in this class will want to become classroom teachers, and if this is your goal I'll do what I can to help you achieve it." An example of follow-through behavior is the work of one local first-grade teacher who sends out congratulation cards to her students when they graduate from high school, 10 or 11 years later.
14. engages in student, peer, and self-evaluation to monitor, assess, and perhaps modify the distribution of attention, higher-level questions and wait-time, and leadership opportunities to various individuals and groups in the class, women and men, African Americans and Whites, and so on.
15. employs a flexible mastery-learning model of instruction (pretest/posttest, carefully constructed teaching units, carefully prepared backup teaching strategies).
16. includes self-confidence and self-esteem building as part of the affective/cognitive curriculum.
17. seeks out and makes professional use of parent volunteers and bilingual/trilingual aides if needed.
18. makes use of informal "interest" and "learning style" inventories to more insightfully address the student's interests, learning preferences, and learning style or strengths.
19. develops a multiability curriculum that allows a variety of academic skills to receive classroom and teacher recognition as important.
20. makes certain that students receive their fair share of instructional resources and technology.
21. creates a collaborative/supportive learning environment—We're all in this together; we're here to learn and grow as individuals and partners; in this class we will be facilitators for each other's success."
22. examines attendance records to get an early start on implementing plans designed to lower the absence rate of specific learners.
23. collects and analyzes data from a survey of television watching to increase his ability to modify patterns of excessive viewing where appropriate, and follows up with a second survey later in the semester.
24. strives to keep academic expectations high and within reach of the learners.
25. teaches students that error, failure, struggle, and success are natural parts of the learning process, particularly when one is studying a wide range of required subjects (which is the basic K–12 reality).

26. works with other teachers to create interdisciplinary units that connect school learning to real-world issues.
27. seeks to create learning experiences that capitalize on and expand students' strengths and weaknesses.
28. uses a variety of instructional materials (videos, computer programs, guest speakers, various print materials, etc.) to present the official curriculum and allows students to provide input to help shape that curriculum.
29. works with other teachers and professional organizations to make certain that students are getting a "fair shake" when it comes to the allocation of resources within the school, school district, and state.
30. develops a plan to learn *all* student names and other background information as quickly as possible in the school semester, constantly uses the names, and encourages students to learn and use each other's names—this reinforces the community-of-learners concept.
31. reveals to students in specific numerical terms the payoff that may follow from hard work in general and a college education specifically (Jaime Escalante, for example, brings back former students who are college graduates to tell his current students how much money they are making). You should help students see the useful things they can do for themselves, their family, and their community after they graduate from high school (and perhaps college).
32. reflects on and analyzes her own pedagogy. For example, if you teach in tracked or quasi-tracked settings, monitor and question your own practices.
    For instance:
    a. Are the teaching strategies employed in one of my classes different from those in another, and, if so, is this warranted?
    b. Am I providing a more challenging curriculum in one section than another, and, if so, is this warranted? Could the degree of challenge in the 'lesser' class be increased?
33. analyzes seating patterns in various sections to see whether racial, ethnic, and/or gender (self-) segregation is occurring; if so, attempts to determine whether this pattern is antithetical to course objectives.
34. accepts, supports, and dignifies the first language (L1) or dialect that students bring to school, and encourages students to use L1 as they develop second-language capability, and also encourages the development of bilinguality but respects the decision of students and parents who opt for monolinguality.
35. supports plans to modify or eliminate tracking systems that channel students away from appropriate educational opportunities (i.e., honors and AP classes in high school).
36. employs portfolio and other forms of authentic assessment that allow the teacher to share the responsibility of assessment with the learner.
37. provides support for, or helps to create, a Future Teachers' Club, and uses this club as a vehicle to help recruit a broader group of individuals into the teaching profession.

B. Examples of Type II MC Teaching

(Communication, planning, and teaching that attempts to establish a positive and collaborative relationship between the home and school so as to [1] place teachers in a better position to collect and use knowledge of a student's family and cultural background to provide sensitive, sensible instruction, and [2] empower parents so they can play a larger role in their child's education)

The teacher:
1. meets with parents of all students early in the year to learn about significant family concerns, values, educational objectives, changes in the health history of the student, and so on.
2. examines the student's cumulative folder in preparation for the family interview.
3. plans classroom social events that include as many students as possible, or that dignify the cultural differences of a family that does not exchange birthday presents, salute the flag, celebrate other mainstream American holidays, and so on.
4. will manifest or allow a different pattern of communication, in cases in which research has demonstrated that such fluency and flexibility promotes student learning (for example, overlapping talk in native Hawaiian students).
5. will individualize instruction to provide maximum continuity in learning for migrant learners whose family mobility annually involves an extended stay in Mexico. This may include the development of learning packets and cassette tapes that students can use while in Mexico.
6. modifies weekend homework assignments for students who travel substantial distances to spend selected weekends with a divorced parent, and so on.
7. will invite parents to visit and observe the class in action when the teacher believes such visits will increase the parent's comfort level with the public school.
8. will use parent-teacher conferences as an opportunity to
   a. manifest cultural sensitivity;
   b. elicit family cultural knowledge;
   c. develop the concept of teamwork between teachers and parents.
9. frequently communicates with parents by letters that express the idea that "we're in this together; we need to work well together and then learn how to cooperate even more; *our success will be your child's success.*"
10. will remain "professionally curious" about each student throughout the course of the year and will be professionally cautious and tentative in using family and cultural background data, to avoid making simplistic or stereotypical judgments.
11. will initiate and support schoolwide efforts to create pertinent parent education activities, such as classes in English as a second language held during school hours in the school cafeteria.

12. will initiate and support schoolwide efforts to help low-income families locate doctors who are flexible in their payment schedules.
13. Encourages parents to schedule face-to-face or telephone conferences throughout the school year to make certain that all of their questions are answered and all of their concerns expressed.
14. supports the efforts to keep adult education courses offered by the school district as inexpensive as possible, particularly for low-income parents and community members.
15. supports efforts by local community leaders to provide community libraries for all communities served by the school, as well as Internet-linked computers in the community libraries and the public schools' libraries and computer labs.
16. creates or supports alternative school programs (schools or choice) where all stakeholders (parents, students, and teachers) sign letters of commitment specifying specific behaviors which will be carried out to reinforce students' efforts to learn.

C. Examples of Type III MC Teaching

(Teaching that attempts to foster cultural pluralism and systematically provide students with in-depth knowledge regarding a wide range of domestic and international ethnic groups and cultures)*

The teacher:
1. uses the social studies and other content areas to make the student aware of the range of cocultures and ethnic groups that interact in various ways to create the American nation and culture.
2. uses the social studies and other content areas to make the students aware of the commonalities and differences between American culture and other cultures, and the positive features of these various cultures.
3. implements units of instruction that are, in fact, historical and contemporary case studies of selected cultures.
4. teaches about cultures in a manner that encourages students to understand and appreciate the various cultures being studied rather than evaluating them exclusively in terms of mainstream American, or other, values.
5. teaches about cultures in an open-minded and flexible manner that encourages students to ask probing questions about their own culture as well as other cultures.
6. Shares the life stories of contemporary Americans who have created healthy bicultural lifestyles, lifestyles which allow for creative participation in two (or more) American cultures, the dominant mainstream American macroculture and the significant, but smaller, cultural worlds (microcultures) created by religious institutions (Catholics, Mormons,

*This type of multicultural teaching simultaneously aims at two of the seven goals discussed in the text. The two are so closely related that for the purpose of the typology, we chose to combine them into one type of teaching.

etc.); the private sector (newspapers, magazines, cable networks, and manufacturing organizations which create products aimed at specific ethnic and cultural groups); nonprofit civil rights organizations (the National Association for the Advancement of Colored People and the Mexican American Legal Defense and Educational Fund, etc.); and public institutions (alternative public schools organized around racial and ethnic themes).

D. Examples of Type IV MC Teaching

(Teaching that attempts to foster intercultural, intergroup, and interethnic understanding and camaraderie within the classroom *and* multicultural appreciation, tolerance, and sensitivity in the community and larger culture)

The teacher:
1. employs multiperspective teaching of history as well as current events (this represents movement away from a Eurocentric and Anglocentric perspective on American and world history).
2. utilizes role-playing of dilemma stories (sociodrama and the materials developed by Fannie R. Shaftel and others).
3. allows for analysis and discussion of the lives and problems of true-to-life "fictional" characters.
4. provides time for student self-disclosure about cultural and/or religious background (keep in mind the supportive, we're in this together, family-like learning environment):
   a. Child of the Week program-sometimes called Star of the Week;
   b. Autobiographical assignment in language arts.
5. carries out the word of the Week program with words like *tolerant, sensitive, supportive, cooperative, multicultural, open-minded, bilingual.* (Cooperation and cooperative learning are so critical to multicultural teaching that *cooperation* should be an ongoing term in the Word of the Week program.)
6. utilizes teacher "witnessing" in praise of diversity:
   "Now, this looks like a very interesting and diverse classroom. Let's see, we have several students who are partially bilingual, several who..." or "Isn't it lovely that we have so many different plants in our community... or planets in the sky... or clouds in the sky."
7. creates opportunities for sister schools and sister classrooms within the same school district or county, pen pals, joint field trips, school visits, and teacher and student exchanges—the idea is to break out of segregated realities that are sometimes imposed by housing patterns and so on.
8. makes students aware of organizations that foster intergroup understanding and cooperation between diverse groups, such as the National Conference of Christians and Jews and the Anti-Defamation League of the B'nai B'rith. (The latter group, in particular, disseminates excellent intergroup instructional materials.) The idea here is to highlight positive examples of intergroup and intragroup cooperation.

9. creates a cooperative learning environment.
10. teaches in a number of ways which makes it clear that the art, music, language(s), history, ethics, and political life of the nation has been decisively influenced by a wide range of individuals, cultures, and ethnic groups. (The *California History and Social Science Framework* will be a helpful resource here.)

E. Examples of Type V MC Teaching

(Teaching that develops in teachers and students the ability and proclivity to think, act, learn, and teach with a multicultural perspective)

The teacher:
1. consistently encourages children, when studying current events and specific historical periods, to wonder whether and why members of one culture or coculture will interpret and react to one situation differently from another because of cultural differences.
2. provides independent study opportunities that pertain to the different ways representatives of various cultures communicate (both verbally and nonverbally).
3. encourages students to read autobiographical and biographical literature in which authors discuss the ways their ethnicity and cultural background influenced their perceptions and responses to various events, both local and distant, familial and nonfamilial.
4. gives specific lessons to show students that members of individual cultures and cocultures perceive, interpret, and respond to reality differently because various cultures have different ways to define and create reality (e.g., categories of time; language concepts and structure; creation stories; gender role socialization; attitudes toward science, progress, family responsibilities, civic responsibilities, etc.).
5. encourages students to read articles about specific issues like educational vouchers in journals which represent different positions on the political spectrum (e.g., the *Nation*, *New Republic*, and the *National Review*).
6. invites students to read six or more consecutive issues of a journal which represents a political orientation different than the one they are beginning to lean toward.
7. Creates opportunities for students to interact with individuals who have been socialized into, or involuntarily become a part of, cultural groups different than that of the students. For example, for a period of six weeks or more, students might: (a) work in a homeless shelter or a home for senior citizens; (b) attend religious services of various faith groups and interview congregational leaders.

F. Examples of Type VI MC Teaching

(Teaching that is aimed at maintaining and expanding freedom and democracy)

The teacher:

1. creates and maintains a democratic decision-making environment in the classroom.
2. attempts to develop in students the ability and proclivity to participate in, and expand access into, various democratic institutions.
3. invites students to explore and share information about the ethnic and cultural identity(ies) handed down to them by their parents and ancestors.
4. invites students to select, study, and share information about other cultural and ethnic groups.
5. teaches units that attempt to reduce racism, sexism, prejudice, and other negative -isms in our society.
6. creates a timeline for the classroom and school which details the growth of democracy in the United States.
7. invites students to read, and report on, important speeches and events associated with the aforementioned growth of democracy.
8. invites local political leaders and elected representatives to participate in various school-based discussion and interviewing opportunities.
9. involves students in analysis, discussion, and voting opportunities which parallel the real world elections held at the local, state, and national levels.
10. invites students to examine and discuss the various meanings and etymology of the terms "freedom" and "democracy."

The Ethnic and Cultural Self-disclosure Inventory

Professor Davidman

Subject: Ethnic and Cultural Self-disclosure Inventory

GENERAL REMARKS

In this class many of our discussions will deal with culture and ethnicity. Your self-disclosure via this inventory will help your professor and classmates listen insightfully and discuss issues sensitively. In this class it is helpful to know where the listeners and speakers are coming from and going to. Tonight, I will share my self-disclosure and then explain how you will use yours next week to introduce yourself to your cooperative learning group. In addition, in attempting to build constructive diversity into each discussion group, I will draw on the information in your written self-disclosure. Please use additional paper to complete your response where necessary.

Self-disclosure Items and Questions

1. Your name: _____

2. Geographically, where are you from? Where do you live now? _____

   _____

3. Your mode of abode (I live with my friends, family, etc.). This is optional.

   _____

4. How long has your family or ancestors been on this continent? _____

   _____

5. Where did your family or ancestors come from before joining the drama "of the Americas"? Or were they always here? _____

6. How many generations of your family, on both sides, have lived in the United States? in (name of state)? _____

7. What languages were or are spoken in your (childhood) home? What languages are spoken in your current domicile? _____

8. Please identify an author, book, film, or ritual you value or have especially enjoyed, and/or a significant event in your life. An important book in your life like the Bible, Koran, or Torah should also be mentioned. _____

   _____

9. Given our opening definitions of race, ethnicity, ethnic group, minority ethnic group, culture, and cultural group, would you be comfortable in describing yourself as a member of a racial, ethnic, and/or cultural group? If so, which groups would you say you are a part of at this point in your life? _____

   _____

10. Have you experienced interpersonal conflict because of your ethnicity, gender, sexual orientation, racial group, cultural group, or an organization you were active in? If so, please describe one or more of these conflicts. Was this conflict resolved in any way and, if so, how? _____

    _____

    _____

11. Do you feel that your racial, ethnic, and/or cultural group membership (and the latter includes gender and sexual orientation) has been a positive feature in your life? If so, briefly explain why. _____

    _____

12. Which person or persons have had the greatest influence on helping to create the person you are today? Provide a few specifics to illustrate the influence. _____

    _____

13. Please try to recall a situation where you challenged an authority figure, or a source of information considered authoritative. Describe the circumstance and results. _____

    _____

    _____

14. Can you think of a situation where someone else challenged authority and it affected your life? If yes, please describe. _____

    _____

    _____

15. Which inequity, or inequities, in our society would you most like to address yourself, and/or see addressed by other individuals or organizations? ___

    _____

    _____

16. In terms of political party or political orientation, how would you describe yourself? _____

_____

_____

17. Please try to recall your earliest memories of discovering that people would or could be treated differently because of their racial, ethnic, gender, or socioeconomic group membership. Pick one memory and describe the circumstances and your feelings. _____

_____

_____

18. In what other courses or setting have you had the opportunity to study and/or discuss multicultural education? _____

_____

_____

19. At this point in your teacher education (or graduate school) program, do you have any opinions about multicultural education that you'd like to share? If yes, please list below. _____

_____

_____

20. Do you have a favorite hobby? If so, please identify. _____

_____

21. If you are currently employed, please describe where and what your current responsibilities are. _____

_____

22. When you have the license or credential you are seeking, in what organization and region would you like to begin, or continue, your career? _____

_____

_____

23. How do you feel about sharing this information with the instructor? Do you look forward to sharing your self-disclosure data in a small-group setting next session?_____

_____

_____

Specially Designed Academic Instruction in English (Sheltered English) Observation Form

Name: _____ Teacher: _____

Date: _____ Grade/Subject: _____

School: _____

- -

Focus: The Use of Specially Designed Academic Instruction in English to Promote Educational Equity.

1. Specifically, what did the teacher do to make her oral remarks comprehensible to the limited English proficient learners (LEP) in her class?

   _____

   _____

   _____

   _____

   _____

2. How did her oral and nonverbal communication differ from communication you have observed in other classrooms?

   _____

   _____

   _____

   _____

   _____

3. Did this teacher make use of cooperative learning groups or partners to increase student comprehension of instructions and lesson content? If yes, how did the groups or partners appear to be functioning?

_____

_____

_____

_____

_____

4. How would you describe the reaction of LEP learners to this form of instruction?

_____

_____

_____

_____

_____

5. From your interview with the teacher, what else did you learn about specially designed academic instruction in English?

_____

_____

_____

_____

_____

Cooperative Learning Group Observation Form

Name: _____   Teacher: _____

Date: _____   Grade/Subject: _____

School: _____

Focus: The Use of Cooperative Learning to Promote Educational Equity.

1. Does this lesson have an instructional focus and, if so, what do you think the teacher would identify as her main instructional objective(s)?
   a. _____
   _____

   b. _____
   _____

2. Was cooperative learning the main instructional strategy in this lesson or one of several that were employed? If the latter, which other strategies were employed?
   _____
   _____
   _____

3. Prior to releasing the students to work in their cooperative groups, what, if anything, did the teacher say to the students to promote effective functioning of groups? (Look for positive group interdependence, individual accountability, etc.)
   _____
   _____
   _____

4. What did the teacher do while the cooperative learning groups were functioning?
   _____
   _____
   _____

5. Were the groups in this class during this learning activity in competition with each other? If so, what effect did this appear to have on the learning?

6. Overall (across all groups in the class), how well did the students appear to be interacting with each other?

7. In the one or two groups you were closely observing
   a. how many of the students were consistently on task in what seemed to be a productive manner?

   b. did students have the same or different responsibilities vis-à-vis the task, or a little bit of both?

   c. did the students appear to be enjoying this learning activity?

8. Were the groups diversely structured in terms of gender and ethnicity?

9. In the group(s) you closely observed, did the member(s) of one cultural (girls/boys) or ethnic (Hispanic, White, Asian, African American, etc.) group appear to dominate the interaction?

10. Did the students in each group appear to be playing special roles at least part of the time—expert instructor, encourager, scribe, reporter, praiser, resource distributor, time keeper, etc.?

11. What did you learn about classroom management from observing these lessons?

12. From your observation of these lessons, what did you not understand?

Position Papers by Albert Shanker

SACRIFICING ACCURACY FOR DIVERSITY*

by Albert Shanker
President of the American Federation of Teachers

We're in the midst of an important change in our school curriculum. By including the contributions of many different groups that have not previously been recognized, we're trying to make a multicultural curriculum that accurately reflects our society.

However, some groups, including the New York State Board of Regents, which has just accepted guidelines for a new social studies curriculum, may end up sacrificing accuracy for diversity. They seem to think that, in order to give kids varied points of view, it is perfectly okay to teach ideas and theories that few or no reputable scholars accept. The Regents' proposal calls this using "noncanonical knowledge and techniques" and "nondominant knowledge sources."

You can see some good examples of what's wrong with this idea in the Portland (Oregon) "African-American Baseline Essays." This mini-curriculum, made up of essays on social studies, science, language arts, mathematics, art, and music, has been adopted or used as a model by school systems all over the country.

The Portland essays present ancient Egypt as an African culture that strongly influenced the development of European civilization, and this is fair enough. It's a view most reputable scholars have agreed with for 40 years, and it corrects distortions of previous historians who were inclined to ignore Egypt's contribution or to disregard the fact that Egypt was an African civilization. But the baseline essays go far beyond discussing Egypt as an African society, and they assert a number of ideas that are inconsistent with the best scholarship. For instance, they maintain that the inhabitants of ancient Egypt were black Africans.

---

*The position papers included in this appendix are reprinted with the permission of Albert Shanker and the American Federation of Teachers. They originally were published in 1991 as part of the "Where We Stand" series of paid advertisements published under the auspices of the American Federation of Teachers.

Scholars of Egyptian history and archeology say that the evidence suggests an entirely different story. Far from being all black (or all white), ancient Egypt, they say, was a multiracial society with a variety of racial types much like that of modern Egypt. In any case, our concept of race—a relatively modern invention—would not have made much sense to the ancient Egyptians, who did not look at people in terms of skin color or hair texture. So the baseline essays not only misrepresent the evidence by insisting that Egypt was a black African society; they distort the example that Egypt has to offer our own multiracial society to make a political point.

The science section of the baseline essays reveals the same preference for politics over scholarship. The ancient Egyptians' excellence in mathematics, medicine, and astronomy is widely acknowledged. For example, we owe our 365-day, 12-month year to them. But kids who learn science from this baseline essay will be told that the Egyptians developed the theory of evolution (thousands of years before Darwin), understood quantum physics and flew around for business and pleasure in full-size gliders—all stuff that no serious scientist believes for a minute. We used to laugh at the Soviets for saying that baseball and everything else of any importance had been discovered or invented in the USSR. These claims for Egyptian science are no more credible, and they are equally political in nature; they are propaganda rather than science. But this is not the biggest problem.

The science baseline essay presents as science stuff that is no more scientific than the Ouija board or mediums or the horoscope in the daily newspaper. Although the essay says it is important to distinguish between science and magic, it treats magic like a legitimate part of science. Kids whose teachers follow the Portland curriculum will be told that the Egyptians could predict lucky and unlucky days with the help of "astropsychological treatises"; and they'll hear how the Egyptians' highly developed "human capabilities" allowed them to see events before they happened ("precognition") or at a distance ("remote viewing"). Ideas like these make good subjects for movies or TV series, but they have nothing to do with science. Kids who are fed this kind of thing are not getting an alternative perspective; they are being cheated.

School boards and teachers accept the legitimacy of what's said in the baseline essays because they assume that the writers have solid credentials—and the introduction to the essays plays along with this. The writer of the science essay is described as a "Research Scientist of Argonne National Laboratories, Chicago," implying that the essay was written by a top-notch scientist, perhaps with the endorsement of a federally funded lab. But it turns out that the writer is not a scientist at all. According to Argonne, he's an industrial-hygiene technician with a high school diploma whose job is collecting air samples.

We all want to improve the achievement of our students. And poor, minority children, whose performance still lags far behind that of white, middle-class kids, deserve the best education we can give them. They're not going to get it if we substitute myths for history or magic for science. Here's how Frank Snowden, a professor emeritus of classics at Howard University, puts it:

Many students already have been misled and confused by Afrocentrists' inaccuracies and omissions in their treatment of blacks in the ancient Mediterranean world. The time has come for Afrocentrists to cease mythologizing and falsifying the past. The time has come for scholars and educators to insist upon scholarly rigor and truth in current and projected revisions of our curriculum. *Tempus fugit!*

THE DANGER OF MULTIPLE PERSPECTIVES

by Albert Shanker
President of the American Federation of Teachers

We are in the midst of a revolution in the teaching of American history. Most people would agree it's long overdue. In the past, our history has been taught as a drama in which white men had all the good roles. It was a spectacular, flag-waving saga designed to create loyalty, patriotism, and sense of the rightness of everything the U.S. did—and it worked. But the picture was incomplete, and it was not honest. It ignored the contributions of women, of African-Americans, of immigrants, of the labor movement and others; it ignored important occasions on which we betrayed our ideals. I don't know anyone today who would defend that kind of patriotic saga of progress or deny that an honest treatment of our history would naturally be multicultural.

But this isn't what some people mean by multiculturalism, and certain popular ideas about the subject are very troublesome. For example, the proposal that the New York State Board of Regents recently accepted, "One Nation, Many Peoples: A Declaration of Cultural Interdependence," sounds reasonable—and certainly the racist language that characterized the "Curriculum of Inclusion," an earlier report to the Regents, has disappeared. But even the latest proposal will encourage intellectual dishonesty and promote divisiveness instead of healing it.

The main point of the report is that history and social studies should be taught from the point of view of "multiple perspectives," and that this should start in the earliest grades. Now, "multiple perspectives" is an excellent phrase. It sounds open-minded, which is what the pursuit of knowledge should be. But when you put the concept into the classroom, what does it mean?

For a teacher presenting a historical event to elementary school children, using multiple perspectives probably means that the teacher turns to each child and asks the child's point of view about the event. To an African-American child this would mean, "What is the African-American point of view?" To a Jewish child, "What is the Jewish point of view?" And to an Irish child, "What is the Irish point of view?"

This is racist because it assumes that a child's point of view is determined by the group he comes from. But is there a single African-American or Jewish or Irish point of view? A child may have a point of view based on the fact that he is rich or poor or that he has read extensively or that he comes from a family of conservative Republicans or Marxists. In a society like ours, we are often, and delightfully, surprised that people do not carry with them the views that stereotypes call for. Is it a teacher's job to tell children that they are entitled to only one point of view because of the racial, religious, or ethnic group they come from? Should schools be in the business of promoting racial stereotypes and fostering differences where they may not exist?

There is another equally serious problem with the idea of "multiple perspectives" as it appears in the report to the New York State Regents. It means that the teaching of history should no longer be dominated by ideas that historians widely accept on the basis of available evidence. It urges, instead, that we open up the curriculum to diverse theories, to "noncanonical knowledge and techniques" and "nondominant knowledge sources." Again, this sounds very open-minded. But what using "noncanonical knowledge" means is that it is okay to teach theories rejected by an overwhelming majority of—and perhaps all—experts in a field because there is little or no evidence for them. It makes ethnic diversity in ideas more important than evidence of their validity.

People who worry about education standards get up in arms when some group tries to get Creationism into the biology curriculum. And they call it an act of educational courage when a school board refuses to purchase textbooks that treat Creationism as a scientific theory. Why? Because the scientific community does not accept the validity of Creationism. Scientists say it is an attempt to pass off a religious view as science. Yet, the Regents' history report assumes that one theory is as good as another as long as the materials are "culturally inclusive." And there seems to be very little resistance on the part of people who would raise a stink if kids were being taught the phlogiston theory in chemistry or the flat-earth theory in geography.

The notion of multiple perspectives that is presented by the Regents' report sounds sensible, but it is dangerous. Schools are supposed to educate our future citizens, scholars, and scientists. They should be places where youngsters learn to think and weigh evidence. But there's little chance kids will learn these basic lessons if the curriculum teaches them that the evidence for an idea is less important than the ethnic perspective of the person presenting the idea.

Schools have also, historically, been places where children of varying backgrounds learned to live together. Assigning kids different points of view based on their ethnic, racial, or religious background will exacerbate conflict or even create it when none exists. Kids who are now happy to think of themselves primarily as Americans may learn to think of themselves primarily as Hispanics or African Americans or Jews.

Throughout the world, countries made up of different peoples are coming apart. It would be tragic if here in the U.S., where almost all feel that they are first and foremost Americans, we adopted a curriculum that would pull us apart.

Appendix 6
Resources for Equity-oriented Teaching

Many resources are available for teachers interested in equity-oriented teaching. The list below is quite selective and far from exhaustive. In a number of cases the selected resource has an extensive bibliography, and two of the resources are themselves annotated bibliographies. The resources are listed under the following subheadings: cooperative learning, parent–teacher communication, general multicultural education resources, sources of children's literature for multicultural education, and sources of information about selected new American immigrant populations.

I. Cooperative Learning
1. Cohen, Elizabeth G. *Designing Groupwork: Strategies for the Heterogeneous Classroom, 2nd ed*. Wolfeboro, N.H.: Teachers College Press, 1994.
2. Johnson, David W., and Robert T. Johnson. *Learning Together and Alone: Cooperative, Competitive and Individualistic Learning*, 4th ed. Boston, Mass.: Allyn & Bacon, 1994.
3. Johnson, David W., and Roger T. Johnson. *Meaningful and Manageable Assessment Through Cooperative Learning*, Edina, Minn.: Interaction Book Co., 1996. Call 612-831-9500.
4. Johnson, David W., Roger T. Johnson, and Edythe J. Holubec, *The Nuts and Bolts of Cooperative Learning*, Edina, Minn.: Interaction Book Co., 1994.
5. Kagan, Spencer. *Cooperative Learning*. San Clemente, Calif: Kagan Cooperative Learning, 1994. This 392 page book is a thorough and excellent resource. It can be ordered from Kagan Cooperative Learning. Call 949-369-6310 or 800-933-2667. Kagan Cooperative Learning offers a variety of texts related to cooperative learning.
6. Kohn, Alfie. "Caring Kids: The Role of Schools," *Phi Delta Kappan* 72, no. 7 (March 1991): 496–506.
7. Slavin, Robert E. *Cooperative Learning: Theory, Research, and Practice*, 2nd ed., Boston, Mass.: Allyn & Bacon, 1995.
8. The December 1989/January 1990 issue of *Educational Leadership* (vol. 47, no. 4) entitled "Cooperative Learning" contains a number of interesting articles and an interview with Spencer Kagan.

II. Parent-Teacher Communication

1. Boruta, Marcia, Janet Chrispeels, and Mary Daugherty. *Communicating with Parents*. San Diego, Calif.: San Diego County Office of Education, 1988. In terms of providing ideas and specific examples for classroom teachers, this is the best resource I have encountered. It can be ordered directly from

   San Diego County Office of Education
   Graphic Communications, Room 212
   6401 Linda Vista Road
   San Diego, CA 92111-7399
   Telephone: 619-569-5391

2. Jones, Linda T. *Strategies for Involving Parents in Their Children's Education*. Bloomington, Ind.: Phi Delta Kappa, 1991. This document is Fastback #315 in Phi Delta Kappa's excellent series on issues and innovations in education.

3. The October 1989 issue of *Educational Leadership* (vol. 47, no. 2) entitled "Strengthening Partnerships with Parents and Community" contains a number of interesting articles and an interview with Joyce Epstein, a leading researcher in this area.

4. The Family Math Project. Write Virginia Thompson, Lawrence Hall of Science, University of California, Berkeley, CA 94720 or call 415-642-1823 to learn more about this project. Briefly, Family Math is a project of the EQUALS program of the Lawrence Hall of Science. It is designed to help parents become more involved in their children's mathematics education. Products include the following:
   a. *The Family Math Book*
   b. *We All Count in FAMILY MATH* (a film about the project)

5. The January 1991 issue of *Phi Delta Kappan* (vol. 72, no. 5) contains a special section on parent involvement with nine stimulating articles. The guest editor is Joyce Epstein.

III. General Multicultural Education Resources

1. Banks, James A. *Teaching Strategies for Ethnic Studies,* 6th ed. New York: John Wiley and Sons, 1997. This is the best single resource for an introduction to *multiethnic* education. The book contains 10 chapters on various American ethnic groups; each of these chapters contains a time line, historical overview, list of teaching strategies, and annotated bibliography. The appendixes and remaining chapters are also quite illuminating.

2. Banks, James A., *An Introduction to Multicultural Education*, 2nd ed., 1998. This 150-page text will serve well in an introductory course in multicultural education, or in a series of workshops on multicultural education. Banks thoroughly explains all of the concepts which are critical to understanding his rich and valuable conception of multicultural education. Chapter titles include: Goals and Misconceptions; Dimensions and School Characteristics; Curriculum Transformation;

School Reform and Intergoup Education; Knowledge Components; Teaching with Powerful Ideas; and several others. The text also contains four useful appendices.

3. Banks, James A. *Multicultural Education, Transformative Knowledge and Action: Historical and Contemporary Perspectives*, New York: Teachers College Press, 1996. This scholarly illuminating text, part of a well-edited multicultural education series for Teachers College Press, will deepen the reader's understanding of the critical relationship between transformative academic knowledge and multicultural education, the difference between mainstream academic knowledge and transformative academic knowledge and other forms of knowledge (popular knowledge, school knowledge, and personal and cultural knowledge), and the historical development of transformative scholarship, and much more. The text, which has four chapters by James A. Banks, also contains chapters by thirteen other authors. The text will prove valuable for new as well as advanced students of multicultural education.

4. Banks, James A., and Cherry A. McGee, eds. *Multicultural Education: Issues and Perspectives,* 3rd ed. New York: John Wiley and Sons, 1997. This text is a series of essays that deal with social class and religion; gender; ethnicity; and language; exceptionality; and school reform, as well as issues and concepts that clarify multicultural education.

5. Bennett, Christine I. *Comprehensive Multicultural Education: Theory and Practice,* 4th ed. Boston: Allyn & Bacon, 1999. This text provides a balance between theoretical materials and teaching strategies. The author's conception of multicultural education strongly links it to global education. For example, the fifth goal in the author's six-goal approach to multicultural teaching is "to increase awareness of the state of the planet and global dynamics."

6. Carrasquillo, Angela L. *Hispanic Children and Youth in the United States.* New York: Garland, 1991. This text is number 20 in a well-conceived and edited series of reference books pertaining to family issues. It is an excellent source for readers seeking general as well as specific information about Hispanic children and youth.

7. Froschl, Merle, and Barbara Sprung. *Resources for Educational Equity: A Guide for Grades Pre-Kindergarten-12.* New York: Garland, 1988. This one-of-a-kind guide will be valuable for all teachers interested in learning more about the general topic of educational equity; it is of particular value for those interested in the special equity concerns of girls and women. The guide treats equity concerns in various school-related areas and provides an annotated bibliography for each of its chapters.

8. Gollnick, Donna M., and Philip C. Chinn. *Multicultural Education in a Pluralistic Society,* 5th ed. Upper Saddle River, N.J.: Merrill, 1998. This well-written and well-conceived text is primarily an introduction to the concepts that are central to a cogent understanding of multicultural education. Each of the following concepts has its own chapter in the text: culture, pluralism, and equality; class; socioeconomic

status, ethnicity, and race; religion, language, sex and gender, exceptionality, and age. Each of these chapters has an insightful discussions regarding educational implications, and the final chapter—"Teaching That Is Multicultural"—builds on these prior discussions to clarify how multicultural education is created in school settings. A final section entitled "Critical Incidents in Teaching," containing seven critical incidents, contributes to this pupose.

9. Grant, Carl A., and Gloria Ladson-Billings, editors, *Dictionary of Multicultural Education*, Phoenix, Ariz.: The Oryx Press, 1997. This is a valuable, illuminating, and timely resource. It provides over 200 definitions, in most cases one- to three-page essays, for a wide range of terms such as affirmative action, border studies, critical theory, culturally relevant pedagogy, dysconscious racism, Ebonics, ethnomathematics, identity politics, institutional racism, and postmodernism. In addition, it contains a very useful appendix entitled "A Sampler of Multicultural Education Resources" which is divided into three parts: organizations; electronic contacts (websites); and federally funded assistance centers.

10. Grossman, Herbert. *Educating Hispanic Students: Cultural Implications for Instruction, Classroom Management, Counseling, and Assessment 2nd ed..* Springfield, Ill.: Charles C. Thomas, 1995. This text provides a good deal of helpful information on teaching Hispanic students; it is particularly valuable because of the wide range of issues it addresses.

11. Hernandez, Hilda. *Teaching in Multilingual Classrooms: A Teacher's Guide to Context, Process, and Content*, Upper Saddle River, N.J.: Merrill, 1997. This text provides a balance between theoretical material and specific classroom teaching strategies. It will be particularly helpful for candidates who have little or no background in second-language acquisition, teaching English learners, and anthropological concepts.

12. Hilliard, Asa, III, Lucretia Payton-Stewart, and Larry Obadele Williams, eds. *Inclusion of African and African-American Content in the School Curriculum.* Proceedings of the First National Conference on the Infusion of African and African-American Content in the School Curriculum, October, 1989. Morristown, N.J.: Aaron Press, 1990. This illuminating series of essays will serve as a useful introduction to Afrocentric education. The book is divided into three major sections: Theory and Rationale; History, Art, and the Spread of African People in the West; Curriculum Methodology and Strategy; it also contains a suggested reading list and a delineation of curriculum aids. Sample essay titles include "The Infusion of African and African-American Content: A Question of Content and Intent," by Wade W. Nobles; "The Cultural Base in Education," by Johnnetta B. Cole; "African People on My Mind," by John Henrik Clarke; and "African Survivals in the Black Atlantic World," by Robert F. Thompson. Inquiries regarding this book should be addressed to Aaron Press, 103 Washington Street, Morristown, NJ 07960.

13. Nieto, Sonia. *Affirming Diversity: The Sociopolitical Context of Multicultural Education,* 3rd ed. New York: Addison Wesley Longman, 2000. This well-written text is noteworthy because it presents an approach to education that is simultaneously multicultural and social reconstructionist; at the same time it presents informative chapters on language, linguistic diversity in the classroom, and the sociopolitical context of education. Nieto defines multicultural education in terms of antiracist education, social justice, and critical pedagogy, among other important elements. The text strikes a balance between social issues, theoretical concerns, and teaching strategies.

14. Quellmalz, Edys S., and Janita Hoskin. "Making a Difference in Arkansas: The Multicultural Reading and Thinking Project." *Educational Leadership* 45, no. 7 (April 1988): 52–55. This article describes the background and results of a three-year project led by reading specialists in the Arkansas State Department of Education and selected Arkansas teachers. The goal of the project is to develop instructional materials that will simultaneously (a) develop the critical thinking ability of students and (b) enhance their knowledge of other cultures and specific multicultural concepts. In 1999–2000 this project was one of several recommended by the Arkansas Governor's office as part of the State's Smart Start program, resulting in a doubling of the number of school districts which have requested staff development training from the Arkansas State Department of Education. In January 1991 the Arkansas State Department of Education published the "McRat Report"; this report, which contains more information about this well-conceived and successful project, can be obtained by writing or calling Martha Shirrell, Reading Section, Arkansas Department of Education, General Division, #4, Capital Mall, Little Rock, AR 72201; 501-682-4377. The project focuses on grades three through eight.

15. Sleeter, Christine E., and Carl A. Grant. *Making Choices for Multicultural Education: Five Approaches to Race, Class, and Gender,* 3rd ed. New York: John Wiley and Sons, 1999. This book describes an approach to education that is simultaneously multicultural and social reconstructionist. Several chapters treat the human relations approach to education, multicultural education, single-group studies, and teaching the exceptional and culturally different. Although each of these chapters contains a section entitled "Recommended Practices," the book is largely conceptual and theoretical in nature. It is a valuable addition to the multicultural education literature.

16. Sleeter, Christine E., and Carl A. Grant. *Turning on Learning: Five Approaches for Multicultural Teaching Plans for Race, Class, Gender, and Disability*, 2nd ed. New York: John Wiley and Sons, 1999. This is the companion piece to the resource listed directly above. Each of the multicultural approaches discussed in *Making Choices* is further illuminated by a thought-provoking set of before and after lessons. The

before and after treatments are followed by a section that explains how the changes made the lesson better in terms of the specific approach under discussion.

17. Sleeter, Christine E. *Multicultural Education as Social Activism*, Albany, NY: State University of New York Press, 1996. This thought-provoking text provides a good introduction to the concepts and literature which strongly connect multicultural education to social action and social justice. Chapter titles include: Multicultural Education as a Form of Resistance to Oppression; Reflections on My Use of Multicultural and Critical Pedagogy where Students Are White; Multicultural Education, Social Positionality, and Whiteness; Teaching Science for Social Justice; and Multicultural Education as a Social Movement.

18. Tiedt, Pamela, L., and Iris M. Tiedt. *Multicultural Teaching: A Handbook of Activities, Information, and Resources,* 5th ed. Boston: Allyn & Bacon, 1999. This is a useful and creative collection of lessons and other resources. The handbook will complement any of the texts above that are primarily theoretical. The text contains a set of well-conceived chapters which include the following: Teaching for Diversity while Promoting Unity; Infusing Multicultural Concepts Across the Curriculum; Learning about Ourselves; Building a Community of Learners; Exploring Language and Linguistic Diversity; and Reflecting on Multicultural Education. The appendix, entitled "Developing Your Multicultural Knowledge Base: Recommended Readings and Resources," is a valuable resource in and of itself.

19. Ramsey, Patricia G., Edwina B. Vold, and Leslie R. Williams. *Multicultural Education: A Source Book,* 2nd ed. New York: Garland, 1998. This excellent source book combines illuminating essays with well-selected, richly detailed annotated bibliographies.

20. *Multicultural Education* is an independent magazine which covers the evolving field of multicultural education. It is published four times a year by Caddo Gap Press, 3145 Geary Blvd., #275, San Francisco, CA 94118. Call 415-922-1911 or fax 415-440-4870. This magazine includes feature articles, promising practices, a listing of multicultural resources, book and film reviews, and perspectives on art, music, and technology. As of January 1, 2000, the subscription rate for individuals was $50.00 per year.

21. *Multicultural Perspectives* is the official journal of the National Association for Multicultural Education (NAME), and its inaugural issue was published in 1999. The journal is published by Lawrence Erlbaum Associates, Inc., 10 Industrial Way, Mahwah, NJ. Call 201-236-9500 or fax 201-760-3735. Regular sections in the journal include: Advancing the Conversation; Multicultural Windows (media reviews); Creating Multicultural Classrooms; The Multicultural Library; Technology; Guide to New Resources; and NAME Conference and Regional News. In 2000-2001 a subscription for an individual costs $45.00. However, NAME members receive a special subscription rate of $21.00 as a ben-

efit of membership. Call 202-628-6263 for membership information, fax your questions to 202-628-6264, or contact NAME via E-mail at nameorg@erols.com.

22. *Multicultural Review* is issued quarterly by GP Subscription Publications, an imprint of Greenwood Publishing Group, Inc. The magazine describes itself as intending "to provide reviews of multicultural materials and information on multiculturalism." The magazine is well edited and complements *Multicultural Perspectives* rather nicely. In 2000 the subscription rate for individuals was $29.95. For subscription information, write to the Greenwood Publishing Group, Inc., 88 Post Road West, P.O. Box 5007, Westport, CT 06881-5007, or call 1-800-225-5800. The fax number is 203-222-1502. A sample copy can be requested at www.greenwood.com.

23. *Teaching Tolerance* is a magazine which is published several times a year by the Southern Poverty Law Center. At the Center's website, www.splcenter.org, the magazine is described as one which "spotlights educators, schools, and curriculum resources dedicated to promoting respect for differences in the classroom and beyond." Subscriptions are available free to teachers, religious and community leaders, healthcare providers, and other educators upon written request on school or organizational letterhead. Send the request to Teaching Tolerence, 400 Washington Ave., Montgomery, AL 36104, or fax it to 334-264-7310.

24. The *Resource Service Catalog of the National Women's History Project* (NWHP). The NWHP is a nonprofit educational project; its address is 7738 Bell Road, Windsor, CA 95492; 707-838-6000. The catalog is an education in itself. Most teachers will learn something useful just from perusing the descriptions of the posters, special units, books, films, and videos that are highlighted in the catalog. This is an organization and set of resources that every multicultural teacher should know about.

25. The first edition of the *Handbook of Research on Multicultural Education* was published by Macmillan in 1995 (ISBN 0-02-895797-0); James Banks is editor and Cherry A. McGee Banks is associate editor. For the field of multicultural education this publication was a major event. The book has 47 chapters, organized into 11 parts. The latter include History, Goals, Status, and Issues (part 1); Research and Research Issues (part 2); Knowledge Construction (part 3); Ethnic Groups in Historical and Social Science Research (part 4); Immigration Policy and the Education of Immigrants (part 5); The Education of Ethnic Groups (part 6); Language Issues (part 7); Academic Achievement: Approaches, Theories, and Research (part 8); Intergroup Education Approaches to School Reform (part 9); Higher Education (part 10); and International Perspectives on Multicultural Education (part 11). This book will serve for many years as a basic reference tool for students, scholars, and advocates of multicultural education.

IV. Sources of Children's Literature for Multicultural Education

1. Kruse, Ginny Moore, and Kathleen T. Horning, with Merri V. Lindgren and Katherine Odahowski. *Multicultural Literature for Children and Young Adults: A Selected Listing of Books By and About Young People of Color, 1980–1990*, 3rd ed. Madison: Cooperative Children's Book Center, University of Wisconsin-Madison, and Wisconsin Department of Public Instruction, 1991. This publication is available from Publication Sales, Wisconsin Department of Public Instruction, P.O. Box 7841, Madison, WI 53170-7841. Inquire about Bulletin #1923 (1-800-243-8782). The well-conceived bibliography section includes the following among its 16 sections: Books for Babies; Books for Toddlers; Fiction for Teenagers; Folklore, Mythology, and Traditional Literature; Issues in Today's World; and Understanding Oneself and Others. Also, please note that in 1997 the Cooperative Children's Book Center and the Wisconsin Department of Public Instruction published *Multicultural Literature for Children and Young Adults: A Selected Listing of Books By and About Young People of Color, Volume Two: 1991–1996.* The authors are Ginny Moore Kruse, Kathleen T. Horning, and Megan Schliesman with Tana Elias. Volume Two follows the same general format as Volume one and in 1999 each could be purchased for $18.00. In addition to these two superb publications, the Cooperative Children's Book Center (CCBC) maintains a website, www.education.wisc.edu/ccbc, which provides more valuable information such as (1) a listing of "Thirty Multicultural Books Every Child Should Know," (2) a regular "Book of the Week" review, and (3) information about "CCBC Choices," a publication which is available on March 15th of each year. The CCBC phone number is 608-263-3720.

2. Tway, Eileen, ed. *Reading Ladders for Human Relations*, 6th ed. Washington, D.C.: American Council on Education, 1981. The primary purpose of *Ladders* is "to advance the cause of better human relations." The volume is organized around five ladders; each ladder is divided into subcategories that are grouped into age-range steps along a continuum from preschool through high school. The five ladders are entitled Growing into Self; Relating to Wide Individual Differences; Interacting in Groups; Appreciating Different Cultures; and Coping in a Changing World.

4. Chelsea House publishes a notable set of 85 biographies of African Americans entitled Black Americans of Achievement. Another set of biographies called Hispanics of Achievement contained 30 titles as of January 2000; a third set, American Women of Achievement, contained 40 stories of women's accomplishments; a fourth set, Great Achievers: Lives of the Physically Challenged, contained 18 hardcover titles and 4 in soft cover; and a fifth set, North American Indians of Achievement, had 21 hardcover titles and 5 softcover titles. The catalogue of Chelsea House includes other collections that should be interesting to classroom teachers, librarians, and curriculum coordinators. The pub-

lisher's address is Chelsea House Pub. P.O. Box 914, 1974 Sproul Road, Suite 400, Broomall, PA 19008-0914. A catalog can be ordered by calling 1-800-848-2665.

V. Sources of Information About Selected New American Immigrant Populations

1. *Handbook for Teaching Cantonese-Speaking Students,* 1989. 71 pp. $8.00 each. Available from the Bureau of Publications, Sales Unit, California State Department of Education, P.O. Box 271, Sacramento, CA 95802-0271; ISBN 0-8011-0824-1. Call Sales Unit at 916-445-1260 for further information. This handbook is designed to assist school personnel in understanding the characteristics of Cantonese-speaking students. The publication is divided into five main sections: Overview of the Cantonese Language Group, Historical and Sociocultural Factors Concerning the Group, Linguistic Characteristics of the Cantonese Language, Recommended Instructional and Curricular Strategies for Cantonese Language Development, and Appendix of Educational and Community Resources.

2. *Handbook for Teaching Hmong-Speaking Students,* 1988. 129 pp. $4.50 each. Available from the Southeast Asia Community Resource Center, Folsom-Cordova Unified School District, 2460 Cordova Lane, Rancho Cordova, CA 95670. Call 916-635-6815 for further information. This handbook is designed to assist school personnel in understanding the characteristics of Hmong-speaking students. The publication is divided into five sections: Overview of the Hmong Language, Historical and Sociocultural Factors Concerning the Group, Linguistic Characteristics of the Hmong Language, Recommended Instructional and Curricular Strategies for Hmong Language Development, and Appendix of Educational and Community Resources. The handbook was developed by Bruce Thowpaou Bliatout, Bruce T. Downing, Judy Lewis, and Dao Yang.

3. *Handbook for Teaching Japanese-Speaking Students,* 1987. 124 pp. $8.00 each. Available from the California Department of Education, Bureau of Publications. ISBN 0-8011-0680-X. See note 1 for phone number and address. This handbook is designed to assist school personnel in understanding the characteristics of Japanese-speaking students. The publication is divided into five main sections: Overview of the Japanese Language Group, Historical and Sociocultural Factors Concerning the Group, Linguistic Characteristics of Japanese, Recommended Instructional and Curricular Strategies for Japanese Language Development, and Appendix of Educational and Community Resources.

4. *Handbook for Teaching Khmer-Speaking Students,* 1988. 152 pp. $5.50 each. Available from the Southeast Asia Community Resource Center, Folsom-Cordova Unified School District. See note 2 for address and phone number. This handbook is designed to help school district personnel understand Khmer-speaking students. The publication is

divided into five main sections: Overview of the Khmer Language Group, Historical and Sociocultural Factors Concerning the Group, Linguistic Characteristics of the Khmer Language, Recommended Instructional and Curricular Strategies for Khmer Language Development, and Appendix of Educational and Community Resources. This handbook was developed by Mory Ouk, Franklin E. Huffman, and Judy Lewis, with contributions by nine others.

5. *Handbook for Teaching Korean American Students,* 1992. $8.00 each. Available from the California Department of Education, Bureau of Publications, Sacramento, CA 95802-0271. Call 916-445-1260 for further information. This handbook is designed to assist school personnel in understanding the characteristics of Korean-speaking students. The handbook is divided into five main sections: Overview of the Korean Language Group, Historical and Sociocultural Factors Concerning the Group, Linguistic Characteristics of the Korean Language, Recommended Instructional and Curricular Strategies for Korean Language Development, and Appendix of Educational and Community Resources.

6. *Handbook for Teaching Lao-Speaking Students,* 1989. 178 pp. $5.50 each. Available from the Southeast Asia Community Resource Center, Folsom-Cordova Unified School District. See note 2 for phone number and address. This handbook is designed to help school district personnel understand Lao-speaking students. The handbook is divided into five main sections: Overview of the Lao Language Group, Historical and Sociocultural Factors Concerning Lao-speaking Peoples, Linguistic Characteristics of the Lao Language, Recommended Instructional and Curricular Strategies for Lao Language Development, and Appendix of Educational and Community Development and Appendix of Educational and Community Resources.

7. *Handbook for Teaching Pilipino-Speaking Students,* 1986. 84 pp. $8.00 each. Available from the California Department of Education, Bureau of Publications. ISBN 0-8011-0291-X. See note 1 for address and phone number. This handbook is designed to assist school personnel in understanding the characteristics of Pilipino-speaking students. The publication is divided into five main sections: Overview of the Pilipino Language Group, Historical and Sociocultural Factors Concerning the Group, Linguistic Characteristics of Pilipino, Recommended Instructional and Curricular Strategies for Language Development, and Appendix of Educational and Community Resources.

8. *Handbook for Teaching Portuguese-Speaking Students,* 1989 102 pp. $8.00 each. Available from the California State Department of Education Bureau of Publications. ISBN 0-8011-0825-XS. See note 1 for address and phone number. This handbook is designed to assist school personnel in understanding the characteristics of Portuguese-speaking students. The publication is divided into five main sections: Overview of the Portuguese Language Group, Historical and Socio-cultural Factors Concerning the Group, Linguistic Characteristics of Portuguese,

Recommended Instructional and Curricular Strategies for Portuguese Language Development, and Appendix of Educational and Community Resources.

9. *Handbook for Teaching Vietnamese-American Students,* 1994. 190 pp. $8.00 each plus $4.95 for shipping. Available from the California State Department of Education, Bureau of Publications. ISBN 8-8011-1083. This handbook is designed to assist school personnel in understanding the characteristics of Vietnamese-speaking students. The handbook is divided into five main sections: Overview of the Vietnamese Language Group, Historical and Sociocultural Factors Concerning the Vietnamese-speaking Peoples, Linguistic Characteristics of the Vietnamese Language, Recommended Instructional and Curricular Strategies for Vietnamese Language Development, and Appendix of Educational and Community Resources.

Appendix 7

Definitions to Facilitate Ethnic and Cultural Self-exploration and Disclosure

1. *Culture*

    A. Thus, culture is one of the most difficult words in the anthropological vocabulary to define. One way of looking at culture is to treat it in terms of [these] different levels and label them accordingly: culture one, culture two, and culture three. Culture one is *your* culture; that is, your personal, idiosyncratic culture, which is made up of everything you are aware of and have experienced. Obviously this means that no two people have exactly the same culture. Culture two is *our* culture. Our culture is composed of those aspects of culture that are held in common by *us*. Us means at least two people at a minimum, but not too large a group as a maximum. . . . The group holding culture two would often be called a subculture in anthropological/sociological terms. Culture two is smaller than national culture, which is culture three, but it is larger than culture one. . . . Culture two is hard to pin down, since it shifts as the groups making it up shift in composition as individuals. One may be an anthropologist and a teacher and a gardener and a kite flyer. If one belonged to as many groups as one had major interests in, one would have to admit to having a multiplicity of cultures. One can do this because of the underlying culture three, which is shared by everyone regardless of the subgroupings.

    George R. Mead, *The Encyclopedia of Anthropology,* 1976 (p. 103)

    B. There is also a fourth level of culture. This level is transnational, or across nation states. We sometimes see writers refer to "Western Culture" or "Asian Culture." Anthony Leeds says that this usage "refers to a congeries of traits which may be ordered in various ways but are distributed over a number of delimitable societies."

    The Encyclopedia of Anthropology, 1976 (p. 103)

    C. Culture is the template or web of meanings by which we organize social and psychological experience.

    Clifford Geertz, *The Interpretation of Cultures,* 1973

D. Culture consists of the behavior patterns, symbols, institutions, values and other human-made components of society. It is the unique achievement of a human group that distinguishes it from other groups.

James A. Banks, *Teaching Strategies for Ethnic Studies,* 1991, 5th ed.

E. Culture is a...dynamic, creative, and continuous process including behaviors, values, and substance learned and shared by people that guides them in their struggle for survival and gives meaning to their lives.

Arvizu, Snyder, and Espinosa, "Demystifying the Concept of Culture: Theoretical and Conceptual Tools" (1980); cited in Hilda Hernandez, *Multicultural Education: A Teacher's Guide to Content and Process*

F. Culture is a system of standards for perceiving, believing, evaluating, and acting.

Ward Goodenough (1971), in *Culture, Language, and Society*

G. Culture is a social group's design for surviving in and adapting to its environment (typically comprised of the geographical, social, and metaphysical environment).

Brian M. Bullivant, "Culture: Its Nature and Meaning for Educators" (1989), in Banks and Banks, *Multicultural Education: Issues and Perspectives,* 1989

H. Culture or civilization, taken in its wide ethnographic sense, is that complex which includes knowledge, belief, art, morals, law, custom, and any other capabilities and habits acquired by man as a member of society.

E. B. Tylor, *Primitive Culture,* 1958

I. Culture is the patterned behavior learned by each individual from the day of birth as he or she is educated (socialized and enculturated) by parents and peers to become, and remain, a member of the particular group into which he or she was born or joined.

George R. Mead, *The Encyclopedia of Anthropology,* 1976 (p. 103)

2. *Macroculture* and *Microculture*

Societies which are multicultural in nature consist of a larger shared *core* culture and many smaller cocultures or subcultures. The larger shared core culture is the macroculture, or total culture. The small cultures are called microcultures.

Derived from James A. Banks, "The Nature of Culture in the United States," in Banks and Banks, *Multicultural Education: Issues and Perspectives,* 1989

3. *Group*

   A. A number of individuals related by a common interest (as in physical association, community of interests, or blood)

                         Merriam-Webster, *Franklin Electronic Dictionary*

   B. A number of people having something in common (as in a habit, interest, occupation, or age)

                         Merriam-Webster, *Franklin Electronic Dictionary*

   C. A group is a collectivity of persons who share an identity, a feeling of unity.

                         James A. Banks, *Multicultural Education: Issues and Perspectives* (p. 13)

   D. A group is [also] a social system that has a social structure of interrelated roles.

                         George A. Theodorson and Achilles G. Theodorson, *A Modern Dictionary of Sociology* (cited in James A. Banks, *Multicultural Education:Issues and Perspectives,* 1989 (p. 29)

   E. The group is the social system that carries a culture.

                         James A. Banks, *Multicultural Education: Issues and Perspectives,* 1989

Note that in modern societies there are numerous groups that individuals can be members of, and that most individuals are simultaneously members of several groups. For example, an individual may identify with a religious group, an ethnic group, a gender group, a racial group, a national group (*nationality*), a group defined by sexual orientation or political affiliation, a professional or occupational group, an age-based group, a service group, and so on.

4. *Cultural Group*

   A. A group of individuals with a shared and somewhat unique culture. The group typically feels a sense of unity and has a "will" to survive which is backed up by specific individual and group behaviors.

                         Leonard Davidman, *EDUC 588 Resource Notebook*

   B. "Cultural Group" and "Social Group" as terms are quite similar and almost synonymous. Indeed, for the purposes of ethnic and cultural group self-disclosure, it is hard to think of a group that is not cultural in some sense, or level, of the term. If a specific social group has an identity or label which is recognized and/or created in a macroculture-like "Gay-Americans" or "recovering alcoholics" or "developmentally disabled" or "African-Americans"—then that social group can accurately be called a cultural group. All groups whose identity are created, negotiated, or given meaning in a specific macroculture are, by that very fact, cultural groups.

                         Leonard Davidman, "Multicultural Education: A Movement in Search of Meaning and Positive Connections," *Multicultural Education,* Spring 1995 (p.10)

5. *Ethnic Group*

   A. A group that shares a common history, a sense of peoplehood and identity, values, behavioral characteristics and a communication system. The members of an ethnic group usually view their group as distinct and separate from other cultural groups within a society. Ethnic groups within the United States include Anglo Americans, Irish Americans, Polish Americans, and German Americans.

   James A. Banks, *An Introduction
   to Multicultural Education* (p. 101)

   B. An ethnic group is a cultural group with several distinguishing characteristics. There are many definitions of "ethnic group," but none on which there is complete agreement by social scientists.

   James A. Banks, *Multiethnic Education:
   Theory and Practice* (p. 53)

   C. The term *ethnic group* has been "interpreted to mean a cultural group, an ancestral group, a racial group, a minority group, an immigrant group, any group that wears colorful clothes and dances at weddings, a group distinguished in certain ways from a supposedly non-ethnic majority, or any combination of these meanings."

   Richard M. Burkey, *Ethnic and Racial Groups:
   The Dynamics of Dominance* (p. 5)

   D. Carlos E. Cortés, history professor at the University of California at Riverside, has written about the five major ethnic groups in America. He identifies these groups as Native Americans, African Americans, European Americans, Asian Americans, and Latino Americans.

   E. An ethnic group is a group that shares a common ancestry, culture, history, tradition, sense of peoplehood, set of economic interests, and a set of political interests.

6. *Ethnic Minority Group*

   An ethnic minority group is an ethnic group that has unique behavioral and/or racial characteristics that enable other groups to easily identify its members. These groups are often a numerical minority within the nation-state and the victims of institutionalized discrimination. Jewish Americans are an example of an ethnic group differentiated on the basis of cultural and religious characteristics. African Americans, Mexican Americans, and Japanese Americans are differentiated on the basis of both biological and cultural characteristics.

   James A. Banks, *An Introduction to Multicultural Education* (p. 101)

7. *Oppressed and Nonoppressed Cultural Groups*

   Oppression is both a social reality and state of mind. Like much else in the social science and popular literature, there is much controversy over who is and is not oppressed. In this course we will consider oppression to exist when the political, economic, and/or civil rights of individuals are systematically diminished or threatened because of their ascribed membership in specific groups. For example, historically, and this extends into the present, African Americans, Mexican Americans, American Indians, women, gay men, and lesbian women have faced discrimination in various social settings. At the same time members of other groups have avoided persistent and pervasive discrimination. For example, vegetarians, environmentalists, educators, Republicans, Democrats, Rotarians, doctors, pacifists, heterosexuals, and so on are groups in which membership carried very little stigma. In addition, it is noteworthy that membership in the latter group (nonoppressed) is, for the most part, voluntary, whereas the opposite holds true for most of the groups who fall in the oppressed category. You can choose to become a nonpacifist or a nonvegetarian; it's not quite so easy to become a nonwoman, or a nonBlack, etc. In addition, vegetarians, conservationists, Republicans, etc. are not visual categories. You can choose to hide your gender orientation and political affiliation, but this is not the case for your gender, color, or handicapping condition (in most cases).

Leonard Davidman, *EDUC 588 Resource Notebook*

8. *Race*

A. A race is a population group or subspecies within the living human species, Homo sapiens, set apart from other subspecies on the basis of arbitrarily selected, commonly visible, or phenotypic criteria. The criteria most often selected are skin color, hair quantity and form, and the shape and form of the body, head, and facial features. A problem is presented, however, by the high variability of such characteristics within any particular population group. Not all genes that transmit all phenotypic characteristics ascribed to a subspecies are transmitted in a cluster. As a result only some members of a particular "race" will have all the criteria for that race, although every member will probably have one or more of the characteristics. The species Homo sapiens is not difficult for specialists to identify, nor is there difficulty in determining its constituent populations, those groups of human beings who inhabit the various areas of the earth. No such clear-cut agreement is possible in determining the nature of subspecies, or races, and many scientists reject the concept of race.

Academic American Encyclopedia, 1980

B. Each of the major divisions of humankind, having distinct physical characteristics.

The Concise Oxford Dictionary of Current English (1990)

C. A tribe, nation, etc., regarded as a distinct ethnic stock.

The Concise Oxford Dictionary of Current English (1990)

D. Race as a meaningful criterion within the biological sciences has long been recognized as a fiction. When we speak of the "white race" or the "black race" or the Jewish race or the Aryan race, we speak in misnomers. . . . Race. . . . pretends to be an objective term of classification, when in fact it is a trope.

Henry Louis Gates, Professor of Afro-American Studies
and Humanities at Harvard, p. 48
in *Loose Canons: Notes on the Culture Wars,*
Oxford University Press (1992)

E. Race is a human invention constructed by groups to differentiate themselves from other groups, to create themselves from other groups, to create ideas about the "other," to formulate their identities, and to defend the disproportionate distribution of rewards and opportunities within society.

James A. Banks, *Multicultural Education,*
Transformative Knowledge and Action:
Historical And Contemporary Perspectives, 1996 (p. 80)

9. *Democracy*

A. Democracy is "A system of government in which ultimate political authority is vested in the people. The term is derived from the Greek words 'demos' (the people) and 'Kratos' (authority)."

Milton Greenberg and Jack C. Plano,
The American Political Dictionary, 10th ed., 1997 (p. 9)

B. Democracy is anything but a "natural" form of association. It is an extraordinary and rare contrivance of cultivated imagination.

Benjamin Barber, *an Aristocracy of Everyone:*
The Politics of Education and the Future
of America, 1992 (p. 5)

C. Democracy …is the environment in which reason is most likely to flourish. Democracy brings reason to bear on common problems. It puts matters of public policy up for public discussion, where they are most likely to be illuminated by evidence and enriched through an open sharing of ideas. Conclusions, when they are finally reached, are always tentative. They can be changed in the light of experience or newly discovered evidence. Thus, the mind of a democrat is never fully closed.

Rodman B. Webb and Robert R. Sherman,
Schooling and Society, 2nd ed., 1989 (p. 86)

D. Making political democracy work is a complex delicate process. Even more complex and precarious is a social democracy: the living together of people endeavoring to follow democratic principles…. Political democracy depends heavily on traditions, customs, and laws. Social democracy depends heavily on the exercise of civility and civitas.

John I. Goodlad, *In Praise of Education,* 1997 (p. 24)

E. Dewey does not see democracy simply as a convenient way to solve problems or pass laws. Democracy is, rather, a means of enhancing intelligence and enriching community life. It is a method of bringing individuals in closer communion with society. The individual is not forced to accept external values or create a wholly private morality. Instead, the individual is given the means to participate in the continued construction and reconstruction of community norms.... The aim of a democratic education is to provide the best possible opportunity for the development of individual and social intelligence.

Rodman B. Webb and Robert R. Sherman,
Schooling and Society, 2nd ed., 1989 (p. 26)

F. A society aiming as high as democracy will seek at all costs to educate all of its students to be democrats, especially if its particular vision of democracy requires that all citizens, not just a few, think and behave democratically.

Walter C. Parker, "Curriculum for Democracy,"
in *Democracy, Education, and the Schools,*
editor, Roger Soder, 1996 (p. 187–188)

I. Selected Data from the FBI's 1996 *Hate Crime Statistics Document*
  1. In 1996 a total of 11,354 law enforcement agencies in 49 states and the District of Columbia participated in the FBI's Hate Crime Data Collection Program (mandated by the 1990 Hate Crimes Statistics Act). These agencies represented nearly 223 million inhabitants of the USA, or 84% of the population. Thus, the data collected below represents approximately 85% of the USA's 1996 population.
  2. In 1996 **twelve** people were murdered in hate-motivated crimes (racial bias motivation = 8; sexual orientation bias = 2; bias against Hispanics = 2). (See page 5 of report.)
  3. In 1996 the total number of bias-motivated criminal incidents reported was 8,759; these 8,759 "incidents" involved 10,706 separate offenses.
  4. Of the 8,759 criminal incidents:
     (a) 5,396 were motivated by racial bias;
     (b) 1,401 were motivated by religious bias;
     (c) 1,016 were motivated by sexual orientation bias;
     (d) 940 were motivated by ethnicity/national origin bias; and
     (e) six (6) were motivated by multiple bias.
  5. Of the 5,396 racially motivated criminal incidents:
     (a) 3,674 (68%) were anti-Black;
     (b) 1,106 (20%) were anti-White;
     (c) 355 (6.5%) were anti-Asian/Pacific Islanders; and
     (d) 51 (.9%) were anti-American Indian/Alaskan Native.
  6. Of the 1,401 criminal incidents which were motivated by religious bias:
     (a) 1,109 (79%) stemmed from anti-Jewish bias;
     (b) 35 (2.5%) stemmed from anti-Catholic bias;
     (c) 75 (5.3%) stemmed from anti-Protestant bias;
     (d) 27 (about 2%) stemmed from anti-Islamic bias; and
     (e) 2 (.14%) stemmed from anti-Atheism bias.
  7. Of the 1,016 criminal incidents motivated by sexual orientation bias:
     (a) 757 (74.5%) were anti–male homosexual;

As of December 1999, the 1995, 1996, and 1997 *Hate Crime Statistics Reports* were available at <www.fbi.gov/publish/hatecrime.htm>.

(b) 150 (almost 15%) were anti–female homosexual;

(c) 84 (8%) were antihomosexual;

(d) 15 (1.5%) were antiheterosexual; and

(e) 10 (almost 1%) were anti-bisexual.

The total number of antigay/-lesbian incidents was 991, 97.5% of total.

8. Of the 940 criminal incidents which were motivated by ethnicity/national origin bias:

(a) 564 (60%) were anti-Hispanic; and

(b) 376 (40%) were motivated by bias toward other groups; these groups are not specified in table one. (See page 7 of report.)

9. Out of a total of 10,706 "hate crime offenses" in 1996:

(a) 4,130 (39%) were intimidation offenses;

(b) 1,762 (16%) were simple assault; and

(c) 1,444 (13%) were aggravated assault.

10. Out of a total of 11,039 victims:

(a) 6,999 (63.3%) were attacked because of their race;

(b) 4,600 (41.6%) of these victims were Black;

(c) 1,445 (13%) of these victims were White; and

(d) 544 (almost 5%) of these victims were Asian/Pacific Islanders.

11. Of the known offenders in 1996:

(a) 66% were White (5,891 out of 8,935)

(b) 20% were Black (1,826);

(c) 1.75% were Asian/Pacific Islanders (157); and

(d) close to .5% were American Indian/Alaskan Native (48).

12. Of 10,706 offenses in 1996…2,723 (25.4%) were committed in California. See Table A8.1 on page 341.

II. Selected Data from the FBI's 1997 *Hate Crimes Statistics Document* and Related Information

1. In 1997 a total of 11,211 law enforcement agencies in 48 states and the District of Columbia participated in the FBI's Hate Crime Data Collection Program (mandated by the 1990 Hate Crimes Statistics Act). These agencies, in 1997, represented nearly 223 million U.S. inhabitants, or 83% of the population. Thus, the data collected below represents approximately 80% of the USA's 1997 population.

2. In 1997 **eight** people were murdered in hate-motivated crimes (racial bias motivation = 5; sexual orientation bias = 3). (See page 5 of report.)

3. In 1997 the total number of bias-motivated criminal incidents reported was 8,049; and these 8,049 "incidents" involved 9,861 separate "offenses."

4. Of these 8,049 criminal incidents:

(a) 4,710 were motivated by racial bias;

(b) 1,385 were motivated by religious bias;

(c) 1,102 were motivated by sexual orientation bias;

(d) 836 were motivated by ethnicity/national origin bias;

(e) 12 were motivated by disability bias; and

(f) 4 were motivated by multiple bias.

Table A8.1. Number of Incidents, Offenses, Victims, and Offenders by Bias Motivation, 1996

	Number of			
	Incidents	Offenses	Victims	Known Offenders
Total	**8,759**	**10,706**	**11,039**	**8,935**
Single Bias Incidents				
Race:	**5,396**	**6,767**	**6,994**	**6,122**
Anti-White	**1,106**	**1,384**	**1,445**	**1,783**
Anti-Black	3,674	4,469	4,600	3,701
Anti-American Indian/Alaskan Native	51	69	71	56
Anti-Asian Pacific Islander	355	527	544	374
Anti-Multi-Racial Group	210	318	334	208
Ethnicity/National Origin:	**940**	**1,163**	**1,207**	**1,095**
Anti-Hispanic	564	710	728	734
Anti-Other Ethnicity/National Origin	376	453	479	361
Religion:	**1,401**	**1,500**	**1,535**	**523**
Anti-Jewish	1,109	1,182	1,209	371
Anti-Catholic	35	37	38	17
Anti-Protestant	75	80	81	44
Anti-Islamic	27	33	33	16
Anti-Other Religious Group	129	139	145	64
Anti-Multi-Religious Group	24	27	27	11
Anti-Atheism/Agnosticism, etc.	2	2	2	0
Sexual Orientation:	**1,016**	**1,256**	**1,281**	**1,180**
Anti-Male Homosexual	757	927	940	925
Anti-Female Homosexual	150	185	192	150
Anti-Homosexual	84	94	99	93
Anti-Heterosexual	15	38	38	4
Anti-Bisexual	10	12	12	8
Multiple Bias Incidents[1]	**6**	**20**	**22**	**15**

[1]There were six multiple-bias incidents. Within these incidents there were 20 offenses, 22 victims, and 15 known offenders.

5. Of the 4,710 criminal incidents which were racially motivated:
   (a) 66% (3,120) were anti-Black;
   (b) 21% (993) were anti-White;
   (c) 7.3% (347) were anti-Asian/Pacific Islander; and
   (d) .8% (36) were anti-American Indian/Alaskan Native.
6. Of the 1,385 criminal incidents motivated by sexual orientation bias:
   (a) 78% (1,087) stemmed from anti-Jewish bias;
   (b) 2.2% (31) stemmed from anti-Catholic bias;
   (c) 4% (53) stemmed from anti-Protestant bias; and
   (d) 2% (28) stemmed from anti-Islamic bias.
7. Of the 1,102 criminal incidents motivated by sexual orientation bias:
   (a) 69% (760) were anti–male homosexual;

    (b) 17% (188) were anti–female homosexual;

    (c) 12% (133) were antihomosexual;

    (d) 1% (12) were antiheterosexual; and

    (e) .8% (9) were antibisexual.

    The total percentage of anti-gay/lesbian incidents was 98% (N = 1,081).

8. Of the 836 criminal incidents which were motivated by ethnicity/national origin bias:

    (a) 58.7% (491) were anti-Hispanic; and

    (b) 41.2% (345) were motivated by bias toward other groups.

9. Out of a total of 9,861 "hate crime offenses" in 1997:

    (a) 39% (3,486) were intimidation offenses;

    (b) 26% (2,564) were simple assault; and

    (c) 13% (1,282) were aggravated assault

    (See page 5 of report.)

10. Nearly six out of ten victims (out of a total of 10,255 victims) were attacked because of their race, with bias against blacks accounting for 39% of the total (N = 3,951). Bias against whites accounted for 21% of the total (N = 1,293).

11. Of the known offenders in 1997, 63% were white and 19% were black. Close to 2% were Asian/Pacific Islanders, and close to .8% were American Indian/Alaskan Native. (See Table Eleven on page 18 of report.)

12. Of 9,861 total offenses against persons in 1997, 2,404 (24.4%) were committed in California. (See Table A8.2 on page 343.)

III. Analysis of the FBI's 1996 and 1997 Hate Crimes Database and Selected Caveats

1. Readers should keep in mind that the total number of offenses committed in California and other states in 1996 and 1997 may be much less than what is indicated by the FBI's data. It may well be the case that law enforcement agencies in California are quite diligent about reporting hate crimes when compared with agencies in other states.

2. In a similar vein, it is worth noting, in the words of the FBI authors who assembled these reports, that while the assembled database is "… not sufficient to allow valid national or regional measures of the volume and types of hate crimes, these data offer perspective on the general nature of hate crime occurrences." (See page 2 of the 1996 report.)

3. In addition, in the foreword of the 1997 report the authors note that "Knowledge about the nature, volume, and scope of hate crime in America may be the most important weapon in struggle against it." However, for this relatively new database to have this effect, more print and electronic journalists and educators will need to become aware of the database, analyze it, and then decide how to "educate" their "public" about the content of the database.

4. We believe that the above-listed summaries answer some questions about the existence of hate crimes in the USA in 1996 and 1997, at the same time that other questions are raised. Conceivably, secondary and university educators could transform some of these questions into

Table A82. Number of Incidents, Offenses, Victims, and Known Offenders by Bias Motivation, 1997

	Number of			
	Incidents	Offenses	Victims[1]	Known Offenders[2]
Total	**8,049**	**9,861**	**10,255**	**8,474**
Single Bias Incidents				
Race:	**4,710**	**5,898**	**6,084**	**5,444**
Anti-White	993	1,267	1,293	1,520
Anti-Black	3,120	3,838	3,951	3,301
Anti-American Indian/Alaskan Native	36	44	46	45
Anti-Asian Pacific Islander	347	437	466	351
Anti-Multi-Racial Group	214	312	328	227
Ethnicity/National Origin:	**836**	**1,083**	**1,132**	**906**
Anti-Hispanic	491	636	649	614
Anti-Other Ethnicity/National Origin	345	447	483	292
Religion:	**1,385**	**1,483**	**1,586**	**792**
Anti-Jewish	1,087	1,159	1,247	598
Anti-Catholic	31	32	32	16
Anti-Protestant	53	59	61	19
Anti-Islamic	28	31	32	22
Anti-Other Religious Group	159	173	184	120
Anti-Multi-Religious Group	24	26	27	11
Anti-Atheism/Agnosticism, etc.	3	3	3	6
Sexual Orientation:	**1,102**	**1,375**	**1,401**	**1,315**
Anti-Male Homosexual	760	912	927	1,032
Anti-Female Homosexual	188	229	236	158
Anti-Homosexual	133	210	214	103
Anti-Heterosexual	12	14	14	14
Anti-Bisexual	9	10	10	8
Disability:	**12**	**12**	**12**	**14**
Anti-Physical	9	9	9	11
Anti-Mental	3	3	3	3
Multiple-Bias Incidents[3]	**4**	**10**	**40**	**3**

[1]The term "victim" may refer to a person, business, institution, or a society as a whole.
[2]The term "known offender" does not imply that the identity of the suspect is known, but only that an attribute of the suspect is identified which distinguishes him/her from an unknown offender.
[3]There were four multiple-bias incidents. Within these incidents, there were 10 offenses, 40 victims, and 3 known offenders.

"invitations to inquiry," inquiries which might result in more knowledge about this database and related questions.

5. Regarding the juxtaposition of 1996 and 1997 data, what are some of the things we learn? Well, from 1996 to 1997:

 (a) There was slightly more law enforcement agencies reporting in 1996 than 1997 (11,354 to 11,211)—in 1996 the reporting agencies represented 84% of the total USA population while in 1997 the number was 83%.

(b) Between 1996 and 1997 a decrease of one percent in any statistic could be explained by the one percent decrease in the size of the population "covered" by the database.

(c) Between 1996 and 1997 there was a 33 1/3% decrease in the number of Americans murdered in hate-crime related incidents (n = 12 to 8).

(d) Between 1996 and 1997 there was an 8% decrease in the total number of bias-motivated criminal incidents reported (n = 8,759 to 8,049).

(e) Between 1996 and 1997 the percentage of hate-motivated criminal incidents motivated by racial bias, religious bias, etc. were quite similar.

1996	1997	
62% racial bias	58.5%	(−3.5%)
16% religious bias	17.2%	(+1.2%)
11.6% sexual orientation bias	13.7%	(+2.1%)
10.7% ethnicity/national origin bias	10.4%	(−.3%)
.7% multiple bias	.5%	(−.2%)

(f) Between 1996 and 1997 the percentages of hate-motivated criminal incidents against Blacks, Whites, Asian/Pacific Islanders, and American Indians/Alaskan Natives were quite similar.

1996	1997
68% anti-Black	66%
20% anti-White	21%
6.5% anti-Asian/Pacific Islander	7.3%
.9% anti-American Indian/Alaskan Native	0.8%

(g) Between 1996 and 1997 the percentages of hate-motivated criminal incidents made against specific religious groups were quite similar.

1996	1997
79% anti-Jewish	78%
2.5% anti-Catholic	2.2%
5.3% anti-Protestant	4%
2% anti-Islamic	2%
.14% anti-atheist	0.22%

(h) Between 1996 and 1997 the overall statistics pertaining to sexual orientation bias were similar, and changes in the subcategories for the most part were negligible.

1996	1997
97.5% total antigay/-lesbian incidents	98%
74.5% antimale homosexual	69%
15% antifemale homosexual	17%
8% antihomosexual	12%
1.5% antiheterosexual	1%
1% antibisexual	.8%

(i) Between 1996 and 1997 the percentage of criminal incidents attributed to anti-Hispanic bias remained fairly constant.

1996	1997
60% (n = 564) anti-Hispanic bias	58.7% (n = 491)
40% (n = 376) anti-other groups	41.2% (n = 341)

(j) In terms of size of their group in the overall USA population Jews are tremendously overrepresented in the hate-motivated religion category. Jews are less than 3% of the overall USA population, but nearly 80% of the religion-based hate crimes in 1996 and 1997 were committed against Jews.

(k) In both 1996 (63.3%) and 1997 (59.3%) a large majority of the total number of hate-crime victims were attacked because of their race. Within this group of "racial" victims Black Americans were significantly overrepresented. In both 1996 (41.6%) and 1997 (39%) Black Americans were nearly 40% of the total number of racial victims, while they account for approximately 14% of the overall USA population. White Americans, on the other hand, who account for more than 60% of the total USA population, were 13% of the racial victims in 1996 and 21% in 1997.

(l) In both 1996 and 1997 the total number of Black American hate-crime victims was about eight times larger than the total number of Hispanic hate-crime victims. In the overall USA population in 1996 and 1997 Hispanic Americans and Black Americans were "roughly" equal.

1996		1997
n = 4600	Black American hate victims	n = 3951
n = 564	Hispanic American hate victims	n = 491

(m)In both 1996 (25.4%) and 1997 (24.4%) California accounted for nearly 25% of the total number of hate crimes (against persons as opposed to property) committed in the USA. In 1996 there were 2723 hate crimes in California and 41% were intimidation crimes and 17.4% were aggravated assault (n = 476). In 1997 there were 2404 hate crimes in California and 40.3% were intimidation crimes and 17.3% were aggravated assault (n = 417).

(n) Invitations to inquiry related to (a) through (m) above and the 1996/1997 FBI hate-crimes database include:
  (1) Why does California account for nearly 25% of the reported hate crimes in the USA?
  (2) Has this "abnormal" statistic led to any political action in Sacramento?
  (3) Which newspapers in our region (or in California) have reported on the FBI hate crimes database, or related issues in the 1996–2000 period?

(4) Why did the number of law agencies reporting drop between 1996 and 1997 nationwide? What happened in 1998?

(5) Do local law agencies in our region participate in the collection and reporting of hate crimes data? Why? Why not?

(6) Why are Black Americans and Jewish Americans significantly overrepresented as hate-crime victims?

(7) Did the 1996/1997 decrease in hate-crime murders and total number of bias-motivated criminal incidents continue into 1998?

(8) Does the FBI know the names of the 20 Americans killed in hate-related crimes in 1996/1997? Will they release these names? How do you contact the FBI?

As of December 1999, the 1995, 1996, and 1997 *Hate Crime Statistics Reports* were available at <www.fbi.gov/publish/hatecrime.htm>.

Appendix 9

Selected Internet Websites

The brief set of websites below is primarily intended to serve as points of departure for preservice and in-service classroom teachers, but may prove interesting for educators with a broader range of interests. All sites listed were on display in December 1999, and hopefully will still be available when readers consult them. The sites are divided into three categories: lesson plans and curriculum resources; multicultural education, civil rights, and educational equity-related organizations; and education-related governmental resources (USA).

I. Lesson Plans and Curriculum Resources
1. The *Multicultural Pavilion* Homepage
   <curry.edschool.virginia.edu/go/multicultural/home.html>
   The Multicultural Pavilion was developed and is maintained by Paul Gorski. As noted in chapter two, with regard to information about multicultural education, this is one of the most thorough and valuable multicultural education-focused sites available. For example, the *Teachers' Corner*, one of ten major categories (links) on the homepage, leads to a page with sections on Multicultural Education, a Guide to Multicultural Education and the Internet, an index of Progressive Education Organizations, a suggested reading list, an Activity Archive (Awareness Activities), a Multicultural Song Index (with the words and titles to a wide range of songs), a website evaluation checklist, and an international photo gallery. *Multicultural Paths-Other Sites*, another homepage category, leads to a page subdivided into general, ethnicity, identity, resources, archives, and special, and each of these has five to seven hot links leading to more multicultural education-related links. For example, the "archives" link has links to African-American literature, essays and reviews, historical documents, historical speeches archives, Native-American literature, online literature for kids, and religious texts.
2. The *AskERIC Virtual Library* Homepage
   <www.ericir.syr.edu>
   ERIC stands for Educational Research Information Center. The AskERIC homepage has links to *About AskERIC*, *Questions and Answer Service*, the *Virtual Library*, *Teaching the Millennium/New and Newsworthy*, *Research and Development*, and *Search the ERIC*

Database. The Virtual Library icon leads to a page divided into: AskERIC Toolbox; AskERIC Information Guides; AskERIC Lesson Plans; Special Projects; Education Mailing List Archive; ERIC Resources, More ERIC Resources, T.V. Series Companion Materials; and the ERIC Conference Calendar and Professional and Commercial Announcements. As of November 22, 1999, the AskERIC lesson plan collection contained more than 1,000 lessons written by teachers from across the United States of America. The lesson plan collection is divided into content areas such as Language Arts, Health, Science, Math, and Social Studies, and each of these categories is further subdivided. Ultimately, the user is led to specific lesson plans which are aimed at specific grade levels. The AskERIC lesson plan collection is a part of the *Gateway to Educational Materials* (GEM) union catalogue, described as a collection which contains thousands of lesson plans, curriculum units, and other educational materials. GEM, which is a project of the U.S. Department of Education's National Library of Education and the ERIC Clearinghouse on Information and Technology, is accessible from the AskERIC Lesson Plans page; in addition, it can be accessed directly at <www.thegateway.org>.

3. The *National Women's History Project* Homepage
   <www.nwhp.org>
   This homepage includes links to:
   (a) an online catalog as well as a link which sets you up to have a free catalog mailed to you;
   (b) a set of favorite links;
   (c) a list of women's history organizations;
   (d) an interesting 15-item quiz with questions and answers;
   (e) information regarding National Women's History Month; and
   (f) a set of ideas to help advance the development of Women's History in various settings.
      In the set of favorite links (on November 22, 1999) we found links to American Maid: Growing Up Female in Life and Literature (ten literature-based women's history curriculum units for grades 3–12); a six-page overview of U.S. Women's History from Compton's Interactive Encyclopedia; and Gifts of Speech (the text of speeches made by influential contemporary women, arranged alphabetically and chronologically). In addition, the online catalog index contains the following categories among others: classroom, math, and science; the women's vote and other rights; and the extraordinary 20th century. The classroom link leads to a number of interesting women's history curriculum products and activities which are available for purchase.

4. The *Internet Resources for Teachers and Students* Homepage
   <www.ets.org/resource.html>
   This page is one of a number of resources made available by the Education Testing Service (ETS) at <www.ets.org>. The Internet Resources page lists a directory with seventeen categories (as of November 22,

1999) including Art and Architecture, English, Health and Physical Science, History and Social Science, Music, Writing, Math and Science, On-line Libraries, and On-line Museums. Each of these categories leads to another set of links, and many of these lead to lesson plans from various organizations. For example, the English category led to these links: *Bartlett's Familiar Quotations*, 9th edition; Fake Out!; The Schoolhouse Project; English; the Shakespeare Web; the Smithsonian Site for U.S. History Materials, and the Internet Book Information Center. Then, clicking on the Schoolhouse Project-English link led to these links (which were part of the Awesome Library Collection described in the next section): drama; languages; literature; philosophy; poetry; public speaking; reading and writing; and standards. The literature link led to another link-filled page which included 'lesson plans,' and the lesson plan link led to 63 items containing hundreds of grade-specific lesson plans from various organizations such as the National Council for Teachers of English (NCTE), the San Diego County Office of Education, and the Columbia Education Center.

5. *The Awesome Library K-12 Education Directory*
   In May 1997, the Awesome Library, under the sponsorship of the Evaluation and Development Institute and the leadership of Dr. R. Jerry Adams, came into being. It stemmed from earlier projects which had been funded by the U.S. Department of Education and other federal agencies. As of November 1999, the site contained 10,000 resources and about 200 of these had received special recognition in the collection (a star) because, as the "About the Awesome Library" page <www.awesomelibrary.org/about.html> indicates, the resource is at least one of the following:
   (a) the source for many other sources on the page;
   (b) a very comprehensive source of information;
   (c) unusually well-organized; and/or
   (d) one which contains essential information for the topic.
       It is quite easy to locate the "star" resources in the collection. For example, to locate all of the social studies resources which have stars, the user simply types in *social studies star* in the database's word search box. On November 24, 1999 this search turned up nine hits which included:
   (a) "By Grade and Standard-California Social Studies for K-12 . . . from the King's County Office of Education." This site provides a directory of lessons organized by the California SCORE Social Studies Framework for K-12.
   (b) "Holiday Listed Alphabetically." This site provides background information on the roots of holidays, and includes other celebrations, such as birthdays.
   (c) "Current Events-Conflict, Peace, the Environment, and Interdependence" from the American Forum for Global Education. This

site provides opportunities for students to work together to solve problems that confront the planet.

One can also use the Keyword search box to seek out lessons on specific topics. For example, typing in *earthquake lessons* turned up two lessons, one related to plate tectonics, the other to statistics. The Awesome Library K–12 Education Directory and overall collection is distinctive because its 24 links include traditional curriculum areas such as Art, English, Math, and Technology; specific roles such as teacher, counselor, nurse, principal, and students; and miscellaneous links like reference, magazines, authors, your town, and lessons. Each of these links leads to other interesting links. The Awesome Library collection is distinctive in another respect, namely the mission of the Evaluation and Development Institute (EDI), the organization which sponsors the library. In its own words, the mission of EDI is to promote "the development of high level knowledge, skills and opportunities for leaders and future leaders across cultures in the service of world peace."

6. The *Teachers First* Homepage
<www.teachersfirst.com>

The Teachers First website is an excellent on-line resource for both pre-service and in-service teachers. On its webpage Teachers First says that it "is a web resource for K–12 classroom teachers who want useful resources and lesson plans to use with their students. Teachers First is a division of Network for Instructional T.V., Inc., a not-for-profit technologies corporation which works with several hundred schools throughout the United States." The site is very well-organized with much useful information. For example, the homepage has a colorful grid with 20 links including content matrix; research tools; professional resources; search options; professional matrix; web tutorial; featured sites; and hot topics. The content matrix link leads to a page with 24 curriculum links such as art, astronomy and space; biology; chemistry; current events; health; math; music; writing; and U.S. History. This page is divided into elementary, middle school, and high school so the user can choose, for example, to look at art lessons (or weblinks) at the elementary, middle, or high school level, and this holds true for all the content areas. In addition, beyond the wide variety of well-conceived lessons which can be reached via the content matrix, this site has a number of other features which will prove helpful for teachers. These include a listing of featured sites with a list of Teachers First lesson plan contest winners, an interactive teachers lounge, an E-mail newsletter which allows the user to receive updates regarding new items in the collection, and links to a fascinating set of reference and library resources. As of November 24, 1999, the latter set of links included the American Fact Finder from the U.S. Census Department; Ask Dr. Universe from Washington State University; the Children's Book Council; the CIA World Factbook; ERIC-the Educational Resources Information Center; the Information Please Kids' Almanac; the Internet Public Library; the Merriam-Webster Dictionary Page; Multicultural Book Review; the Quotation Center; and Roget's Thesaurus. Go to <www.teachersfirst.com/reference.htm> to see brief descriptions of these and other resources.

7. *The Gifts of Speech: Women's Speeches From Around the World* Homepage was developed and is maintained by Sweet Briar College in Virginia.

   The Gifts of Speech homepage states that "Gifts of Speech is dedicated to preserving and creating access to speeches made by influential contemporary women." However, some of the speeches are by historical figures such as Lucretia Mott and Elizabeth Cady Stanton. As of November 25, 1999, there were approximately 220 women featured in the collection, some with one speech and others with several. Some of the women included in the collection are Madeleine Albright, Benazir Bhutto, Pearl Buck, Marian Wright Edelman, Ruth Bader Ginsberg, Doris Kearns Goodwin, Chandrika Kumaratunga, Toni Morrison, Eleanor Holmes Norton, Wilma ManKiller, Eleanor Roosevelt, and Betty Shabazz. The site can be browsed by year, by topic, or alphabetically by name. This rich collection can be used for a variety of creative instructional purposes in English and history classes and beyond.

8. *The Social Science Education Consortium (SSEC)* Homepage

   On its homepage the SSEC notes that it is a not-for-profit corporation whose offices are in Boulder, Colorado. The SSEC mission is threefold, namely, "...to provide leadership for social science education, to promote a larger role for the social sciences in education, and to close the gap between frontier thinking in the social sciences and educational practice." As a part of its leadership effort, the SSEC provides a small set of well-conceived, richly detailed lesson plans for elementary and secondary teachers. Although sparse in number (12 lesson plans as of November 1999), the authors believe this collection of lessons will be particularly helpful for candidates who are learning how to write, critique, and implement lesson plans in elementary and secondary social studies methods courses. Veteran teachers may also find this thoughtfully constructed collection valuable. The titles of the twelve lessons are:

   Elementary Level
   - Education in Two Cultures: A Day in the Life
   - Just a Dream: How People Change the Environment
   - What Makes a Good Citizen? Models in Literature

   Middle/High School
   - Black Towns in the West: A Case Study of the Exodusters
   - Cross-Cultural Communications
   - Education in Two Cultures: A Day in the Life
   - How Tolerant Should U.S. Laws Be of Cultural Practices?

- Images of Place: Using the Internet to Explore American Cities
- Junk Science and Juries
- Prelude to the Trail of Tears: *Worcester v. Georgia*
- Technology Learning Stations
- Social History Expressed in Fashion

9. The *Public Broadcasting Station (PBS) Online- Teacher Source* Homepage

   This site, as of November 25, 1999, among other valuable features, such as media, literacy, and adult learning resources, listed 1,300 video-related lessons in five broad areas: the arts and literature; health and fitness; math; science and technology; and social studies. The site is well-organized and offers much more than a collection of informative lesson plans. For example, at the math page one can: (a) select recommended books or websites; (b) get information about grants and conferences; (c) get information about professional development via video and web for graduate credit; and (d) choose to see the titles of lessons for specific grade levels. The grade level titles can be further categorized around specific content areas like measurement, geometry, or data analysis. Thus, with a few clicks one can see all of the measurement-related lessons for the middle-school grades. The lessons included in this collection revolve around video segments shown on popular PBS shows like "NOVA" and "Newton's Apple." It is quite possible that these videos will be a part of local school district, county, and university video collections.

10. The *Discovery Channel School* Homepage

    was created and is maintained by Discovery Communications, Inc. Teachers interested in learning more about the Discovery Channel's videos and related resources will find this website quite helpful. In addition to a set of video-related lesson plans for grades K–6 and 7–12, the site also provides an advance organizer for upcoming Discovery Channel programs, a set of learning adventures, and opportunities to participate in online discussions. As of November 1999, the set of approximately 400 lessons were categorized into 14 areas. These included ancient history, animals, astronomy, earth science, economics, human body, literature, life science, oceans, physical science, space science, technology, U.S. history and world history. For most of the lessons listed the following information is available: a lesson overview, lesson vocabulary, questions, activities, standards, and links. In addition to the lessons and aforementioned resources, this site also makes available another valuable resource, namely a link *to Katy Schrock's Guide for Educators* <schooldiscovery.com/Schrockguide/index.html>, an informative list of Internet websites which Ms. Schrock has found useful for enhancing curriculum and professional growth. We found this collection of websites to be quite educational. Some of the categories employed are agricultural education; history and social studies; health, physical education, and fitness; math; science, technology, and Y2K; special education; search engines, reference sources; Internet information, and shopping.

II. Selected Multicultural and Civil Rights-Related Organizations
1. The *American Association of University Women* (AAUW) <www.aauw.org>
2. The *American Civil Liberties Union* (ACLU) <www.aclu.org/>
3. The *Anti-Defamation League of B'nai Brith* <www.adl.org>
4. *ASPIRA*, a national nonprofit educational organization that works with Latino Youth. <www.incacorp.com/aspira>
5. The *Children's Defense Fund* (CDF), a national advocacy organization for children and youth. <www.childrensdefense.org>
6. *Educators for Social Responsibility* (ESR), an organization which provides curricula and professional development for teachers and others concerned about diversity, mediation, and peace education. <www.benjerry.com>
7. The *Harvard University Civil Rights Project* <www.law.harvard.edu/groups/civilrights>
8. Human Rights Watch <www.hrw.org/>
9. The *National Association for Bilingual Education* <www.nabe.org>
10. The *National Association for Ethnic Studies* <www.KSU.edu/ameth/naes>
11. The *National Association for Multicultural Education* (NAME) <www.inform.umd.edu/NAME>
12. The *National Coalition for the Homeless* <nch.ari.net/wwwhome.html>
13. *People for the American Way* <www.pfaw.org/>
14. The Southern Law Poverty Center <www.splcenter.org>
15. The *Women's Educational Equity Act Resource Center* <www.edc.org/WomensEquity/>

III. Education-Related Governmental Resources
1. The *United States Department of Education* Homepage <www.ed.gov/>
This page provides access to a varied, large, and informative set of databases and documents. Some of the major categories/links on the page are research and statistics; publications and products; funding opportunities; a list of the site pages which are most popular; and other sites.
2. The *Publication and Products* Page of the United States Department of Education <www.ed.gov/pubs/index.html>
Major categories/links on this page include the database of ED publications in ERIC; collections of research syntheses; educational research

and practice-reports and studies; and guides to the U.S. Department of Education.

3. The "*Other Sites*" Page of the United States Department of Education <www.ed.gov/EdRes/index.html>
This page provides links to U.S. Department of Education-funded Internet Resources. These include the comprehensive regional assistance centers; equity assistance centers; star schools program sites; regional educational laboratories; and curricular resources and networking projects.

4. The *National Center for Education Statistics* (NCES) Homepage <www.nces.ed.gov>
Major categories/links on this page include Encyclopedia of ED Statistics; NCES Fast Facts; What's New; Electronic Catalogue; and search NCES.

5. The *U.S. Department of Education-Office of Civil Rights* Homepage <www.ed.gov/offices/OCR/index.html>
Major categories/links on this page include about us; what's new; publications and products; related links; search; and contact us.

6. The *Office of Bilingual Education and Minority Languages Affairs* (within the U.S. Department of Education) Homepage <www.ed.gov/offices/OBLEMA>
Major categories/links on this page include about us; OBLEMA News; funding opportunities; technical assistance; and FAQ.

7. The *U.S. Census Bureau* Homepage <www.census.gov/> (part of the U.S. Department of Commerce)
Major categories on this page include about the bureau; publications; access tools; search; related sites; and American fact finder.

8. The *Educational Resources Information Center* (ERIC) Homepage <www.accesseric.org>
This is the systemwide website for all components of the federally supported ERIC system. From this page you can quickly visit the web pages for the U.S. Department of Education; the National Library of Education; the various ERIC sites (clearinghouses and other components); ERIC's special projects; and searching the ERIC database.

Text Evaluation Form for Course Instructors

Name (optional): _____

Address: _____

City: _____ State: _____ Zip: _____

School: _____

Course Title: _____

Office Phone: _____

- -

1. Which chapters in *Teaching with a Multicultural Perspective* did your students read? _____

   _____

2. For the objectives in your course, how could these chapters be improved?

   _____

   _____

3. In terms of new content, what would you add to this text to make it more useful for your course? What would you delete? _____

   _____

   _____

4. What did you like most about this text? least? _____

   _____

   _____

5. Do you plan to continue using this text? _____

          Please mail to
                Patricia Davidman
                University Center for Teacher Education
                California Polytechnic State University
                San Luis Obispo, CA 93407

Index